Hundred Years of Sociology in India: Evolving Issues, Emerging Trends

Abha Chauhan · Ajailiu Niumai ·
Tattwamasi Paltasingh
Editors

Hundred Years of Sociology in India: Evolving Issues, Emerging Trends

Indian Sociological Society
Estd. 1951

Springer

Editors
Abha Chauhan
Centre for Kashmir Studies
Central University of Himachal Pradesh
Dharamshala, Himachal Pradesh, India

Ajailiu Niumai
Centre for the Study of Social Inclusion
University of Hyderabad
Hyderabad, Telangana, India

Tattwamasi Paltasingh
Department of Sociology
Sambalpur University
Burla, Odisha, India

ISBN 978-981-96-1316-8 ISBN 978-981-96-1317-5 (eBook)
https://doi.org/10.1007/978-981-96-1317-5

This Springer imprint is published by the registered company Springer Nature Singapore Pte Ltd.
The registered company address is: 152 Beach Road, #21-01/04 Gateway East, Singapore 189721, Singapore

Introduction

We are happy to present the Volume titled *Hundred Years of Sociology in India: Evolving Issues, Emerging Trends* based on papers presented during the 47th All India Sociological Conference of the Indian Sociological Society (ISS) held at the University of Science and Technology Meghalaya (USTM) from 20th to 22nd December 2022. The Conference was attended by more than 1000 delegates from different parts of the country. The three-day event comprised an Inaugural Session, three Plenary Sessions, including one Regional Session on the Northeast, three Memorial Lectures, 28 Research Committees (RCs) and 01 Adhoc Group Technical Sessions, and a Valedictory Session in which the RC Convenors presented their reports. Some of the papers, like the Keynote Address, the Presidential Address, and the Memorial Lectures, are published in the ISS Journal *Sociological Bulletin*.

The papers were presented in the four different Technical Sessions of RCs with diverse themes spreading over three days of the Conference. It is from these RC presentations that we received 24 papers for this Volume, which, though specific to their respective RCs, were largely in consonance with the main theme of the Conference 'Hundred Years of Sociology in India: Exploring Trajectories for the Future'. The papers, spread over five parts have focussed on the origin, growth, and development of the discipline of Sociology and the evolving issues and emerging trends related to the subject in different areas and regions of the country. These parts are: (I) *Sociology in Regions: Evolving Issues*; (II) *Indigenizing Sociology in India*; (III) *Sociology from Margins: Caste, Religion and Gender*; (IV) *Sociology of Care*; and (V) *Employment, Education and Environment: Emerging Trends.*

The teaching of Sociology in India started a little more than a hundred years ago with the first Department of Sociology and Civics at the University of Bombay in 1919, though the subject began to be taught in 1914. It was subsequently introduced at Mysore and Calcutta Universities in 1917, followed by those in Osmania and Poona. The two Schools, the Bombay School and the Lucknow School (1919–1921) as they are called, laid the foundation of Sociology in India and its subject matter. These produced the 'pioneers' of Sociology in India, followed by generations of Sociologists who became distinguished scholars in their own rights. Soon after India's independence in 1947, departments of Sociology opened in different places, and by the twenty-first century, Sociology was taught in more than 3250 colleges, universities, and other institutes. It can be said that over the past hundred years, the discipline of Sociology has established itself well, institutionally and professionally. The papers in Part I of this Volume deal with the emergence of Sociology in India in general, with a focus on some regions and states like Northeast India (Tiplut Nongbri, Ajailiu Niumai, Baharul Islam Laskar), Uttar Pradesh (Shweta Prasad), and Karnataka (R. Indira).

The Indian Sociological Society (ISS) was registered in 1951 in Bombay with the initiative of Prof. G. S. Ghurye, who was also its first President (1951–1966) with around 100 Life Members. Till 2022, there have been 28 Presidents, 47 All India Sociological Conferences, 72 Volumes (with many Issues) of the *Sociological Bulletin* since 1952, and 5566 Life Members. Many significant changes occurred in the ISS over the years, particularly in tune with those of the International Sociological Association (ISA), with the introduction of features like Research Committees, Regional Associations, Memorial Lectures, and the Lifetime Achievement Awards. The two Journals—*Bharatiya Samajshastra Sameeksha* (*Sameeksha*, Hindi) and E-Journal—*Explorations* (English) were also introduced subsequently. The *Sociological Bulletin* and *Sameeksha* have been published by Sage since 2017–2018. The ISS also has its online triannual Newsletter and Website. The ISS office shifted to Delhi in 1989 and to its own premises at Vasant Kunj, New Delhi, in 2017.

As Sociology was established in India in the 1950s, the issues of development, nation-building, community development, education, industrialisation, rural transformation, and forms of social stratification like caste, class, ethnicity, and gender became important. Initially, the debates centred around the contradictions of colonialism and nationalism, Indology and Sociology (book-view and field-view), tradition and modernity, and Sociology and Anthropology.

The end of the twentieth century and the beginning of the twenty-first century witnessed the issues of liberalisation, globalisation, empowerment, and environment, leading to the emergence of new trends of concern and analysis, such as climate change, natural and health disasters, and increasing social inequalities and resistance movements by tribals, Dalits, women, and farmers among others. Studies related to identity assertions, popular culture and media, LGBT and queer studies, conflicts and violence, and the COVID-19 pandemic gained momentum. The theoretical perspectives such as phenomenology, post-modernism, post-structuralism, subaltern, and standpoint theories became important, challenging the earlier ways of looking at society from the lenses of Indology, civilisational or functional perspectives.

The era of concepts beyond Dominant Caste and Sanskritisation, like intersectionality, social exclusion, and new technology, seemed to have arrived, giving more space and power to people. The papers in Parts III, IV, and V deal with contemporary issues surfacing in the discipline like digital Sociology (Abdul Matin) and information society (Srabanti Choudhuri), Sociology of care and ageing (Samita Manna and Soumyajit Patra, Tattwamasi Paltisingh, Anagha Tendulkar), environmental movements (Anoop K. A.), gulf migrants (Antony Palackal and Lekha N. B.), current emerging trends of communalism (Arvinder Ansari), problems of marginalised groups (Sudha Khokate) and Dalit movement (B. B. Malik and Vijay Laxmi Mall), new agrarian issues (B. B. Mohanty), gig economy (Joseph M. T.), gender studies (Leena Pujari), drug addiction (Pirzada Athar Hussain), Sociology of sports (Sanjay Tewari), and Sociology of work and industry (Pranjal Sarma).

The urge for critical analysis of the Western paradigm, and the need for indigenisation and contextualisation was felt from the beginning and was reflected by various sociologists. Some papers in Part II on 'Indigenizing Sociology in India' focus on this theme while bringing out the contributions of the pioneers of Sociology in India (Biswajit Ghosh, Gayatri Bhattacharya). A paper on Political Sociology (B. K. Nagla) in this part points out to the diversification of Sociology as a discipline into varied fields over the years. The issues of usefulness and popularity of the subject, its conceptual and methodological rigour, the quality of teaching and research, its relevance to higher education, market, and job prospects, projects, syllabus and curriculum, pedagogy, language, funds, and other related aspects of Sociology continued to be discussed on various platforms. Many sociologists see the appropriateness of the subject and the task of sociologists as playing a meaningful role in development, policy-making, and designing a good society. The reflexive and liberating role of Sociology, as reflected in the papers of this Volume, is built into their works as they continue to play a crucial role as teachers, researchers, activists, social thinkers, policy-makers, and administrative and academic sociologists.

Sociology, thus, in the last hundred years, is seen and understood as an academic and professional discipline, critical and engaging, relevant for policy-making, development planning, and nation-building, with an emancipatory role towards civil society. The papers in this Volume have looked at several issues evolving from varied perspectives, from historical to contemporary times, suggesting the content and emerging trends of Sociological teaching and research in India today. We thank all the paper presenters and plenary speakers at the 47th All India Sociological Conference who took out time to finalise their papers and contributed to this Volume. This is the first Volume of its kind brought out by the Indian Sociological Society (ISS) revolving around the theme of the conference, encouraging members to participate and present papers in the ISS annual conferences. We hope that this precedence continues for the forthcoming Conferences of the ISS. We are thankful to the publishing team of Springer Nature Singapore Pte Ltd. for bringing out this Volume, timely and meticulously.

Postscript As we move towards the publication of this Volume, we are pained by the sudden demise of our colleague and friend, Prof. Baharul Islam Laskar of the University of Science and Technology Meghalaya (USTM), on 12 August 2024. The Indian Sociological Society (ISS) and the Editors of this Volume acknowledge with gratitude his contribution to the discipline of Sociology and his exemplary role as the

Organising Secretary of the 47th All India Sociological Conference at the USTM, Meghalaya, in December 2022. We are grateful to him for his paper in this Volume on Northeast India, and thank Prof. Abdul Matin for finalising it.

Prof. Abha Chauhan
President ISS: 2022–2023

Prof. Ajailiu Niumai
MC Member

Prof. Tattwamasi Paltasingh
MC Member

Contents

Part I
Sociology in Regions: Evolving Issues

Chapter 1
Researching India's Northeast: Challenges and Possibilities

Tiplut Nongbri

Abstract The paper maps the challenges and possibilities of sociological research in India's Northeast. Combining textual evidence and personal experience, the paper brings out the limitations of the Euro-centric and nation-state perspectives to make sociology meaningful to students of the Northeastern region. Strongly critiquing methodological nationalism as highly insensitive to societies and cultures at the margins, the paper calls for reflexivity and a shift from a view from above to a view from below. It also brings out the importance of Northeast as a site for testing and validation of theories. The complexity and diversity of the region, contradictions and paradoxes, shifting and multiple identities, and fast pace of change that descended on the region provide ample scope for scholars to venture into new areas of research and experiment with new approaches and paradigms.

Keywords Tribes · Religion · Marginalisation · Migration · Racial discrimination · Methodological nationalism

Introduction

The establishment of the Department of Sociology in Dibrugarh University in 1967 in the then-undivided state of Assam created a new chapter in the growth and development of Sociology in the region. Till this time, students interested in the study of society had to join the allied Department of Anthropology established in 1948 at Gauhati University or seek admission in universities outside the region. Today, students of Northeast interested in Sociology no longer have to make this difficult and expensive choice. With over a dozen universities offering post-graduate and doctoral programmes in Sociology and Social Anthropology the students are spoilt for choice. During its over five-and-a-half decade-long journey Sociology has made

T. Nongbri (✉)
Formerly at Centre for the Study of Social Systems, School of Social Sciences, Jawaharlal Nehru University (JNU), New Delhi, India
e-mail: tiplutnongbri81@hotmail.com

A. Chauhan et al. (eds.), *Hundred Years of Sociology in India: Evolving Issues, Emerging Trends*, https://doi.org/10.1007/978-981-96-1317-5_1

significant progress in teaching and research but is also encumbered by a number of challenges.

It is no exaggeration to say that research in and on the Northeast is fraught with a number of challenges that researchers elsewhere do not usually experience. In the first place, the Northeast as an entity rarely figured in social science discourse that could serve as a theoretical base for research. Early writings on the Northeast are confined to the plains of Assam with a cognitive silence on the hills inhabited by tribes and indigenous communities. Even after Sociology came on the scene, research on the Northeast remains sketchy with vast areas shrouded in ambiguity.

Two inter-related factors can be discerned that contributed to this state of affairs. The *first* is Northeast's geo-political location at the extreme periphery of India with 98% of its borders connected to foreign lands and only 2% with India and inhabited by people deemed to have little in common with the general population. This has not only pushed Northeast away from the national historical and intellectual consciousness, but also led to the neglect of their history, society and culture as distinct entities that deserve to be studied in their own right. The *second* stemmed from the dominance of the upper caste and upper-class perspective in the practice of sociology, which leaves little space for the history, polity and cultural specificity of marginal groups and regions. Notwithstanding increasing contestations from scholars in the margins,[1] teaching and research in sociology continues to be informed by the world-view, vocabulary and perspectives of the dominant groups, the majority of whom belong to the upper strata of the Hindu caste system.

The end result is that the knowledge produced rarely equips students with the ability to apply what they learn in the classroom to their lived reality which is generally at sharp variance with what they studied. This comes out sharply in the literature on Dalits and tribes, two marginalised groups in Indian society.

To illustrate how this affects research, let me share my experience researching tribal religion for my doctoral degree carried out under the Department of Sociology, University of Delhi. Although much time has passed, the situation has not changed much in many aspects. Trained in the ethnographic tradition of Malinowski and the British School of Anthropology where the subject of study was generally the 'primitive other' and the 'field' an alien space in the colonial backwaters of Africa, Asia and/or the Pacific islands, I had little by way of methodological resource to draw from to work in my own society.

Secondly, there was hardly any book on tribal religion that could serve as a reference point for my study. The Sociology of Religion syllabus on which I was trained was dominated by the ideas of Durkheim, Marx, Weber, Malinowski and Evans-Pritchard which are based either on the beliefs of Australian aborigines and African tribes that bear little resemblance to the society I was studying, or on world religions such as Christianity and Islam. Books on Indian religion were restricted to Hinduism, with Srinivas' *Religion and Society among the Coorgs* as the master text, whose central concern is the Hindu ritual complex.

---

[1] See for instance, V. Kumar (2010), V. Xaxa (2010), T. Nongbri (2003, 2006).

The problem got further complicated when I turned to writings on tribes. While colonial ethnographers and missionaries consider tribes as 'animists' and 'worshipers of demons' (Biwar in Gurdon 1907/1975; Morris 1910, 54), Indian sociologists led by G. S. Ghurye (1943) view tribes as 'Backward Hindus' who have no religion of their own. Not only was there any interrogation of this view, rather looking at the entity primarily from the prism of caste, tribes have variously been described as 'non-sectarian Hindus' (Shah 2005) and 'structural equivalent of jati' (Beteille 1986). Informed by the civilisational approach, Indian writings on tribes largely revolved around their isolation or integration with caste or with tribe-caste continuum, which ended up not only ignoring the heterogeneity of tribes but also devaluing local customs and cultures specific to communities.

Today the debate has shifted from the tribe-caste continuum to whether 'tribes' and 'indigenous peoples' are synonymous categories or different. However, the theoretical and ideological position remains largely unchanged with the voice of the dominant groups prevailing, drowning out the minority voice of the subaltern.

Indicative of the continued dominance of the Ghuryean perspective, in a special issue of *Seminar*[2] edited by Surinder S. Jodhka on 'India's Religious Minorities: A Symposium on Exclusion, Identity and Citizenship' out of 14 papers in the journal covering Hinduism, Jainism, Buddhism, Sikhism, Zoroastrianism, Islam, Christianity and Dalit worldview there is not a single paper on tribal religion or tribal worldview—*an omission that raises serious question about Indian Sociology's sensitivity to diversity.*

The exclusion of tribal religion is not confined to scholarly writings but on the socio-political plane as well. In the Indian Census, there is no place for tribal religion in the list of religions drawn up by the government but pushed into the amorphous category 'Others'. This act not only reaffirms the view advanced by Indian sociologists that tribes have no religion of their own, but is also strongly suggestive of the homogenisation process at work.

It cannot be denied that there are many tribes in India who have borrowed from or assimilated into the Hindu ritual complex as a process of acculturation. It is also *equally true that there is a large number who by no stretch of the imagination can be described as Hindus, backward or otherwise.* This is particularly true of tribes in the Northeast whose traditional belief system and lifeworld is a far cry from Hinduism with its hierarchical system of caste and physical representation of their numerous gods and goddesses.[3] The tendency to paint all tribes with the same brush

---

[2] Seminar (2009).

[3] Even outside Northeast India, the classification of tribes as Hindus has not been without resistance. During the 2011 census enumeration, the tribes of Madhya Pradesh and Chattisgarh alleged that the census enumerators ignored their linguistic and religious identity. Led by the Gondwana Gantantra Party, the Gonds of Mandla and Jabalpur submitted memorandums to the office of Registrar General and Census Commissioner of India and the Director Census Operations, Bhopal to put a stop to the practice of recording their religion as 'Hindu' and language as 'Hindi' and to register them as per their indigenous belief and language as these are critical to their identity ('Tribals alleged Census Irregularities in Madhya Pradesh, Chattisgarh-Religious and linguistic identities overlooked during the counting exercise', *The Hindu*, March 2, 2011).

ignores the diversity of tribes and amounts to what Professor Oommen calls 'cultural monism' (2010, 21).[4]

Methodological Nationalism at Work

It is not in the meta-narratives and metropolitan universities alone that the cultural specificities of marginal groups are ignored, the same kind of methodological nationalism[5] is at play in Northeast India as well. In his paper 'Sociology in Northeast India: A Synoptic View' Nanda (2010)[6] brought into sharp focus the failure of universities in the Northeast to address the socio-cultural and geo-political specificity of the region. Pointing to the continued dominance of conventional courses which largely revolved around models developed by European and American thinkers in the sociology syllabi of many universities, he states, 'like elsewhere in the country, in this region too, sociology of the common person, minorities and the marginalized sections does not find place' (p. 146). The disconnect between the subject matter fed to the students and the cultural and political specificity of the region comes out sharply in Indian Sociology, a compulsory paper taught both at the under-graduate and post-graduate levels. Heavily influenced by the Dumotian perspective, which sees Indian society as coterminous with Hinduism, there is little of Northeast in the course that focuses on mainstream Hindu culture.

The Hindu-centric approach not only ends up marginalising cultures and traditions that lie outside the pale of Hinduism, but also seriously affects the capacity of the students to translate what they learn in the classroom and textbooks into tools for their betterment. 'Tribal students in particular, exhibit difficulty in relating to several aspects of Indian Sociology as the categories and concepts used in the discourse... which are deeply embedded in Brahminic ideology and ethos appear alien to these students' (ibid, 149).

Causal Factor

It is not difficult to understand the reasons behind this approach, Sociology made its entry in Northeast India twenty years after Independence when the country was still caught up in the process of nation-building, which called not only for the building of infrastructure but also for the promotion of unity among the people. Nation-building in the Northeast was particularly an onerous task given the region's socio-cultural diversity, sensitive geo-political location, and social and economic backwardness.

---

[4] Oommen (2010).

[5] Briefly, methodological nationalism means an approach that looks at things from the lens of the nation-state and an uncritical acceptance of derived theories and paradigms.

[6] Nanda in M Chaudhury (ed) (2010).

Adding to the problem, was the social and political unrest in many parts of the region, fuelled partly by ethnic aspirations and partly by policies enforced by the state, which did not take people's consent into consideration. This process was to have a significant impact on Sociology teaching and research in the region. The imperative of nation-building called for the creation of a united and singular India bound by a common culture, ideology and ethos. What better agencies than universities to carry out this agenda?

While this approach may seem pragmatic and politically correct to many, what we fail to recognise is that national unity cannot be built by forced homogenisation or erased history. Neither can we build a good knowledge base on faulty and misguided information. This militates against the very premise of Sociology and the scientific method which treats value neutrality and the collection of accurate and foolproof data as the cornerstone of the discipline.

Research output in the early years of Sociology in the region also reflects the nationalist agenda. A review of books published between 1970 and 1990 (Kumar 1999)[7] shows that a large number of books are in the nature of tribal ethnography of individual tribes providing account of their culture, tradition, polity, economy, laws, customs, demography and land use pattern. Prominent among the topics are economic development and the impact of various government schemes, electoral politics and emerging educated elite and leaders. Many of the books are compilations of papers presented at seminars funded by the North Eastern Regional Centre of the Indian Council of Social Science Research. According to Kumar, the books are mostly descriptive in nature, lacking both in methodological and theoretical rigour. Understandably enough, a cursory reading of some suggests the works are primarily intended to serve as a knowledge pool for administrators.

It needs to be recognised that methodological nationalism is highly constraining to sociology in general and the researcher in particular. It limits the researcher's ability to see structures and processes that lie below and beyond the nation-state. It also leads to blind and uncritical acceptance of derived theories and paradigms framed in contexts and situations different from the empirical world being studied. This is not to undermine the value of standard theory and models, the efficacious use of which has immensely contributed to the understanding of the workings of society. But these cannot be used uncritically across the board without refining them to suit the field being studied.

From Challenges to Possibilities

If research on Northeast India is beset with a number of challenges major part of which is tied to the way in which Sociology is practised, this is also where the possibility lies for sociologists in the Northeast to come up with path-breaking research using new research tools and perspectives that could shed new light on the society and culture

[7] Kumar (1999).

of the region. For this to happen scholars would need to think out of the box and be willing to be innovative and move out of their comfort zone. Recent publications on the region show this is happening in several disciplines, including Sociology. But for this to take place on a scale that could make a difference, Sociology would need to reconfigure and reinvent itself in a major way.

For a start, Sociology would need to shed off its disciplinary-centric approach which has stifled its growth. It should also be more cautious in the application of the Durkhemian dictum that *'the social can be explained only by the social'* and the allied postulate that *'facts' are 'externally verified' observations.*[8] This narrow conceptualisation not only leaves out a wide range of issues from the purview of Sociology but also limits its explanatory potential. Nowhere is this more visible than in the study of tribes and indigenous communities, many of whom are concentrated in India's Northeast, and whose life-worlds, beliefs, and values are deeply embedded in nature. It would not be far wrong to say, ethnocentrism apart, the tendency to restrict sociological analysis to the social and the externally verifiable commanded by the Durkhemian approach, prevented sociologists from arriving at a proper understanding of tribal religion. The denial of tribal religion as a distinct entity with its own philosophy, rites and ceremonies in tune with the world they live in, stemmed from this narrow perspective. A more ecological reading would show, that tribal or folk religion is not ideologically empty but underlined by strong social and ecological philosophy. Tribal belief represents the close link that exists between humans and nature and their mutual interdependence in which each draws from and feeds the other. Their rites and ceremonies may lack the complexity of more advanced religions, are an expression of this inter-connectedness.

Further, we live in an age where planet Earth and its institutions are seriously threatened by forces that seem to lie beyond our control: climate change, bio-diversity loss, natural calamities like floods and forest fires. These processes seriously question the adequacy of our sociological paradigm and the anthropocentrism of our discipline that views humans and human society as the centre of the world detached from nature. This cannot be farther from the truth. Human being, the most dominant organism on earth is intricately linked to nature. The air he breathes, the water he drinks, the food he eats and the products he uses and throws away all come from nature. Any change in nature affects human life in significant ways. In turn, how humans live, and the products they make, consume and dispose off affect nature. This reality calls for a change in our approach towards the natural world and a re-working of our theoretical tools and paradigms to take stock of the effect of the natural on the social world. It also calls for a recognition of primal cultures and worldviews as an embodiment of a sustainable way of life and ecological prudence.

Northeast offers a viable ground for the testing and validation of theories not only on religion but on other aspects as well. The complexity and diversity of the region, contradictions and paradoxes, shifting and multiple identities, and fast pace of change that descended on the region provide ample scope for scholars to venture into new areas of research and experiment with new approaches and paradigms. We

---

[8] Durkheim (1895).

can identify many areas old and new that call for systematic exploration. Listed below are some of the issues scholars may wish to take up.

Need to Problematise the Concept 'Northeast'

In the first place, we need to problematise and deconstruct the concept 'Northeast'. Although Northeast is accepted as a natural entity in popular discourse, it is an enigma with a contested identity. Its popular conception (Seven Sisters) as a geo-political space confined to the territorial limits of Arunachal Pradesh, Assam, Manipur, Meghalaya, Mizoram, Nagaland and Tripura ignores its shifting and multiple identities. Even Sikkim, the eighth state, tends to get lost in this imagery. The conceptualisation of the entity Northeast has undergone a series of transformations over the years. From what was originally conceived as a 'frontier' of the British empire (Pemberton 1835; Mackenzie 1884), the Northeast has metamorphosed into a 'region' with a distinct identity of its own within independent India's nation-state. In recent times, following India's new economic initiative to forge closer economic ties with the ASEAN countries post-liberalisation, the Northeast has been described as a 'bridgehead' that connects India with South, South-East and East Asia (Cf Nongbri and Shimreiwung 2017, p. 18).

The shifting identity of the Northeast is rarely captured in works on the region. While its peripheral status is emphasised by the use of such epithets as 'Mongolian fringe' and 'cultural other' there is little serious engagement with the concept 'Northeast'. The tradition of village study and study of small groups and communities that dominate sociological research rarely prepare students to look at mega entities, such as regions; this is generally considered the domain of geography or economics. Engaging with different conceptualisations is important in sociological research as well, as concepts are not empty words but abstractions of social reality. This act can help us unravel the complex history and power dynamics that underline the origin of the entity we know as Northeast and its current place in India's polity.

Another issue that calls for close scrutiny is the 'crisis of development' that plague the contemporary Northeast. While the region is endowed with vast human potential[9] and an abundance of natural resources,[10] it is sorely lacking in development. Northeast ranks lowest in all parameters of development. According to data released by the Ministry of Statistics and Programme Implementation, Government of India as on 1 March 2021, barring Assam and Tripura all the Northeastern states lie at the

[9] The region is noted for its good literacy rate. Barring Assam literacy of Northeastern states is higher than the national average for both males and females.

[10] According to one estimate Northeast has 864 metric tons (mt) of *coal*; 421 mt of *hydro carbon*; 154 mt of gas in oil equivalent. Large *shale* formation in Arunachal & Assam that could yield *15 billion tons of recoverable oil*; 60,000 megawatts of *power potential* (*1/3 of India's run off* flows from NE—described in national documents as *National Waterways II* (largest after Ganga) extraction of which is at different stages of completion. Indian government under UPA II even promised to evacuate/sell power to Bangladesh.

bottom 6 of the list of states, higher only to Andaman and Nicobar island in terms of GDP. Together, the eight Northeastern states' contribution to the country's GDP is a meagre 2.8%.[11]

The critical question that arises is why underdevelopment when the Northeastern states have been treated as Special Category States with 10% of all union budget channelised to the Northeast? Even after scrapping of its Special category status in 2015, with the dissolution of the Planning Commission and the formation of NITI Ayog, Northeast remains the favoured destination of central funding. To address its special needs, a new scheme, *the PM's Development Initiative for Northeast* (PM-DevINE) has been adopted with effect from the 2022 financial year, executed through the North-Eastern Council.

Vision 2020 Document attributes Northeast's under development to the devastating effect of partition; poor infrastructure; top-down approach; ethnic conflict and insurgency; poor governance; and anomalous status of MyDONER and NEC. This calls for close scrutiny of the development model followed, the policies adopted and the system of governance prevailing in the region. This is necessary because the colonial account reveals that underdevelopment is a new phenomenon absent in the past.

There is also a need to revisit India's partition. Partition not only disrupted trade routes but also burdened the region with the need for new infrastructure. Land and riverine routes through which goods and services passed were brutally snapped plunging the region into economic crisis. The once vibrant social and economic space is reduced to an economic hinterland and military zone bristling with security personnel to guard the newly created international border. Revisiting partition will not only help us to understand its effect on the economy[12] but also on the society and polity particularly in the interim period between the transfer of power and promulgation of the Indian Constitution. Re-examining the political manoeuvrings and negotiations which took place during the period can throw light on current processes such as ethnic movements and insurgency activities. For example, states like Manipur[13] and Tripura claim that they have been coerced to sign the Instrument of Merger with India (Cf. Karlsson 2011, p. 256).[14]

Another area that calls for investigation is the history and geography of the Northeast prior to the arrival of the British. Except for the plains of Assam and Manipur, major parts of the Northeast are shrouded in ambiguity. The dearth of information makes understanding the region highly problematic. Northeast has a rich store of oral

---

[11] Indian States by GDP 2019–20, Source: Ministry of Statistics and Programme Implementation, GOI.

[12] Accounts by colonial historian Edward Gait and administrator BC Allen show that poverty and want was not only absent in Assam (erstwhile Northeast) but the people were also industrious and prosperous. If that was the case, what accounts for Northeast's present economic predicament?

[13] In Manipur, the refusal of Government of India to accept the democratic government the erstwhile kingdom had elected in 1948 (Manipur Constitution Act) and appointed Dewan to oversee administration led to protests and formation of UNLF.

[14] Bengt B Karlsson, *Unruly Hills: Nature & Nation in India's Northeast*, New Delhi, Orient BlackSwan, 2011, p. 256.

tradition—myths, legends and folklore which can be effectively sourced to reconstruct the history of the region. This exercise will not only help us have a better understanding of the past, but also why the Northeast is seen as the cultural 'other' in the popular imagination, which has put Northeast folks at the receiving end of violence and discrimination when they come out of the region for education and employment.

The 121 years of British rule (1826–1947) in the Northeast also left a large amount of material and visual resources that provide valuable fodder for research. While historians and social anthropologists are increasingly turning to this resource not only to reconstruct the history and society of the Northeast but also to interrogate the politics of knowledge production salient to colonialism (see for instance, Joy Pachuau 2014; Pachuau and Willem van Schendel 2015; Natasha Nongbri 2021; Avitoli Jimo 2021).[15] Sociologists have yet to come forwards to access this valuable resource.

Fast Pace of Change

Added to the above is the fast pace of change that descended on the region, especially in the post-liberalisation period rendering the familiar unfamiliar even for those born and bred in it. While the material condition has remained more or less unchanged, the intrusion of the forces of modernisation, globalisation, market and IT, along with the consumerist and materialist values have not only shaken the foundation of the subsistence-based economy but also loosened the social fabric of society.

This calls for a close examination of the effect of globalisation on the society and culture of the Northeast. In recent years Northeast India has not only attracted a large number of international funding agencies, namely, World Bank, ADB, IFAD, etc., but has also become the favoured destination of tourists. IFAD in particular has been involved in working with local communities in mainstreaming gender, natural resource management and formation of women's Self Help Groups (SHGs). It would be interesting to see how this affects the status of women in society.

We also need to explore more deeply into the process of modernisation and change, which has given rise not to the dissolution or abandonment of the old as modernisation theorists would have us believe, but to the pluralisation and hybridisation of culture. How do we handle this theoretically? For example, where do we locate Khasi matriliny today with an increasingly large number of people taking their father's surname as their identity but staunchly adhering to clan exogamy based on matrilineal principle for the purpose of marriage? Locating the Khasi kinship system within the rigid classification devised by sociologists becomes a challenging task indeed.

---

[15] Joy Pachuau 2014, *On being Mizo*; Joy Pachuau and Willem van Schendel 2015: *The Camera as Witness. A social history of Mizoram, Northeast India*, Cambridge University Press: Natasha Nongbri in T. Nongbri and R. Bhargava (2021); Avitoli Jimo, in T. Nongbri and R. Bhargava (2021)

Beyond Northeast, New Areas of Research

In recent times, the large-scale migration of people from the Northeastern states to India's metropolitan cities for education and employment has opened up new areas of research. This has not only shifted the field from the region to the cities but also brought back long-used concepts, such as race and ethnicity into circulation, albeit with a new face doused in violence and discrimination. Recent publications on the subject have also thrown up new ideas, such as 'pan-Northeast solidarity' and 'racial discrimination' (see for instance, McDuie-Ra 2012; Nongbri and Shimreiwung 2017) that call for deeper interrogation.

Migration into the cities has also put the spotlight on dress and fashion sported by the youth of the Northeast. The increasing popularity of Korean fashion and Korean pop culture among the youth has not only exposed them to attacks from self-styled nationalists but also reinforced their 'otherness' in the eyes of the 'mainlanders'. In 2014, a student from Arunachal Pradesh lost his life after being beaten up by shop-keepers in Delhi's Lajpat Nagar market for sporting a Korean hairstyle.[16] This calls for an explanation of why Northeast youth opted for Korean instead of Indian fashion. According to Kharsyntiew, Northeast youth sport Korean fashion to 'lay claim to a political space that is often dominated by mainstream discourse' (Kharsyntiew 2018).[17] While this calls for close investigation, the popularity of Korean fashion among Northeast youth could also be seen as an expression of their desire to re-establish and rebuild the fractured connectivity with cultures and society across the border. Contrary to what historical texts proclaim about Northeast's isolation there is rich evidence which suggests that its people were part of a wide network of trade, friendship and migration spanning South Asia, South East Asia and China. The oral history of many Northeast communities confirms this fact, challenging the isolation theory.

A related issue in the context of Northeasterners in the city that calls for exploration is food: the culinary, taste and consumption pattern of the people which has a close link to their culture and identity. While the eating and sharing of food has received wide attention in Indian Sociology the same cannot be said in the context of the Northeast. There is hardly any study that addresses the issue of food.[18]

In recent times, food has emerged as an important marker of the identity of people from the Northeast. Northeast folks in India's metropolitan cities are judged not so much by their looks or attire as by the food they eat—seen as eaters of beef and

[16] The wide media coverage of the incident and strong protests by Northeast migrants against discrimination forced the Union government to set up a special committee under Shri M.P. Bezbaruah, a retired Indian administrative officer to examine the issue and suggest measures for remedial action.

[17] Kharsyntiew in Vandenhelsken et al. (2018).

[18] Food is an important marker of identity and status. It is both a unifying and differentiating element. Sharing of food signifies oneness, and restriction on food sharing signifies the unbridgeable gulf of social distancing. A focus on food will not only help us understand the problems faced by Northeasterners away from their homeland, but also the dynamics of ethnic relations within the region.

smelly food—food that are highly repulsive to the mainland sensibility. In a recent film *Axone* which focuses on the experience of Northeasterners in India's capital city, New Delhi, Northeast filmmaker Nicholas Kharkongor cogently brings out the uneasy relations between the Hindu landlords and the Northeast tenants because of their love for the smelly fermented beans, a must have item in the menu of most northeast people, especially in times of celebration.

Concluding Remarks

Returning to the point made at the outset about the neglect of Northeast in Sociology, a perusal of the list of courses offered in some of the Sociology departments in the Northeast indicates the emergence of a new consciousness of the importance of integrating the socio-cultural and socio-political specificities of the region in the syllabi. Out of 12 universities whose syllabi I was able to access, 6 universities: Assam, Dibrugarh, Tezpur, Nagaland, Cotton State University and University of Science and Technology Meghalaya (USTM) have included *Sociology of Northeast India* in the syllabi. Mizoram does not have a course specifically related to Northeast but has two allied courses *Sociology of Tribes* and *Sociology of Marginalised Community*. In apparent recognition of the cultural proximity and growing economic importance of South-East Asia to Northeast India, Nagaland and Cotton universities have come up with a course *Sociology of South-East Asia*. Another important course, *Sociology of Globalization* has been introduced in Assam, Dibrugarh and Sikkim universities. Other courses, seemingly designed to meet the socio-economic needs of the region, have also found their entry in the syllabi. These are courses as—*Sociology of Human Resource Management* in Dibrugarh and Tripura, *Sociology of Entrepreneurship Development* in Nagaland and *Science, Technology and Society* and *Rural Society and Indigenous Technology* in USTM.

This is an encouraging development indeed, but more needs to be done to sensitise students to the distinctiveness of Northeast India and its rich socio-cultural and historical heritage. Also, to achieve the desired result, it needs to be accompanied by a change in perspective in the servicing of the courses. The materials presented in the earlier part of the paper strongly affirm the need for an interdisciplinary approach. It also calls for a shift from a view from above to a view from below. The theoretical advantage of the view from below is that it not only takes note of the specificities (social, cultural and regional) of the entity or phenomenon being studied but also of the structural location of the observer. The view from below has revolutionised research on Dalits and women. The same needs to be incorporated in studies of tribes, other marginalised groups and societies at the margins, like those in India's Northeast.

Stated differently, this calls for greater reflexivity and triangulation of method and perspective. This is necessary because the empirical world is not unidimensional but multifaceted, it is also highly complex and fluid. The same phenomenon can be studied in different ways and from different perspectives. No single perspective is adequate to understand the empirical world because it is complex and multifaceted. Nowhere is this more true than in India's Northeast.

References

Beteille A (1986) 'The concept of tribe with special reference to India'. Eur J Sociol 27:297–318

Durkheim E (1964, first published 1895) The rules of sociological method. The Free Press, Collier Macmillan Publishers

Ghurye GS (1943) The aborigines so-called and their future. Institute of Politics & Economics, Poona

Gurdon PRT (1907) The Khasis. Reprinted in 1975 by Cosmo Publications, Delhi

Jimo A (2021) 'We were the other: visuality in colonial writings'. In: Nongbri T, Bhargava R (eds) Materiality and visuality in North-East India: an interdisciplinary perspective. Springer, Singapore, pp 23–35

Jodhka SS (2009) Special issue on India's religious minorities: a symposium on exclusion, identity and citizenship. Seminar (ed) 62

Karlsson B (2011) Unruly hills: nature & Nation in India's Northeast. Orient BlackSwan, New Delhi

Kharsyntiew T (2018) 'Youth fashion and the identity of resistance in Northeast India.' In: Vandenhelsken M, Barkataki-Ruscheweyh M, Karlsson B (eds) Geographies of difference: explorations in northeast Indian studies. Routledge, London, pp 159–174

Kumar N (1999) Survey of research in sociology and social anthropology in north-east India. Regency Publications, New Delhi

Kumar V (2010) 'Teaching caste and the Hindu social order: Dalits in India Sociology.' In: Chaudhuri M (ed) Sociology in India: intellectual & institutional practices. Rawat Publications, Jaipur, pp 360–380

Mackenzie A (1884) History of the relations of the government with the hill tribes of the North East Frontier of Bengal. Reproduced in The North East Frontier of India. Mittal Publication, 2001

McDuie-Ra D (2012) Northeast migrants in Delhi: race, refuge and retail. Amsterdam University Press, Amsterdam

Morris JH (1910) The history of the welsh Calvinistic Methodists' foreign mission to the end of the year 1904. University of Illinois at Urbana-Champaign, CM Book Room

Nanda SK (2010) 'Sociology in Northeast India: a synoptic view'. In: Chaudhuri M (ed) Sociology in India: intellectual and institutional practices. Rawat Publications, Jaipur, pp 139–153

Nongbri T (2003) 'Tribal studies in India: themes & perspectives'. In: Development, ethnicity & gender: select essays on tribes in India. Rawat Publications, Jaipur & Delhi, pp 18–57

Nongbri T (2006) Tribe, caste and the indigenous challenge in India. In: Karlsson BG, Subba TB (eds) Indigeneity in India. Kegan Paul, London, pp 75–95

Nongbri N (2021) 'Representing tea, creating consumers: tea advertising in late colonial India'. In: Nongbri T, Bhargava R (eds) Materiality & visuality in north-east India: an interdisciplinary perspective. Springer, Singapore, pp 129–150

Nongbri T, Shimreiwung AS (2017) Migration, identity & conflict: lived experience of northeasterners in Delhi. Rawat Publications, Delhi & Jaipur

Oommen TK (2010) Scheduled castes, scheduled tribes and the nation: situating G. S. Ghurye. In: Occasional paper, series 7, Second G. S. Ghurye memorial lecture, Department of Sociology, University of Mumbai

Pachuau Joy LK (2014) Being Mizo. Oxford University Press

Pachuau Joy LK, Willem van Schendel W (2015) The camera as witness. A social history of Mizoram, Northeast India.Cambridge University Press, Cambridge

Pemberton (1835) The Eastern Frontier of Bengal

Shah AM (2005) Sects and Indian social structure. Occasional paper (new series), no 1. Department of Sociology, Delhi School of Economics, University of Delhi

Xaxa V (2010) 'Tribes as indigenous peoples of India'. In: Chaudhuri M (ed) Sociology in India: intellectual & institutional practices. Rawat Publications, Jaipur, pp 340–359

Chapter 2
Hundred Years of Sociology in Karnataka: Growth Trajectory and Current Challenges

R. Indira

Abstract Sociology in India has traversed one hundred years, and just as we are celebrating this journey, new challenges are emerging for the discipline. This is the situation in Karnataka, one of the first states in the country, where sociology made its beginnings as early as in 1917. From falling enrolments to dwindling employment opportunities and questions being raised about its job relevance, sociology is facing a crisis situation in the state. There are serious gaps in the subject content, pedagogical practices, skills imparted and attempts at enhancing the employability of students. Also, the hurried imposition of NEP in the state without adequate preparation could not bring any meaningful change in the curriculum quality or in the teaching–learning practices. But all these challenges do not undermine the relevance of sociology to our times. The need of the day is to enhance the contemporaneity of the discipline and develop new skills in students which enhance their job prospects. The paper seeks to trace the shifts that have emerged in the growth path of the discipline, locate the gaps and identify the way forward.

Keywords Karnataka · NEP · Regionalisation · Sociology

Sociology in Karnataka: Historical Roots

The journey of sociology in Karnataka can be traced back to the year 1917 when A. R. Wadia travelled from Wilson College, Mumbai to Mysore to head the Department of Philosophy at Maharaja's College, University of Mysore. The discipline got a fillip by the interest which Bajendranath Seal, the then Vice-Chancellor of the University of Mysore evinced in introducing sociological perspectives in the study of philosophy. Along with A. R. Wadia, Bajendranath Seal took the initiative to introduce social philosophy and sociology at the University of Mysore, which was the first university to be established in Karnataka and the sixth in the country.

R. Indira (✉)
Formerly Professor of Sociology, University of Mysore, Mysuru, Karnataka, India
e-mail: ramaraoindira@gmail.com

A. Chauhan et al. (eds.), *Hundred Years of Sociology in India: Evolving Issues, Emerging Trends*, https://doi.org/10.1007/978-981-96-1317-5_2

The beginnings of sociology in the country happened around the same time in the universities of Calcutta (1917), Bombay (1919), Lucknow (1921) and Mysore (1917). In Mysore, the subject was offered in the Department of Philosophy due to the keen interest evinced by A. R. Wadia in sociology. In fact, the credit for having introduced the first undergraduate programme in sociology in the country goes to Karnataka, when in 1928–29 A. R. Wadia charted the B.A. pass course in sociology for being introduced in the University of Mysore. He also ensured that the subject became an integral part of the BA. Honours course in Social Philosophy.

The stage for starting a full-fledged Department of Sociology in the University of Mysore was laid when a year's master's programme in sociology by dissertation was introduced in 1949. In 1955 a regular two-year postgraduate programme in sociology was introduced at the University of Mysore.

With the introduction of taught courses in the curriculum at the undergraduate and postgraduate levels, the process of formation of sociology began in earnest and it also marked the gradual emancipation of sociology from social philosophy as an academic discipline (Jayaram 2011).

With new universities being established in different parts of the state, independent departments of sociology began functioning in all these universities. These included the departments set up in Karnatak University, Dharwad (1957), Bangalore University, Bengaluru (1965), Gulbarga University, Kalburgi (1980), Mangalore University, Mangaluru (1981), Kuvempu University, Shivamogga (1987), Karnataka State Open University, Mysuru (1996), Karnataka State Akka Mahadevi Women's University, Vijayapura (2003), Tumkur University, Tumakuru (2008), Rani Chennamma University, Belagavi (2010), Davanagere University, Davanagere (2010) and Vijayanagara Krishnadevaraya University, Bellary (2011).

The process of bifurcating and trifurcating existing universities and setting up new universities in districts that were hitherto under the jurisdiction of established universities began in 2016, with Bangalore University being trifurcated into three separate universities. While the newly set up Bangalore City University has an independent Sociology Department, the Bangalore North University set up at Kolar with all colleges in Kolar district and colleges in select regions of Bangalore's Rural and Urban districts has not established a postgraduate department of sociology. Though efforts are being made by teachers and associations of sociology to impress upon the university and state administration that the establishment of a PG department would help the growth of the discipline in the region, it has not happened so far. In 2020 the Raichur PG Centre was bifurcated from Gulbarga University and established as a separate university.

In the 2022–23 academic year eight new universities were established in Karnataka by pulling out select districts from the jurisdiction of existing universities. These included the Hassan, Mandya and Chamarajanagar Universities separated from the University of Mysore, Kodagu University from Mangalore University, Koppal University from Vijayanagara Krishnadevaraya University, Bidar University from Gulbarga University, Bagalkot University from Rani Chennamma University and Haveri University from Karnatak University. With the exception of Haveri University, independent departments of sociology are not functioning in any of the new universities. However, PG courses continue to be offered in government colleges in these universities.

All these new universities were postgraduate centres of the universities from which they were separated, and the only change one could notice in these institutions was the filling up of administrative positions such as those of the Vice-Chancellor, Registrar and Registrar of Evaluation and no academic or infrastructural quality enhancement is seen. Leave alone the new universities, even in the established universities; the number of permanent faculty is constantly on the decline. It is not uncommon to find university departments running with a single permanent faculty or no permanent faculty. With a virtual freeze being imposed on appointments in the state for more than a decade, the situation seems to be very discouraging and is seriously affecting the growth of the discipline. The growth of sociology at the postgraduate level is mostly a success story of numbers with the discipline being offered in nearly 20 state universities, but with hardly any scope for academic upgradation.

For nearly sixty years after the first postgraduate course in sociology was started at the University of Mysore, master's courses were offered only in university departments. It was only in the year 2007 that the Government of Karnataka decided that postgraduate courses would be offered in select government colleges in different parts of the state. The reason behind this decision was projected as 'altruistic', with the state claiming that 'universities are located in urban centers, and all aspirants, especially women and students from vulnerable groups could not travel long distances or afford to stay in hostels. Keeping such factors in view, the government argued that opportunities for postgraduate education must be brought closer home. It is needless to mention that political pressure and the pull of local power blocks played a major role in deciding which college gets to open a P.G. centre. It was seen as a matter of prestige and academic considerations did not always matter' (Indira and Shanthi 2023).

In Karnataka today, PG courses in sociology are being offered in most universities and at least 20 degree colleges across the state. However, there is virtually no student or faculty mobility between these institutions. Neither is there any academic interaction leading to curriculum review nor for identification of innovative pedagogical practices. A major share of the teaching is assigned to guest faculty many of whom have started teaching PG courses just after completing their post-graduation. The situation that prevails in the state vis-à-vis guest teachers has been brought out by Indira and Shanthi in their article under reference when they write.

> 'Another issue of growing concern in Karnataka, which also has a bearing on declining admissions, is the increasing dependence on teachers known as 'guest faculty' in many departments and colleges across the state. There is more than one reason for such a situation. First, is the superannuation of almost all the senior faculty in virtually every department, and the vacant positions not being filled up… In a given department, if the number of teachers is at least five, the need for guest faculty is not actually felt. However, this is not the case in all the postgraduate departments or postgraduate centres of universities offering the master's programme in sociology. A classic case is that of a department, which has only one permanent teacher and fourteen guest teachers, which includes post-doctoral research fellows and those with other national fellowships. There is also the case of a postgraduate centre of a university, which is being run by nine guest faculty. In yet another department, there is one permanent

teacher and three guest teachers. A similar situation prevails in many first-grade colleges too. Many of the guest faculty have no hands-on experience of teaching or any kind of academic exposure. The obvious consequence of such a situation is either a drastic decline in student enrolment or the closure of the course itself. What is disturbing is the complacent attitude of the state administration which is not proactively clearing the blocks that are coming in the way of making permanent faculty appointments' (Indira and Shanthi 2023, p. 10).

Sociology is also being offered at the undergraduate and pre-university levels in Karnataka. As per the latest available data, there are 412 government, 315 government-aided and 829 private un-aided first-grade colleges in the state. Regional differences notwithstanding sociology is offered in at least 60% of the government and aided colleges as an elective, but only about 10–20% of the private colleges offer the option of choosing sociology as a major subject. It is learned that only in about 35% of the private colleges the arts stream is offered. A majority of government-aided colleges are science or commerce colleges. The same situation more or less prevails in the 2818 pre-university or +2 level colleges in the state. While sociology is offered as an independent elective in 60% of the government and government-aided colleges only in about 10% of the nearly 2000 private colleges, the option to study sociology is available.

There are nearly 35 private/deemed universities in the state, but with the exception of three of these institutions, sociology is not offered as an independent branch of study in others. For that matter, most of these institutions offer education in technology, management and other allied streams, and humanities and social sciences are not considered as areas attracting students.

In a state that played a pioneering role in introducing sociology courses at different levels of the higher education system, it is unfortunate that the discipline is gradually losing its base. It is time to reflect on the factors that are bringing about this situation and re-build the discipline by making a 'situational analysis' of the gaps as well as opportunities for change.

Present Scenario

Before proceeding to discuss a new model for making sociology relevant to contemporary situations, it is important to analyse the state-of-affairs in the discipline in the state. In their essay 'Sociology in Karnataka: Looking Back on its Century Old Trail', Indira and Shanthi observe that,

> 'One of the most disturbing shifts that have taken place in the status of the discipline of sociology in the state of Karnataka relates to the dwindling number of aspirants at all the three levels. Today, the presence of sociology is generally limited to government or private-aided colleges, and it hardly finds a place in the expanding private sector, as most private colleges do not find it a worthy source of investment. Also, it needs to be investigated if one of the key stakeholders in the knowledge transmission system-the teachers, have not been able to convince students, parents, administrators and the private managements about the potential of sociology and its practical applicability' (Indira and Shanthi 2023, p. 6).

The growing lack of interest in the discipline is primarily due to the dis-connect between the buzzword 'placements' and sociology. The state of Karnataka has witnessed a huge rise in the number of employment opportunities in such sectors as information technology, biotechnology, hospitality sector, media management and health care. Given the fact that sociology is not considered a professional course and little is being done in most institutions to give the 'feel of the field' to students there is an increasing hesitation on the part of students and their families to opt for this subject or institutions to offer courses in sociology. The general impression that after pursuing a programme in sociology for 3, 5 or 7 years as the case maybe it does not necessarily lead them towards a job acts as the main de-motivating factor. Falling enrolments, parental disinterestedness and failure of the system to respond to changes taking place both in academia and the world at large have put the discipline on the back burner.

NEP: An Experiment that Really Did not Make Much Headway?

Karnataka wanted to be the first state to introduce the NEP model in the country and in the 2021–22 academic year, the 4-year BA Honours Course with 8 semesters with option to exit at each stage was introduced in all the state universities. A Committee with teachers in PG Sociology departments and government degree colleges was formed. Some interactive meets were held by inviting senior faculty, but since there was no formal procedure in place to initiate a consultative process or have the curriculum peer-reviewed, the course content approved by the Expert Committee was accepted by the government and classes commenced.

The curriculum has three-course categories, viz. Discipline Specific Core Course (DSC), Discipline-Specific Elective (DSE) and Open Elective. While students who opt for sociology are expected to study DSC and DSE courses, students of other streams or those who have chosen other majors, such as Economics and History can opt for Open Electives offered by the Sociology Departments of their respective colleges. The teaching however is done by the sociology faculty. While the DSC courses fall in the category of mainstream sociology courses, open electives include such courses as social media, social entrepreneurship, tourism management and disaster management. The irony is that these courses are offered by the sociology department but students who have opted for sociology as a major (the NEP structure also reduced the number of majors from three to two) do not have access to these supposedly job-oriented courses. The two major lacunae that I see in the current arrangement are that neither are teachers formally trained in pedagogical practices to be followed in teaching the new courses nor is source material available in Kannada, which is the medium of teaching–learning in at least 90% of the colleges.

The recent decision of the state to give up the 4-year BA Honours model and bring it back to the three-year pattern has led to changes being brought out in the course content, reshuffling of courses across semesters and removal of certain critical courses proposed in the 2020–21 model. This action will further jeopardise the discipline's interest and throw up serious challenges in the path of making sociology 'relevant'.

Regionalisation of Teaching–Learning and Research

The ultimate objective of education is not just information dissemination, but instilling in the learners, skills that enhance their capacities to achieve 'social mobility'. While it is very important to give freedom of expression in the language of one's choice, what needs to be taken seriously is the social divide that is being created because of the inability to use English as the medium of communication. In a recent interview that was held in a college to fill up vacant teaching positions in sociology, not one out of the 30+ aspirants who attended the interview could communicate in English. This is one of the few institutions that still has English medium sections and knowledge of English was a necessity. This is a clear indication that in the changing social milieu degrees per se do not ensure employment. In his article 'Sociology in a Regional Context', Shah (2000) wrote,

> 'Regionalisation of sociology and social anthropology in all the linguistic regions of India seems to be an inevitable process. It needs to be accepted as a fact. Serious discussions are necessary to examine its consequences in every region and to establish an appropriate relationship between it and pan-Indian as well as world sociology and social anthropology'.

What Shah wrote two decades ago has emerged as one of the biggest challenges in Karnataka today, with Kannada being the most widely used medium of teaching and research in sociology. Till about 1990s, most government and government-aided colleges at least in urban centres offered instruction in both English and Kannada medium, and at the postgraduate level, they had the option to write their examination in Kannada. It was mostly in undergraduate and +2 level colleges in rural regions that only Kannada medium was being offered. The private un-aided colleges are almost exclusively English medium colleges.

Today majority of the students, mostly first-generation learners in +2, undergraduate and postgraduate level state universities have had all their education in the regional language. It is also true that a major portion of teaching is done in Kannada. With more and more graduates who have had their entire education in the Kannada medium, entering the teaching profession, either as permanent or guest faculty at all levels of education, teaching–learning goes on almost entirely in Kannada. Today, except in a few city-based private colleges and a few university departments, the English medium is virtually non-existent. It is needless to say that students who obtain their education in English medium would have an edge over others because English speaking skills are today a necessity and not a luxury.

The issue that needs to be addressed in this connection is about the preparedness of the discipline to provide the right direction to students and teachers by making available information sources, data bases, and translations of mandatory readings in all languages. Is that happening? I would unhesitatingly say 'yes', but only in a very limited way. The concerns expressed by Indira and Shanthi in their writing on sociology in Karnataka bring out the need to exercise caution in this matter:

> 'While on the subject of vernacularization, it is also important to recognize the role that textbooks written in Kannada played in popularizing the subject, especially at the undergraduate and pre-university levels. The contributions of some senior teachers both in junior and first-grade colleges who took pains to write books or translate English classics into Kannada must be acknowledged. However, with the passage of time and the increase in the proportion of students writing their examinations in the vernacular language, a great deal of commercialization of textbook writing has taken place. One of the challenges for controlling the quality of textbooks in Kannada lies in subjecting these publications to a rigid review process and rejecting those that do not fulfill the standard norms.
>
> While it is true that the use of the vernacular medium as a source of knowledge transmission at different levels of learning, and also in research programmes has to be supported, the limited availability of translations or research-based literature in the discipline makes it difficult for students and the research community to update/widen their knowledge horizons. Given the fact that a large number of research students who write their theses in Kannada are not conversant with English or other languages, their reference base is also very limited' (Indira and Shanthi 2023).

With both knowledge forms and transmission patterns widening in multiple ways, if those who are engaged with the discipline do not take the issue of regionalisation seriously and do not find viable alternatives sociology would be further marginalised.

Future Paths

With a history of more than 100 years, why is sociology facing a crisis situation in the state of Karnataka? Is it because the system and its stake-holders, barring a few exceptions are not making an effort to reorient the focus of the discipline and the pedagogical practices? Is the discipline being pushed to a state of complacency because of its reluctance or even refusal in many cases to engage in a critical review process? Has the time not come for engaging in a consultative process involving persons from within and outside the fraternity to redesign the process of teaching and research? Here are a few suggestions for addressing these questions.

- There is an immediate need to subject the sociology curriculum at all levels to a rigid and critical peer review process by involving entrepreneurs with innovative ideas both from academia and industry. There is a need to bring a convergence between the theory and practice of sociology. Novel subject areas which give a sense of contemporary relevance to sociology must be introduced.
- The priority today is to take sociology beyond the classroom. It is also equally important to take it into medical, engineering, law, management and other classrooms. The thrust must now be on 'doing sociology' and not just 'learning sociology' and imagining that it would bring its rewards. It is the field that must be the focal point and not just 'grades' that are slowly losing their value.

- Courses on research methodology, which instil fieldwork and writing skills in students must be introduced both in undergraduate and postgraduate levels. Given the fact that Karnataka today has taken up major research-based evaluation projects, we must train our students to find placements in this sector.
- It is very important to instil digital and speaking and writing skills both in Kannada and English in our students and faculty desirous of equipping themselves with new skills. Knowledge of AI, Big data analysis and integrating technology into curriculum delivery practices must be given both to students and faculty.
- It is of critical importance to identify the sectors which are future employers of sociology graduates and apprise them of the relevance of the discipline of sociology in their respective work areas. This not only opens up employment opportunities but also serves as a value addition to the discipline.

I would like to conclude by quoting Mukherji (2006) who in his presidential address to the XXXI All India Sociological Congress held in 2005 at Jammu had said,

> 'Our society is now a living professional organisation. But let there be no mistaking that it will thrive only as long as we continue to engage with teaching and research in sociology as they relate with the change and transformations in our country and the world, and make our voices heard' (Mukherji 2006, p. 172).

References

Indira R, Shanthi G (2003) Sociology in Karnataka: looking back on its century old trail. In: Nagla BK (ed) Sociology in India: regions and histories. Rawat Publications, Jaipur

Jayaram N (2011) Sociology in Karnataka: the formation and decline of a discipline. In: Patel S (ed) Doing sociology in India: genealogies, locations, and practices. OUP India: Kindle Edition

Partha Nath Mukherji (2006) Sociology for what? rethinking sociology in an era of transformatory changes. Sociol Bull 55(2):172–200

Shah AM (2000) Sociology in regional context. In: Situating sociology—a symposium on knowledge. Institutions and practices in a discipline. Indian Seminar.Com. https://www.india-seminar.com/2000/495/495%20a.m.%20shah.htm

Chapter 3
Sociology in Northeast India: Beginning to Present

Ajailiu Niumai

Abstract Sociology as a discipline was formally introduced in Northeast India during the late 1960s. This development has played a crucial role in shaping our understanding of the region's social dynamics. This chapter will examine the trajectory of sociology in Northeast India. Secondly, it examines the contributions of some sociologists to the growth of sociology in the region. Finally, it will examine the reasons for creating a regional sociological association that promotes collaboration among scholars from both the region and beyond. Sociology as a discipline in Northeast India still grapples with the need for localised theoretical models that move beyond mainstream Indian sociological paradigms, which often overlook the region's specificities.

Keywords Sociology · Anthropology · Tribe · Northeast region · Contributions

Introduction

Sociology in Northeast India has an anthropological orientation and it was confined to the ethnographic study of certain indigenous tribes by the colonial administrators cum anthropologists during the colonial period. The development of sociology as a discipline in Northeast India is rooted in ethnology since the colonial administration emphasised on documenting ethnographic reports and monographs on tribes and ethnic communities. The concept of 'tribe' in Northeast India is a colonial construct and did not exist earlier. It was used by the colonial administrators to describe certain communities, and it has since been adopted by academics and researchers to refer to these groups. Some of the earliest works on the sociology of Northeast India

A. Niumai (✉)
Centre for the Study of Social Inclusion, University of Hyderabad, Hyderabad, India
e-mail: ajainiumai@uohyd.ac.in

Department of Sociology, University of Johannesburg, Johannesburg, South Africa

A. Chauhan et al. (eds.), *Hundred Years of Sociology in India: Evolving Issues, Emerging Trends*, https://doi.org/10.1007/978-981-96-1317-5_3

were written by colonial administrators and anthropologists such as Pemberton, R, B. (1827), Yule (1844), Oldhan 1854), Godwin (1873), Mackenzie (1884), Soppit (1969), Chambers (1889), Hodson (1905, 1911), Shakespear (1914), Hutton (1921a, b), Mills (1922, 1926), Von Furer Haimendorf (1938), and the like. These works reveal that the sociology of Northeast India is the study of the social, cultural, economic, and political life of the communities in the region. Sociology could not evolve as a discipline on its own during the colonial period and hence, it co-joined with anthropology. Virginius Xaxa affirms that "*Sociology has a very late entry in the Northeast India. In Eastern India, it was Anthropology that has a historical priority, a hangover of the colonial division of sociology and anthropology.*"

This chapter will address three issues. It will trace the origin of sociology in Northeast India; secondly, it examines the contributions of some sociologists to the study and development of sociology in the region; and thirdly, examine the reasons for creating a regional sociological association. Northeast India is often dominated by the question of subjugation and hegemony which leads to certain kinds of assertions for sub-nationalism, ethnic identity, and sovereignty (Biswas and Suklabaidya 2008). And, the assertion of autonomy becomes problematic in the region due to a combination of historical, political, social, and economic factors. While autonomy is a legitimate expression of cultural and political aspirations, challenges arise that make the process complex and sometimes contentious.

The Northeast region was not a sociological entity in the past since it has been excluded from the mainland intellectual discourse. Dibrugarh University is the first in Northeast India to introduce sociology in 1967. Gradually, a few Universities in the region established the department of sociology. Initially, they offered post-graduate, Master of Philosophy (MPhil), and Ph.D. programmes. MPhil was discontinued in 2022 under the National Education Policy 2020. Later, various colleges offered under-graduate courses in sociology. The department of sociology and its faculty in various institutions, universities, and colleges in the Northeast region focus on the social issues specific to the region. In this context, we can argue that these departments and faculty contribute collectively to what could be informally referred to as a '*sociology of Northeast India*' because of their shared emphasis on studying the socio-cultural, ethnic, tribal, religious and political complexities of the region. There isn't an established or recognised school of Northeast India Sociological tradition in the same sense as Bombay School and Lucknow School.

Some important questions arise as to what drives sociologists to examine not only contemporary society but also the historical context that shapes it? Why has sociological research on Northeast India been scanty? Studying the past helps sociologists identify patterns and trends, allowing them to analyse how certain aspects of society have evolved. Therefore, the regional particularity of Northeast India opens up a methodological question as it is different from both the models of mainland India or of highland Burma as proposed by Leach (1973) and the like. Referring to the past allows sociologists to explore the historical underpinnings of current societal dynamics and make informed observations about the future trajectory of societies. In fact, sociologists can trace the origin of these issues and gain insights into their development. Sociological research on Northeast India has been scanty for several reasons. For instance, the region has been marginalised in the context of academic attention making it difficult for researchers to conduct rigorous studies. Secondly, the Northeast has experienced various natural and man-made calamities like landslides, floods, ethnic conflicts and insurgencies, which directly hinder researchers from conducting their work effectively. The current ethnic conflict in Manipur which started on 3 May 2023 between the Meitei and Kuki-Zo communities has, at times, made research activities difficult due to safety concerns and restrictions on mobility. This continues to be a major barrier that must be addressed in our discussions and planning.

This study employed a qualitative research method, especially purposive sampling to interview nine sociologists who have worked on the Northeast region and contributed towards the development of sociology as a discipline. Most of them are retired and one of them M. N. Karna passed away on 19 April 2023. I contacted the selected respondents via telephone and took their consent to write about their contributions. And, I engaged in face-to-face conversations and individual interviews even through email with selected respondents between March–August 2023. The contributions of two sociologists will be based on secondary sources. I formulated unstructured questionnaires for the interview. Most of them preferred to send their responses through email, which led to accurate and insightful data. The online interviews via email provided flexibility to respond at their convenience, allowing them to carefully consider their responses over time. Additionally, it provided conciseness of expression which is useful in this study.

Contributions of Some Sociologists and the Growth of Sociology Departments in Colleges and Universities

The contributions of P. K. B. Nayar, T. K. Oommen, S. M. Dubey, M. N. Karna, Virginius Xaxa, Tiplut Nongbri, A. C. Sinha, and Biswajit Ghosh particularly in Assam, Meghalaya, and Tripura will draw special attention in this section. I also interviewed Pranjal Sarma to know the current thrust areas of the department of sociology at Dibrugarh University as it is the first department of sociology in the region. The illustrious works of T. K. Oommen especially on tribes (Adivasis) are important in Northeast sociology. He has published a book titled "Social Inclusion in Independent India: Dimensions and Approaches" by Orient BlackSwan (2014). He has referred to the people of the Northeast as one of the socially excluded categories of India in Chap. 11, "Refugees, Foreigners, Outsiders and North-East India: Need for Differing Approaches for Social Inclusion." He said, "*The first paper I published on the theme of tribe (Adivasis) was a paper titled 'The Rural–Urban Continuum Re-examined In The Indian Context' in Sociologia Ruralis, the official organ of the European Rural Sociological Society. I have described the circumstances that prompted me to publish the paper in this journal in my book: 'Trials, Tribulations and Triumphs,' published by Konark Publishers in 2018, Chap. 11 particularly pages 135 onwards. It is clear that the Indian sociological establishment did not publish my paper because my position did not fall in line with their thinking. I have argued in my paper that the tribes (Adivasis) have a distinct identity, a perspective that is not acceptable by most Indian social scientists. As you know, G. S. Ghurye considered tribes as backward Hindus, M. N. Srinivas imagined their absorption to Hinduism through Sanskritization, N. K. Bose thought of tribes as undergoing the Hindu mode of absorption, and Surajit Sinha postulated a tribe-caste continuum,* etc. *That is, conceding a specific identity to Adivasis was not acceptable to Indian sociologists and social anthropologists.*" Oommen's work remains important for Northeast Sociology, as it validates the region's pluralities and contestations, pushing for analytical frameworks that resists homogenization. After two decades of India's independence, the first post graduate (PG) programme in sociology was established at Dibrugarh University and P. K. B. Nayar moved from Kerala to join as the first faculty. P. K. B. Nayar recalls, "*When Dibrugarh University advertised the post of Reader in their newly started Department of Sociology in 1967, I applied for it since I had been working as Lecturer in social sciences in the Kerala University. I was appointed as Reader and Head of the Department of Sociology even without an interview in Dibrugarh. I had a very good time though both the place and the University had been new to me. I drafted the Post Graduate Programme in Sociology and helped in the selection of two Lecturers in Sociology. One is a male (I think his name is Chauhan) and the other was the daughter of the Principal of the neighbouring college known as Dibrugarh Hanumanbux Surajmal Kanoi Commerce College. The University had only two other Social Science Departments at that time - Political Science and Anthropology. Thereafter, I continued there for a year but resigned during the summer vacation. The main reason was that my parents were old and I had to catch three planes without connecting flights, which would take two days, to reach home. However, I joined the USAID Programme in New Delhi because there were direct train and plane services to Trivandrum. I was invited by the Department of Sociology, Dibrugarh University in 1989 (I do not remember the exact date) for two weeks' Visiting Professorship. Dibrugarh had changed a lot since my departure but I soon adjusted to the environment. Dibrugarh will be always remembered by me with a lot of sweet memories. My colleagues, office staff and students there were very affectionate and loving.*"

While remembering his stint at Dibrugarh University, P. K. B. Nayar said, "*The Vice-Chancellor (Dr. N. R. Seth) will take me to all places where he was invited and will ask me to speak without notice. After one or two meetings, I got myself prepared for a possible speech whenever I went with him for meetings. In October 1967, when the University was formally inaugurated by Dr. Thrigun Sen (then Minister for Education in the Union Cabinet), I was an invited speaker. I published an article titled 'Dibrugarh University: Challenge and Response' in the ASSAM TRIBUNE (Daily) on that day. In my speech, I said that the Dibrugarh University will be breaking new ground in educational matters in Upper Assam.*" His one-year service was significant in laying the foundational ethos of the department and marked a formative moment in the institutionalisation of sociology in the region.

After P. K. B. Nayar left the department, S. M. Dubey joined the Department of Sociology in 1968. He took major initiatives for the upgradation of sociology as a discipline in Northeast India. He realised that there were several misgivings about sociology in Northeast India. The contents of sociology and studies in sociology did not appropriately deal with sociological discourse, which is now considered as mainstream sociology. In 1969, the Department of Sociology, Dibrugarh University established the Centre for Sociological Study of Frontier Region and started a journal titled *The North Eastern Research Bulletin*. Both the Centre and the Journal played a significant role in the growth of sociological research in this region. The first issue of the journal came out in 1970. Unfortunately, the Centre stopped functioning due to a shortage of manpower and financial support from concerned authorities and the government (Saikia 2017). This journal publishes papers, research notes, and book reviews every year by the Registrar, Dibrugarh University, Assam. In 1969, the first undergraduate Department of Sociology was established in Jorhat College under Dibrugarh University. Gradually, the establishment of universities in the Northeast region paved the way for sociology to take root.

One of the important contributions in this direction in Dibrugarh, Assam was later made by the historian Sheila Bora on the women question in Northeast India where she pointed to various roles and statuses of women at home and work-place. Pranjal Sarma asserts that "*with a vision of promoting critical understanding and building better societies, the Department of Sociology at Dibrugarh University fosters interdisciplinary cooperation to generate scientific knowledge and critical thinking among its scholars. The department serves as a hub for research and teaching, encompassing various specialized areas within sociology, such as Industrial Sociology, Urban Studies, Rural Studies, Sociology of Education, Social Change and Development, Tribal Studies, and Gender Studies. The curriculum is thoughtfully designed to meet the manpower needs of diverse industrial organizations and both public and private sectors. I had the privilege of serving as the Head of the Department, where I played a crucial role in overseeing the department's affairs and promoting a nurturing academic environment.*" At present, the faculty members include Pranjal Sarma, Seema Verma Borabora, Jyoti Prasad Saikia, Upasona Sarmah, Bikash Dena, Kuheli Das, Bhairab Hazarika, Rhishika Baruah, Anannya Gogoi, Dhriti Sonowal, and Pooja Chetry. The retired faculty members are B.N.Borthakur, S.C. Sarmah, Prasanta Bordoloi, D. Doley, Ashwini Kr. Bora, and Joyanta Borborah. Their contributions have enriched the department. The evolution of sociological enquiry at Dibrugarh University has been marked by an enduring commitment to regional relevance and interdisciplinary engagement.

The second Department of Sociology jointly with Anthropology in Northeast India was established at the North-Eastern Hill University (NEHU), Shillong in 1976 with a Master of Arts (MA), Master of Philosophy (MPhil), and Doctor of Philosophy (Ph.D.) programmes with the joining of Prof. G. S. Aurora. Initially, it was housed in a private bungalow in a residential area with twenty-one (21) MA students and one lecturer where classes used to be conducted in a garage. Gradually, the strength of the faculty increased to five and later, it increased to seven faculty with a total of sixty students in 1980. Under the leadership of Prof. G. S. Aurora, Dr. A. P. Sinha and Dr. A. C. Sinha were recruited as Readers including two lecturers viz; Mr. C. Nunthara and Mr. M. K. Rao. Subsequently, Dr. Virginius Xaxa, Dr. Nikhilesh Kumar, Dr. C.

L. Imchen, Dr. M. N. Karna, Dr. P. M. Chacko, Dr. P. S. Dutta, Dr. I. L. Aier, Dr. A. K. Nongkynrih, and Prof. Tiplut Nongbri joined the department. Some of them left the department after they served for a few years or retired and one of them Prof. A. K. Nongkynrih passed away in 2021. Currently, the Department of Sociology has six faculty members viz; Prof. B. Panda, Prof. D. V. Kumar, Prof. Rekha Shangpliang, Prof. Kedilezo Kikhi, Mr. Md. Yusuf Khan, and Dr. Rashi Bhargava. The Department of Sociology at NEHU played a significant role in shaping the study of sociology in the region. The faculty members have been instrumental in shaping Northeast Sociology by fostering regionally grounded scholarship, promoting ethnographic research, and nurturing a generation of sociologists attuned to the region's diverse social realities. The contributions of four eminent sociologists who have worked at NEHU and whom I have interacted and interviewed will be highlighted briefly. Unfortunately, due to word limitations, analysing the contributions of other senior sociologists is not feasible in this chapter.

I would like to emphasize Virginius Xaxa's perspective since he worked in the Department of Sociology at NEHU from 1978 to 1990. He affirms that, "*the setting up of the NEHU at Shillong was the major development in the spread of sociology in the region, although Dibrugarh University was the first to have a Department of Sociology. The Department at NEHU began as the Department of Sociology and Social Anthropology. However, it was bifurcated into two different departments of Sociology and Anthropology in 1982. Subsequently, its teaching of sociology spread to some colleges in Assam. The NEHU as a University cared for the Hill regions of Northeast India. Nagaland, Meghalaya, and Mizoram were the key constituents of the NEHU, as unlike Assam, Manipur, and Tripura—they did not have a university then. Accordingly, there were campuses of NEHU in Nagaland and Mizoram. Though the NEHU was administratively confined to a few pockets, it attracted a large number of students especially tribal students from other states of the region such as Assam, Manipur, Tripura, and Arunachal Pradesh. The spread of the Department of Sociology is associated intricately with the spread of the central universities and the subsequent development of private universities including the private colleges.*"

Virginius Xaxa recalls, "*My contribution to the understanding of Northeast India in general and tribes, in particular, has been more in the form of participation in seminars and conferences than in the form of writing. As for the writings are concerned, it has not been tribes of the Northeast per se except in more recent times. An earlier reference to tribes has been more in the context of the comparative study of tribes across tribal regions in India with a focus on movements, identity, development,* etc. *In my recent writings on the Northeast, I have focused on aspects of social differentiation, social exclusion, and social inequality. However, my key contribution has been in respect of the supervision of the M. Phil. and Ph.D. theses of a good number of students from the Northeast and shaping their ideas and perspectives.*" Xaxa has also worked at the Tata Institute of Social Sciences in Guwahati from 2011–2016 and Tezpur University, Assam from 2016 to 2018 and he has made significant contributions to the study of sociology especially on issues related to indigenous communities, land rights, identity, social exclusion, inequality, and development.

Tiplut Nongbri recalls her stint at NEHU, "*The brief period I spent at the NEHU was a homecoming of sorts. It provided me with a chance to engage with students who hailed from various tribes and communities of the region, each bringing their own set of unique stories and experiences. This period enabled me to reflect and refine my perspective of the region seeing from close quarters many of the social and political dynamics that textbooks rarely provide. The most memorable was seeing gender in action and the role of the political class in perpetuating the subordination of women.*[1] *This reaffirmed my ideas on gender inequality, intra-tribal and inter-tribal relations, and the importance of collective action to bring about transformation in society. The short stint at NEHU also gave me the opportunity to meet and interact with local scholars and community leaders, whose works and insights became invaluable to my subsequent work.*"

In the context of challenges, while doing research in sociology, Tiplut Nongbri said, "*Some challenges propelled me to use my regional and socio-cultural identity, to convey the richness of North Eastern societies, their power and gender dynamics, unique kinship structure, and tribal complexities, to the wider academic community. My research projects often took me back to my roots, where I worked closely with people on the ground, understanding their histories, struggles, and aspirations. These engagements provided valuable insights not only into the interplay of gender, kinship, and ethnicity in North Eastern societies but also the power of Sociology and its theoretical tools to uncover the hidden dynamics in human society. For instance, while my birth and upbringing in the Khasi family helped me in no small way to understand the intricacy of the matrilineal system, long seen as a haven for women, it was sociology and the methodological tools it developed that opened my eyes to the inner dynamics that lie beyond and below the surface level. Some of the papers*[2]*I wrote clearly illustrate this fact. The research not only exploded the myth that matrilineal descent confers superior status to women but also unequivocally exposed the sordid way in which a woman's body and her sexuality are reduced to a site where ethnic politics are fought and debated.*" Tiplut Nongbri's reflections on her time at NEHU and her research journey embody a deep reflexive and regionally grounded sociology that challenges both disciplinary silences and dominant national frameworks. Through her insider-outsider perspective as a Khasi sociologist, Nongbri

[1] *On this, see 'Meghalaya State Commission for Women and the Politics of Empowerment' Chap. 7 in Tiplut Nongbri A Situational Analysis of Women and Girls in Meghalaya, National Commission for Women, New Delhi, 2006.*

[2] *See in particular, 'Ethnicity and Gender: Ethnic Politics among the Khasi', Chap. 8 in Tiplut Nongbri, Development, Ethnicity and Gender: Select Essays on Tribes in India, Rawat Publications, Delhi & Jaipur, 2003 and 'Researching the Khasi: Encounter with the Self' Chap. 16 in N Jayaram (ed) Knowing the Social World: Perspectives & Possibilities, Orient BlackSwan, Delhi, 2017, pp. 323–344.*

(1991), *Language, Region and National Identity* (Sage 1999), *Agrarian Structures and Land Reforms in Assam* (2004), and *Democracy, Pluralism and Conflict* (2006), *Socio-economic aspects of ethnic identity in North-Eastern India* (2013), and *Language, Region and National Identity* (2020). His latest work before his demise is *Power to People in Meghalaya: Sixth Schedule and the 73rd Amendment* (2021).

expands the epistemological horizons of Indian sociology, making Northeast India's social worlds both visible and intellectually indispensable.

I would also like to mention the contributions of the two other eminent sociologists, viz; M. N. Karna and Awadhesh Coomar Sinha (A. C. Sinha). M. N. Karna taught sociology at NEHU and he was also the Honorary Director of the North-Eastern Regional Centre of the ICSSR at Shillong and Director of A. N. Sinha Institute of Social Studies, Patna.

M.N. Karna taught at Patna University and IIT, Kanpur too. His areas of research focus on social movements, land relations, and agrarian studies in North East India. His major works are *Land Relations in North-East India* (1987), *Social Movements in North-East India* (1991). A. C. Sinha contributed to the Sikkimese and Nepalese studies in the region. He has served as the Head of the Department of Sociology and Dean of the School of Social Sciences, at NEHU. His areas of research are political sociology, Himalayan studies, and sociology of environment. Some of his major works include *Politics of Sikkim* (1975), *The Indian North-East Frontier and the Nepalese Immigrants* in N. K. Rustomji and C. Ramble (Eds.), *Himalayan Environment and Culture* (1990), with Pariyaram M. Chacko, I. L. Aier—*Hill Cities of Eastern Himalayas: Ethnicity, Land Relations and Urbanisation* (1993), *Beyond the Trees, Tribes and Tigers: Historical Sociology of Eastern Himalayan Forests* (1993), *The Nepalis in North East India: A Community in search of Indian Identity*, edited with Subba (2003), *Verrier Elwin's idea of civilization: An analysis* in T. B. Subba & S. Som (Eds.), Between Ethnography and Fiction: Verrier Elwin and the Tribal Question in India: Colonial Anthropology versus Indological Sociology Elwin and Ghurye on Tribal Policy in India (Chap. 6), Orient Blackswan (2005), *Cultural Change Among the Tribes of Northeast India* in Subba, T. B., Puthenpurakal, J., & Puykunnel, S. J. (Eds.), Christianity and Change in Northeast India (2015), and *Northeast India: History of the Present and Predicament of the Future in Communities, Institutions and Histories of India's Northeast*, Routledge (2021). Both Karna and Sinha taught sociology and mentored several Ph.D. students who are serving as faculty in various universities and colleges across India. Their contributions stand as foundational pillars in the development of Sociology in the region, both in terms of scholarship and institution building. They not only produced rich empirical work but also played crucial roles at NEHU and other institutions in embedding sociology. Their legacies continue to inspire scholarship that is historically informed, regionally embedded and sociologically rigorous.

The third Department of Sociology in Northeast India was opened in Mizoram on 28 July 1982 at Pachunga University College. The fourth Department of Sociology was introduced in Tripura in 1985 in a prestigious government college named Maharaja Bir Bikram College (MBBC), which later became a state-aided university. A senior teacher of the Department of Political Science Dr. Jagadish Gan Chaudhuri was temporarily given the additional charge of the department, and a few guest teachers were appointed to manage the academic load of the BA general course. The curriculum of The University of Calcutta was followed in ditto as all colleges of the state of Tripura were then operated under its jurisdiction. The department got its first full-time Assistant Professor when Biswajit Ghosh joined on 24 August 1986.

Biswajit Ghosh said, "*Sociology then became a very popular option to many Arts graduates and the venue of the department had to be shifted to a bigger classroom because of student pressure. Nearly 80 students were admitted every year to the BA Sociology course of the college. Though the examination process was then managed and controlled by the Department of Sociology of The University of Calcutta, sociology students of Maharaja Bir Bikram College (MBBC) were found to pass with high grades.*" Before leaving MBBC in September 1993, Biswajit Ghosh was able to establish the discipline on its strong footing as MBBC was then the only college in Tripura offering Sociology to its students.

The fifth Department of Sociology was established at Assam University, Silchar in July 1995. Prof. Nirakar Mallick joined as the founding faculty on 20 July 1995. Other faculty who joined the Department of Sociology include Dr. Aradhana Das, Prof. Arvind Chauhan, Prof. Manjit Singh (retired from Punjab University), Prof. Humayun Bakth, Prof. V. P. Singh, Prof. Pariyaram Chako, Prof. N. Sudhakar Rao, Prof. G. Ram, Prof. Jhimli Bhattacharjee, Dr. Bijaya Kumar Behera, Dr. Ruma Debnath, Dr. Rajiya Shahani, and Dr. Shailendra Kumar. Some of them left the department after serving for a couple of years. They introduced two courses on Northeast India, viz; Sociology of Northeast India and Culture and Development in Northeast India.

The sixth Department of Sociology was established at Nagaland University on 6th September 1997 under the School of Social Science at the University headquarters Lumami campus with 25 student intake capacity in the initial stage. The Ph.D. programme started in the department in 2003. Today, the faculty members include Temjensonang, Toshimenla Jamir, Athungo Ovung, Sandeep Gupta, Yamsani Srikanth, Pitheli K Jimo, Dipika Paul, and Suraj Beri. Previously, A. Lanunungsang Ao, S. Nzanbemo Lotha, Kelhouputuo Theunou, and K. Rajendra Singh worked in the department but have now retired. The seventh Department of Sociology was established at Tezpur University, Tezpur in Assam in 2006. Prof. Chandan Kumar Sharma is the pioneer of the Department of Sociology. The other faculty members include Amiya Kumar Das, Rabin Deka, S. S. Sumesh, Nirmali Gogoi, Sarmistha Das, Subhadeepta Ray, A.S. Shimreiwung, and Pamidi hagjer. Virginius Xaxa and Chandrasekhar Bhat made a meaningful impact on the Department during their time at Tezpur University. Today, it is among the better-known Departments of Sociology in the region.

The eighth Department of Sociology was established at Sikkim University in 2008. The faculty members are Sandhya Thapa, Binod Bhattarai, Srijana Singh, Swati Akshay Sachdeva, K. Indira, Shankar Narayan Bagh, and Sona Rai. The ninth Department of Sociology came into existence at Rajiv Gandhi University, Arunachal Pradesh in 2010 under the leadership of the Vice-Chancellor Prof. Tamo Mibang and Prof. Maqitul Hussain. The academic session started in August 2011. Prof. Hussain was given the Head-in-charge and later, Bikash Bage took over as the head of the Department and pioneer in 2012. Later, other faculty members like Padi Hana, and Nani Umie joined the department. The department started its M.Phil and Ph.D programmes in 2015 and Post Graduate course in 2022. The tenth Department of Sociology was established at Gauhati University in 2011. The faculty members include

Shabeena Yasmin Saikia, Kaberi Das, Swarnali Basumatary, and Ritwik Rupam Sarma. The M.A. programme in sociology was launched in Gauhati University in 2009 under the auspices of the Department of Political Science which later became an independent department. The eleventh post-graduate Department of Sociology was formed in Tripura University (A Central University) in 2011. At present, the only faculty member is Parama Chakma. The twelfth Department of Sociology was established in Manipur University in 2012. The faculty members include Kshetri Rajendra Singh (retired), Mayanglambam Lilee Devi, Takhellambam Deepamanjuri Devi and Yumlembam Khogen. The thirteenth Department of Sociology was established at Mizoram University in April 2015. The faculty members are R.K. Mohanty, R. Lalhrualliana, B. Lalzarliana, and Samuel L. Chuaungo. The fourteenth and fifteenth Departments of Sociology were introduced with the post graduate programme in Cotton University (faculty members are Draghima Basumatary, Indrani Sarma, Pratisha Borborah, Jyoti Das, and Sima Shree Bora), and Assam Women's University, Guwahati (faculty members include Kuki Boruah, Rimlee Das, and Himakshi Choudhury). Gradually, many more departments of sociology were established in both central and state universities including colleges in the Northeast region.

Sociology is also offered at the Tata Institute of Social Sciences, Guwahati (faculty members are Stephen Pamei, and V. Sawmveli), Indian Institute of Technology (IIT) in Guwahati (faculty members include Ngamjahao Kipgen, Sawmya Ray, Sambit Mallick, Visakh Madhusoodanan Subha, and Rituparna Patgiri), National Institute of Technology, Dimapur in Nagaland (A. Wati Walling is the sociology faculty member), and in some deemed and private universities in the region. Subrat K Nanda in his chapter titled 'Sociology in Northeast India' in Maitreyee Chaudhuri's (2010) edited book on 'Sociology in India: Intellectual and Institutional Practices,' mentioned that sociology is taught in North Eastern Regional Council of Indian Council of Social Science Research (ICSSR), Shillong; Institute of Peace and Conflict Studies, Guwahati; Tribal Research Institute, Guwahati; Tribal Research Institute, Itanagar; and Omeo Kumar Das Institute of Social Change and Development (OKDISCD), Guwahati. Sociological courses are taught to the B.Tech students, postgraduate and Ph.D students in IIT Guwahati. Sociological courses are also taught to the students of Assam Agricultural University in Jorhat and Central Agricultural University in Imphal. Nursing colleges in different parts of the region also teach a few sociological courses to their students. There has been institutional spread but sociology is not perceived as of any special import either as a career option or as a fruitful research endeavour. Nonetheless, these institutions often engage with the unique socio-cultural context of Northeast India in their research and teaching. I am not able to elaborate on all the research themes of each department due to the constraint of the word limit in this chapter. From the above narratives, it is clear that some people from outside the Northeast region have come there to nurture the discipline of sociology. Later on, the local scholars from the region and also people from outside the region joined the departments of sociology and enhanced the quality of research and teaching. The Northeast India has played a significant role in advancing sociological discourse, with North Eastern Hill University hosting the 18th All India

Sociological Conference (AISC) in May 1987 on the theme 'Sociology and Social Transformation,' when Victor D'Souza was the President of the Indian Sociological Society (ISS), followed by Tezpur University organising the 43rd AISC in 2016 with the theme 'Rethinking Sociological Traditions of India,' when Sujata Patel served as the President of the ISS, and more recently, the University of Science and Technology hosting the 47th AISC under the theme 'Hundred Years of Sociology in India: Exploring Trajectories for the Future,' when Abha Chauhan was the President of the ISS.

Formation of The Northeast India Regional Sociological Association

On 29 September 1973, Prof. S. M. Dubey with a group of enthusiastic research scholars established the North-East India Sociological Association (NEISA) in Dibrugarh University, Assam, and the first conference of the Association was held in September 1973. To form this association, a convention was held in September 1973. Dubey (1978) mentioned that the Department of Sociology and the Centre of Sociological Study of the Frontier Region of the Dibrugarh University in collaboration with the North East India Sociological Association (NEISA) organised a three-day national seminar in March 1975 on "*Sociological Perspectives on North East India.*" This was the first attempt to debate the region from a sociological perspective with a special focus on social structure, political sociology, and sociology of economic development. All the papers presented were published in his edited volume including some additional published articles from the *North Eastern Research Bulletin* (Saikia 2017). NEISA was registered as a society in Guwahati, Assam in 1975 but it became defunct within a few years.

On 3 December 2021, the author created a WhatsApp group dedicated to Northeast India Sociology. This initiative aims to create a unified platform that promotes active sociological discussions, connect with others, share new research trends in the region, and work towards establishing a Northeast Sociology network. The response from the sociology community was impressive, with over one hundred individuals participating in the group. There was a thirst for sociological discourse among the sociology fraternity from the Northeast region to come together under one umbrella. Many members felt the need to form an association since they wanted a platform to network, disseminate ideas, knowledge, and information. However, the like-minded members felt that it was not a good idea to call one hundred members of the WhatsApp group for a meeting. Therefore, they decided to invite faculty members from ten Universities in the region and had its first meeting on 7 December 2021. And, NEISA was formed on 3 January 2022. This is keeping in trend with the marriage of new media with traditional academic disciplines and the questions asked in the WhatsApp group have contributed to a new direction in debates of forming a brand new NEISA. This initiative filled the vacuum that existed for a long time among the Northeast sociology fraternity.

Before forming NEISA, the author consulted seniors like Tiplut Nongbri, Virginius Xaxa, R. Indira, C. S. Bhat, and a few other scholars to gather their ideas, suggestions, and inputs. NEISA did not conduct an election but nominated sixteen (16) Core Members aka Managing Committee (MC) Members among themselves from eight states. There is a general consensus that the MC should have representatives from all the eight states of Northeast India. Tiplut Nongbri is the Senior Advisor to NEISA. In 2022, NEISA opened a savings bank account in Punjab & Sind Bank in Manipur using the life membership fees of R.K. Mohanty and the author. The author took the initiative to draft the Memorandum of Association (MOA) and Byelaws, actively seeking and incorporating valuable suggestions from Prof. Tiplut Nongbri, Prof. Chandan Kumar Sharma, Prof. M. Amarjeet Singh, Prof. R. K. Mohanty and Prof. Temjensonang. The suggestions were meticulously polished and approved by members in a Managing Committee meeting, paving the way for the registration of the Society. Its temporary Head Office is C/o Head, Department of Sociology, University of Tezpur, Assam, and it may be relocated to any place in North East India from time to time for the Society to function.

The following are the first office bearers:

President—Prof. A. C Sinha (retired from NEHU).

Vice-President—Prof. Chandan Kumar Sharma (Tezpur University).

Secretary—Prof. Ajailiu Niumai (University of Hyderabad).

Joint Secretary—Prof. Biswambhar Panda (NEHU) and Prof. M. Amarjeet Singh (Jamia Millia Islamia).

Treasurer—Prof. R. K. Mohanty (Mizoram University).

Managing Committee Members—Prof. Kedilezo Kikhi (Tezpur University), Prof. Kshetri Rajendra Singh (Manipur University), Prof. Temjensosang (Nagaland University), Dr. Aphun Kamei (Delhi School of Economics), Dr. Rekha M. Shangpliang (NEHU), Dr. Bikash Bage (Rajiv Gandhi University, Arunachal Pradesh), Dr. Indrani Sarma (Cotton University, Assam), Dr. Upasana Sarma (Dibrugarh University), Dr. Sandhya Thapa (Sikkim University), Dr. Khuraijam Bijoykumar (North East Studies, JNU, Delhi), and Dr. Sharmila Chottaray (Tripura University).

A. C. Sinha could not make himself available to function as the President of NEISA due to his prior commitments, so Chandan Kumar Sharma was unanimously nominated as the President in May 2023 by the Managing Committee Members. Temjensosang is nominated as the Vice-President and the other office bearers remain the same. In 2022, NEISA was officially affiliated with the Indian Sociological Society (ISS) as one of the regional sociological associations. And, it has been officially registered as a Society under The Societies Registration Act, 1860 in Guwahati, Assam on 2 May 2024 named "Sociological Association of North Eastern India" (SANEI). It is important to note that the name NEISA could not be utilized, as a society by that name had already been registered in 1975. The formation of SANEI is crucial for addressing the unique socio-cultural dynamics and challenges faced by communities in the region. This association will provide a platform for sociology fraternity who works on the region to come together, fostering collaboration that is essential for tackling the diverse sociological issues often neglected in mainstream discourse. One of the main goals of SANEI is to facilitate meaningful dialogue, and advocate for social change and inclusion that the region rightfully deserves.

SANEI organises the Occasional Special Lecture Series twice a year. In 2022, Professor T. K. Oommen delivered the first Special Lecture Series on "*Exclusion and Inclusion of North East India,*" held online on 18 August 2022, where around one thousand faculty, scholars, and students from various parts of India and overseas attended. The second Special Lecture Series on "*The Near Future of Indian Higher Education,*" was delivered by Satish Deshpande on 21 January 2023. Rowena Robinson delivered the third Special Lecture Series on "*New Possibilities for Indian Sociology: Quantitative, Collaborative and Comparative Research,*" held on 6 September 2023. The Fourth Special Lecture Series on "*Crisis of globalisation and Indian responses*" by Prof. Anand Kumar was held online on 15 March 2024. This lecture was in collaboration with the Department of Sociology, Sikkim University. Prof. R. Indira delivered the Fifth Special lecture Series on '*Teaching and Researching Sociology in the Regional Language*' on 6th December 2024. This event was organised by SANEI in collaboration with the Department of Sociology, Manipur University. SANEI is the youngest Regional Sociological Association in India and yet vibrant and active.

Sociological Themes in the Region

The major sociological themes which have been studied by the earlier sociologists in Northeast India were tribal studies, insurgency, ethnicity, religion, culture, tribal family and kinship, gender, political dynamics, tribal development, status of tribal women, social movements, and the like. In the 1990s and early 2000s, the major themes shifted to the sociology of education, medical sociology, identity politics, demography, the rise of middle class, minority rights, human rights, land rights, inheritance and customary laws, changing family relations, ecology and environment, impact of development projects, indigenous medicine, Non-Profit organisations (NGOs), and the like. In recent times, new emerging research trends in sociology focus on indigenous knowledge systems, identity and marginality, food studies, racism, LGBT rights, sexuality, land and forest rights, gender based violence, trafficking of women and girls, drug smuggling, sociology of crime, illegal migrants, migration and diaspora studies, environmental studies, women's reproductive health, surrogacy, IVF, social policy, development, livelihood, rural transformation, conflict and peacebuilding, and the like. The course on Sociology of Northeast India is currently being offered in several sociology departments across colleges and universities in the region.

Sociology has been taught in regional language at under-graduate level in Northeast India especially in Assam. And, teaching in regional language is one of the hindrances for the students to get exposure at national level (Jyoti Saikia 2017: 58).

Thus, teaching sociology in regional language at the under-graduate level in Northeast India becomes a constraint for the development of the discipline. P.K.B. Nayar (2007) asserts that teaching sociology in regional languages also contributed to difficulties in the subject for its takers. We don't have translations of classical sociology books into regional languages in the Northeast region. Hence, there is an absence of quality textbooks in regional languages and a lack of terminology that fails to ensure standards in the teaching of sociology in the region.

Conclusion

The sociology of Northeast India suffers from inadequate conceptual and theoretical development. Hence, it is imperative that we shift focus toward empirical research to establish a strong theoretical framework. The application of mainstream sociological concepts like sanskritisation, westernisation, and modernisation must be critically evaluated to effectively understand the unique context of the region. The emergence of young scholars exploring their societies is promising, yet this shift poses significant challenges regarding methodology and theoretical frameworks. Collaborative efforts between scholars from both within and outside the region are essential for enriching the discipline of sociology. The advancement of sociology in the region hinges on our ability to cultivate indigenous knowledge systems, adopt interdisciplinary and multidisciplinary approaches, and prioritize community-based participatory research. Furthermore, fostering inter-regional scholarly collaborations will be crucial in driving sociological inquiries forward.

References

Biswas P, Suklabaidya C (2008) Ethnic life-worlds in North-East India: an analysis, sage studies on India's North East. Sage publications, New Delhi

Chambers OA (1889) Hand book of The Lushai Country. Printed by the Superintendent of Government Printing, India

Dubey SM (1978) North East India—a sociological study. Concept Publishing Company, New Delhi, New Delhi

Godwin-Austen HH (1873) On Garo Hill tribes. J Anthropol Inst Great Brit Ireland 2:391–396. https://www.jstor.org/stable/2841459

Von Furer-Haimendorf C (1938) The Naked Nagas. London, 2nd edn. Calcutta, 1962

Hodson TC (1905) Manipur and it's tribes. J Roy Soc Arts LIII:545

Hodson TC (1911) The Naga tribes of Manipur. London

Hutton JH (1921a) The Angami Nagas, with some notes on the neighbouring tribes, 2nd edn. Bombay, London 1969

Hutton JH (1921b) The Sema Nagas, 2nd edn. Bombay, London, 1968, forward by Henry Balfour

Karna MN (ed) (1987) Land relations in North-East India. Gian Publishing House, Delhi

Karna MN (ed) (1991) Social movements in North-East India. Indus Publishing Company, New Delhi

Karna MN (2004) Agrarian structures and land reforms in Assam [Hardcover]. Regency Publications, New Delhi
Karna MN (2006) Democracy, pluralism and conflict. Rawat publication, Jaipur
Karna MN (2013) Socio-economic aspects of ethnic identity in North-Eastern India. Publisher unknown
Karna MN (2020) Language, region and national identity. Pac Rev 48(1):176–186. https://doi.org/10.1177/0038022919990105
Leach ER (1973) Political systems of highland Burma: a study of Kachin social structure. Routledge, UK
Mills JP (1922) The Lhota Nagas: with an introduction and supplementary notes. London
Mills JP (1926) The Ao Nagas. With a foreword by Henry Balfour, London
Mackenzie A (1884) History of the relations of the government with the hill tribes of North East Frontier of Bengal. Calcutta
Nayar PKB (2007) Sociology's quest for 'society': an enquiry into the current pursuits and needed concerns in the discipline. Sociol Bull 56(2):172–194
Oldham T (1854) On the geological structure of part of the Khasi Hills, with observations on the meteorology and ethnology of that district. Carbery (4)+78+(2)+lxxiipp
Oommen TK (2014) Social inclusion in independent India: dimensions and approaches. Orient BlackSwan, Hyderabad
Pemberton RB (1827) The Nagas, App. 13 in Wilson's Documents of the Burmese War, Calcutta
Saikia JP (2017) Sociology in North East India. Nat J Soc Sci Res 1:53–59. The Assam Kaziranga University, Jorhat, Assam
Shakespear LW (1914) History of upper Assam. Upper Burmah and North-Eastern Frontier, London
Soppit CA (1969) The Kachcha Nagas, 1884 in Verrier Elwin's book—Nagas in the nineteenth century. Oxford University Press, Bombay
Sinha AC (1975) Politics of Sikkim. Thomson Press, Haryana
Sinha AC (1990) The Indian north-east frontier and the Nepalese immigrants. In: Rustomji NK, Ramble C (eds) Himalayan environment and culture, IIAS, Shimla, pp n/a
Sinha AC, Chacko PM, Aier IL (1993) Hill cities of eastern Himalayas: ethnicity, land relations and urbanisation. South Asia Books, New Delhi
Sinha AC (1993) Beyond the trees, tribes and tigers: historical sociology of eastern Himalayan forests. Har-Anand, New Delhi
Sinha AC, Subba TB (2003) The Nepalis in North East India: a community in search of Indian Identity. Indus Publishing Company, New Delhi
Sinha AC (2005) Verrier Elwin's idea of civilization: an analysis. In: Subba TB, Som S (eds) Between ethnography and fiction: Verrier Elwin and the tribal question in India: colonial anthropology Vs indological sociology Elwin and Ghurye on tribal policy in India (Chapter 6) [Hardcover]. Orient BlackSwan, Hyderabad
Sinha AC (2015) Cultural change among the tribes of northeast India. In: Subba TB, Puthenpurakal J, Puykunnel SJ (eds) Christianity and change in Northeast India. Concept Publishing, New Delhi
Thomas CJ, Karna MN, Gassah LS (2021 and 2023) Power to people in Meghalaya (Sixth Schedule and the 73rd Amendment). Generic Publishers
Yule H (1844) Notes on the Khasia Hills, and people. J Asiatic Soc Bengal 152:612–631

Chapter 4
Journey of Sociology in Uttar Pradesh

Shweta Prasad

Abstract Sociology has completed 100 years of its journey in India. Despite deep Western hegemonic influences since its inception, the discipline has evolved over the years to focus on India-specific issues, approaches, and methods which is very much evident in the contributions of some of the leading sociologists from India. As the discipline is maturing, the focus is shifting to newer areas of study, not to say that these areas were not at all focused upon earlier. The recent focus on the Sociology of regions has been in trend for the past few years. However, it is more explicit now than ever before. This sudden focus and recognition of the Sociology of regions has motivated sociologists to generate region-specific knowledge to build a Sociology of India. The present paper is an attempt to develop a sociology of Uttar Pradesh, one of the largest and most diverse states of India. The paper builds upon the contributions of the first and second generations of sociologists from this region who have been associated with the institutions of higher education. Using narrative as a method of primary data collection, the paper focuses on the contributions of sociologists from this region who have already made their presence felt strongly on the Indian knowledge landscape mainly through the influential academic pursuits associated with well-recognized intellectual centers of Sociology in Lucknow and Varanasi. Contributions of individual sociologists from Uttar Pradesh have also been presented in the paper.

Keywords Uttar Pradesh · Sociologists · Regional sociology · Lucknow School · Sociology in Varanasi

Introduction: Need for Regional Sociology/ies

In the context of India, the field of sociology has recently celebrated its centenary milestone which led to the decision to organize an all-India conference on the theme to discuss the journey of Sociology in India so far. Thereafter, another conference in

S. Prasad (✉)
Department of Sociology, Banaras Hindu University, Varanasi, Uttar Pradesh, India
e-mail: shweta1@bhu.ac.in; shweta1_bhu@yahoo.co.in

A. Chauhan et al. (eds.), *Hundred Years of Sociology in India: Evolving Issues, Emerging Trends*, https://doi.org/10.1007/978-981-96-1317-5_4

Lucknow in April, 2023 on the theme "Sociology 'in' and 'of' regions" highlighted the significance of studying regional sociology. As distinct approaches that aim to comprehend the social and cultural characteristics of a specific spatial and ecological area (Book of Abstracts 2023), both "sociology in regions" and "sociology of regions" are significant for a comprehensive understanding of sociology in a region.

A country marked by profound diversity, India, showcases distinct regional landscapes, each presenting its own array of challenges and opportunities concerning the advancement of sociology within these specific contexts. Given the intricate web of regional diversities that sociology encounters in India, it is apt to use the word "sociologies" rather than "sociology" which acknowledges the multifaceted nature of the discipline in India as it navigates the distinct challenges and opportunities presented by various regions. In the absence of these regional sociologies, the broader discipline of Indian Sociology would be like "a tree without roots" as these localized perspectives serve as crucial lenses through which to comprehend and engage with the intricate social fabrics of diverse Indian regions. By venturing beyond a monolithic approach, regional sociologies illuminate the region-specific dynamics, cultural nuances, historical underpinnings, and socio-economic variations that shape societies. Such granularity is imperative for fostering a comprehensive understanding of the complexities inherent to India's social landscape.

The endeavor to write regional sociologies contributes to a more holistic and accurate portrayal of India's societal tapestry. It allows for the acknowledgment and exploration of regional intricacies, thus enriching the overarching discipline while ensuring its relevance and resonance within the diverse realities of the nation. Explaining the significance of writing regional sociologies, Ashok Kaul opines, "in view of our rich past and unexplored philosophies and narratives, regional sociologies can find common grounds of episteme that needs to be explored" (20 July 2023).

R. K. Mukherjee (Book of Abstracts 2023) also underscores the paramount importance of grasping the historical and cultural underpinnings that mold a region's trajectory and the lived experiences of its populace, thereby giving rise to the concept of regional sociology. Mukherjee had advocated for a holistic approach that extends beyond the mere examination of social and economic structures to encompass the broader tapestry of environmental, historical, and cultural dimensions intrinsic to the region.

This comprehensive lens enables us to unravel the intricate interplay between society and its surroundings, shedding light on how this dynamic interrelationship shapes the course of regional development. Furthermore, this approach unveils the genesis and evolution of sociology as an academic discipline within the confines of that specific area. In essence, the dual pursuit of regional sociology and the sociology of regions elucidates the multifaceted narratives woven into the fabric of a given geographical context, facilitating a deeper understanding of the interwoven dynamics that govern the social order and its intricate connections with the environment.

In light of the above facts, the objective of this paper is to chart out the evolution of "sociology" within the geographical confines of Uttar Pradesh, a region known for its profound socio-cultural, political, and historical heritage.

Journey of Sociology in Uttar Pradesh

The landscape of sociology in Uttar Pradesh is underpinned by three distinct pillars: the Lucknow School,[1] Sociology in Varanasi, and Independent Scholars whose affiliations may not align directly with either of these aforementioned hubs of sociological knowledge. While the Lucknow School has garnered recognition within the annals of Indian sociology, the commensurate contributions of the scholars of Varanasi to the discipline's advancement in Uttar Pradesh, remain largely overlooked. Yet, an equitable portrayal of sociology's trajectory in Uttar Pradesh necessitates an acknowledgment of the pivotal role played by the social thinkers and sociologists in Varanasi as well.

The advancement of sociology in Uttar Pradesh has been shaped by the collective endeavors of these three pillars.

I. *The Lucknow School*

The inception of Sociology in the region is intrinsically linked to the activities and influence of these entities. Notably, the Department of Economics and Sociology at Lucknow University in the early 1920s stands as a pioneering educational establishment, not just within Uttar Pradesh but on a national scale, as a catalyst for the dissemination of Sociological knowledge.

While assessments concerning the contributions of the Lucknow School to the discipline's progression have elicited divergent viewpoints, their imprint on the sociological landscape remains conspicuous. This recognition is grounded in distinctive attributes, characterized by "its vision of sociology and social science having a historical civilizational anchorage, its sense of unease with positivistic, utilitarian and the general evolutionary constructions and premises of the western sociology, its openness towards historicity, culture and values in the formulation of sociological concepts and their theoretical underpinnings, and its methodological eclecticism" (Singh 2004:145 as cited in Thakur 2013).

An intellectual force to reckon with (Singh 1984), having a multidisciplinary orientation, the Lucknow School of Sociology occupies a significant position in the history of Indian sociology. The pioneering works of stalwarts such as Radhakamal Mukerjee (1889–1968) and Dhurjati Prasad Mukerji (1894–1961), helped develop an unquestionable legacy for this School of Sociology. Dhirendra Nath Majumdar (1903–1960), a social anthropologist by training, was another towering researcher and academician associated with this School. Awadh Kishore Saran (1922–2003) was yet another prominent figure of the Lucknow School of Sociology.

Radhakamal Mukerjee, a seminal figure in the field, played a pivotal role in the establishment and leadership of the Department of Economics and Sociology at Lucknow University. His pioneering endeavors encompassed a multidisciplinary scope, making substantial contributions to Economics, Sociology, Ecology, and Demography. During the initial decades of the previous century, Mukerjee adeptly interconnected these realms to foster a more promising societal trajectory. His pioneering research endeavors and written contributions are deeply imbued with the tenets of the nationalist movement, which fervently championed the creation of an all-encompassing, forward-looking, and modernistic paradigm encompassing Economics, Sociology, and, to a certain extent, History. Echoing contemporaneous thinkers, Mukerjee ardently advocated that a profound understanding of Indian society could best be achieved through indigenous approaches intrinsic to the Indian context. The corpus of his scholarly works, including "Foundation of Indian Economics" (1916), "Border-Lands of Economics" (1925), "The Social Structure of Values" (1949), and "The Dynamics of Morals" (1951), stands as enduring testimonies to Mukerjee's significant contributions within the realm of social sciences in India. These seminal works collectively underscore his lasting impact on the field, traversing disciplinary boundaries to illuminate pivotal facets of Indian society, culture, and their intricate interrelationships.

Dhurjati Prasad Mukerji, acclaimed as one of the foundational figures in the establishment of Sociology in India, espoused a firm adherence to the Marxist methodological framework in his sociological investigations. Through an array of seminal research contributions and literary works, including "Personality and Social Science" (1924), "Modern Indian Culture: A Sociological Study" (1942), "On Indian History: A Study in Method" (1943), "Views and Counterviews" (1946), and "Diversities" (1958), he adeptly delineated a methodological orientation that left a lasting imprint on the trajectory of Indian Sociology.

Central to his scholarly pursuits were core facets of Indian society, including "Indian personality," "Indian middle-class," "Indian culture," and the intricate tapestry of "social and cultural traditions." Mukerji's intellectual endeavors bore witness to his deft handling of the dualistic interplay between "tradition' and "modernity." These diametrically different forces exerted discernible influences on Indian societies, engendering a nuanced amalgamation of values and cultural syntheses. His insightful exploration of this dynamic duality elucidated the evolving ethos of Indian societies as they navigated the coexistence of enduring traditions and the evolving contours of modernity.

Dhirendra Nath Majumdar, an anthropologist by training, holds a notable association with the Lucknow School of Sociology. He obtained his doctorate from Cambridge University in 1935, on "Cultural Change Among Hos," which was published later as "A Tribe in Transition" in 1937. His research endeavors manifest an unmistakable continuity with the methodological legacy set forth by B. Malinowski.

Majumdar's body of work bears testimony to his methodological alignment, notably evident in volumes such as "Races and Cultures of India" (1944), "The Affairs of a Tribe: A Study in Tribal Dynamics" (1950), "Social Contours of an Industrial City: Social Survey of Kanpur" (1960), and "Himalayan Polyandry, Structure, Functioning and Culture Change: A Field Study of Jaunsar-Bawar" (1963). These seminal contributions resonate within the domain of Social Anthropology, enriched through the conduit of the Lucknow School of Sociology in India. His academic pursuits underscore the School's enduring legacy, and these contributions collectively serve as invaluable references that extend our understanding of diverse facets within the realm of Social Anthropology.

Awadh Kishore Saran's noteworthy tenure within the Lucknow School of Sociology spanned between 1946–1966. His contributions, imbued with an Indological perspective, have significantly enriched the landscape of Indian sociology. His scholarly impact materialized prominently through an array of authored works. Notable among these are "On the Intellectual Vocation" (1996), "Traditional Thought: Towards an Axiomatic Approach" (1996), "Sociology of Knowledge and Traditional Thought" (1998), "Hinduism in Contemporary India" (2007), and "On the Theories of Secularism and Modernization" (2007).

Saran had reorganized some of his scholarly outputs post-retirement and two of these books were posthumously published. This nuanced timeline of publications illuminates a noteworthy facet that interfaces with both his personal and professional trajectory within the realm of research and academic authorship, offering a discerning lens into the intricate interplay between life experiences and scholarly contributions within the Indian context.

The trajectory of this sociological School demonstrated an enduring growth pattern that transcended generations, with subsequent cohorts of sociologists who were steeped in its legacy. Among these, scholars like Abha Avasthi, Rajesh Misra, and A. K. Srivastava, to name a few, have made noteworthy contributions while remaining affiliated with the School.

Of particular significance is Rajesh Misra, who has left an indelible mark on the Lucknow School of Sociology. His scholarly pursuits have been particularly dedicated to the comprehensive study of the middle class within India. Moreover, Misra has conducted in-depth research on socio-cultural movements within the Uttarakhand region of the former Uttar Pradesh. Furthermore, his active engagement with the ISS underscores his commitment to the broader sociological community and its intellectual discourse. A. K. Srivastava too has made manyfold contributions in the areas of Political Sociology, Family Studies, Environment and Society, etc.

Thus, the Lucknow School of Sociology emerged as a profound intellectual force that has left an indelible mark on the landscape of Indian sociological thought. The multidisciplinary orientation, historical anchorage, and methodological eclecticism of this School stand as enduring hallmarks. The School has enriched the sociological discourse through its diverse yet interconnected explorations of Indian society, culture, and history.

II. *Sociology in Varanasi*

The roots of the sociological discourse in Varanasi draw from a diverse array of literary sources, as well as scriptures, which were not initially intended for scientific sociological inquiry. Yet, within this eclectic blend, an intellectual tradition took shape. This tradition seamlessly interwove social philosophy with the fabric of social reality. It placed a pronounced emphasis on comprehending cultural norms and the intricate tapestry of social institutions. A noteworthy aspect of this tradition was the fervent assertion of the freedom to inquire, a stance championed with vigor, albeit by a minority, as highlighted by Dube (1977, p. 3).

In the historical backdrop of colonial India, the endeavor to establish institutions and organizations tailored to specific geographical contexts was notably exemplified by the establishment of the Benares Institute in Varanasi (1861) within Uttar Pradesh. This initiative aimed to catalyze, advocate, and amplify modernistic paradigms and a scientific ethos among the emerging generation across diverse disciplines. The overarching objective was to contribute to the collective betterment of society, both in the present and in the times to come.

These institutional endeavors, spanning various regions of India were instrumental in setting a robust groundwork. This foundation laid a firm platform for the initiation of pioneering endeavors with a multidisciplinary orientation. These early initiatives progressively paved the way for scholars and researchers to gravitate toward a more subject-specific and methodologically nuanced approach. This evolutionary trajectory ultimately facilitated the emergence of sociology as an autonomous discipline.

Varanasi, a seat of learning since ancient times, has contributed significantly to the growth of the discipline in this region. Sociology in Varanasi developed out of the combined efforts of some of the institutions as well as a few sociologists who played important roles during its formative years. Speaking about the existence and evolution of Sociology in Varanasi, Anand Kumar asserts "Varanasi was an interdisciplinary nucleus which created a continuous flow of sociological knowledge since the 1930s. Foundation of Banaras Hindu University (BHU) in 1916 and establishment of Kashi Vidyapeeth in 1921 were landmarks in the chronology of the sociological journey of India" (Anand Kumar, personal interview, April, 2023). He further adds, "Formation of Sociology departments at BHU and Kashi Vidyapeeth in the mid-1960s, along with the establishment of Gandhian Institute at Rajghat, was the next turning point" (ibid.). The intellectual community in Varanasi is credited with the publication of some significant periodicals that generated sociological knowledge for this region of Uttar Pradesh and beyond.

One of the leading figures associated with sociological scholarship in Varanasi was *S. K. Srivastava.* A postgraduate in Anthropology from Lucknow University, Srivastava was appointed as the Malviya Professor of Sociology at Banaras Hindu University in 1965 and became the Founder of the Department of Sociology at BHU. He has worked on social stratification, mobility, and ethnography. His ethnographic study on the *THARUS-A Study in Culture Dynamics* received international recognition in 1995 at the Norwegian Institute of International Affairs, OSLO. He contributed to the discipline of Anthropology and Sociology as an elected Foreign Fellow of the American Anthropological Association and Indian Sociological Society as well. Another prominent sociologist from BHU, Varanasi was *Harish Chandra Srivastava* who mostly contributed to theoretical aspects in sociology. He "developed an intellectual, philosophical and theoretical model to understand the Indian society" (personal interview with Satyendra Tripathi, 29 April 2023). His writings in Hindi have been a boon for the students of this region who struggle to get a quality book in the Hindi language. Prof. S. K. Srivastava (2011) and Prof. Satyendra Tripathi (2014) both received the ISS lifetime achievement award.

Discussions on the Sociology of Gender were first started by *Girija Saklani* in BHU during the 1970s. According to Anand Kumar, "BHU was one of the leading institutions to focus on women's issues during those days in North India. Even Delhi was not talking about women's issues, when BHU started discussing it under Girija Saklani" (Anand Kumar, personal interview, April 2023).

Taking the tradition further, *Surinder Jaitley* has contributed immensely to the Sociology of Gender and was instrumental in establishing the Centre for Women's Studies here as one of the first three centers to be established by the University Grant Commission in India in the 1980s. Centre for Women's Studies and Development, Banaras Hindu University is one of the pioneering centers of the country in the area of Women's Studies, and since then, it has been contributing significantly to evolve a gender-friendly society in Uttar Pradesh in general and Varanasi, in particular. Due to its excellent performance, the UGC Visiting Committee declared the center as one of the Nodal Centres in 1997, which is the highest recognition of excellence accorded to any Women's Studies Centre in India (www.bhu.ac.in).

Anand Kumar who started his teaching career at BHU, found sociology to be at a crossroads. He states that "I joined BHU in late 1979 and taught there till 1989. It was post- Emergency period that created demystification of sociology and disappointment about sociologists. At the same time, it was a period of enlargement of the Sociological field with emergence of gender issues, peasant questions, diminishing democracy and realignment of social forces" (personal interview, April 2023). Anand Kumar has focused on studying poverty, peasant problems, ITM pollution of the Ganges, projects related to rural women of the Centre of Social Research, and the promotion of the Institute of Peace Research and Action (IPRA). He reveals "the foundation for many of his contributions, were laid during his stint at BHU." His studies on poverty and movements were initiated here which he developed later when he joined JNU at New Delhi.

In recent years, *Ajit Pandey* has contributed significantly to the discipline. He initially worked on tribal studies, particularly in the kinship framework—kinship and social stratification, kinship and tribal equality, tribal economy, etc. He informs that in tribal societies, kinship plays an all-pervasive role affecting cultural, political, ideological, and other aspects of life as well. However, over the period, Pandey shifted to sociological theories and research methodology. Toward the end of his career, Pandey focused more on subaltern studies and is still working in this area. According to him, "out of 5 sites of exclusion, I have worked on Dalits and tribal. After this, I plan to focus on gender, peasantry (he treats peasantry as a site of exclusion) and religious minorities."

In short, the sociological discourse in Varanasi stands as a remarkable testament to the confluence of diverse literary sources and philosophical underpinnings that gave rise to a unique intellectual tradition. With an emphasis on understanding cultural norms, social institutions, and the pursuit of free inquiry, this tradition resonates as a beacon of scholarly vigor. As Varanasi continued to evolve as a seat of learning, notable figures like S. K. Srivastava, Harish Chandra Srivastava, and Girija Saklani contributed pioneering works driving sociology's evolution. The tradition finds resonance in contemporary scholars like Anand Kumar and Ajit Pandey, who continue to explore new dimensions, from subaltern studies to sociological theories. Varanasi's enduring sociological journey illuminates the intrinsic connection between academic pursuit and societal transformation, paving the way for a more inclusive and insightful understanding of Uttar Pradesh's social fabric.

III. *Contributions of Individual Sociologists*

Other than the contributions of the stalwarts from the Lucknow School and Varanasi, Sociology in Uttar Pradesh has enriched and benefitted from the contributions of many individual sociologists, not belonging to any School as such. These individual sociologists have played crucial roles in enriching the discipline through their academic endeavors, and also by establishing departments of sociology at various places in this region. Institution building to carry forward the sociological legacy of the region has been one of the most important contributions of these sociologists. It is interesting to note and worth mentioning here that many of them have, directly or indirectly, been related to the Lucknow School which speaks volumes about the influence of Lucknow School on sociologists in this region.

One such name is of *B. R. Chauhan*, an alumnus of Lucknow School. Starting his journey of teaching Sociology in Rajasthan in the late 1940s, Chauhan shifted to Agra Institute of Social Sciences, and then to Meerut University where he was the founder and Head of the Department of Sociology. He mainly worked on rural sociology and has made significant contributions to the discipline through his writings such as *A Rajasthan Village* (1967), *Towns in the Tribal Settings* (1970), and *Rural–Urban Articulations* (1990). His book in Hindi, titled *Samaj vigyan ke Prerak Shrot* (1994), dealing with the founding fathers of sociology has been widely appreciated. As President of the ISS, he played a crucial role in strengthening the Indian Sociological Society. His latest work, *Rural Life: Grass Roots Perspectives* (2009), is based on field experiences and assessment of published work over eight decades of intensive studies in villages of Uttar Pradesh.

R. N. Saxena, one of the first few Presidents of the Indian Sociological Society in the late 1970s, has played an important role in building various departments of sociology in Rajasthan, Maharashtra, and U.P. He was the founder and Director of the Institute of Social Sciences, Agra, who also established the Department of Sociology at Aligarh Muslim University (AMU), Aligarh. A sociologist of international repute, Saxena, has worked mainly on caste and tribes in India. Another prominent figure from AMU, who contributed significantly to the discipline of Sociology, is *Noor Mohammad* who worked on criminology initially but shifted to development studies and research methodology in later years. Editor of Sociological Bulletin and Organizing Secretary of the All-India Sociological Conference in 1998, the conference where the creation of research committees was formalized due to the long-standing efforts of T. K. Oommen, can also be counted as his significant contribution toward the discipline of Sociology in India.

Other than these sociologists, many others, including Indian and foreign researchers and academicians, have conducted studies in Eastern and Western U.P. and these studies contain important information on socio-economic, cultural, and political life in this region of India. In this context, we can trace and highlight a number of quality research works and their relevant and useful outcomes for researchers, academicians, and policy makers. For instance, the book "Don't Marry Me to a

Plowman: Women's Everyday Lives in Rural North India" (1996) as an outcome of the extensive fieldwork with participant observations done by Patricia Jefferey and Roger Jeffery, unveils the untold, unseen, and largely neglected emotional aspects of the general countryside women of North India through Western Uttar Pradesh. This book, with great narratives, examples, and shared emotion-based information by women throws light on the social, cultural, economic, and modernity-related realities of society bringing women to the front stage of society.

In the intricate tapestry of Uttar Pradesh's sociological landscape, the contributions of individual sociologists have woven threads of profound significance. While the legacy of the Lucknow School and sociology in Varanasi stand as pillars, these sociologists, in their individual capacities, have uniquely enriched the discipline. Their endeavors span from pioneering research and academic writings to the establishment of sociology departments across the region. Their contributions collectively bear testimony to the intricate socio-cultural fabric that defines Uttar Pradesh and the invaluable role sociology plays in comprehending its complexities.

State of Sociology in Uttar Pradesh and the Way Forward

Thus, the journey of sociology in Uttar Pradesh reflects a rich and dynamic tapestry of academic inquiry that has evolved over the years. Uttar Pradesh, as one of India's most culturally and socially diverse regions, has provided a fertile ground for sociological exploration due to its intricate societal complexities, historical heritage, and contemporary challenges.

The establishment of departments of sociology and research centers within universities has further bolstered the field's growth. These academic spaces have facilitated the exploration of diverse socio-cultural phenomena, ranging from rural–urban dynamics, caste and class interactions, gender relations, political processes, and religious practices, to environmental concerns. The sociological gaze in Uttar Pradesh extends beyond theoretical frameworks, delving into the intricate connections between societal issues and policy implications.

Uttar Pradesh's unique demographic makeup and historical significance have propelled sociologists to engage in interdisciplinary collaborations, linking sociology with anthropology, political science, economics, history, and other disciplines. This interdisciplinary approach enriches the understanding of complex social dynamics and contributes to more holistic insights.

However, challenges persist. The state's immense diversity can sometimes make it difficult to generalize findings across the entire region. Besides, being a Hindi-speaking state, the students of sociology in most of the universities in Uttar Pradesh choose Hindi as a medium of instruction, which deprives them of quality books, which are mostly available in English. Furthermore, issues related to access to education, healthcare, and economic opportunities continue to be pressing concerns that sociology seeks to address in Uttar Pradesh. Uttar Pradesh's massive population;

deep-rooted social inequalities based on caste, class, and gender; increasing rural–urban divide; gender-related challenges, such as discrimination and violence against women; environmental challenges related to pollution, deforestation, and resource depletion; and maintaining the autonomy of sociological research in the face of political interferences pose a series of challenges for most of the disciplines including sociology. Addressing these challenges requires a multidimensional approach, involving not only sociological research, but also collaboration with policymakers, grassroots organizations, and communities. Overcoming these obstacles will enable sociology in Uttar Pradesh to contribute more effectively to societal understanding, policy formulation, and positive change.

Overall, the state of sociology in Uttar Pradesh reflects an evolving landscape that is responsive to the multifaceted challenges and opportunities presented by the region's societal fabric. As it navigates the interplay of tradition and modernity, regional distinctiveness, and global influences, sociology in Uttar Pradesh remains an essential discipline for unraveling the intricacies of its dynamic.

As sociology in Uttar Pradesh enters the future, it must reckon with the challenges posed by a diverse cultural landscape, social inequalities, and the rapid pace of urbanization. However, with a rich legacy to draw upon, along with the dynamism and resilience of its sociological community, the discipline is poised to continue to unravel the intricacies of society, shaping meaningful narratives that reflect the region's complexities and aspirations. Through interdisciplinary collaborations and a continued dedication to context-specific research, sociology in Uttar Pradesh can illuminate pathways toward social progress and contribute meaningfully to a deeper understanding of the state's societal dynamics.

Notes

1. The nomenclature "school" has evoked contention concerning the Lucknow School. Addressing the application of the term "school" for Lucknow school, Madan (2007 as cited by Manish Thakur), highlights the absence of a formally declared "school" and underscores the lack of a unified pedagogical and research approach within the Lucknow School. Madan's reservations revolve around the absence of uniformity and formal proclamation. However, Harvey's conceptualization of "schools," particularly in the sociological context, provides illumination. Harvey elucidates that a "school" refers to an assemblage of academics and researchers, constituting an identifiable intellectual entity, irrespective of administrative boundaries. Consequently, the pursuit of homogeneity should not be the primary criterion when characterizing such academic clusters.

References

Book of Abstracts (2023) Sociology of and in regions: pedagogy, practices and possibilities. In: Midterm ISS international conference, Department of Sociology, University of Lucknow in collaboration with ISS, New Delhi

Dube SC (1977) Indian sociology at the turning point. Sociol Bull 26(01)
Kaul A (2023) Evolving relevance of sociology @epaper.GreaterKashmir.com
Singh Y (2004) Ideology and theory in Indian sociology. Rawat Publications, Jaipur 2004:145 as cited in Manish Thakur (2013) Radhakamal Mukerjee and the politics of disciplinary erasure: a preliminary note @https://serialsjournals.com/abstract/30852_3.pdf. Retrieved 29 August 2023
Singh Y (1984) Image of man: ideology and theory in Indian sociology. Chankya Publications, Delhi

Chapter 5
Sustainable Development Goals and Their Performance in Northeast India

Baharul Islam Laskar

Abstract From a global viewpoint, the Sustainable Development Goals (SDGs) for every region, country, state, or district are equally important. Development can be understood through a variety of sociological and psychological frameworks. The diverse landscape of Northeast India (NEI) presents a multitude of concerns and obstacles to sustainable development. Out of 103 districts that were reviewed, 62.1% were classified as Front Runners on all 17 SDGs, while 37.9% were classified as Performers, according to the available statistics. East Sikkim, Gomati, North Tripura, West Tripura, and Serchhip are the five districts in Northeast India that performed the best in terms of the Sustainable Development Goals (SDGs). Many differences are evident in the indicators used to measure progress toward SDG 3 and SDG 6. Pregnant women in the Tuensang District of Nagaland had the lowest score at 4.9 out of a possible 124.8 in the Imphal West District of Manipur. The proportion of rural residents receiving potable water from piped sources is also highest in Kolasib district, Mizoram, at 97.5%, and lowest in Darrang district, Assam, at 1.44%. Some states and districts are doing better than others on some metrics, but not all of them. Consequently, that's where the focus should lie.

Keywords Sustainable Development Goals (SDGs) · Northeast India · Healthy lives · Well-being · Clean water and sanitation

Introduction

The health and well-being of people depend on multiple factors, including accessibility and availability of water, its quality and sanitation facilities, and related norms and values of people. The respective national governments and the United Nations (UN) are trying their best to ensure minimum requirements or facilities needed to

B. I. Laskar (✉)
Department of Sociology and PA Sangma Centre for Tribal Studies, University of Science and Technology, Baridua, Meghalaya, India
e-mail: blaskar69@gmail.com

A. Chauhan et al. (eds.), *Hundred Years of Sociology in India: Evolving Issues, Emerging Trends*, https://doi.org/10.1007/978-981-96-1317-5_5

keep people healthy and contribute toward individual, national, and global development. The UN has notably framed the Millennium Development Goals (MDGs) in 2000 to be achieved by 2015, and later the Sustainable Development Goals (SDGs) in 2015 to be achieved by 2030. The 17 SDGs of the 2030 Agenda for Sustainable Development, provide a shared design for present and future peace and prosperity for people and the planet. The SDGs are a crucial demand for action by all countries in a global partnership. The SDGs are framed to address the intersecting challenges of widespread income inequality between and within countries, disparities in access to resources, obstinate degradation of the environment, and numerous other problems tied to existing systems of economy and government (Lencucha et al. 2023).

SDG 3 (ensuring healthy lives and promoting well-being) and SDG 6 (clean water and sanitation) are closely related and are of great relevance for the diverse Northeast India. SDG 3 addresses all major health priorities—reproductive, maternal, newborn, child, and adolescent health; communicable and non-communicable diseases; universal health coverage; and access for all to safe, effective, quality, and affordable medicines and vaccines. SDG 3 sets specific targets, in which health emergencies such as COVID-19 pose a global risk and have shown the critical need for preparedness. The United Nations Development Programme (UNDP) highlighted huge disparities in countries' abilities to cope with and recover from the Covid-19 crisis (UN 2023a). The pandemic provides a watershed moment for health emergency preparedness in all countries (Laskar 2020; Laskar 2021a).

Numerous experiences at various stages have gone into setting the aims for SDG 6. One example is the 1977 Mar del Plata conference in Argentina, which established an Action Plan on "Community Water Supply" and said that everyone should have access to water that meets their fundamental needs in terms of quantity and quality. On 22 March 1992, the United Nations General Assembly established World Water Day; on 19 November 2013, it became World Toilet Day. The Millennium Development Goals, adopted in 2000, called on nations to cut in half the number of people without access to clean water for drinking and basic sanitation facilities by 2015. The United Nations General Assembly (UNGA) proclaimed 2003 as the International Year of Freshwater, and 2008 was the International Sanitation Year. The United Nations General Assembly formally acknowledged the right to access clean water and sanitation in 2010. Water and sanitation must be accessible and managed sustainably for all people by 2030, according to SDG 6. Because of the many ways in which they contribute to a more prosperous society, less poverty, and a healthier environment, water, and sanitation are seen as crucial to sustainable development by the United Nations. Water shortages are becoming increasingly common as a result of human activities such as overexploitation, pollution, and global warming. United Nations estimates put the number of people without access to safe drinking water at 2.2 billion and the number of people without access to decent sanitation at around 4.2 billion (UN 2022). Unsafe hygiene practices are prevalent and have a multiplicative impact on people's health, especially when it comes to rates of maternal, newborn, and child mortality. Improving water quality through pollution reduction and improvement of water and sanitation management through increasing community involvement and promoting efficiency are important in all areas of use.

Sociology of development allows us to understand the society in a more global context, in which the issue of personal and national development is an important discourse. There are diverse sociological and psychological paradigms to construe development. The works of Spencer (1873), Morgan (1877), Confucius (1928), Raul Prebisch (1949), Smelser (1959), Geertz (1963), Parsons (1966), Weber (1967), Organski (1967), Marx and Angels (1968), Huntington (1968), Rostow (1971), Foucault (1972), Bourdieu (1972), Giddens (1973), Dos Santos (1973), Wallerstein (1974), Amin (1976 and 1990), Frank (1978), Cardoso and Faletto (1979), Flora and Torres-Rivas (1989), So (1990), Beck (1992), Chickering and Reisser (1993), and others may be noted.

Selected Reviews

It is envisioned that ensuring healthy lives and promoting well-being at all ages is important to building prosperous societies, although inequalities in healthcare access still persist. It is noted that more than six million children still die before their fifth birthday each year, and only half of all women in developing regions have access to the health care they need. As access to good health and well-being is a human right, the SDG offers to ensure that everyone can access the highest standards of health and health care (UN 2023b).

In fact, all the SDGs are interrelated and interdependent, particularly health and well-being. Reduction of poverty leads to improved health and well-being, while good health leads to effective poverty reduction. Similarly, the connection between food consumption and health is highly context-dependent; access to education is associated with better health, at both individual and community levels; endorsing gender equality leads to easy health gains; improving water quality and sanitation and its access lead to improved health; affordable energy leads to both economic development and the availability of other basic services; economic progress leads to health advantages; development stages are related to typical patterns of health challenges; dropping inequalities in income, wealth, education, health care services, and access to power can contribute to the attainment of health and well-being goals; sustainable consumption and production is strongly linked with health; many health impacts from climate change are direct; health of marine systems is directly related to human health in coastal areas; changes to the environment can affect health; peace, justice, and strong institutions are vital factors of health improvements; and operative partnerships are crucial for achieving health (Howden-Chapman et al. 2017).

To implement the 2030 Agenda for Sustainable Development, nations and regions of the world are trying their best. For example, the European policy for health and well-being developed the roadmap for its implementation. It proposed five strategic directions and four enabling measures to achieve better, more equitable, and sustainable health and well-being for all at all ages. The five strategic directions are advancing governance and leadership, leaving no one behind, preventing disease and addressing health determinants by promoting multi- and intersectoral policies throughout the life course, establishing healthy places, settings, and resilient communities, and strengthening health systems toward universal health coverage (UHC). The four enabling measures are financing and investment for health, multi-partner cooperation, health literacy research and innovation, and monitoring and evaluation (WHO 2021).

It is observed that there are six issues with regard to improving the quantity and quality of health services in India. These are the resources earmarked for health needs to increase; health resources need to be used in a fair and just manner including regulation of private sector health provision; the balanced allocation of health resources particularly between towns and villages; accessibility of rural areas; the more efficient use of health workers; and the successful implementation of policy (Borooah 2018). It is opined that India has one-sixth of the world's population and a large share of the world's poor. The barriers to achieving the health-related Millennium Development Goals (MDGs) are structural and cultural issues including inefficient and inadequate health systems, inadequate social support, and a general lack of health awareness (Chang et al. 2011).

It is comprehended that the benefits of having access to an improved drinking water source can only be fully realized when there is also access to improved sanitation and observance of good hygiene practices. Beyond the direct advantages of people being hydrated and healthier, access to water, sanitation, and hygiene (WASH) has deep socio-economic impacts, particularly for women and girls. A few specific impacts of WASH are—(i) The disease and time burden linked with lack of access to WASH prevent many adults from earning a living or fulfilling their potential in professional showgrounds; (ii) Many children in low-income communities with no access to WASH are unable to attend school, particularly in the case of girls in rural areas; (iii) There are multiple morbidity and mortality from diseases directly caused by unsafe water, inadequate sanitation and poor hygiene practices, which also contribute to child malnourishment, i.e., physical and mental under-development. For universal execution of the rights to access safe water and sanitation, we need well-resourced, capable institutions delivering services and changing behavior in robust and suitable ways (UN 2023c). The interaction between WASH and disease is well established. For example, diarrhea is often caused by a lack of clean water for proper handwashing and a lack of toilets, which further contributes to contaminating drinking water and water resources in many localities. The WHO estimates that 50% of malnutrition is connected with repeated diarrhea or intestinal worm infections from unsafe water or poor sanitation or hygiene (Worley 2014).

A study in India shows that the incidence of WASH-related diseases was at 5.7% of all outpatient visits and 6.9% of all hospital admissions, which were associated with restrictions in daily activities of sick people and out-of-pocket expenditure. It suggests for holistic strengthening of WASH facilities to mitigate the avoidable burden of diseases (Goyanka 2021). Another study among residents of urban slums in Kolkata in India reflects that over 90% of households had access to piped water, 6% reported access to continuous supply, 45% of adult women in 2019 spent 20 min daily to fetch water, 80% used shared improved latrine facilities, and unhygienic behavioral patterns predisposing to food- or water-borne diseases were also noted.

It recommends awareness generation and sustainable community mobilization for food hygiene to ensure community well-being (Kanungo et al. 2021).

A study of five Indian states i.e., Karnataka, Madhya Pradesh, Rajasthan, Uttar Pradesh, and West Bengal indicates that the children and mothers who were from Open Defecation Free (ODF) areas confirmed better health and nutritional indicators than those who were from the non-ODF areas, which were having statistically significant differences in the values. For example, the prevalence of diarrhea in the last month preceding the survey was 15.1% in ODF areas and 22.1% in non-ODF areas, stunted children were 33.7% in ODF areas and 39.6% in non-ODF areas, and 19.6% and 29.0% of women's BMI was below normal in ODF and non-ODF areas, respectively (GoI 2017). A study on the impacts of the Swachh Bharat Mission (SBM) across 320 villages in five states viz., Bihar, Madhya Pradesh, Maharashtra, Rajasthan, and Uttar Pradesh, found that after building household toilets, 93% of women feel safe not being miffed by someone or impaired by animals, and also reported no longer being afraid of contracting health infections while defecating. Similarly, 94% of the men also reported that they are free from facing snake and other animal attacks while defecating in contrast to 7% when they did not own a toilet (SRCPT 2021).

It is noted that the northeastern states have taken many initiatives to implement and localize the SDGs. But to achieve the targets it is suggested to have a multi-approach, concerted and coordinated efforts, and focus on sectors where the region has inherent advantages. It is also noted that the Covid pandemic has cast some doubts on the feasibility of achieving the goals as per the original timelines (Singh 2022). It is suggested that the SDGs can be achieved only through inclusive development, i.e., regional variation should be addressed properly. It found that uneven human development across the states in the northeast region is quite significant, and also exposed that the socio-economic components are having a positive role in determining the level of human development in the region (Nandi 2017).

Therefore, it is clear that there are a number of studies encircling the SDGs. However, the achievements in the performance of the SDGs having facts and figures are limited. So, this study is proposed to evaluate the same in the context of northeast India, particularly focusing on the SD Goals 3 and 6.

Methods

Goals 3 and 6 in particular have seen varying degrees of success between countries, states, and districts when it comes to achieving the SDGs. This paper makes an effort to assess how well Goals 3 and 6 have worked within the framework of eight states in Northeast India. An investigation at the district level is done using the existing literature and data on the subject. The status is evaluated in this study using the North Eastern Region District SDG Index Report and Dashboard 2021–22 released by the NITI Aayog, Government of India. Researching the demographics and basic statistics of Northeast India (NEI) is necessary before examining the water and sanitation

Table 5.1 Basic data on NEI, 2011

State	Total population	Sex ratio	Population density	Literacy rate (%)	Area (%)	Urban population (%)	ST (%)	Decadal growth (%)
Arunachal Pradesh	1,382,611	938	17	65.38	32	22.9	68.8	26.03
Assam	31,169,272	958	398	72.19	30	14.1	12.4	17.07
Manipur	2,721,756	992	115	79.21	8	32.5	35.1	24.50
Meghalaya	2,964,007	989	132	74.43	9	20.1	86.1	27.95
Mizoram	1,091,014	976	52	91.33	8	52.1	94.4	23.48
Nagaland	1,980,602	931	119	79.55	6	28.9	86.5	−0.58
Sikkim	607,688	890	86	81.42	3	25.2	33.8	12.89
Tripura	3,671,032	960	350	87.22	4	26.2	31.8	14.84
NER	45,587,982	956	174	74.48	–	18.5	–	18.27
All India	**1,210,193,422**	**940**	**382**	**74.04**	**–**	**31.2**	**8.6**	**17.70**

Source Compiled from Census of India, 2011

situation, as well as the health and welfare of the eight states in the region. Arunachal Pradesh, Assam, Manipur, Meghalaya, Mizoram, Nagaland, Sikkim, and Tripura are the eight member states that make up the Northeast India Institute (NEI). There are more dialects than ethnic groups, and the hilly states are home to a largely tribal population that exhibits some degree of intra-tribal variation (Laskar 2021b).

Table 5.1 reflects that the total population of the region comprises 3.77% of the country's population, while it varies from 31,169,27 i.e., 68.37% in Assam to 607,688 (1.33%) in Sikkim. Similarly, the sex ratio (992 and 931), population density (398 and 17), literacy rate (91.33 and 65.38%), proportion of geographical area (32 and 3%), urban population (52.1 and 14.1%), and scheduled tribe (94.4 and 12.4%), and decadal growth (27.95 and −0.58%), vary extensively from state to state. Therefore, the socio-demographic situation of each of the states has its own significance and accordingly the needs for each of the SDGs. It is noteworthy to mention here that the geographical area of the region is comprised of both plains and the majority of hills, so the needs and quality of health and well-being, and water and sanitation are varied in the region.

Findings from the Northeast India: 17 SDGs

Although there are many concerns and obstacles, the government has already achieved significant progress in recent years toward reaching the SDGs. In order to assess the SDGs' achievement in NEI, districts are ranked from Aspirant (score 0–49), Performer (50–64), Front Runner (65–99), and Achiever (100) using a composite score that goes from 0 to 100. The aggregate score and ranking of districts for all 17

Table 5.2 State-wise number and % of districts in each performance category for all SDGs

State	Aspirant (%)	Performer (%)	Front runner (%)	Achiever (%)	Not available (%)
Arunachal Pradesh	0	12 (48)	13 (52)	0	0
Assam	0	4 (12.12)	23 (69.7)	0	6 (18.18)
Manipur	0	1 (6.25)	8 (50)	0	7 (43.75)
Meghalaya	0	10 (90.91)	1 (9.09)	0	0
Mizoram	0	1 (9.09)	7 (63.64)	0	3 (27.27)
Nagaland	0	11 (91.67)	0	0	1 (8.33)
Sikkim	0	0	4 (100)	0	0
Tripura	0	0	8 (100)	0	0

Source Compiled from NITI Aayog (2021)

SDGs is as follows: out of 103 districts, 64 (62.1%) are considered Front Runners, while 39 (37–9%) are considered Performers (Table 5.2). There is data available for all districts of Arunachal Pradesh, Meghalaya, Sikkim, and Tripura for each performance category, but no data for the other states. Notably, data is not available for 43.75% of Manipur's districts, 27.27% of Mizoram's, 18.18% of Assam's, and 8.33% of Nagaland's districts, respectively.

Further, it depicts that majority of the districts are Front Runner in the states of Sikkim (100%), Tripura (100%), Assam (69.7%), Mizoram (63.64%), Arunachal Pradesh (52%), and Manipur (50%); while majority of the districts are Performers in Nagaland (91.67%) and Meghalaya (90.91%). No districts are in the category of either Aspirant or Achiever.

With total NEI scores of 75.87, East Sikkim, Gomati, North Tripura, West Tripura, and Serchhip are the top five districts in the country. In Table 5.3, one can see which districts in each state have the best and worst total scores on all seventeen SDGs. It reproduces regional differences in test results. Further variation is seen in the highest range districts, with scores ranging from 64.07 in Kohima to 75.87 in East Sikkim. Likewise, the lowest range districts have scores that range from 53.00 in Kiphire to 71.93 in Khowai. Hence, it is evident that even the lowest-ranking districts in Sikkim and Tripura have lower scores than the highest-ranking districts in Arunachal Pradesh, Assam, Meghalaya, and Nagaland.

Goal 3

Index scores for Objective 3, out of 120 districts considered for ranking and calculation, 103 had index scores between 31 and 76%. Twelve districts (or 78.6% of the total) are considered to be in the lead, seventy-one are considered to be performing at a satisfactory level, and eighteen are just aspirants, according to the data. Among

Table 5.3 Highest and lowest ranked districts by state on performance of 17 SDGs

State	Highest rank (score)	Lowest rank (score)
Arunachal Pradesh	Papum Pare (68.87)	Kra Daadi (55.60)
Assam	Kamrup Metropolitan (71.73)	Dima Hasao (62.67)
Manipur	Imphal West (72.13)	Tamenglong (64.93)
Meghalaya	East Khasi Hills (66.27)	North Garo Hills (56.87)
Mizoram	Serchhip (74.87)	Lawngtlai (63.40)
Nagaland	Kohima (64.07)	Kiphire (53.00)
Sikkim	East Sikkim (75.87)	West Sikkim (71.87)
Tripura	Gomati and North Tripura (75.73)	Khowai (71.93)

Source Compiled from NITI Aayog (2021)

the best performing districts in Mizoram are Champhai (76), Sikkim's East Sikkim (74) and North Sikkim (73) districts, Arunachal Pradesh's Upper Siang (72) and East Siang (71) districts, and Mizoram's Saiha (71). While North Garo Hills (43) in Meghalaya and South West Khasi Hills (31), East Jaintia Hills (32), and West Jaintia Hills (40) in Meghalaya are the worst performing districts in Northeast India, Mon (41) and Zunheboto (43) in Nagaland are the worst performers in Nagaland (Niti Aayog 2021).

A look into state-wise performance on Goal 3 (Table 5.4) shows that in Arunachal Pradesh 16% of districts are Aspirants, 68% are Performers, and 16% are Front Runner districts. In Assam and Tripura, 100% of districts are Performer districts. In Manipur, 88.89% of districts are Performers and 11.11% are Front Runners. In Meghalaya and Nagaland, 63.64% of districts are Aspirant districts and 36.36% are Performers. In Mizoram and Sikkim 25% of districts are Performers, and the rest 75% are Front Runners. Therefore, the two best performing states are Mizoram and Sikkim, while the two worst performing states are Meghalaya and Nagaland. Figure 5.1 depicts the performance categories of the number of districts for SDG 3.

A further glance into state-wise and district-wise performance on Goal 3 (Table 5.5) demonstrates widespread variations across states and districts. In Arunachal Pradesh, the top performing district is Upper Siang (72) and the bottom performing district is Longding (47). In Assam, the top and the bottom performing districts are Darrang (64) and Karimganj (54). In Manipur, the top and the bottom performing districts are Bishnupur (65) and Senapati (54). In Meghalaya, the top and the bottom performing districts are West Garo Hills (53) and South West Khasi Hills (31). In Mizoram, the top and the bottom performing districts are Champhai (76) and Lawngtlai (51). In Nagaland, the top and the bottom performing districts are Longleng (55) and Mon (41). In Sikkim, the top and the bottom performing districts are East Sikkim (74) and West Sikkim (59). In Tripura, the top and the bottom performing districts are Dhalai and West Tripura (60) and Sepahijala and Unakoti (55). Figure 5.1 displays the performance of districts (top and bottom) on SDG 3.

Table 5.4 State-wise % of districts in performance categories for SDGs 3 and 6

State	SDG 3			SDG 6		
	Aspirant	Performer	Front runner	Aspirant	Performer	Front runner
Arunachal Pradesh	16	68	16	0	4	96
Assam	0	100	0	7.41	40.74	51.85
Manipur	0	88.89	11.11	0	0	100
Meghalaya	63.64	36.36	0	9.09	45.45	45.45
Mizoram	0	25	75	0	0	100
Nagaland	63.64	36.36	0	0	9.09	90.91
Sikkim	0	25	75	0	0	100
Tripura	0	100	0	0	12.5	87.5

Source Compiled from NITI Aayog (2021)

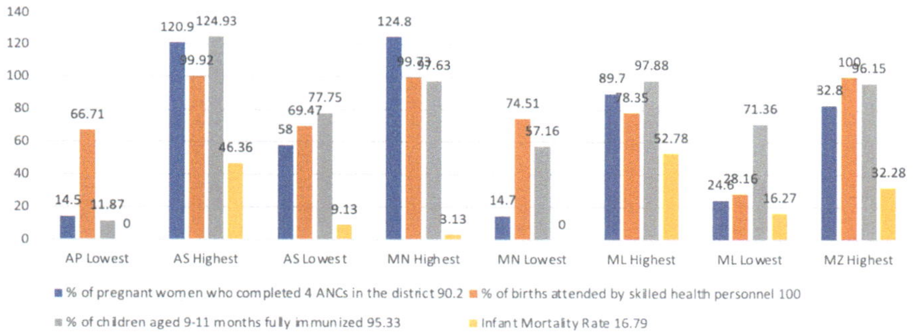

Fig. 5.1 Highest and lowest scores of districts on SDGs 3 and 6 by state. *Source* Prepared from data available in NITI Aayog (2021)

A look into the selected health indicators (Table 5.6) shows that the performances of the districts and states are quite different. For example, the highest scores of pregnant women who completed 4 ANCs range from 124.8 to 77.2, while the lowest scores range from 4.9 to 14.5. Similarly, the highest scores on births attended by skilled health personnel range from 100 to 78.35, while the lowest scores range from 28.16 to 61.56. Similar trends are observable for other selected indicators too. Figure 5.2 reflects the highest and lowest district scores on selected health indicators by state.

Table 5.5 Performance of districts (top and bottom) On SDGs 3 and6 by state

State	District	SDG 3 score	District	SDG 6 score
Arunachal Pradesh	Upper Siang	72	Lower Dibang Valley	93
	Longding	47	Namsai	51
Assam	Darrang	64	Jorhat	76
	Karimganj	54	Darrang	42
Manipur	Bishnupur	65	Churachandpur	88
	Senapati	54	Imphal East	74
Meghalaya	West Garo Hills	53	West Khasi Hills	82
	South West Khasi Hills	31	South West Garo Hills	46
Mizoram	Champhai	76	Kolasib	96
	Lawngtlai	51	Saiha	83
Nagaland	Longleng	55	Kohima	93
	Mon	41	Mokokchung	61
Sikkim	East Sikkim	74	North Sikkim	91
	West Sikkim	59	East Sikkim	83
Tripura	Dhalai and West Tripura	60	West Tripura	78
	Sepahijala and Unakoti	55	South Tripura	61

Source Compiled from NITI Aayog (2021)

Goal 6

The 103 districts (out of 120) that were considered for the ranking and calculation had index scores ranging from 96 to 42 according to the findings for Goal 6. Among the 103 districts that were considered, 81 are considered front-runners (78.6%), 19 are considered performers (18.4%), and 3 are considered aspirants (2.91%). The five best performing districts are as follows: Kolasib (96 points), Lower Dibang Valley (93 points) in Arunachal Pradesh, Kohima (93 points) in Nagaland, Mamit (91 points) in Mizoram, and North Sikkim (91 points) in Sikkim. Alternatively, the three worst performing districts in Assam are Darrang (42), South West Garo Hills (46), and Morigaon (48) (NITI Aayog 2021).

A look into state-wise performance on Goal 6 (Table 5.4) shows that in Arunachal Pradesh 96% of districts are Front Runners and rest 4% are Performer districts, and in Assam, 51.85% are Front Runners, 40.74% are Performers, and rest 7.41% are Aspirant districts. In Manipur, Mizoram, and Sikkim 100% of districts are Front Runners. In Meghalaya, 45.45% each are Front Runners and Performers, and the rest 9.09% are Aspirant districts; in Nagaland, 90.91% are Front Runners, and the remaining 9.09% are Performers; and in Tripura, 87.5% are Front Runners and rest 12.5% are

Table 5.6 Highest and lowest district scores on selected health indicators

State	% of pregnant women completed 4 ANCs in the district		% of births attended by skilled health personnel		% of children aged 9–11 months fully immunized		Infant mortality rate		Total physicians, nurses, and midwives per 10,000	
	District	Score	District	Score	District	Score	District	Score	District	Score
AR	Lohit	90.2	Upper Subansiri and West Kameng	100	East Siang	95.33	East Siang	16.79	Papum Pare	29.05
	Anjaw	14.5	Longding	66.71	Kra Daadi	11.87	8 districts	0	Longding	5.83
AS	Kamrup Metropolitan	120.9	Jorhat	99.92	Kamrup Metropolitan	124.93	Kamrup Metropolitan	46.36	Kamrup Metropolitan	17.22
	Dima Hasao	58	Dhubri	69.47	Dibrugarh	77.75	Sivasagar	9.13	Tinsukia	4.84
MN	Imphal West	124.8	Imphal West	99.73	Imphal West	97.63	Ukhrul	**3.13**	Tamenglong	19.49
	Thoubal	14.7	Tamenglong	74.51	Ukhrul	57.16	Chandel	**0**	Imphal West	5.00
ML	South West Garo Hills	89.7	South West Garo Hills	78.35	South West Garo Hills	97.88	South West Khasi Hills	52.78	East Garo Hills	12.14
	West Jaintia Hills	24.6	South West Khasi Hills	28.16	North Garo Hills	71.36	East Garo Hills	16.27	South West Khasi Hills	4.74
MZ	Aizawl	82.8	Serchhip	100	Champhai	96.15	Kolasib	32.28	Champhai	26.98
	Lawngtlai	22.6	Lawngtlai	61.56	Mamit	70.23	Serchhip	8.90	Lawngtlai	4.92
NL	Kohima	77.2	Mokokchung	98.39	Kiphire	79.84	Kiphire	22.01	Mokokchung	12.89
	Tuensang	4.9	Mon	69.09	Zunheboto	35.45	Longleng	0	Dimapur	5.35
SK	North Sikkim	83	North Sikkim	100	South Sikkim	98.87	West Sikkim	41.96	East Sikkim	50.88
	East Sikkim	55.9	South Sikkim	99.07	East Sikkim	92.17	North Sikkim	4.81	West Sikkim	13.93
TR	West Tripura	90.5	West Tripura	99.29	West Tripura	152.79	Unakoti	26.26	West Tripura	18.82
	Dhalai	56.3	North Tripura	76.07	Sepahijala	54.24	Khowai	8.83	North Tripura	9.59

Source Compiled from NITIAayog (2021)

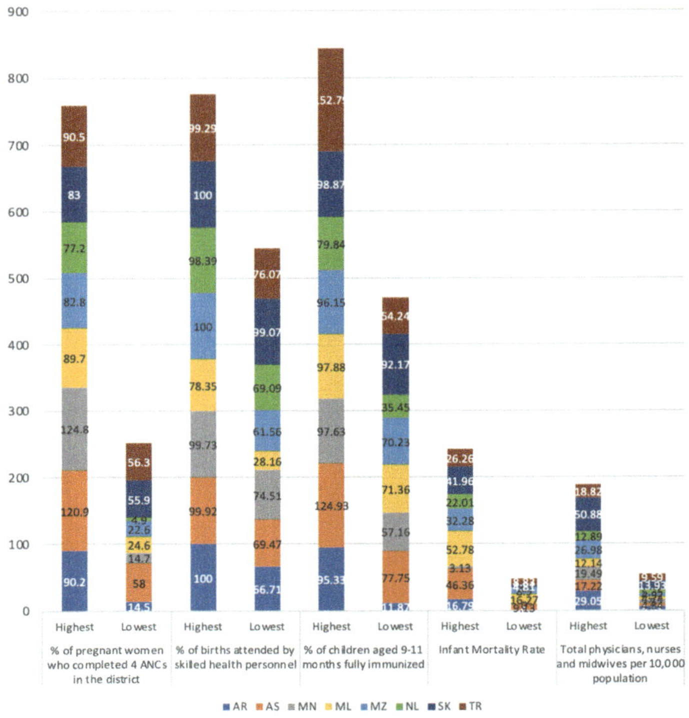

Fig. 5.2 Highest and lowest district scores on selected health indicators by state. *Source* Prepared from data available in NITI Aayog (2021)

Performers. Therefore, the three best performing states are Manipur, Mizoram, and Sikkim, followed by Arunachal Pradesh, Nagaland, and Tripura; while the two worst performing states are Meghalaya and Assam.

A further glance into state-wise and district-wise performance on Goal 6 (Table 5.5) demonstrates widespread variations across states and districts. In Arunachal Pradesh, the top performing district is Lower Dibang Valley (93) and the bottom performing district is Namsai (51). In Assam, the top and the bottom performing districts are Jorhat (76) and Darrang (42). In Manipur, the top and the bottom performing districts are Churachandpur (88) and Imphal East (74). In Meghalaya, the top and the bottom performing districts are West Khasi Hills (82) and South West Garo Hills (46). In Mizoram, the top and the bottom performing districts are Kolasib (96) and Saiha (83). In Nagaland, the top and the bottom performing districts are Kohima (93) and Mokokchung (61). In Sikkim, the top and the bottom performing districts are North Sikkim (91) and East Sikkim (83). In Tripura, the top and the bottom performing districts are West Tripura (78) and South Tripura (61). Figure 5.1 displays the performance of districts (top and bottom) on SDG 6.

Looking at some of the SDG 6 targets now reveals much more variety in how the states and districts are doing. Based on the data presented in Table 5.7, the districts of Manipur, Meghalaya, Mizoram, Nagaland, and Sikkim had the highest percentage of rural residents using an upgraded drinking water source, while Darrang, an Assam district, had the lowest percentage at 17.13%. In Darrang district of Assam, just 1.44% of the rural population has access to piped water for drinking, but in Kolasib district of Mizoram, 97.50% do.

Bishnupur, a district in Manipur, has the lowest performance rate (52.6% of the population lives in households with an enhanced sanitation facility), while Champhai, a district in Mizoram has the greatest performance rate (98.3% of the population). Longleng in Nagaland has 97.3% of its schools equipped with working restrooms for female students, whereas Dibang Valley in Arunachal Pradesh has the lowest performance rate at 40%. Figure 5.3 shows the top and bottom performing districts by state on certain measures of water and sanitation.

Conclusion

The general picture for Northeast India (NEI) appears to be better, at least in comparison. In addition to the other SDGs, SDG 6 (access to clean water and sanitation) and SDG 3 (ensuring healthy lives and fostering well-being) are tremendously vital. There is a great deal of diversity among the SDGs and their metrics, especially among SDGs 3 and 6. There is, of course, a lot more that can be done to improve performance. There are differences from one state and one district to another. Certain states and districts are doing better than others in some metrics, but not all of them. So, to boost a state or district's performance, more coordinated and all-encompassing initiatives are needed. Local requirements, geographical constraints, and cultural acceptability must all be considered simultaneously.

Table 5.7 Highest and lowest district scores on selected indicators of clean water and sanitation

State	Using an improved drinking water source		Getting safe and adequate drinking water within premises through PWS		Improved sanitation facility		Schools with functional toilet facility for girls	
	District	Score	District	Score	District	Score	District	Score
AR	Lower Dibang Valley	100	Lower Dibang Valley	60.71	–	–	Lower Dibang Valley	97.03
	Namsai	18.60	Namsai	12.79	–	–	Dibang Valley	40
AS	Jorhat	84.94	Hailakandi	68.85	Dima Hasao	83.8	Kamrup Metropolitan	91.71
	Darrang	17.13	Darrang	1.44	Cachar	57.6	Hailakandi	51.76
MN	All districts	100	Imphal West	88.11	Chandel	85.2	Churachandpur	91.83
	–	–	Imphal East	46.72	Bishnupur	52.6	Ukhrul	44
ML	All districts	100	West Khasi Hills	53.59	South Garo Hills	88.4	Ri Bhoi	79.10
	–	–	West Garo Hills	10.85	South West Garo Hills	71.4	South West Garo Hills	48.08
MZ	All districts	100	Kolasib	97.5	Champhai	98.3	Champhai	97.15
			Lawngtlai	41.94	Lawngtlai	90.3	Lunglei	76.08
NL	All districts	100	Kohima	92.99	Mokokchung	96.7	Longleng	97.30
	–	–	Mon	10.30	Dimapur	81.1	Kiphire	71.32
SK	All districts	100	North Sikkim	95	South Sikkim	91.7	West Sikkim	96.01
			East Sikkim	29.78	North Sikkim	83.8	North Sikkim	85.59
TR	West Tripura	89.75	Unakoti	74.13	West Tripura	80.2	West Tripura	91.23
	South Tripura	70.24	North Tripura	54.78	Unakoti	61.8	Dhalai	65.08

Source Compiled from NITI Aayog (2021)

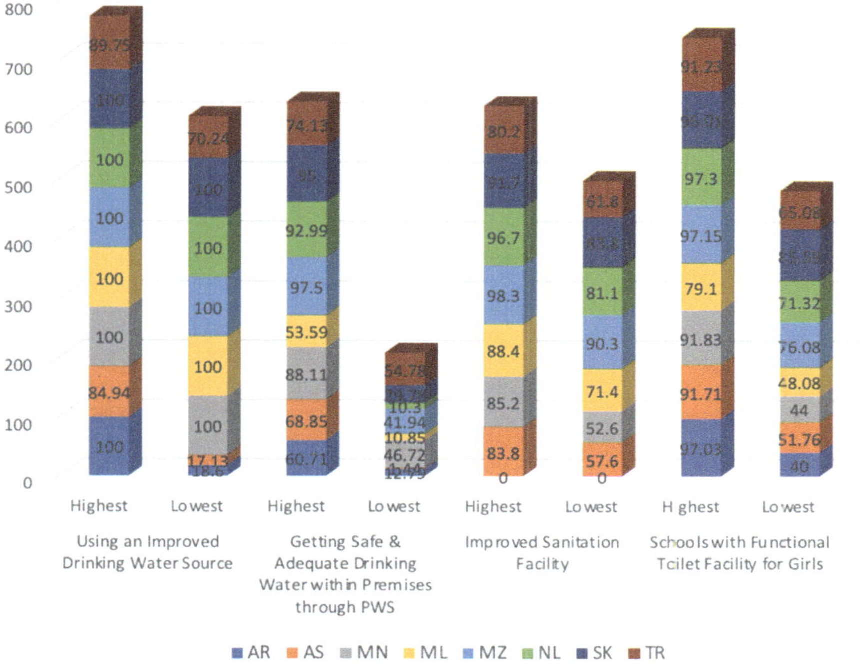

Fig. 5.3 Highest and lowest district scores on selected indicators of clean water and sanitation by state. *Source* Prepared from data available in NITI Aayog (2021)

References

Amin S (1990) Mal-development: anatomy of a global failure. Pambazuka Press

Amin S (1976) Unequal development: an essay on the social formations of peripheral capitalism (Trans by Brian Pierce). Monthly Review Press

Beck U (1992) Risk society: towards a new modernity. Sage Publications

Borooah VK (2018) Health outcomes and policy in India. In: Health and well-being in India. Palgrave Macmillan. https://doi.org/10.1007/978-3-319-78328-4_1

Bourdieu P (1972) 1977. Outline of a theory of practice (Trans Richard Nice). Cambridge University Press

Cardoso FH, Faletto E (1979) Dependency and development in Latin America (Trans by Marjory Mattingly Urquidi). University of California Press

Chang J, Srivastava J, Patel I, Balkrishnan R (2011) India's progress towards the health related millennium development goals—child mortality. Indian J Pharm Pract 4(4):9–13

Chickering AW, Reisser L (1993) Education and identity, 2 ed. Jossey-Bass

Confucius (1928) The great digest (Trans and Commentary E. Pound). New Directions Publishing

Dos Santos T (1973) The crisis of development theory and the problem of dependence in Latin America. In: Bernstein H (ed) Underdevelopment and development: the third world today. Penguin Books, pp 57–80

Flora JL, Torres-Rivas E (1989) Central America: sociology of "Developing Societies." Monthly Review Press

Foucault M (1972) The archaeology of knowledge and the discourse on language. Pantheon Books
Frank AG (1978) Dependent accumulation and underdevelopment. Macmillan
Geertz CJ (1963) Agricultural involution: the processes of ecological change in Indonesia. University of California Press
Giddens A (1973) The class structure of the advanced societies. Barnes & Noble
GoI (2017) Review of health data in selected ODF and non-ODF districts under the SBM (Report of Findings). Ministry of Drinking Water and Sanitation (MoDWS), Government of India
Goyanka R (2021) Burden of water, sanitation and hygiene related diseases in India: prevalence, health care cost and effect of community level factors. Clin Epidemiol Glob Health 12:1–8
Howden-Chapman P, Siri J, Chisholm E, Chapman R, Doll CNH, Capon A (2017) SDG 3 ensure healthy lives and promote wellbeing for all at all ages. https://council.science/wp-content/uploads/2017/03/SDGs-interactions-3-healthy-lives.pdf. Accessed 27 April 2023
Huntington SP (1968) Political order in changing societies. Yale University Press
Kanungo S, Chatterjee P, Saha J, Pan T, Chakrabarty ND, Dutta S (2021) Water, sanitation, and hygiene practices in urban slums of eastern India. J Infect Dis 224(Supplement_5):S573–S583
Laskar BI (2020) Emergence and re-emergence of communicable diseases—an analysis of Covid-19. In: Matin A, Joshi PC, Laskar BI (eds) Covid crisis: social science perspectives. ABS Books
Laskar BI (ed) (2021a) Sociology of Covid-19 pandemic: Indian experiences. LAP LAMBERT Academic Publishing
Laskar BI (2021b) Sociology of north east India. Rawat Publishers
Lencucha R, Kulenova A, Thow AM (2023) Framing policy objectives in the sustainable development goals: hierarchy, balance, or transformation? Glob Health 19:5
Marx K, Angels F (1968) Selected works. Lawrence and Wishart
Morgan LH (1877) Ancient society. MacMillan & Company
Nandi GC (2017) Regional variation and development perspectives: a study of north east India. Int J Res Anal Rev (IJRAR) 4(2):556–565
NITI Aayog (2021) North eastern region district SDG index report & dashboard 2021–22. NITI Aayog, Government of India
Organski AFK (1967) The stages of political development. The University of Chicago Press
Parsons T (1966) Societies: evolutionary and comparative perspectives. Prentice Hall
Prebisch R (Nov 1949) Growth, disequilibrium and disparities: interpretation of the process of economic development. Estudio Económico de América Latina y el Caribe, Naciones Unidas Comisión Económica para América Latina y el Caribe (CEPAL), no 1105
Rostow WW (1971) The stages of economic growth. Cambridge University Press
Singh IJ (01 Jan 2022) Sustainable development goals: a road map for the north-eastern states. Econ Polit Wkly 57(1)
Smelser NJ (1959) Social change in the industrial revolution. University of Chicago Press
So AY (1990) Social change and development: modernization, dependency and world-system theories. Sage
Spencer H (1873) The study of sociology. King
SRCPT (2021) Access to toilets and the safety, convenience and self-respect of women in rural India. Sambodhi Research and Communications Pvt. Ltd.
UN (2022) Water and sanitation. https://sdgs.un.org/topics/water-and-sanitation. Accessed 16 Mar 2022
UN (2023a) Goal 3: ensure healthy lives and promote well-being for all at all ages. https://unric.org/en/sdg-3/. Accessed 27 Mar 2023
UN (2023b) Good health and well-being: why it matters. https://www.un.org/sustainabledevelopment/wp-content/uploads/2018/09/Goal-3.pdf. Accessed 26 Apr 2023
UN (2023c) WASH—water, sanitation and hygiene. https://www.unwater.org/water-facts/water-sanitation-and-hygiene/. Accessed 24 Mar 2022
Wallerstein I (1974) The modern world-system, vol 1. Academic Press
Weber M (1967) The protestant ethics and the spirit of capitalism. Unwin

WHO (2021) Health and well-being and the 2030 agenda for sustainable development in the WHO European Region: an analysis of policy development and implementation. World Health Organization. https://apps.who.int/iris/bitstream/handle/10665/339795/WHO-EURO-2021-1878-41629-56873-eng.pdf. Accessed 26 Apr 2023
Worley H (2014) Water, sanitation, hygiene, and malnutrition in India. Population Reference Bureau

Part II
Indigenizing Sociology in India

Chapter 6
Indigenizing Sociology in India: Contributions of Some 'Pioneers'

Biswajit Ghosh

Abstract The social conditioning of Indian sociology in its early days was deeply influenced by the colonial experience, the memory of the past glory, and the project of future political and cultural emancipation. The pioneers of Indian sociology uniformly shared certain visions of Indian society and preferred sociology to reflect on those. They spoke and wrote on a wide variety of issues while countering the over-arching European criticisms. While doing so, they laid the foundations of a number of new fields of study and advocated new approaches, categories, and methods. As against the domination of western discourses, they strongly argued and worked for indigenizing sociology in India, thereby, laying the foundation of 'Sociology for India'. Despite many common threads in their thinking, their paths were different.

Keywords Indian sociology · Pioneers · Nationalism · Tradition · Personality · Perspectives

Introduction

The social conditioning of Indian sociology in its early days was deeply influenced by the colonial experience, the memory of the past glory, and the project of future political and cultural emancipation. Though Indian social scientists took time to respond to the challenges of colonialism and defend Indian identity, the constant growth of nationalism provided the ideological milieu in which the pioneers of Indian sociology along with many other social scientists joined cultural and political elites to counter 'investigative modalities' (Cohn 1996) and colonial construction of knowledge. The response of social scientists was delayed as 'social science as a profession itself was a byproduct of colonial impact rather than the anti-colonial struggle' (Singh 1984, p. 156). Notwithstanding their ambivalence towards western social sciences for historical reasons, they gradually started advocating new approaches, categories,

B. Ghosh (✉)
Former Vice Chancellor and Professor of Sociology, The University of Burdwan, Bardhaman, West Bengal, India
e-mail: bghoshbu@gmail.com

A. Chauhan et al. (eds.), *Hundred Years of Sociology in India: Evolving Issues, Emerging Trends*, https://doi.org/10.1007/978-981-96-1317-5_6

and methods to study Indian society and culture. Nationalist ideas played a prominent role in the works of a host of nineteenth and twentieth-century Indian social scientists like Sarat Chandra Roy, Bhupendranath Dutta, K. P. Chattopadhyay, Tarak Nath Das, B. S. Guha, N. K. Bose, Surajit Sinha, and many others 'who were socially committed and contributed to nation-building through their analytical writings and research' (Guha 2019, p. 158).

Though one can notice many common threads in their thinking, nationalist ideas of pioneers like G. S. Ghurye and N. K. Bose were criticized for arguing for a vertical integration of Indian society where Brahminical ideals were given prominence and the secular and materialistic trends were ignored (Bose 2007; Guha 2019). It should, however, be acknowledged that these pioneers started theorizing in a context when the 'colonial paradigm' of Indian society and culture exaggerated its segmentary cleavages and 'offered a deeply fractured picture of Indian society' (Singh 1986, p. X). During the colonial period, many British, Missionary, and European writings on Indian society and culture used conceptual categories which were Eurocentric in cognitive and value terms. Some of those concepts also intended to distort history, exaggerate its segmentary cleavages, and undermine its tradition. As a corollary, while colonial interest and intellectual curiosity of the western scholars led to the development of Indian sociology and social anthropology, such development was equally influenced by the concern of Indian pioneers to indigenize the discipline.

The early 'pioneers' of Indian sociology, therefore, responded sceptically to the ideological formulations of Indian reality by European scholars (Ghosh 2019). They not only refuted the ideological biases in western interpretations, but they also demonstrated the organic unity of Indian society and endowed Indian social science with new methods and contents. As Singh (1984) argues, a deeper historical orientation was integral to their conceptual framework of sociology. Gupta's (1972) pioneering work refuted the allegation that Indian sociology was 'adaptive', 'routinized', and 'tradition-bound'[1] since its inception (cited by Sharma 2019, p. 8). She rather exhibited how 'philosophical thought about society as a whole and an attempt to carry out a secular solution of social problems characterised the early precursors of sociology in India' (Gupta 1972 p. 83). This led them to provide 'a plural and multidimensional thrust to sociology in India' (Sharma 2019, p. 7). Let me investigate these strands of thought in the writing of primarily three Indian pioneers, namely Benoy Kumar Sarkar (1887–1949), Radhakamal Mukerjee (1889–1968), and Dhurjati Prasad Mukerji (1894–1961).

The Social and Intellectual Context

It is interesting to note that nationalism provided the overall social context in which these pioneers grew up. They had many significant things in common. The Bengali intelligentsia of the 1890s—the decade of birth of these pioneers—were participants in a new phase of the renaissance led by luminaries like Rammohan Roy, Ishwar Chandra Vidyasagar, Bankim Chandra Chattopadhyay, Swami Vivekananda,

Mahatma Gandhi, and Rabindranath Tagore. Events like the partition of Bengal and the Swadeshi movement of 1905 influenced their thinking deeply. Commenting on this context, Yogendra Singh wrote,

> Bengal played a domineering role in both emergence of a critical middle class of intellectuals, poets, artists and reformers as also in sponsoring vigorous philosophical and meta-theoretical dialogue with the western traditions which at that time had an overwhelming global presence. Sociologists such as B. K. Sarkar and B. N. Seal focused particularly on critically evaluating the western philosophical and theoretical paradigms of social sciences as to their relevance in studies of the Indian society, its culture and traditions.....Sarkar's views are a representation of the intellectual-cultural waves that were overtaking Bengal in early twentieth century, which had a deep impact upon the formation of the normative and epistemological horizons of Radha Kamal Mukherjee's discourses in social sciences. (Singh 2016, p. 4)

Interestingly, as a student of Presidency College, Benoy took a direct part in anti-British movements and declined to accept state government scholarship and the job of a Deputy Magistrate. Though he refrained from joining any active politics, as a nationalist, Benoy felt it essential to lift the country from embarrassment and put it on an equal footing with the West. In this respect, he admired Vivekananda's effort to illuminate Indian honour globally and his proclamation of conquering the world. Benoy, therefore, set his major task of discovering the real identity of India. It would be interesting for us to note how many other Indian pioneers also set a similar target in the milieu in which they were debating, researching, and writing despite the British agency targeting them. Radhakamal, for instance, was arrested by the British police for his sympathy for the 'terrorists' under the disguise of adult education. Benoy was also not allowed to return to India from abroad for long doubting his proximity with the revolutionaries (Bhattacharyya 1990, p. 66). The colonial government not only forced him to change his argument about British rule in India, it also tried to pacify him by offering him a teaching post at the University of Calcutta. Benoy's acknowledgement about politics being 'a luxury which the progeny of the poor cannot afford' (cited by Bhattacharyya 1990, p. 67) should be read in that context.

In Bombay also, G. S. Ghurye (1893–1983) 'made a sustained effort to move away from the colonial legacy of sociology' (Momin 1996, p. vi). He, however, started nurturing anti-colonial nationalism by stressing more on the Indian tradition of harmony and assimilation. The ideology of narrow and exclusivist nationalism promoted by Brahmin elite like Vishnushastri Chiplunkar from Pune influenced him greatly (Momin 1996, p. vii). Interestingly, no Indian sociologist/anthropologist opposed nationalism and all were affected by it in one way or another.

More importantly, given their common social and intellectual milieu, these pioneers accepted Indian society as the obvious and natural object of their professional attention. They also designed India's future on the larger canvas of world-historical processes. As they inherited the legacy of social reform in the country, the issues related to challenges of nation-building and economic development concerned them the most. Another interesting uniformity is seen in their reflection about the civilizational unity of India as a plural society.

The members of Lucknow school[2] of Indian sociology, namely Radhakamal Mukerjee, D. P. Mukerji, and Dhirendra Nath Majumdar (1903–1960)—called 'trinity' in the history of Indian sociology—were also worried about the culturally alienating effects of modernization. The Sociology Department at the University of Lucknow started stressing interdisciplinary studies in social sciences since 1921. Their training in disciplines like economics and history[3] had probably influenced them to look beyond disciplinary boundaries. This school emerged as a major critique of western modernity and proposed indigenous ideas about the relation between tradition and modernity. This school, argues Madan (2013), had contributed to a wide variety of conceptual and practical issues including cultural values, institutions, and practices of Indian society. It had stressed more on conceptual issues and 'became famous for its engagement with the question of post-colonial social and economic reconstruction and its concern with grass-roots issues and problems' (Momin 2013, p. 207).

While the Lucknow School offered a clear alternative to western and colonial explanations of Indian society and culture, the Bombay School, which is the oldest Indian institution of teaching and research in sociology, had contributed differently towards the development of Indian sociology including its professional expansion. Momin (2013, p. 207) argues that this 'school has made a pioneering contribution to sociological research by emphasising fieldwork and by ingeniously synthesising the sociological, Indological, and historical perspectives'. G. S. Ghurye, the main ideologue of this school, rejected some of the premises of colonial knowledge notwithstanding his bias for 'Hindu/Brahminical nationalist ideology' (Upadhya 2002, p. 27). Being trained in Sanskrit and Indology, he was deeply influenced by the Orientalist explanation of Indian society. He, therefore, suggested the homogenization of Indian tribes by ignoring their socio-cultural diversities. Pradip Bose (1996, p. 72) also felt that Ghurye's narrative of caste, one of his major contributions, 'completely accepts the epistemological authority of the orientalists and colonial discourse' and his understanding of caste 'lacks any indigenous perspective towards this subject'. Yet, Ghurye encouraged A. R. Desai to undertake a materialist explanation of Indian nationalism. Dirks (2013, p. 239), therefore, considered him 'one of India's first postcolonial intellectuals' as he fought for Indian intellectual autonomy and self-sufficiency while championing the cause of Indian social science.

Indian Sociology and Interpretation of Indian Tradition

During British rule, the plea for the development of indigenous sociology took different forms. The large group of liberals, for instance, did not hesitate to use western concepts, explanations, and categories, they only preferred such adoption to match Indian reality. The liberal camp also included those who advocated and practised Indology for the development of Indian sociology. Like them, the Orientalists also looked at Indian reality from a purely textual perspective and were charmed by its philosophical traditions. Scholars like A. K. Saran (1922–2003) have, however, argued that acceptance of western social science would lead to permanent alienation of Indian intellectuals from their rich cultural heritage. He 'practised a theoretico-philosophic stream, rooted in India's past glory and civilisational uniqueness' (Sharma 2019, p. 8). According to Madan (2013), Saran favoured the exploration of 'traditional thought' and critiqued the concept of modernity including the ideas propagated by evolutionists, positivists, and Marxists. He was a theist and hence, to him, the notion of social science was an anathema (Madan 2013, p. 44).

The influence of Orientalist and Indological thinking about India can clearly be discerned in the early writings of Benoy. Thus, the beginning of what is called *Sarkarism* (Mukhopadhyay 2015, p. 212) was marked by the emphasis on dichotomy between the East and West. He also criticized the western pedagogic ideals and philosophy of life. In the spirit of *Swadeshi* ideas, he wanted to build India, by not emulating Europe, but by asserting Indian uniqueness and safeguarding the beauty of Indian values. Following the Orientalists, Benoy first argued that Indian (Hindu) culture gave importance to spiritualism and thereby undermined material prosperity. Later, while translating Sukracharya's *Nivisara* in 1910, Benoy changed his views completely and put forward a new thesis that East is equal to the West. Four volumes of this translation were published under the general title *Positive Background of Hindu Sociology* (1914, 1921, 1926, and 1937). As the title of the book itself speaks, Benoy here informed us that the past of the Hindus was full of secular, mundane, and materialistic activities. He found a high degree of overlap of both the Hindu and the Buddhist traditions with the ideals of western positivism. It was only after the industrial revolution that India/Asia lagged behind. Though Benoy did not present his ideas systematically, it is possible to understand the bewilderment that many other social scientists of his time faced in presenting anti-colonial and anti-western sociology.

In his theory of progress also, Benoy brilliantly brought in the Indian case to argue that progress is the property of humanity since its inception. Proposing a multilinear theory of progress, Benoy argued that there is no ultimate goal of progress and it is not a stage-wise movement. Challenging Comte's notion of progress, he argued that progress is dialectical and man's life and society develop through disharmony. He, therefore, wrote, 'No *dwanda* (conflict), no progress' (Sarkar, 1941, cited by Bhattacharyya 1990, p. 476). Much before the publication of Lewis Coser's celebrated book *Functions of Social Conflict* (1956), Benoy claimed that conflict provides a creative agency for progress. As it is apparent, he opposed any kind of deterministic theory of progress and change. To explain this process, he used the concept of 'creative disequilibrium' (cited by Bhattacharyya 1990, p. 475). The process of disequilibrium can be noticed at a personal level, inter-human level, and also in society and culture. Since progress is a ceaseless, continuous, and universal process, it cannot be the typical feature of the West only. Such solid reasonings about the 'fundamental unity of men' allowed Benoy not only to challenge the colonial view that Indian society and culture were static and despotic but also to argue contrarily that like its glorious past, India's future will be equal to that of the West.

Among the pioneers, Radhakamal Mukerjee is 'credited with having played a foundational role in the shaping of social sciences in general and sociology in particular' (Thakur 2012, p. 89). His vision of sociology was also rooted in the Indian tradition though he was more universalistic and interdisciplinary in his approach. Though his arguments about the western paradigm of social sciences coincided with those of Benoy, Singh (2016) feels that Radhakamal was more systematic and constructive in explaining the limits of western discourses. He found the western social science model including the Marxian one inadequate for explaining Indian social life. Since the western method of an individualistic conception of man and social reality cannot be applied to understand Indian social reality, he supported Sir Brajendra Nath Seal's argument that western academics had undervalued Indian civilization without taking her distinctiveness into account (Sen 2020). Seal's comparative method for the study of culture attracted his attention. Using this method, he came to the conclusion that beneath the seeming variations of cultural traits of any culture, there is a decisive rhythm of harmony (Sen 2020). Notwithstanding appreciating the scholarly spirit of the West, he challenged their practice of division of knowledge into several branches. He argued 'The philosophy of social science aims at discovering the structure of the real, whole or complete man and society' (Mukerjee 1960:1). He used Indian categories and resources from art, architecture, history, and culture to argue that India should be seen in Indian terms. He believed that harmony is the basic value of life and he found this harmony amply illustrated in the Indian scheme of life of previous ages.

Like Benoy and Dhurjati, Radhakamal also argued that Indian culture has viewed man as a responsible member of a community. In the Indian context, therefore, man is not an isolated individual. Unlike Indian culture, western society has relegated superior human values and traditions to the background in order to promote objectivity and instrumentality. This allowed them to treat nature as objects for satisfying human greed. Radhakamal's criticism of the notion of scientific and instrumental western progress allowed him to argue for the ecological balance that we all desperately seek today (Oommen 2015). During Radhakamal's time, western scholarship failed to realize the importance of the unity and oneness of human civilization. Radhakamal's penetrating analysis led him to defend Oriental civilization, where men relish the beauty and charm of nature as they give importance to the intrinsic qualities of life, including social cohesion. By arguing in this way, Radhakamal also defended his idea of 'cosmic humanism' which balances man and society with the vertical and ontological order. As compared to the West, Indian society sees man first as a social creature, as human beings are value-creating and value-fulfilling animals. This influences their personality, their social relationships, and the functioning of groups and institutions. It may be noted that Mukerjee noted dynamic reciprocity among the components of his triad, namely man, the structure of society, and values leading to the totality of the society. While providing a solid theoretical framework to discuss issues of Indian society, he engaged himself in the field work to understand the impending socio-economic issues.

Dhurjati also equally expressed his concern for the development of a unique approach to interpret and understand Indian society and its past. Thus, for him, Indian culture is essentially social. India might or might not have had history, politics, or economics in the western sense of the term, but it had a society and had too much of it (Mitra 2015). Unlike the west, India's history, economics, and philosophy have always been centred in social groups and rooted in social realities. The limitations of western sociology for Dhurjati also signify the limitations of western culture and society. By contrast, he stressed on the creative aspects of Indian tradition in maintaining stability and cohesion. Hence, the first and immediate task for Indian sociologists is to study the social tradition. And to do so, Indian sociologists should become Indian first by sharing their traditions and learning languages like Sanskrit and Persian.

To him, our conception of freedom is different, because our conception of man is *purusha* and not the 'individual' of the west. Hence, Indian sociologists will have to accept that the group is the major unit of such analysis and reject the individual. Like bees and beavers, Indians are almost regimented people though they mostly do not feel restricted. He, however, recognized the problem of 'group tyranny' hindering proper growth of personality and leading to stagnation. In such a context, idealizing or worshipping tradition becomes dangerous. To overcome this problem, Dhurjati argued for individual autonomy. He believed that culture could be recreated by infusing it with fresh vigour. A balance can be maintained between the freedom and surveillance of the individual choice. Individuation and sociation thus must go hand-in-hand.

To Dhurjati, traditions are the 'reservoirs of collective experience and collective wisdom' which help an individual to relate an abstract with the concrete, a part to the whole, and link the past with the present and future (Mitra 2015, p. 239). He divided tradition, that is *parampara* meaning succession, into three categories namely: primary, secondary, and tertiary. While it is the primary tradition which is most authentic and close to Indian society, it is the secondary tradition which is seen as an influence of the Muslim rule. In the tertiary traditions, conceptual thought differences survived evidently. He, thereby, rejected the western fiction that the Indian mind was 'annexed and possessed' by religion.

Such arguments led Dhurjati to claim that traditions are not static. He refuted the European charge that Indian tradition is changeless. Like other aspects of social life, tradition also changes. He noticed instances of adjustment, accommodation, and assimilation in Indian tradition. From such a point of view, tradition does not obstruct modernization. It rather is a condition for such transformation as it allows a person to choose between alternatives and thereby develop a synthesis between the existing and the new pattern. Modernity must, therefore, be defined in relation to, and not in denial of, tradition. He thus wrote,

> The value of Indian traditions lies in the ability of their conserving forces to put a break on hasty passage. Adjustment is the end product of the dialectical connection between the two. Meanwhile [there] is tension. (Mukerji 1958, p. 76).

He identified *Sruti, Smriti, Anubhava* as the major forces of change in tradition. The third one *Anubhava*, meaning personal experience, is radical. Many Indian saints contributed to changes in socio-religious order because of collective experience. This means Indians need not modernize them by blindly following the West. Being concerned about the contradictory role of the new middle class in British India in defending and consolidating colonial rule, Dhurjati advised them to 'de-alienate' and perform *samajdharma* (Mitra 2015). Being influenced by Tagore, he reasoned that there could be no genuine modernization through imitation. Only a self-conscious person may modernize by synthesizing internal and external ideas. The influence of Buddhism, Islam, and British commerce and culture can clearly be noticed in Indian tradition. Due to such synthesis, Dhurjati advised us not to consider Indian tradition as a perfect replica of either Hindu, Islamic, or western mode of living.

Dhurjati's analysis about the nature of tradition, in general, and Indian tradition, in particular, became intriguing when he argued that tradition and modernity are not dialectically opposed like British colonialism and Indian nationalism. Rather, there is very strong evidence of the interplay of the two, as modernization does not mean departure of the tradition. Tagore's life trajectory allowed him to argue how the influence of the West could not demean his loyalty to traditional values. He wrote, 'His (Tagore) saturation with Indian traditions was deeper; hence he could more easily assimilate a bigger dose of western thought' (1943/1972: 75–76). Dhurjati, therefore, optimistically argued about the capacity of tradition to adjust and tolerate western influences. The flexible capacity of the Indian tradition to assimilate several tribal cultures as well as dissenting voices led him to claim that Indians are *Varansankara*—mixed race.

As against the European propaganda of the adverse role of tradition in India's development, Dhurjati argued the opposite. In doing so, he postulated the possibility of the emergence of newer and better alternatives out of the synthesis. This means modernity cannot be explained without relating it with tradition. Even if a conflict develops in the intermediate stage, the dialectical triad will finally reflect a movement towards coincidence of opposites.

Nature of Sociology

Interestingly all our pioners saw sociology as a synthesis of different social sciences and not an individualistic science. One of the most important aspects of their works was a departure from the western notion of sociology as a concept of metaphysical individualism.

For Benoy, sociology, as an 'architectonic' science (Bhattacharyya 1990, p. 202) deals with all types of inter-human relationships under two major branches: theoretical and applied sociology. For him, sociology is the study of each and every social phenomenon. As for him, the discipline lacks any strict boundary, he accommodated the study of every phenomenon within the scope of this 'specialized social science'. For him, anthropology and history constitute the foundation, politics represents the goal and psychology allows sociology to begin.

Radhakamal has equally stressed on the need for an interdisciplinary social science that could discover the unity of social sciences. Like many other pioneers of his time, he criss-crossed the knowledge base of social sciences like economics, sociology, demography, and social work in an effort to bridge the gap between theory and practice. The preoccupation of the western social sciences with analytic and specialized treatment of social relations and processes did not allow them to develop an 'integrative and comprehensive theoretical pattern'. Though Radhakamal did not deny the importance of the natural science method, he preferred a philosophical setting while applying any method (Sen 2020). A perfect mixture of natural science approach and spiritual or metaphysical orientation is desirable to grasp the essence of culture and civilization.

In a similar vein, Dhurjati argued that the task of sociology is to integrate the specialized social sciences in a holistic fashion. It should correct the imbalance that happened due to the overspecialization of social sciences and provide an epistemological understanding of society. He thus wrote, 'Sociology has a floor and a ceiling like any other discipline'. But its specialty 'consists in its floor being the ground floor of all types of social discipline and its ceiling remaining open to the sky' (Mukerji 1958, p. 229). Like Radhakamal, he criticized the fellow social scientists of his time for ignoring the totality of knowledge and seeking 'a mad career of purity' (Mitra 2015, p. 256). Though hopeful about the future of sociology, Dhurjati argued for a 'differently oriented' discipline in India. It is worth noting here that western sociological theory, in general, and its Parsonian version, in particular, did not satisfy him because of its overweening accent on the 'individual' or the 'actor-situation'. He, therefore, considered the western notions of 'progress', 'equality', 'social forces', and 'social control' excessively ethnocentric and mechanistic.

Methodology

The pioneers of Indian sociology gave importance to ontological and epistemological issues of the discipline. They were opposed to the positivist postulate of atomism and the positivist procedure of dividing the 'multi-dimensional world' in which human beings live into isolated entities. Benoy, for instance, found it difficult to align himself with the sociological system of western sociologists because they stressed a particular aspect of the social existence of human beings. He was also opposed to the western practice of 'monistic interpretation of social phenomenon' (Saha 2013, p. 7). Comte's positivistic determinism was as fallacious to him as was Marxian economic determinism. However, in the early 1920s, Benoy expressed his liking for positivistic methods. He then wrote,

> We have to proceed to the historical, philosophical, economic and political studies exactly in the spirit in which the archaeologist or rather the students of positive science have been attacking their problems (Sarkar 1922: 330).

However, he gradually understood the limitations of the positivistic method for a social scientist and, thereby, started prescribing comparative methods and stressed on the idea of pluralism for scientific analysis. He himself used this method to argue about the fundamental unity of human beings across space. He grounded the strategy of pluralism on relativism as opposed to the practice of absolutism under monism (Saha 2013).

Radhakamal's arguments, on the other hand, are firmly premised upon the epistemology of hermeneutics and interpretivism rather than positivism. He however, began with a structural functional approach to ascertain the interdependence between the economic sphere and the social–historical-cultural order of Indian society. Such dependence on the western paradigm of social sciences, despite national self-awareness, was a central feature of many Indian social scientists of that time including, Radhakamal (Thakur 2012 p. 104). Later, however, he used the 'trans-disciplinary' approach and comparative methods for a comprehensive appraisal of Indian social reality. By rejecting the utility of imperialistic positivistic method, he then brought in indigenous notions of dharma, sangha, and transcendental values to challenge western ideological hegemony and cultural dominance.

Dhurjati was equally influenced by these traditions as he gave importance to subjectivity, relied on history and philosophy, and critiqued positive, objective, and inductive methodologies for analysing society. He was not a Marxist. He noted down the limitations of the Marxian approach to study Indian society. Unlike the Marxists, he did not analyse everything in terms of class conflict as caste conflicts overshadow them in India. To him, class struggle is noticed in Indian history only marginally. Our history is rather marked predominantly by cultural synthesis and value assimilation. Secondly, most of the Marxists were not aware of the socio-economic history of India. And third, the way economic pressures work is not similar to any mechanical force. They may change and act differently. He, therefore, preferred to call him a 'Marxologist' as he stressed on the utility of the dialectical method for studying economic changes in India. By finding dialectical linkages between tradition and modernity, colonialism and nationalism, and individualism and collectivism, Dhurjati expanded our vision of the applicability of methods.

But, at the same time, Dhurjati stressed on *Sruti, Smriti,* and *Anubhab* as methods to understand and interpret non-economic aspects of Indian social life. The first two are dialectical exegesis, while the third is personal experience. He did refer to the hermeneutic tradition of conducting research popularized by Dilthey. He argued that studying personality calls for the use of subjective and individualistic judgements and insight. Hence, it requires a different kind of understanding than that used in physical sciences (Mitra 2015). For instance, while conducting social research, we often fall back on our memories. Understanding a phenomenon, a symbol, requires the use of *Anubhab.* The method of case history entirely depends on *Smriti. Sruti* or popular folk tales, myths, etc., are also used in social research. Despite being tolerant of western ideas and concepts, Dhurjati brilliantly contributed to the development of indigenous sociology by highlighting the limits of western concepts, theories, and methods to explore and explain the totality of Indian social life.

Concept of Personality

As against the western concept of an individual, all our pioneers stressed on the multi-dimensional personality of a man. It is important for us to note that a strong concern for analysing the concept of human personality was felt by all of them in order to oppose the western explanation of man-society relations. Personality, for Radhakamal, is the entire way in which an individual adjusts in different directions: biological, social, ideal, cosmic, and transcendental. Human personality always looks for higher spiritual values of any civilization at different levels. Herein, he used the concept of *cosmic humanism,* which is similar to Benoy's idea of universal man, to argue that there is continuity between personality and universe, between social order and cosmic order. Radhakamal's argument about the invisibility of society and the possibility of the development of a general theory of society emanates from such a belief (Thakur 2012).

Like Radhakamal, Benoy also believed that humanity is the same everywhere. Hence, he did not like differentiating human beings based on their caste, region, or religion. He strongly believed that human beings across space and culture are endowed with qualities like dynamism, power, and creativity. These qualities are used everywhere to create and recreate social order. This means no force can permanently control human beings. Herein, again, Benoy talked against the Durkheimian or Marxian notion of determinism. To explain the creative nature of human power, Benoy used the concept of 'creative disequilibrium'. Being a plural person, a man is always involved in a war between good and evil. A person can never be either totally good, or totally bad. Taking an example, he explained that as against a traditionalist, a naughty person 'begins his life with a doubt, with a question, with a challenge' (Sarkar 1938, p. 120). The four basic instincts of a human being, namely *Kama, Kanchana, Kirti, and Karma* contribute to four different spheres of creation. Such an explanation allowed Benoy to confront the western notion of a rational, scientific man of the West as against the so-called irrational and illogical variety from the East. Much before Edward Said, Benoy questioned the alleged inferiority of the East and thereby posed a big question to the construction of Orientalism.

As compared to Radhakamal and Benoy, Dhurjati's sociology centred around the problem of the development of personality in relation to Indian culture and society (Mitra 2015, p. 239). Personality to him is 'the synthesis of the double process of individualization and socialization of uniqueness of individual life' (Mukerji 1924, p. 11). He criticized the western notion of personality as it stresses only on 'achievement' to count the success of a person. Echoing Radhakamal's concern, Dhurjati also argued that the West unduly stressed on domination over nature for human advantage. In the West, the individuals had, therefore, become either destructive or passive. A 'free' individual should also be a 'socially committed' individual. An individual should remain rooted in his tradition, as any integrated development requires the right balance between the social aspects of living with the achieved ones. Technological advances should not curtail human freedom. Development should not destroy humanism.

Conclusion

It, therefore, appears that the pioneers of Indian sociology uniformly shared certain visions of Indian society and preferred sociology to reflect those concerns. They spoke and wrote on a wide variety of issues as it was impossible for them to concentrate on a few themes to counter the overarching European criticisms. Madan (2011) feels that as our pioneers were in a great hurry to deal with a wide variety of subjects, they could not go deep into any of them. The lack of any single, rigorously worked-out theoretical framework also bothered Benoy and Dhurjati. Yet, they contributed to laying the foundations of a number of new fields of study. Being concerned about the future of India, they also came forward with elaborate suggestions about its social and economic progress. Despite the common goal, their paths were, however, different.

Madan (2011) has argued that the founders of sociology in India also contributed significantly to the making of a 'modern' social consciousness, without losing their cultural roots. As they started imagining India in an atmosphere of self-discovery and self-assertion, they, in one way or another, argued against any Eurocentric reductionism in explaining Indian society and culture. As against the domination of western discourses, they strongly argued and worked for indigenizing sociology in India. This laid the strong foundation for arguing in favour of 'Sociology for India'.

Notes

1. Edward Shils (1961, cited by Gupta, 1972, p. xii) had argued that social scientists from colonial countries and colonial universities are at best adept in 'adaptive researches', 'routinised' sciences which require no original thinking or creativity.
2. I do agree with Jayaram (2013) that it is simplistic to argue that scholars of both Lucknow and Bombay schools had argued unanimously about all aspects of social reality. The idea of a school offering coherent ideas and orientation cannot be found in the case of both schools of sociology. Notwithstanding certain striking similarities, they maintained differences.
3. For Ghurye also, history and sociology are almost the same (Pramanick 1994, p. 290).

References

Bhattacharyya SK (1990) Indian sociology: the role of Benoy Kumar Sarkar. The University of Burdwan, Burdwan

Bose P (1996) A narrative of caste: Ghurye on caste and race in India. In: Momin AR (ed) The legacy of G. S. Ghurye: a centenary festschrift. Popular Prakashan, Bombay, pp 61–73

Bose P (2007) The anthropologist as 'scientist'? Nirmal Kumar Bose. In: Uberoi P, Sundar N, Deshpande S (eds) Anthropology in the east: founders of Indian sociology and anthropology. Permanent Black, Ranikhet, pp 290–329

Cohn B (1996) Colonialism and its forms of knowledge. Princeton University Press, Princeton

Dirks N (2013) G.S. Ghurye and the politics of sociological knowledge. Sociol Bull 62(2):239–252

Ghosh B (2019) Study of Indian society and culture: methods and perspectives. Kerala Sociol 47(1):13–29

Guha A (2019) Colonial, Hindu and nationalist anthropology in India. Sociol Bull 68(2):154–168
Gupta BD (1972) Sociology in India. Centre for Sociological Research, Calcutta
Jayaram N (2013) Introduction: the Bombay School—so-called—and its legacies. Sociol Bull 62(2):195–203
Madan TN (2011) Sociological traditions: methods and perspectives in the sociology of India. Sage Publications, New Delhi
Madan TN (ed) (2013) Sociology at the university of Lucknow. Oxford University Press, New Delhi
Mitra A (2015) Dhurjati Prasad Mukerji—from the problem of personality to the plane of sociology. In: Mukhopadhyay AK (ed) Bengali intellectual tradition—from Rammohun Roy to Dhirendranath Sen. K. P. Bagchi and Co., Kolkata, pp 235–263
Momin AR (1996) Introduction. In: Momin AR (ed) The legacy of G. S. Ghurye: a centenary festschrift. Popular Prakashan, Bombay, pp v–xiii
Momin AR (2013) Revisiting the legacy of the Bombay School of sociology. Sociol Bull 62(2):204–216
Mukerjee R (1960) The philosophy of social science. Macmillan and Co., Ltd., London
Mukerji DP (1924) Personality and the social sciences. The Book Company, Calcutta
Mukerji DP (1958) Diversities: essays in economics, sociology and other social problems. People's Publishing House, New Delhi
Mukerji DP (1943/1972) Tagore: a study. Manisha Granthalaya, Calcutta
Mukhopadhyay AK (2015) Benoy Kumar Sarkar—the theoretical foundation of Indian capitalism. In: Mukhopadhyay AK (ed) Bengali intellectual tradition—from Rammohun Roy to Dhirendranath Sen. K. P. Bagchi and Co., Kolkata, pp 213–234
Oommen TK (2015) Radhakamal Mukerjee on social ecology: filling up some blanks. Sociol Bull 64(1):15–35
Pramanick SK (1994) Sociology of G.S. Ghurye. Rawat Publications, Jaipur
Saha S (2013) Benoy Kumar Sarkar (1887–1949): a tryst with destiny. Sociol Bull 62(1):4–22
Sarkar BK (1922) Futurism of young Asia and other essays on the relations between the East and the West. Julius Springer, Berlin
Sarkar BK (1938) Greetings of young India: messages of social and cultural reconstruction (Part 1). N.M. Chowdhury and Co., Calcutta
Sen S (2020) Radhakamal Mukerjee's views on civilization. Burdwan J Sociol 1(1):35–47
Sharma KL (2019) Indian sociology at the threshold of the 21st century: some observations. Sociol Bull 68(1):7–24
Singh Y (1984) Image of man: ideology and theory in Indian sociology. Chankya Publications, Delhi
Singh Y (1986) Indian sociology—social conditioning and emerging concerns. Vistaar Publications, New Delhi
Singh Y (2016) Changing discourses in social sciences: relevance of Radhakamal Mukherjee. Sociol Bull 65(1):3–18
Thakur M (2012) Radhakamal Mukerjee and the quest for an Indian sociology. Sociol Bull 61(1):89–108
Upadhya C (2002) The Hindu nationalist sociology of G.S. Ghurye. Sociol Bull 51(1):28–57

Chapter 7
Personality, Music and Community in the Sociology of D.P. Mukerji

Gayatri Bhattacharyya

Abstract D. P. Mukerji's concept of Purusha or Person as a creative agent endowed with a sense of responsibility to the rest of his/her native community and world at large offers an alternative template for sociology as understood in the west which foregrounds atomistic and atomized individuals. A solitary explorer in the realm of sociology of music in the hundred-year-old narrative of sociology in India, D.P. seeks to demonstrate that every art-form, music in particular, offers a means to develop personality and stimulate unity among human beings. It is exemplified in the practice of Indian music. Contrast of the ideas of Mukerji and Weber reveals their differences in assessment of the role of rationalization and capitalism in the development of music, culture and society. Overemphasis on rationalization and capitalistic interests block, according to D.P., innovativeness of Personality and creativity in music. His analysis reveals the vitality of Indian music in the modern era, as evidenced in the aesthetically satisfying blending of words and melody in Rabindrasangeet. But D.P.'s anxiety in what he deemed declining standard of Indian music blurred his vision of the innovations by the post-Tagore generations in the creation and enjoyment of music through the vicissitudes of time and social conditions.

Keywords Person/Purusha · Dhyan-murtis of Ragas · Raginis · Sangeet

Nurtured in an ambience of cultivation of arts and scientific temper, trained academically in history and economics, Dhurjati Prasad Mukerji (D.P.) came to embrace sociology, the '(n + I)th' discipline with great expectations. Sociology, the newly emerging branch of knowledge, appeared to him to have been striving for a synoptic and synthetic view of life and reality and, it would, he hoped, help him develop his Personality, i.e. his specificity or specific identity as a Person, endowed with autonomy and ability for making rational judgment about the humans and things and also with a sense of responsibility to the rest of his native community and the humanity at large.

G. Bhattacharyya (✉)
Calcutta University and Currently Senior Fellow, I.C.S.S.R, New Delhi, India
e-mail: gayatrib18@gmail.com

A. Chauhan et al. (eds.), *Hundred Years of Sociology in India: Evolving Issues, Emerging Trends*, https://doi.org/10.1007/978-981-96-1317-5_7

Mukerji's sociological venture in exploring the nature of person is distinguished by ever-perfectible personality that constantly recreates her/himself in originative and dialectical interaction with the surrounding reality carrying on and reshaping the inherited tradition. The immediate empirical referent is the Indian society, his native society, which has proverbially been known as a *tradition-laden* society. D.P. considered tradition a process and a product of bequeathing by the preceding generation of what is inherited and acquired by it to the Persons in the succeeding generation. He did not, of course, remain bewitched with traditionalism (Madan 2007, 2011, 2013; Mitra 2015).

Person, Individual and Bureaucracy

Worried about the fate of atomized individuals in 'modern' societies which form the 'reference group' for most of the societies in today's world, D.P. sought to project the vision of a world lived in and continually reconstituted by Persons. Person is distinguished from Individual (claimed to be originated by modern societies) by virtue of the former's potentialities for exercising autonomy and creative ability as well as their sense of responsibility to the fellow-beings and empathy with their weal and woe. The aforementioned qualities are hardly discernible in cases of 'independent but virtually isolated units of modern societies, bolstered by bureaucracies' of gargantual might and measure which smother their individualities and rob them of the warmth of human and humane relationships with others around. The Bengali or Sanskrit equivalent of Person is, as used by D. P., *Purusha* which for many suggests a male being. But differences in sex, status and ethnic group are without significance in his conceptualization of *Purusha* or Person though D.P.'s formulation seems somewhat problematic (cf. Bhattacharyya 2010).

However, Man is man only among men. Those humans who remain imprisoned by calculations of instrumental rationality emphasized in capitalist society that breeds selfishness, or, at the least, self-centredness, are deprived of the opportunities for fruition of human faculties and potentialities. The way to avert it lay, D. P. believed, in transition of societies of India and other countries to the socialist order. Though he had an undying faith in socialism, his scepticism regarding the probability of success of the desired transition in the face of growing ascendancy of technocracy and bureaucracy becomes evident in his 'Man and Plan in India' (Mukerji 2002/1958: 35—88). He apprehended subversion of the person by the bureaucracy in both capitalist and socialist systems. A different but feasible milieu emerging out of Mukerji's sociological imagination may be experienced in the life of a collectivity, marked by openness and dynamism and comprised of persons having communion with their fellow-beings.

The freedom, cherished and practised by the person, is gained through cooperation and alliance, which, in turn, enables one to perform higher deeds. In contrast with dissocialized individuals, embroiled in the rat-race engendered by the hegemony of the variants of capitalist economy encircling the globe, the person, liberated from the 'versus-sense' afflicting individuals and guided by the spirit of association and alliance, gets empowered to lay down and preserve the foundation of a habitable world. D.P. writes, therefore, 'a cooperative, affiliative person (purusha) is real, an individual is not' (Mukerji 2009: 45/Mukhopadhyay 1957: 20). Not forced to grope for the way out of the irreconcilability of facts and forces, as viewed from the logical frame of the dichotomy of either/or, Purusha proceeds in life through resolution of contradictions to reach the goal of '*living well and living better in and through the ecological balance between plant, animal and human communities*' (Mukerji 2004: xxvi/1932: emphasis added). This is the objective that inspires 'the development of personality' through the application of Reason. D.P.'s *Purushavad* or personalism reconciles, in particular, the contradiction manifested in the opposition between tradition and experimentation, which remains unresolved in case of asocial, unreal individuals.

Personality, Culture and Music

D.P. has all through sought to highlight the dual aspect of personality—its distinctiveness and originality and its communion with the rest of the community of which it is a creative part. This duality becomes clearly evident in the interaction between the different art forms including music and the development of personality.

The foregoing idea of *person as pictured by D.P. is melded with a notion of culture* that nourishes and is nourished by such institutions as express a fundamental belief in collective and mutual development rather than the individual's advancement celebrated by bourgeois society. This notion of culture initially suggesting the idea of cultivation or growth came to refer early in the nineteenth century to 'a general state or habit of mind' associated with the ideal of human perfection. 'We must not forget', writes D.P., 'that the Sanskrit equivalent of culture is *sanskriti*, which means reorientation or recreation' (Mukerji 2002/1958: 307). D.P., combined the documentation of culture as a way of life with the meaning of culture as the corpus of intellectual and imaginative works through which social groups and persons seek to explore and express meanings or understanding of their lives. Music eminently facilitates the process. D.P. observes:

> 'After all, music is an integral part of living; living together means a social process, and a genuinely active social process demands not merely an understanding but also an active release of the desires and ethos of peoples who not only express themselves in various forms of art, but who in the present disposition of affairs, are prevented from doing so. Social classes can come closest together through music, ...' (2002b/1945: 38).

The statement cited above occurs in D.P.'s *Indian Music: An Introduction* (1945) wherein he proved to be a solitary explorer in the realm of sociology of music in the hundred—year—old narrative of Indian sociology. D. P. had written a long chapter, 'Sociology of Modern Indian Music' in the book, *Modern Indian Culture* (1942). His cultivation of musical knowledge and taste, started in his early youth (Bose in Mukerji 1975), gained continuous refinement throughout his life. He religiously listened to the performance of male and female maestros of classical Indian music in Calcutta and Lucknow (Mukerji n.d. & Mukerji 1955). He had wide and intimate acquaintance with Bengali music and musicians. He wrote prolifically in Bengali on classical and regional music (Mukhopadhyay 1987). He had working knowledge of European music also (Mukhopadhyay 2002: passim). An acclaimed connoisseur of music, D. P. had the rare privilege of becoming co-author with Rabindranath of the book, *Sur O Sangati* (Thakur and Mukhopadhyay 1935). His own *Katha O Sur* (1938) was reprinted more than once. Mukerji displayed the exceptional ability to combine his musical knowledge and sensibility with sociological imagination. He listened to the performers of 'Baiji Gharana' (personal anecdotes from my aunt, Snehalata Chaudhuri, a former lecturer in an inter-college in Lucknow) with due reverence.

The prefatory note to *Indian Music* concludes with D.P.'s statement: 'I am not ashamed of the sociological stamp in my treatment of music'. It may be contrasted with Marc Perlman's expostulation regarding Nazir Ali Jairazbhoy's 'remarkable' book, The *Rāgs of North Indian Music: Their Structure and Evolution* (1971). It 'focuses on formal "musicological" analysis to the exclusion of sociological factors' (Perlman 2011). In 2014 came out *Indian Music and Its Assessment: A Sociological Perspective* by Israt Jahan, a performing vocalist in Hindustani Music who has also formal training in both sociology and musicology. It, however, contains no reference to D.P.'s work (cf. also Das Gupta 2007).

Sociological Import of D.P.'s Discourses on Music

The sociological import of D.P.s discourses on music is patent in the opening passage of his tiny but significant work of 1945:

'Indian music, being music, is just an arrangement of sounds; being Indian it is certainly a product of Indian History. But the features of the sound-pattern were common to India and Europe up to the period when both had a similar social and cultural background… In both regions religious and folk-music had been the inevitable context of classical music; in both classical music at moments of crisis had drawn from people's music for fresh life, elaborated it at leisure, and imposed sophisticated forms upon it in return. Music was equally intimate with the functions of collective living and equally susceptible to the genuine influences that worked upon the culture pattern. So long as the princely courts and princely dignitaries and the strongly entrenched guilds fixed the rules of living, Indian and European music alike betrayed the rudiments of melody and harmony. Since then, the tempo of change has been slower in India than in Europe accounting, partly, at least, for the so-called 'spirituality' of her music' (2002b/1945: 1).

Overall, D. P. seems anxious to establish a sort of equivalence in music between the two regions. This anxiety is explicable if one consults the footnote on page 29 of

Indian Music where D.P. makes an oblique and cryptic reference to the musical insensibility of Britishers such as Beverley Nichols and Leo S. Amery, British Secretary of State for India and Burma during 1940–1945. Even a cursory glance at Chap. 6, 'Musical Interlude' of *Verdict on India* (1944) by Nichols (though D.P. himself has not mentioned the book) reveals the ludicrous ignorance of some of the Britishers of the nature of Indian music and their vitriolic attack on the same. D. P.'s Sociology of Music sought, therefore, to highlight the specific identity (if not uniqueness) of Indian music simultaneously with its commonality with Western music.

The Two Pioneers in Sociology of Music: Mukerji and Weber

Distinctiveness of Mukerji's work in sociology of Indian music becomes pronounced when it is compared with a similar venture of Max Weber in relation to European music. Weber was himself adamant that aesthetic value judgment and sociological analysis must be clearly separated (Weber 1949: 32–33, cf. also Freund 1969: 268–269). This dictum would not have been countenanced by Mukerji. Also, Weber's emphasis on contribution of capitalism and the bourgeoisie to the 'development' of music and his relative neglect of individual performers and performances would have been unacceptable to D.P.

The Rational and Social Foundations of Music by Weber points for the first time to the rational harmonic system as a 'unique element to Western art' and Weber's sociology of music is considered crucial to understanding Western music (Martin 1995). Rationalization conceived as the universal historical process at work is central to Weber's sociological oeuvre. He was intrigued at the possibility of detecting the process at work in the 'irrational' arena of culture. This was the template used by Weber to investigate the rise of Western music (Weber 1949: 29 ff.)

Two key moments in music's rationalization were, according to Weber, the development of modern musical instruments and modern music notation. The process worked through the evolution from ancient to modern music which eliminated the mystical and 'irrational' qualities. It culminated in the unique development of chordal harmony in the West (Turley 2001: 679). The simple principle of a distance between tones in the music that a musician might make or a singer might sing was replaced by the organized, standardized, 'rationalized' principle of chordal harmony. It did not occur for a variety of reasons in the Chinese, Indian and Hellenic experiments. (Weber 1958: 97). To bolster his argument of rationalization, Weber linked cultural, economic, social, technical and even climatic factors in his account of the evolution of music in the West (Käsler 1988: 170). Weber's thesis is epitomized in his conclusion, regarding the innovation of the piano as the 'specifically modern keyboard instrument'.

> ...the particular sonorous effects of its expressive tone oscillations permitted it [the clavichord] to yield before the hammer piano only when *a small stratum of musicians and amateurs with delicate ears no longer decided* over the fate of musical instruments, but

when *market situations prevailed* and the production of music became capitalistic (Weber 1958: 118; emphases added).

The accentuation of the difference between the two systems of music of India and Europe is traced by D. P. to the technical discovery of the keyboard of the tempered scale in Europe which facilitated the replacement of voice—the previous ground of harmonic music—by instrumental music, thus opening the path to harmony. In India too, instruments dominated courtly music in the Mughal period that proved to be a highly creative phase of the classical or Hindustani music. 'But then India did not change over to the tempered scale….' (Ibid.: 7). So 'the genuine difference between the two types of music today is between one style of melody grounded on the tempered scale with distinct and clear intervals separating two consecutive notes, and another type of melody based on chromatic [diatonic? Cf. Chakraborty 2001, footnote on p.8) scale facilitating *mirh*, i.e. glides from one note to another so characteristic of the music of instruments' traditionally used in India.

Sjoberg and Cain (1971) and Turley (2001), however, think that Indian music production system provides a perfect counter-system analysis to western music production/notation. Highly formalized, it possesses many parallel elements to Western music like rhythm, melody scales and structured sections. But, they think, 'Indian music system has its own unique elements' (Turley 2001: 648). It is based on Rag (Rāga) and Tāl(a). Rag is the melody line and Tal is the rhythmic form. One may point out that Shruti (microtone, with an interval smaller than the rāgas), Shuddha and Chhaya-lag (pure ragas and ragas with shades of others) are some of the terms found in the lexicon of Indian classical music only (Deva 2015, Gangoly 1948). Further, the significance of the master and his trained students has kept the musician an important part of Indian music (Turley 2001: 649). D. P. had much earlier explained some of the aforementioned special features of Indian music.

D.P. On the Nature and State of Indian Music

Though tiny in size, *Indian Music* examines various aspects of the system of Indian music and its evolution, the instruments used in it, the system of *ragas* as well as the *gharanas*. It considers mainly the Hindustani music prevailing in the Northern and Eastern part of India and passingly refers to the Karnatic style prevalent in South India (2002b/1945:11). Barring a few decorations (*alamkars*), 'the Hindustani music of the North is built on the same principles as those of the Karnatic music (of the South)… The essentials of this common Indian music have been traced to the pre-Muslim period' (Ibid. 2). A note of lamentation on the presumed degeneration of Indian classical music runs through the work though D. P. repeatedly assured himself and his audience that '… Indian music is not dead'.

The innovation displayed by the Indian musicians reveals the 'composite culture' of India: 'Muslim masters took Hindu pupils, and vice versa. The songs, when they were not descriptive of nature and royal grandeur, were invariably particularly of the

Krishna–and the Shiva–cycles of legends. Some of the most devout songs to Hindu deities were actually composed by Muslims. Since then no change has occurred in the attitude of Muslim musicians towards such songs (Ibid. 4).

D. P., however, receives a jolt. 'In the last four or five years', writes he in 1945, 'one has been hearing of a new item, Islamic songs, in the programme of the All-India Radio. Even then, the structure, the sentiment, the execution remains (sic) identical, only the names of holy places and saints remaining Muslim e.g. *Kawali, Soz, Nat, Mārcia* are also cast in exactly the same classical mould which India evolved during the Muslim period as one product in joint endeavour. The same remark applies to the *secular* note songs of Muslims. *There is no Pakistan in Indian music at least'* (2002b/1945: 4; emphasis added). Indian personality has been in the making through ages along the lines of Indian music nurtured by the composite culture of India.

D. P. showed that the evolution of Indian classical music from Ālāp, Dhrupad, Dhamar or Holi, through Khayal, to Thumri, Dadra, Tappa, 'is a procession from the abstract and the divine to the concrete and the human, with an increasing prominence of the verbal' (2002b/1945:15). There are many styles in Hindustani music (which is pro facto Indian classical music from the Mughal period) that can easily be linked with the various *Deshi* styles in which 'meaning' dominates music. D. P. continues, the social urge has expressed itself in Indian music in the humanization of the abstract modes as also in the collectivisation of the same because these non-classical, so-called 'inferior' styles are sung in groups whereas the classical is almost invariably a solo performance (Ibid. 16). Openness of *Marga* or classical or sophisticated music to the *Deshi* or folk-music and simultaneous observance of fidelity of the composers and executants to the basic structure of a *rāga* made up of a cluster of notes, arranged traditionally in a special way, and their exercise of culturally approved freedom (not license) in their delineation and execution have, according to D.P., sustained the authenticity of and creativity in Indian music.

The above fact is illustrated in several aspects of Indian music such as (a) *Gharana*; (b) Classification of *Ragas* (according to their appropriateness for time sequence—morning (Bhairon or Lalit), noon (Sarang), evening (Purvi), night (Darbari Kanada), seasons, for the rains (*Megh* or *Mallar*) and *Basant*, *Hindol* and *Kaafi* in spring); and *rasa* (feeling or emotion), *bhava*; and (c) cultivation of the art of listening. If a raga or rhythmic melody in classical music is a structure, the *gharana* is a style of rendition—the two shape the possibility of expressing the beauty of the raga distinctly—but leave an enormous amount of free play for performance (Patke 2007: 48).

In the absence of any fixed and print format of the Notation system, music has been purveyed through the system of *Gharanas* or schools providing oral instruction.

A certain degree of standardization of the *Rāgas* and *Rāginis* has been a feature of the system of classical music of India. An artist contemplates the archetype of a specific raga/ragini. All types of raga 'tend to conform to the angelic type of each *rāga*... The attainment of the *Dhyan-murti*, the angelic, the divine, or the archetypal form, which can be sensed only by contemplation, is the supreme endeavour of every artist. Musicians believe that if the proper notes of a raga are struck, the presiding spirit, *devata*, stands out in the fullness of being, (Mukerji 2002: 26). D. P. notes

O.C. Gangoli's *Rāgas and Raginis* Vol. II (1935) that pictorializes the ragas and their moods—emotions and colours. The musician singing a song or playing a raga is expected not to depart widely from but to conform to the moods and notes and rhythmic line of the raga to the best of her/his ability.

The circulation of the *cultural capital* thus accumulated depends on a process of continual interaction of systems of patronage, performance, contexts and *audience acculturation.* D. P., therefore, valorizes the art of listening which has, as if, unobtrusively assumed a *quasi-institutionalized shape* in the culture of Indian classical music. Since the Indian music is, as it has been noted above, mainly contemplative, 'at least the two contemplaters, the musician and the listener, must meet. The third is the accompanist' (2002b/1945: 26). The Indian musician sincerely attempts in the space for executing any rhythmic music line or *rāga* to bring up the contemplated image or dhyan-murti of the raga and 'unfold it before the vision of the sympathetic listener'. Modern listeners, D. P. regrets, often fail the contemplative musicians.

Sangeet—Melody and Words—Rabindra Sangeet

In the next breath, D. P. admires the 'new experimenters ... And Tagore is the tallest of them' (2002b/1945: 30). The first aspect of Tagore's musical experiment is to give emotion its due place in music. (Mukerji 1990/1931: 770). The second cognate aspect of Tagore's music is that simultaneously following the classical make-up in the mixture of ragas, 'in reality it was more dependent on words than on music itself' (Mukerji 1961: 180). This particular feature made Tagore the creator of a new genre of music (Mukhopadhhyay 2000/1938). Like Mukerji, but independently of him, Jairazbhoy writes that modern Indian music could be said to have begun with the songs of Rabindranath Tagore (1975: 238).

The new genre created by Tagore was termed by Mukhopadhyay Rabindra Sangeet. The successful union of words and melody, as accomplished in Tagore's songs, 'produces a new *rasa* that is different from the *rasa* of either one alone... So we better call this new creation *Sangeet*... As it is impossible to distinguish between form and essence, the rasa of sangeet should be regarded as distinct from the rasa of melody and the rasa of poetry...' (Mukhopadhyay 2021/1938: 89). The poet has tried to create songs 'where the words and the tune have achieved a true union, as Shiva and Shakti in the figure of Ardhanārishwar' (Tagore 2008: 677). The perfection of a work of art, the poet reminds, consists in the harmony achieved between its component parts, e.g. words and tune in a musical composition.

D.P. is eloquent on the originality, beauty and variety of Rabindra sangeet. But, he registered also his difference with Tagore regarding proper rendition of Hindustani music. The poet had reservations regarding the elongation of *taan* and display of all richness and nuances of a ragini by a performer at one go. The artist 'must beware of prolixity—he must remember that reticence is more significant than garrulousness' (Tagore 2008: 680). Agreeing in principle to this view of the poet, D.P. sought nonetheless to highlight that each attempt of rendition of a musical piece set in a raga/ragini is 'a *process of revealing* the multi-layered nuances of the relevant raga/ragini. And, the audience is required to have patience with the performance and the performer' (Thakur and Mukhopadhyay 1987/1935). D.P. thought that the model set by Tagore was followed in their respective ways by Atulprasad Sen, Dwijendralal Ray and a few others such as Kazi Nazrul Islam in the world of Bengali music. Much of the rest appeared to D.P. insufferable.

Even Rabindra sangeet, so highly valued by D. P., might, because of its faulty rendition, prove irksome. Regarding the Modern Bengali Songs, D. P. remarked, 'They are beyond my comprehension. There is no *raga* or blending of *ragas* at their base. At the most, they may evoke, though in very few cases, a vague image of a raga... These songs are new, very new, and do not have any other quality than newness (Entry on 12–11-59 in *Jhilimili*—Mukhopadhyay 1987: 281–282). Elsewhere he writes that modern Bengali song is loathsome to the ear (Entry on 01–12-59 in *Jhilimili* Mukhopadhyay 1987: 283). The fall of standard in music including classical music of India was attributed by D. P. to the lack of appropriate cultural ambience that might be sustained by adequate financial and cultural support from the society and polity. With the decline of patronage by the Nawabs and Rajas, the newly emerging Middle class in the new dispensation under the British rule and in the post-colonial period was expected to undertake the responsibility for sustenance of the musicians and music. But D. P. noticed with regret the failure of the Indian, particularly Bengali, middle class in playing the historical role in ensuring continuity and development of art and culture in the country.

Music, Middle Class and Capitalism

Max Weber and later scholars such as Jürgen Kocka (1995) noted the positive role of the European bourgeoisie in the development of art and music and musical instruments in the West. The Indian middle class, because of its comprador role in colonial India and the ersatz nature of its culture was no peer for its European counterpart. Unable to provide succour to the dying tribe of musicians of classical line and distanced from the folk life and culture, they seemed to D. P. to be a 'spurious middle class' (Mukerji 2002a/1948: 23) lacking the choice and appropriate action for developing a social purpose (a characteristic of Person in D.P.'s weltanschauung) which might have sustained the tradition of Indian music and musicians. Don Martindale joins issue with D. P. on this point. Only a curious definition of social purpose would, retorted Martindale, identify the objectives of the princes who patronized the musicians but 'exploited their societies for their own requirements—as constituting a true social purpose, while the objectives of the contemporary middle classes—who struggle for the best possible life for themselves and their children are not' (1974: 59). D. P. is slightly misunderstood. Only this much may be told here: the 'babus' of colonial India (Bengal in particular) were in general given more to enjoyment of sensual pleasures and vulgar forms of amusement than to enjoyment of healthy recreation (cf. Singha 1956/1868). Enjoyment of the latter calls for the development of adequate and appropriate infrastructure and supportive system 'for the sustenance of the artists and professionals in art and music'. The middle class in colonial and post-colonial India seemed to D.P. to have failed in the task. Mukerji's succeeding generations also seem to remain worried about 'the middle class' callous insularity. The bulk of the Indian Middle class could hardly 'break from their individualistic insularity towards conscious and collective action in the public sphere' (Varma 2007: xix, also cf. Chakrabarti 2010; Joshi 1986).

The situation has changed a little with the passage of time. But, the middle class (and along with it the masses) seemed to have been gripped by a frenzy of sensationalism and intoxication with the bizzare. The subtle, sublime and genuinely delightful aspect of music gets subverted beyond redemption. Resuscitation of 'The Lost World of Hindustani Music' seems highly implausible under the circumstances (Mukherji 2006). But going back to the folk and building a culture that will add to the enjoyment of what is new and beautiful was the desirable course. That was not being done because of an all-pervading epigonism and craze for exotica and the outre presented by the west/modern.

The most serious threat to the cultivation of music and musical taste in modern India lies in the manipulation of technological innovations for the practice and spread of music by interested parties with ulterior motives. D.P. reproachfully remarks, 'Vulgarity of public taste in music is artificially created and deliberately fostered'.

In *Modern Indian Culture* D.P. is more sharply critical of those who commodify music for the market and control and exploit it for their selfish gain. The role of radio, stage and film in spreading and altering the culture of music cannot be denied. But, these three agencies are not innocent. D.P. noticed that in his own milieu the 'film and gramophone companies were driven by capitalist concerns'. Mukerji notes that, under the pressure of strong financial groups they tend to oust new efforts. And they camouflage their profit motives by referring to public taste. The public taste being what it is, there is no sense in making it worse. *It is rank hypocrisy to appeal to demand when the supply alone is ready to exploit the demand–supply Eq.* (2000/1948: 176; emphasis added).

Affinity of the Views of D.P. And the Frankfurt School: Culture Industry

The above problem also engaged the minds of scholars of the Frankfurt School. Around 1944, Theodor Adorno and Max Horkheimer expressed in *Dialectic der Aufklarung* (*Dialectic of Enlightenment*, 1979) serious concern over the emergence and working of 'Culture Industry' in modern western societies, which breeds mass culture smothering every element of individuality in creation as well as enjoyment of music and other works of art. Adorno and Horkheimer, in particular, illustrate the process with reference to the psychedelic impact of the syncopated rhythm of jazz on the listeners or participants. They are rendered into helpless, powerless entities that prove ridiculous in their expressive impulses. Jazz is, observe Adorno and Horkheimer, '"the expression of our time" only in so far as estranged from its unruly origins and taken over by the huge organization of the *culture industry*, it has hardened and now is crammed into the people in the service of the naked profit motive so that many millions hardly have the opportunity to hear any other music as an alternative' (TFISR: 112–113, emphasis added).

Culture industry thrives on the insidious nexus of monopoly of capitalism, technological innovations in mass persuasion, production and standardization of cultural objects and popular taste. 'Under monopoly all mass culture is identical...' (Adorno and Horkheimer 1979: 121).

It is claimed that standards in production and consumption relating to enjoyment of music and other cultural objects were based primarily on consumers' needs, and for that reason were accepted with so little resistance. 'The result is the circle of manipulation and retroactive need in which the unity of the system grows stronger. No mention is made of the fact that the basis on which technology acquires power over society is the power of those whose economic hold over society is greatest. A technological rationale is the rationale of domination itself. It is the coercive nature of society alienated from itself' (Adorno & Horkheimer 1979: 121). Its tentacles have spread into every nook and cranny of society and human psyche today.

Creative Industries—The New Horizons in Music?

Beginning from Weber, the Western scholars of music and sociology of music, have been concerned overwhelmingly with European 'art' music, that is, far from being concerned with music in societies, they limit their scope to what is in fact one of the traditions of music making in the western world, not and never has it been the music of the majority of the people (Martin 1995, viii). Add to it their Eurocentrism.

Attachment, explicit or implicit, to the idea of 'superior' quality of classical music or art music has resulted, in the thinking of D. P. and Frankfurt School scholars, into the neglect of the opportunities for creativity provided by the relatively recent versions of 'light music or popular music'. They could not visualize the possibility of the emergence of the forces and processes countervailing the eclipse of 'personality' of creators and consumers of music by profiteering forces in the music world. Culture industry so much criticised by Adorno has come to be replaced by 'creative industries' widely known in today's world. The latter offers 'relative autonomy to professionals and artists' and facilitate the active role of the audience. They make room for specific involvement of practices of resistance against the totalizing uniformity of culture and 'commodification of art' engendered by the culture industry. Whereas the culture industry still appeared to emphasize 'the abstract collective component of culture, a constant appeal to the productivity of the individual occurs in the creative industries' (Raunig 2011: 201).

The fact is very much in evidence at the emergence of varieties in popular music as Pop Punk, Britpop, Indie and so on. 'Indie', a popular music genre of Britain of 1990s, was derived through the abbreviation of 'independent' and aimed at reconciling the commercial nature of pop with the musicians' preferences and creative innovations (Hesmondlagh 1999: 35). 'Indie' culture is now spread worldwide. The Indians seem to have undergone a similar experience. For instance, artists in different parts of India such as Bihar, U.P., Delhi or Mumbai have in present times come to 'enjoy more freedom in their dealings with music behemoths' because of significant changes in the character and working of 'culture industry' (Tripathy 2012: 60). Tripathy analyses with the help of data of fieldwork the process of phenomenal rise of vernacular music industries in Bhojpur's Maithili/Magahi dialects and their contribution to the creative activities of scores of males and females and also to the making of and promotion of Bhojpuri or Bihari identity across the country. 'It is, in fact, possible to think of the Bhojpuri *culture industry* in terms of three concentric circles': (1) the inner circle of Bhojpuri movies, (2) the next circle of CD/VCD industry and (3) the outer circle of 'live-show' industry' (Tripathy 2012: 59; note here how the pejorative connotation ascribed by Adorno to culture industry has been dropped). The live-show industry has proved 'the real daily provider for thousands of professionals', keeping the CD industry afloat despite the financial drain caused by copying (2012: 60). The local singers (some of whom are producers of CDs of their performance), small producers and the live-show audience who 'are part customers, and part traditional patrons—sponsors', are the mainstay of the new system (2012: 60).

Taking her cue from 'thinking about *popular music* in Trinidad', Tejaswini Niranjana shows how music becomes related to the 'structure of social aspiration and issues of social mobility' in India as well (Niranjana 2013: 43). It is illustrated in the impact of 'language-music conjuncture' on the social role played by the Hindustani music in the Dharwad—Hubli region in negotiating the language conflict in Karnataka during the rise of Karnataka 'nationalism'. The suturing of the gap or potential conflict between the social aspiration of music and the potential desire of Dharwad district for the unification of Karnataka along linguistic lines was made possible, suggests Niranjana, 'because of the way in which Hindustani music took hold of the cultural imaginary' (2013: 47, also cf. Bhindikar 2007). Hindustani music here has been part of the 'cultural labour' undertaken in the region. Cultural labour suggests the nature of 'the work involved in cultural practice and performance, and the nature of performers' activity, through teaching, singing, playing, notating, evaluating and arguing about music'. Cultural labour 'references a visible aspect of social transformation and social process, the latter to be seen as marked by elusive shifts in ways of living, thinking and creating' (2013: 47). The formation of the taste for Hindustani Sangeet in Dharwad is shown to be one result of such shifts.

A different kind of response—reaction—to the Indian classical music comes from Dalit Quarters: 'Music essentializes caste identity' (Kumar 2021: 63). The traditional music thrives, allegedly, on the 'binaries of sonic' leading to 'the distinction between "Classical" (usually seen as the preserve of the upper castes) and "folk" (associated with Dalit musical traditions) forms of music' (2021: 63). Feeling of this kind has its roots in the humiliation of Dalit musicians by the casteists among the Indians. Even an Irula tribeswoman, Nanjiyamma, was trolled by the casteists on her winning the National Film Award for the Best Female Playback Singer for the year 2022 at the 68th National Film Awards (Karthika 2022).

Radhika Kumar's ire was caused by remarks of the casteists against the Dalit rapper Sameer Samos when he performed the creditable job of raising a considerable sum from crowdfunding to meet his expenses at the Oxford University. As a counter-response to the elitist and casteist attitude, the Dalit musicians offer a radical imagination of music that breaks open the binaries of the sonic while adopting multiple genres, technologies (including digitization) and emerging soundscapes. 'To embrace and assert their caste while simultaneously echoing the hope for a future that rejects caste', observes Kumar, 'forms the subtext of Dalit musicians and their songs'.

The above-noted fact is not quite unexpected. Nettl notes that culture units, nations, minorities, even-groups, social classes, education strata all identify themselves by adherence to particular repertoiries and styles of music in today's world (1985). Proliferation of varieties of music within the boundaries of a nation-state may, of course, co-exist with the search for the especial identity of the country's music vis-à-vis that/those of other countries/nation-states. The euphoria and emotional exuberance expressed over the event of winning by the song, Natu, of Telugu film R, the Golden Globe Award in 2023 for its being the Best Original Song is a pointer to the intense desire of a country for recognition of its music by the rest of the world. The award to Natu is 'a first for any Asian song'. The song is claimed to have showcased everything that the film is about and the film is 'so rooted to our culture and traditions, and not in any other country's feelings' (Ram Charan in *TOI* 24 May 2023). Alongside claim of this kind, concern also is expressed by the Indians, over how to make Indian music intelligible for and likable to the international audience though '*saara khel to saat suron ka hi hai*'. The fact that most humans can no longer conveniently exhibit their cultural specialities by dress, social structure, material culture or religion has, reminds Nettl, given music an increased role as emblem of ethnicity (Nettl 1985). The different facets of interface of music as emblem of ethnicity and the multilayered and multifaceted socio-political and cultural identity of the humans present complex sociological problems to explore. D. P. or Adorno or Horkheimer and the like-minded did not envision it.

Two more points be made before concluding. D.P.'s apprehension regarding the future of the quality and quantity of Bengali songs and the middle class' responsibility for it seems to prove somewhat correct from the 1990s. New Bengali songs no longer greet the ears of the Bengali (Acharya 2017; Pathak 2014). Happily, however, D.P. seems to be incorrect regarding his relative neglect of the role of the females in Indian music. They have been found in increasingly larger number to demonstrate their virtuosity in music, both vocal and instrumental, with the passage of time and changes in the milieu of music in the country' (cf. Bhirdikar 2007 and Maciszewski 2007). The male-centric music world either in this country or abroad is changing slowly but steadily.

Conclusion

The world of music facilitates the enjoyment of non-instrumental values and aesthetic pleasures which contribute to the realization of the creative potentialities of human personality. It provides an ideal for a liveable human life which connects human beings—groups as well as individuals. Social and economic forces and cultural practices of socially significant groups may and do help or hinder the realization of the ideal. Attention to the interplay of different factors and forces operating in the realm of music which is also a terrain for contestation of various kinds will promote a better understanding of the development of personality and the socio-cultural reality with which it is related dialectically, shaping and being shaped by it. D. P. made the beginning. Why should the posterity refrain from enriching the legacy he bequeathed to them?

References

Acharya S (2017) 'Nagar Jeevaner Bangla Gaan O Ei Samay' (Bengali Song and Life in the City: At this time). In Mukhopadhyay AK (Ed). Shilpa, Samaj SO (Art, Literature and Society). Kolkata: Bagchi KP. pp 179–198
Adorno TW, Horkheimeer M (1979) Dialectic of enlightenment (John Cumming Tr). London: Verso
Bhattacharyya G (2010) Dhurjatiprasader 'parsan' dharanay manabee (Woman in the concept of 'Person' of Dhurjatiprasad). In Mukhopadhyay 2010:734–747
Bhirdikar U (2007) The spread of north indian music in maharashtra in the late nineteenth and early twentieth centuries; socio-cultural conditions of production and consumption. In Amlan Dasgupta (Ed) 2007:220–238
Chakraborty A (2001) Dhurjatiprasad: Anubade-Anubhave. Kolkata: Suchetana
Chakrabarti D (2010) 'D.P. Mukerji and middle class in India' in sociological bulletin. 59(2), pp 235–255
Das GA (Ed) (2007) Music and Modernity: north Indian classical music in an age of mechanical reproduction. Kolkata: Thema
Deva BC (2015) An introduction to Indian music. Publications Divisions, Govt. of India, New Delhi
Freund J (1969) The sociology of max weber (Mary Ilford Tr). New York: Vintage Books
Gangoli OC (1948/1935) Ragas and raginis: a pictorial iconographic study of indian musical modes. Bombay: Nalanda Publications
Hesmondhalgh D (1999) Indie: the institutional politics and the aesthetics of a popular music genre. In Cultural Studies 13(1). pp 34–61
Jairazbhoy NA (1971) The Rāgs of North Indian Music: their structure and evolution. Faber and Faber Ltd., London
Jairazbhoy (1975) 'Music' In a cultural history of India (Basham AL Ed) 212–242, New Delhi: Oxford
Joshi PC (1986) Lucknow school of economics and sociology and its relevance today: some reflections in sociological bulletin. 35(1), pp 1–27
Karthika VK (2022) What is the caste of music? In EPW 26 2022 57(48). Postscript 1
Kocka J (1995) The middle classes in Europe. In J Mod Hist 67(4):783–806
Radhika K (2021) Songs of protest. In EPW. 56(43) pp 63–64)
Maciszewski A (2017) Nayika ki yadgar: North Indian Women Musicians and their Words. In Amlan Dasgupta (Ed.) 2017:156–217

Madan TN (2007) Search for synthesis: the sociology of D. P. Mukerji. In Uberoi, Patricia, Nandini Sundar and Satish Deshpande (Eds). Anthropology in the East: Founders of Indian Sociology and Anthropology: Ranikhet: Permanent Black. pp 256–289

Madan TN (2011) Sociological traditions: methods and perspectives in the sociology of India. Sage, New Delhi

Madan TN (2013) Sociology at the university of lucknow: first half century. New Delhi: O.U.P

Martin PJ (1995) Sounds and society: themes in the sociology of music. Manchester University Press, England

Martindale D (1974) Sociological theory and the problem of values. Charles E. Merrill Publishing Co, Columbus, Ohio

Mitra A (2015) Dhurjati prasad mukerji: from the problem of personality to the plane of sociology in Amal Kumar Mukhopadhyay (Ed) The Bengali Intellectual Tradition, Kolkata: K.P. Bagchi & Co

Mukerji DP (2002/1958) Diversities. New Delhi: Manak

Mukerji DP (2002a/1942) Indian culture: a sociological study (Reissue, with A. Mitra's Introduction, of the 1979 revised and enlarged edition of Modern Indian culture: a sociological study of 1948. New Delhi: Rupa

Mukerji DP (2002b/1945) Indian music: an introduction. New Delhi: Rupa & Co.

Mukerji DP (2004/1932) Basic concepts in sociology, New Delhi: Rupa

Mukerji DP (2021) 'Words & Melody' excerpts from D.P.'s Bengali book *Katha O Sur* (translated from Bengali into English by Kalpna Bardhan) In Ideas, Thoughts & Memories: Bengali Literary Messages (Bardhan, Tr & Ed) Kolkata: Anustup

Mukerji (1972/1943) Tagore: a study (Satyen Bose, Intr.) Calcutta: Manisha Granthalay

Mukerji (1955) The great masters i have heard published in Radio Sangeet Sammelan

Mukerji (1961) Tagore's music a centenary volume: Rabindranath Tagore. New Delhi : Sahitya Akademi. pp 180–186

Mukherji KP (2006) The Lost World of Hindustani Music. Penguin Books, Gurgaon

Mukhopadhyay KP (1410) *Khayal–O–Hindustani Sangeeter Abakshaya*. Kolkata: Dey's Publishing

Mukhopadhyay (1956) (BE 1363) *Amra O Tanhara* (We and They). Kalikata: Indian Associated Publishing Co. Pvt. Ltd

Mukhopadhyay (1957) *Baktabya* (Statements) Kalikata: Bidyoday Library Pvt. Ltd

Mukhopadhyay (1987) *Dhurjati Prasad Rachanabali*, Vol. Dey's Publishing, III (compiled by Subir Bhattacharya) Kolkata

Mukhopadhyay DP (2002/1985) *Dhurjati Prasad Rachanavali* (Collection of works by Dhurjati Prasad in Bengali) Vol. I. Kolkata: Dey's Publishing

Mukhopadhyay (2010/1987) *Dhurjati Prasad Rachanabali* Vol. II. Kolkata: Dey's Publishing

Mukhopadhyay DP (2000/1938) *Katha O Sur* (Words and Melody). Kolkata: Rabindra Bharati

Music (1975) In a cultural history of India. Basham AL (ed) 212–242, New Delhi: Oxford

n.d. 'My Musical Memoirs' (unpublished, perhaps lost, partly translated in Bengali by Chinmohan Sehanobis in *Parichaya* and *Sahitya Patra*

Nettl B (1985) The western impact on world music: change, adaptation and survival. Schirmer Books, New York

Niranjana T (2013) 'Music in the Balance: Language, Modernity and Hindustani Sangeet in Dharwar'. In EPW 48(2) pp 41–48

Pathak A (2014) Aa mori bangla gaan bolei day sarbo? (shall we give up our responsibility by just exclaiming about Bengali songs?). In ABP

Patke RS (2007) Thinking dialectically of North Indian Classical Music. Das Gupta (ed.) 2007:32–59

Perlman M (2011) The Rāgs of North Indian Music, Forty Years Later. In Ethnomusicology. 55(2) (Spring/Summer 2011), pp 318–324

Raunig G (2011) 'Creative industries as mass deception'. In *Critique of Creativity: Precarity, Subjectivity and Resistance in the 'Creative Industries'*. (Gerald Raunig, Gene Ray and Ulf Wuggenig (Eds). London: MayFly Books

Shaw K (2013) Independent creative subcultures and why they matter. In Int J Cult Policy. 19(3) pp 333–352
Silbermann A (1995) The sociology of music (Corbet Stewart Tr.). London: Routledge
Kaliprsanna S (Hutom Pyancha) (1956/1868) Hutom Pyanchar Naksha O Anyanya Samaj-Chitra (Amusing narrative by Hutom Pyancha and other glimpses of society). Brajendra Nath Bandyopadhyay, Sri Sajanikanta Das (Eds) Kalikata: Bangiya Sahitya Parishat
Rabindranath T (2006) The english writings of Rabindranath Tagore. Vol. Three (Sisir Kumar Das Ed). New Delhi: Sahitya Akademi
Rabindranath T (2008) The english writings of Rabindranath Tagore Vol. Four (Nityapriya Ghosh Ed). New Delhi: Sahitya Akademi
T.F.I.S.R. (The Frankfurt Institute for Social Research) (1973) *Aspects of Sociology* (Max Horkheimer and Theodor Adorno) Preface. Heinemann, London
Rabindranath T, Mukhopadhyay DP (1987/1935). *Sur O Sangati.* In Dhurjati Prasad Rachanabali Vol. III (Subir Bhattacharya, compiler). Kalikata: Dey's Publishing
Rabindranath T, Mukhopadhyay DP, Sur OS (1935) Kalikata: Bhamali Bhavan (Reproduced in *Dhurjati Prasad Rachanabali* Vol. III)
Turley AC (2001) 'Max weber and the sociology of music'. In Sociological Forum 16(4) pp 633–653
Verma PK (2007) The great Indian middle class. New Delhi: Penguin Random House, India
Weber M (1958) The rational and social foundations of music. (Don Martindale, Johannes Riedel, Gertrude Neuwirth Ed, Intr). U.S.A. Southern Illinois University Press
Weber M (1949) The methodology of social sciences. (Edward A Shils, Henry A Finch, Tr & Ed) New York: The Free Press
Weber M (1971) Max weber: the interpretation of social reality (Elridge JET Tr, Intr). London: Nelson
Weber M (1978) Max weber: selections in translation. (Runciman WG (Ed), Matthews F (Tr)) Cambridge: Cambridge University Press
Zahan I (2014) Indian Music and Its Assessment: A Sociological Perspective. Kanishka Publishers, New Delhi

Chapter 8
Rise of Agrarian Studies in Indian Sociology

B. B. Mohanty

Abstract The paper traces the development trajectory of agrarian studies in Indian sociology. It narrates its journey from village studies, through rural sociology to agrarian sociology and subsequent emergence as one of the core branches of Indian sociology over a period of three decades beginning with the 1960s. It is noted that the study of agrarian social structure peaked twice in Indian sociology, the first time in the 1970s in the aftermath of the green revolution and the second time in the 2000s following neoliberal reforms. Though there are ups and downs, agrarian studies continue to be one of the core areas of Indian sociology and are likely to receive greater sociological attention in the decades ahead in the context of ongoing rapid changes in the rural-agrarian economy and society.

Keywords Rural sociology · Village studies · Colonialism · Agrarian change · Neoliberalism

Sociology and Agrarian Studies: The Global Background

Although sociology as a discipline emerged in the nineteenth century it did not consider agrarian studies as the area of its interest till mid of the twentieth century even though analysis of the agrarian structure and relations goes back to the classic doctrines of the political economy of the eighteenth and nineteenth centuries. Originated in the West which was undergoing transition to capitalism, sociology was mainly concerned with problems of industrial capitalism and understanding of capitalist modernity. Agrarian economy and society were not the subject of its interest for quite a long time and the classical sociologists developed theories and concepts to study Western capitalist development and modernization. Although Marx and, more specifically, Weber wrote on agriculture and peasants, their writings did not generate much sociological interest. Later, Lenin's extensive research into the nature and dynamics of the peasant culture and production and the subsequent fascinating

B. B. Mohanty (✉)
Department of Sociology, Pondicherry University, Puducherry, India
e-mail: mohantybb99@gmail.com

A. Chauhan et al. (eds.), *Hundred Years of Sociology in India: Evolving Issues, Emerging Trends*, https://doi.org/10.1007/978-981-96-1317-5_8

Lenin-Chayanov debate covering a number of key issues on the political economy of agrarian change provided insightful ideas. A wealth of literature flourished from this debate that analysed historical as also contemporary developments in peripheral political economies and in advanced capitalist formations that led to sociological research and analysis across the globe.

After the Second World War, with the availability of new and meaningful evidences on agrarian history, industrial and commercial evolution and demographic changes, the volume of research grew and new directions in historical research emerged which ultimately generated fresh insights and discourses. Of these, the Dobb-Sweezy debate in the 1950s and Brenner's debate in the 1970s on the Marxist explanation of the transition from feudalism to capitalism in the light of the European experience were both crucial and significant contributions to the discourse. Meanwhile, the rise of the anthropology of peasantry based on the theory of cultural relativism as developed by Kroeber and extended by Robert Redfield expanded the scope of agrarian studies in sociology and anthropology. Besides, three pioneering studies in the 1960s and 1970s (Barrington Jr Moore's *Social Origins of Dictatorship and Democracy,* Eric Wolf's *Peasant Wars of The Twentieth Century* and James Scoot's *The Moral Economy of the Peasant*) opened up explorations of agrarian change beyond Europe and Russia in terms of themes, concepts and methods and stimulated sociological research and debates on peasant movements, politics and agrarian change. As a result, agrarian studies emerged as the core of scholarly research and debates in development sociology.

Emergence of Agrarian Studies in Indian Sociology

Though sociology was introduced as a discipline in India in the 1920s, agrarian issues were not recognized as subjects of its interest for many decades notwithstanding the fact that the Indian rural-agrarian economy and society experienced substantial changes during the British Raj days in terms of land, labour and credit relations leading the commercialization of agriculture, growing impoverishment of peasantry, social inequality, tension, mobilization and movements. Agrarian studies emerged as a distinct field of sociological inquiry only in the 1960s, after nearly four decades of the existence of sociology as an independent discipline.

Unlike the West, where sociology originated in response to the problems aroused by the growth of industrial capitalism, in India, it was primarily developed to serve the interests of the colonial empire. Sociologists were trained to engage in studying village communities, the caste system, tribal life, religious beliefs and practices. In short, in India, sociology during this period was not critical; it was rather in complete isolation from society to buttress colonial interests. However, the critical writings of Karl Marx, Henry Maine and Baden-Powel in the later part of the eighteenth century based on an evolutionary perspective provided insights for understating agrarian structure and change. Few studies by scholars like Mann and Kanitkar on Deccan village, Thomas Coats on a village in Lonikand, and Wisers on the *jajmani* system tangentially touched upon agrarian relationships. However, the available studies were descriptive and ethnographic, mostly drawn on British anthropological tradition. Though a few attempts were made that were critical of colonial policies in the last phase of British rule, they did not influence subsequent sociological analysis for many years. Of late, it was realized that empirical village studies are required to provide a field view to correct the "book view" and "upper caste view".

In fact, sociology as a distinct discipline grew fast in independent India and was greatly shaped by rural-agrarian studies. After independence, sociology in India continued to have a British ethnographic orientation and was closely associated with social anthropology. The influence of American sociology became visible with the beginning of the planned economic development and both the British and American traditions continued together as they were not antagonistic and emphasis was given more on community studies at the micro-level based on an ethnographic-cultural approach. American anthropologists like Robert Redfield and Milton Singer influenced largely the village studies. A series of village monographs were published in the 1950s. Most of them provided a general account of the social, economic and cultural life of the rural people though some of the later studies focused on specific aspects of the rural social structure, such as stratification, kinship or religion. The focus of these studies was mostly on inter-caste hierarchy, factionalism, *jajmani* relations, the relation between caste and class, etc. Both village and caste studies went together in the research framework. The structural–functional method emerged as a distinct theoretical line in the analysis of first-hand material about single villages and castes. The village was treated as a functional whole with different caste groups constituting its parts and assuming different roles and positions. Most of the studies have adopted Redfield's analytical model applied to the study of village social structure. The social organization of production, class structures, conflict and tension among various groups were largely ignored by these village studies. Some of these issues were taken up by the subsequent studies undertaken in the 1970s and thereafter (for example, Epstein 1973; Djurfeldt and Lindberg 1975; Breman 1974; Mencher 1978; Harriss 1982; Gough 1989). Overall, village studies provided a panoramic view of the structural diversity of village communities in rural India, which subsequently set the foundation for systematic studies on rural-agrarian change.

Rise and Fall of Rural Sociology: The growth of rural sociology in America in the 1920s had an impact on Indian sociology. The conventional approach to the understanding of Indian social realities through the lenses of rural-village studies changed with the realization of the growth of urban centres, cities, industrial establishments, as well as the urban population. The rise in rural–urban differences led to the branching of sociology into rural sociology, urban sociology and industrial sociology. The horizon of earlier village studies expanded under the sub-discipline of rural sociology for a broader understanding of village life and rural social structure. *Introduction to Rural Sociology in India* was brought out by A R Desai in 1949 (published by the Indian Society of Agricultural Economics) as a part of the series in Readings in Agricultural Economics which was revised and enlarged with a new title *Rural Sociology in India* with essays on diverse issues like inter-caste relations, rural stratification and power structure, land reforms, cooperatives, *panchayat raj*, community development programmes and agrarian unrest. Agrarian studies or agrarian sociology did not emerge as a distinct field of study in sociology. Rural studies flourished for two decades between 1970 and 1980. Development studies emerged as a new area of research during this period. In the course of the 1980s, emphasis was laid on studies on rural development with the introduction of a host of development schemes like IRDP and NREP in the late 1970s. A number of studies were undertaken to assess the impact of these programmes, especially on the rural poor. Many scholars also analysed the role of different rural cooperatives and land reforms in rural development (Baviskar 1980; Radhakrishnan 1989).

The growing involvement of NGOs in rural development led many scholars to analyse their role in rural development (Khan and Thomas 1989). The National Institute of Rural Development which was started in the 1960s to serve as a repository of knowledge on rural development for assisting the government in policy formulation in rural development brought out the *Journal of Rural Development* in 1981 to disseminate the research studies on rural development issues. Put succinctly, the distinction between agrarian sociology and rural sociology was not clearly drawn. Rural was considered synonymous with agrarian and this continued in some form or other even in the 1980s and thereafter. However, in the course of the 1980s, rural sociology declined following the failure of community development programmes, the *panchayati raj* system, rural cooperatives and land reforms. Which formed the main themes of rural sociology. Meanwhile, the theory of dominant castes was challenged by the rich peasant thesis, and the traditional *jajmani* and joint family system lost their relevance with the expansion of urban influences. These developments contributed to the declining importance of rural sociology. With the increasing penetration of capitalist relations in agriculture following the green revolution, the analysis of the social framework of agriculture and the emerging relationship among various agrarian categories required a new perspective, which ultimately led to the emergence of agrarian studies.

Rise of Agrarian Studies

The series of studies undertaken by Daniel Thorner marked a new departure. Thorner's book *The Agrarian Prospect in India* (1956) that described the relationship existing between the hierarchy of power and prestige in the village and the hierarchy in agricultural production of the owner, cultivating tenant and labourer and the model of *malik, kisan* and *mazdur* provided a meaningful understanding of agrarian relationships. Besides, some of the essays written by Thorners in *Land and Labour in India* (1962), particularly on the employer-employee relationships in agriculture and the critical appraisal of the existing agricultural statistics, opened up many areas for scientific inquiry. P.C. Joshi's work on land reforms also provided new insights. Joshi (1969a, b, 1971) concentrated on land reform measures, the rationale behind their formulations, the implementation of such programmes and their consequences from a Marxist perspective.

Since the early seventies, the studies on agrarian social structure and change have taken a distinctive shape with Andre Beteille's study (1974) that explained social relationships existing among various agrarian categories, the pattern of inequality and conflict arising from ownership, control and use of land and highlighted some of the important conceptual problems involved in agrarian analysis. However, Beteille did not himself undertake any substantial analysis of agrarian relations based on village research. Bremen's (1974) study about the breakdown of the *hali* system of labour relations in south Gujarat was the first analysis of its kind of agrarian relations based on two villages. Subsequently, a number of studies were undertaken within the Marxist framework on agrarian class relations, differentiation of peasantry emphasizing tension, conflict and contradictions (Chakravarti 1975; Djurfeldt and Lindberg 1975; Alexander 1975; Joshi 1975; Mencher 1978). In fact, agrarian studies peaked in the 1970s and generated many interesting debates.

The changes in the Indian agrarian economy and society following the introduction of the green revolution generated exciting debates on a wide range of issues, including the mode of production, social inequality, the relationship between caste and class, which led to many sociological studies. The mode of production debate, which arguably was central to the study of the political economy of India's agrarian change, was greatly enriched by sociological insights. Though economists contributed substantially to this debate the empirical analysis by a few sociologists made it more meaningful (for example, Mencher 1974, 1978; Pathy 1975; Omvedt 1972; Gupta 1980) and influenced sociological studies during the 1980s as well as the 1990s.

A separate discourse among sociologists emerged around mainly the appropriateness of the caste or class model to the study of Indian rural society. While a group of scholars argued for caste as the basic unit of studying social inequality, the other group, led by scholars of Marxist orientation, emphasized on the usefulness of the class basis of social inequality. The debate has evoked many historical and empirical studies, which highlighted the interlinkage between caste and class in different parts of the country. The dominant caste thesis, which was advanced by Srinivas (1959) based on the numerical strength of a caste and predominant landholding position, and other criteria like education and urban sources of income, was challenged by the rich peasant thesis (MacDougall 1979). It was argued that a class of rich peasants has emerged in the countryside with the introduction of capitalist relations in agriculture that dominate the socio-political institutions in villages. Yet another line of argument was that though the dominant castes and dominant class are not necessarily congruent, they were not completely independent. The caste basis of these agrarian classes was observed by many sociologists (Harriss 1981; Gough 1989; Breman 1985). The complex interplay of class and caste in peasant movements and other arenas of rural social existence and politics has been highlighted by many subsequent studies.

In the 1970s, a debate also emerged among social scientists relating to the impact of agricultural modernization, particularly the green revolution on the trend of inequality. While one group subscribed to the view that the effects of agricultural modernization instead of removing the earlier inequalities have created further inequalities the other group holds that new measures have reduced the inequalities and brought prosperity to the peasants of all categories. Many sociologists contributed significantly to this debate (for example, Epstein 1973; Mencher 1978; Breman 1974). Though the debate on the mode of production disappeared inclusively towards the mid-1980s, the debate on social inequality continued to remain active in the 1980s and also in the 1990s. Dhanagare's (1987) analytical account of the studies conducted in the different parts of the country, especially from Punjab, Haryana and Tamil Nadu, and many subsequent analyses made by Gough (1989), Harriss (1981) and others enriched this debate. An interesting debate surfaced among economists on whether the conditions of agricultural labourers had improved or deteriorated with the advent of the green revolution. Though sociologists have not made quantitative analysis of large-scale macro-level data their rich qualitative analysis provides an account of conditions of agricultural labourers, the emerging changes in labour relations, the nature of exchanges in labour, the emerging pattern of labour molisation, etc. (Breman 1974; Oommen 1975).

The study of agrarian mobilization and movements became an important area of sociological research towards the mid-seventies. The thesis advanced by Barrington Moore that the Indian peasantry is traditionally docile and was not able to play any revolutionary role provoked many scholars to probe it further. Gough (1974), Dhanagare (1983), Desai (1979, 1986) and Mukherji (1979) challenged this thesis and provided an account of the widespread peasant struggles in pre and post-independent India. The role of the middle peasant as advocated by Wolf (1969) generated a debate in the Indian context. While one group led by Alavi (1973) emphasized the revolutionary potentialities of the middle peasants and others like Dhanagare and Gough (1968) pointed out the ability of the poor peasants and agricultural labourers to lead struggles. Many subsequent studies provided insights into understanding the pattern of mobilisation of Indian peasants in the post-independence period (Oommen 1985; Mukherji and Chatopadhaya 1981; Mukherji 1987). The impact of agrarian struggles on the social structure has also been analysed by a few sociologists (Oommen 1975; Radhakrishnan 1989).

Though in the 1970s and 1980s, the issue of peasant movements became the core of sociological discourse, the 1990s witnessed a decline in the interest of sociologists in these studies. However, the massive growth of "new farmers" movements with the emergence of Shetkari Sangasthan and the Bharatiya Kisan Union during the 1980s highlighted issues like the demand for remunerative prices, subsidies in agricultural inputs, irrigation and electricity charges, non-payment and waving of loan, etc., representing all classes of farmers and agricultural labourers encouraged sociologists to study these movements. The reasons for and background to the emergence of these new farmers' movements and their class character were analyzed by a few sociologists (for example, Omvedt 1994; Dhanagare 1994; Lindberg 1994). Some sociologists like Omvedt (1993) and Arora (2001) tried to relate these movements to the discourse on new social movements. The relationship between traditional socio-cultural institutions and farmers' mobilisation was analysed by sociologists like Sahay (2004).

Neoliberalism and Agrarian Studies

From the 1990s, the influence of global capitalism and neoliberal reforms set in motion a process of agrarian change on an unprecedented scale and pace. It marked a shift from the planned slow growth to market-driven rapid growth facilitated by new technology of farm production and substantive changes in the government's development policy. Though a new agenda of research emerged in sociology, some of the old debates have not disappeared. The studies on issues like capitalist transition, social inequality, land reforms and rural development, as well as caste and class interaction continued. Besides, writings on new issues like the agrarian crisis and farmers' distress, labour migration, environmental and ecological movements, etc., emerged.

Though the studies on agrarian distress and farmer suicides were largely made by economists, many sociologists provided useful insights. While the economists attribute these suicides mainly to agro-economic problems like crop failure, indebtedness, growing cost of cultivation, etc., sociologists pointed to a complex of sociological reasons like the disintegration of community and kinship support systems, breakdown in traditional values, and growing individualization (Mohanty 2005; Vasavi 1999).

Greater penetration of capitalist elements into the rural economy prompted many sociologists to revisit the old debate on social inequality and the contours of caste-class interaction. Few sociologists indicated the rising trend of inequality in terms of landholding structure, use of agricultural machinery, and application of agricultural inputs among various castes and agrarian classes (Mohanty 2000; Sahay 2002). It was also argued that, though agricultural modernization has improved, and benefitted various categories of agrarian population, the extent of prosperity being relative to the resource ownership position, the large farmers appropriated the lion's share of the development measures and dominated the socio-economic and political spheres of rural society. It was viewed that as the modernizing measures were introduced without removing the earlier inherited inequalities, they generated further inequalities (Mohanty 1999). In a recent study, Sahay (2015) explains how the higher castes, through control over land, use various means such as labour hiring and wage payment, and informal credit arrangement exercises their dominance over the lower and marginalised castes in villages. In a subsequent analysis, Sahay (2020) while indicating the rising trend of social inequality calls for a closer examination of how caste and class function in the context of changing dynamics of agrarian structure.

With neoliberal changes, there was a renewed interest in reviving the debate on capitalist transition. It was initiated by the contribution of some scholars like Chatterjee (2008), who ruled out the possibility of agrarian transition in India in the near future. Following the framework of transition advanced by Sanyal (2007), he argued that under the present conditions of postcolonial development in the context of a globalised economy, the narrative of capitalist transition was no longer valid. Challenging Gupta's (2005) hypothesis on the vanishing trend of village and agriculture in India, Chatterjee concluded that such a transition was unlikely to take place in India due to the state interventions in response to the "demand politics" of electoral democracy. According to him, though with the continuing rapid growth of global capitalism, more and more primary producers lost their means of production, the government policies and programmes which were launched under the conditions of democratic politics tended to reverse the effect of this primitive accumulation. Mohanty and Lenka (2019) explained the variations in the ongoing agrarian transitions across states. The recent study of Sahay (2020) reveals a high level of landlessness and agrarian inequality, but without landlordism. Mohanty (2016) provides a comprehensive and critical account of the ongoing discourse on agrarian transition in the context of neoliberal reforms.

Though land reforms were an important area of research and policy debate in the first two decades of planned development, they disappeared in the 1980s as the pace of land reforms slowed down. A new debate has emerged among most of the developing countries revolving around two dominant approaches to land reform: neoliberal and populist. While the neoliberal land reforms attempt to create or restore private rights to property for the purpose of improving the smooth functioning of rural markets (usually markets in land, credit and agricultural inputs) and increasing efficiency and production through security of title, the populist reforms try to restore the connection between the peasant communities and land, improving social justice by distributing resources to the poor. In India, while provisions are made for the protection of land rights of these weaker sections, resources are provided for government officials and private companies to legitimate land grabs, indicating a kind of policy ambivalence. In this context, how and for whom this contradiction gets resolved constitutes India's "new" land question, which has assumed importance. Several studies indicated the adverse impact of neoliberal policies on the landholding pattern of weaker sections (Saxena 2011; Still 2014; Chakravarti 2016).

With the advent of neoliberal globalization, which pursued rapid transformation of the agrarian rural economy, the emerging pattern of labour migration generated a new debate. A good number of studies were undertaken on labour migration. Based on his analysis of the declining importance of agriculture and village economy, Gupta (2005) indicated the sign of the "vanishing village" and the rising trend of rural-to-urban migration. To him, "the village is as bloodless as the rural economy is lifeless. From rich to poor, the trend is to leave the village" (2005, p. 757). Similar arguments were also put forth by others. On the other hand, a group of scholars of neoliberal orientation subscribed to the view that though the effects of neoliberal reforms created opportunities for employment in the urban industrial sector, the surplus labouring poor in rural India were unable to take up these employment opportunities due to a lack of necessary human capital. In their view, those who migrated from rural to urban areas were mainly the richer ones (Dubey et al. 2006; Srivastava 2011; Kundu and Saraswati 2012). Yet a number of micro-level studies indicated circular or seasonal labour migration due to poverty and deprivation (Breman 1996). It is argued that migrant labourers remained footloose, a phenomenon which has led to the continual circulation rather than the permanent out-migration of workers from the countryside. Studies were also made to document the diverse impact of neoliberalism on various categories of rural and agrarian populations (for example, Mohanty 2019).

Conclusion

Though the study of agrarian social structure emerged as a subject of study in India in the recent past, it has become a well-established branch of Indian sociology. While the early community and village studies provided useful insights for the meaningful understanding of agrarian relationships, the growth of rural sociology as a sub-discipline of sociology and studies on rural development programmes also contributed to the enrichment of agrarian studies. The study of agrarian structure peaked twice in Indian sociology, the first time in the 1970s during the aftermath of the green revolution, and the second time in the 2000s following neoliberal reforms. While the nature of capitalist elements in agriculture, rural class structure, caste and caste dimensions of social inequality, conditions of agricultural labourers and peasant mobilization and movements were the major areas of sociological inquiry in the 1970s, themes of studies in the 2000s relate to agrarian transition, farmers' distress and suicides, indebtedness and labour migrations although some of the old questions were also debated further. Though there are ups and downs, agrarian studies continue to be one of the core areas of Indian sociology. As the majority of the population continues to live in villages and depend on agriculture, and given the rapid changes in the rural economy and society, issues afflicting the rural-agrarian population are likely to receive greater sociological attention in the decades ahead.

References

Alavi H (1973) Peasant and revolution. In Gough K, Sharma HP (eds) Imperialism and revolution in South Asia. Monthly Review Press, New York, pp 291–337

Alexander KC (1975) Agrarian tension in Thanjavur: National Institute of Rural Community Development

Arora V (2001) 'Politics of class(ness) in the farmers' movement in India: validity of the new social movement paradigm. Sociol Bull 501(84–121)

Baviskar BS (1980) The politics of development: sugar cooperatives in Maharashtra. Oxford University Press, Delhi

Beteille A (1974) Studies in agrarian social structure. Oxford University Press, Delhi

Breman J (1996) Footloose labour: working in India's informal economy. Cambridge University Press, Cambridge

Breman J (1974) Patronage and exploitation: changing agrarian relations in south Gujurat. University of California Press, Berkeley, CA

Breman J (1985) Peasants, migrants and paupers: capitalist production and labour circulation in west India. Oxford University Press, Delhi

Chakravarti A (1975) Contradiction and change: emerging patterns of authority in a Rajasthan village. Oxford University Press, Delhi
Chakravarti A (2016) If we had land, we would be human: the implications of landlessness in a Bihar Village. In: Bhagat-Ganguly V (ed) Land right in India policies, movements and challenges. Routledge, New Delhi, pp 15–30
Chatterjee P (2008) Democracy and economic transformation in India. Econ Pol Wkly 43(16):53–62
Desai AR (ed) (1986) Agrarian struggles in India after independence. Oxford University Press, New Delhi
Desai AR (ed) (1979) Peasant struggle in India. Oxford University Press, Delhi
Dhanagare DN (1983) Peasant movements in India, 1920–50. Oxford University Press, Delhi
Dhanagare DN (1987) Green revolution and social inequalities in rural India. Econ Polit Wkly 22(19,20,21):AN 137–144
Dhanagare DN (1994) The class character of politics of farmers movement in Maharashtra. J Peasant Stud 21(3 & 4):72–94
Djurfeldt G, Lindberg S (1975) Behind poverty: the social formation of a Tamil village. In: Scandinavian institute of Asian studies monograph series 22. Curzon Press, Lund
Dubey A et al (2006) Surplus labour, social structure and rural to Urban migration: evidence from Indian data. Eur J Dev Res 18(1):86–104
Epstein TS (1973) South India: yesterday, today and tomorrow. Macmillan, London
Gough K (1968) Peasant resistance and revolt in south India. Pac Aff 14(4):526–544
Gough K (1974) Indian peasant uprising. Econ Polit Wkly 9(32–34):1391–1412
Gough K (1989) Rural change in southeast India, 1950s to 1980s. Oxford University Press, Delhi
Gupta D (1980) Formal and real subsumption of labour under capital: the instance of share-cropping. Econ Pol Wkly 15(27):98–106
Gupta D (2005) Whither the Indian village: culture and agriculture in 'Rural, India.' Econ Polit Wkly 40(8):751–758
Harriss J (1981) Capitalism and peasant farming: a study of agricultural change and agrarian structure in northern Tamil Nadu. Oxford University Press, Delhi
Harriss J (1982) Capitalism and peasant farming: a study of agricultural change and agrarian structure in northern Tamil Nadu. Oxford University Press, Delhi
Joshi PC (1969a) Agrarian social structure and social change. Sankhya 31(b):479–490
Joshi PC (1969b) Land reforms in India. In: Desai AR (ed) Rural sociology in India. Popular Prakashan, Bombay, pp 444–475
Joshi PC (1971) Land reforms in agrarian change in India and Pakistan since 1947. In: Joshi PC, Dutta (eds) Studies in Asian social developments. Tata McGraw Hill, New Delhi
Joshi PC (1975) Land reforms in India, trends and prospects. Allied Publishers, Delhi
Kundu A, Saraswati LR (2012) Migration and exclusionary urbanisation in India. Econ Polit Wkly 47(26–27):219–227
Lindberg S (1994) New farmers' movements in India as structural response and collective identity formation: the cases of the Shetkari Sanghatana and the BK. J Peasant Stud 21(3&4):95–125
MacDougall J (1979) Dominant castes or rich peasants? Econ Pol Wkly 14(12/13):625–634
Mencher JP (1978) Agriculture and social structure in Tamil Nadu: past origins, present transformations and future prospects. Allied Publishers Private Ltd., New Delhi
Mencher JP (1974) Problems in analyzing rural class structure. Econ Pol Wkly 9(35):1495–1503
Mohanty BB (1999) Agricultural modernization and social inequality—case study of Satara district. Econ Pol Wkly 26(34):50–61
Mohanty BB (2000) Agricultural modernization in rural Orissa: land transfer and ownership pattern. Sociol Bull 49(1):63–90
Mohanty BB (2005) We are like the living dead: farmer suicides in Maharashtra. J Peasant Stud 32(2):243–276
Mohanty BB (ed) (2016) Critical perspectives on agrarian transition: India in the global debate. Routledge, New York
Mohanty BB, Lenka PK (2019) Small farmers' suicide in Odisha. Econ Polit Wkly 54(22):51–59

Mohanty BB (2019) Agrarian transformation in western India: economic gains and social costs. Routledge, New Delhi
Mukherji PN (1979) Naxalite movement and the peasant revolt in north. In: Rao MSA (ed) Social movements in India Delhi: Manohar Publication
Mukherji PN, Chattopadhyay M (1981) Agrarian structure, proletarianisation and social mobilization. Sociol Bull 30(2):137–162
Mukherji PN (1987) Study of social conflicts: case of Naxalbari peasant movement. Econ Polit Wkly 22(38):1607–1617
Omvedt G (1972) India and the colonial mode of production: comment. Econ Pol Wkly 7(42):1669–1670
Omvedt G (1993) Reinventing revolution: new social movements and the socialist tradition in India. M. E. Sharpe Inc., New York
Omvedt G (1994) We want the return for our sweat: the new peasant movement in India and the formation of a national agricultural policy. J Peasant Stud 21(3&4):126–164
Oommen TK (1975) Agrarian legislations and movements as sources of change. Econ Polit Wkly 10(40):1581–1584
Oommen TK (1985) From mobilization to institutionalization: the dynamics of agrarian movements in 20th century Kerala. Popular Prakashan, Bombay
Pathy J (1975) Social stratification in an Orissa village. Econ Polit Wkly 10(23):893–901
Radhakrishnan P (1989) Peasant struggles: land reforms and social change in Malabar 1836–1982. Sage Publications, Delhi
Sahay GR (2002) Caste and agrarian economic structure—a study of rural Bihar. Sociol Bull 51(2):195–217
Sahay GR (2004) Traditional institutions and cultural practices vis-à-vis agrarian mobilisation: the case of Bhartiya Kisan union. Sociol Bull 53(3):396–418
Sahay GR (2020) Landlessness and agrarian inequality without landlordism. Econ Pol Wkly 55(34):50–56
Sahay GR (2015) Dominance of Jats is unabated: caste and dominance in the villages of western Uttar Pradesh. Contrib Indian Sociol 49(2):216–249
Sanyal K (2007) Rethinking capitalist development: primitive accumulation, governmentality and post-colonial capitalism. Routledge, New Delhi
Saxena KB (2011) Land reforms: unfinished agenda or reversal of policy. In: Mohanty M (ed) India-social development report 2010: the land question and the marginalised. Oxford University Press, New Delhi
Srivastava RS (2011) Labour migration in India: recent trends, patterns and policy issues. Indian J Labour Econ 54(3):411–456
Still C (2014) Dalits in Neoliberal India: mobility or marginalisation? Routledge, New Delhi
Srinivas MN (1959) The dominant caste in Rampura. Am Anthropol 61(1):1–16
Vasavi AR (1999) Agrarian distress in Bidar: market, state and suicides. Econ Pol Wkly 34(32):2263–2268
Wolf ER (1969) Peasant wars of the twentieth century. Harper & Row, New York

Chapter 9
Political Sociology: Reflections on Specifics of Contemporary Indian Polity

B. K. Nagla

Abstract Political Sociology is a branch of sociology that studies the sociological analysis of political phenomena which range from State to civil society to other aspects such as citizenship, social movements, and the sources of social power. In simple terms, Political Sociology is the study of power and the relationship between societies and political conflicts. The ideologies of Political Sociology were discussed by the founding fathers of sociology such as Karl Marx, Emile Durkheim, and Max Weber to theorists such as Gellner, Anthony Giddens, Jurgen Habermas, and Michael Mann. The sociology of politics covers a vast area of research including everything from revolutions to municipal elections, from historical studies of party systems to abstract theories of collective behavior. It would be impossible in a single essay to properly review the entire field of Political Sociology. Therefore, in this paper, we focus briefly on the basics of the discipline of Political Sociology with specifics to the Indian Context.

Keywords Political Sociology · State and society · Nation-state · Power and authority

Introduction

A new combination of sociology and political science has given birth to Political Sociology. It tries to relate general sociological theories to the available body of knowledge of political science and sociology especially to understand political behavior in a social setting.

The paper is a modified version of the special lecture delivered on Political Sociology in India at RC 15, 47th All India Sociological Conference, University of Science and Technology Meghalaya, 20–22 December 2022.

B. K. Nagla (✉)
M. D. University, Rohtak, Haryana, India
e-mail: bnagla@yahoo.com

A. Chauhan et al. (eds.), *Hundred Years of Sociology in India: Evolving Issues, Emerging Trends*, https://doi.org/10.1007/978-981-96-1317-5_9

Ideologies and questions are asked such as 'Why should one vote? What difference does it make if we do not vote? What will be the conclusion?' Political Sociology was originally concerned with social trends, the dynamics, and structures of formal political processes, and understanding the different types of frameworks. Students who study and specialize in Political Sociology, learn about the questions which were brought up in Medieval History and how governments have been coming down for ages. Political sociologists generally started understanding the sources and consequences of revolutions, the role of political institutions, state development, political outcomes, and the use of power and decisions. In this context, the present paper deals with:

I. Political Sociology as a sub-discipline
II. Reflections on specifics of contemporary Indian polity.

The paper is based on published works in various books and journals particularly ICSSR volumes of *Survey of Research in Sociology and Political Science*, Nagla's edited volume of *Political Sociology* (1999), Gupta's book on *Political Sociology in India: Contemporary Trends* (1996), and his paper on 'Engaging with Events: The Specifics of Political Sociology in India' (1996), writings of Bendix and Lipset (1957), Lipset (1966) on *Political Sociology* etc.

The paper starts with the conceptual clarification of Political Sociology as a sub-discipline and discusses its relationships between sociology and political science. Taking the current discourse, the paper presents some of the alternative views about the significance of Political Sociology. It claims that, despite persistent controversies, looking into the research tradition of Political Sociology is a useful resource to grasp the identity of the sub-discipline. Accordingly, the paper explains the relationship between state and society as the central issue that cuts across theoretical and methodological diversity. Finally, the text takes the nation-state as the most typical configuration of the relationship between state and society in modern history taking the context of Political Sociology in India.

Political Sociology as a Sub-discipline

Political Sociology is a fairly young discipline. Although its roots can be traced to nineteenth-century scholars such as Karl Marx and Alexis de Tocqueville, its systematic development in the USA and Europe dates from only the 1930s (cf. Coser 1966). In the late 1950s and early 1960s, Political Sociology was firmly established as a distinct sub-field of sociology with the publication of works such as Ralf Dahrendorf's *Class and Class Conflict in Industrial Society* (1959) and Seymour Martin Lipset's *Political Man* (1960).

In the mid-1950s, scholars set out to differentiate Political Sociology from political science. Bendix and Lipset, for example, maintained that 'political science starts with the state and examines how it affects society, while Political Sociology starts with society and examines how it affects the state' (1957, p. 87). The boundary between the two disciplines, however, was never as distinct as suggested by Bendix and Lipset and has since become increasingly blurred. In an essay published in 1967, Lipset and Rokkan also correctly noted: 'The term Political Sociology has come to be accepted both within sociology and political science as encompassing the overlap between the two parental disciplines' (Lipset and Rokkan 1967 p. 438). Their definition of the field is still the most concise: 'Political Sociology can be defined as the study of the interrelationship between society and polity, between social structures and political institutions' (Lipset and Rokkan 1967, p. 440). This is explained briefly as:

> Political Sociology analyses the interaction between politics and society. It studies the interrelationship between society and polity, between social structures and political institutions. Indeed, political institutions are themselves social structures. Political structures include physical structures (geographical and demographic), and social structures (technical skills, institutions, and cultures).

Political Sociology as a formal discipline has come into being only after the Second World War. It started in the USA to indicate the close relationship between sociology and political science. In Europe, the works of Weber, Michels, Mosca, Pareto, and Siegfried were relevant to emerging concerns of what eventually became two fields.

It is debatable whether various scholars were sociologists or political scientists. Thus, one analysis argues that major sociologists in the late nineteenth century were, for the most part, political sociologists or sociological political scientists (Lepawsky 1964, p. 32). We may mention here that William Graham Sumner's chair at Yale was called 'political and social science,' and Laster Ward, the first President of the American Sociological Society, contributed much to politics (ibid:33). Franklin Giddings had been a Professor of Politics before holding the first chair of sociology at Columbia University (1894), a career pattern that was somewhat like that followed by another 'father' of American sociology, Edward A. Ross.

Conversely, several scholars who formulated basic concepts and methods in political science were identified with sociology during their academic careers. For example, Arthur Bentley in his major classic work, '*The Process of Government,*' introduces the concepts of interest group and process in political science; he received his basic training in sociology and teaching at the sociology department of the University of Chicago (Lepawsky 1964, p. 34; Small 1905, p. 209ff).

Political Sociology is a branch of sociology mainly concerned with the analysis of the interaction between politics and society. Politics is about power in social situations. Politics occurs when there are differentials in power or authority. Power occurs in all societies and if we equate politics with power relations, then politics also is endemic to social life. Harold Lasswell provides the variable meaning of 'influence and the influential' and 'power and the powerful' (Lasswell 1958:23). This viewpoint is to understand *power, authority,* and *influence* as characteristic social control processes within the sociological tradition, and not unique to any social group. As Dahl defines it, 'A political system is any persistent pattern of human relationship that involves, to a significant extent, power, rule or authority' (Dahl 1963, p. 6).

This is to say that there are no differences in the way power is used in different social groups, simply that in some form or another it is a potential feature of almost any kind of social relationship. Max Weber, for example, sees power as simply the ability of one group (or individual) to enforce its preferences on others. He defines power as 'the chance of a man or a number of men to realize their own will in a communal action even against the resistance of others who are participating in the action' (Weber 1948, p. 180).

Therefore, Political Sociology is concerned with power in its social context. There are diverse conceptualizations of power (Lukes 1978), which have their relevance within theories of politics. In addition to the central notion of 'power,' there are others concerning such related notions as 'authority,' 'influence,' and 'force' or 'violence,' which will also need to be examined in the context of theoretical schemes.

As we all know, power is the key concept in Political Sociology. Political Sociology analyzes power by separating it from influence. *Power* is distinct from the influence which involves a coercive element. There may be diverse components within coercion like force, domination, and manipulation. Manipulation does not involve force. *Force* is the use of physical coercion to impose one's will on others. It is a narrower concept than power since one may exercise power without using force. Nevertheless, it is often appealing to equate force with more. Power is legitimized into authority, of course, by virtue of the political skill and political resources of the power holder. The concept of authority is more limited than that of power. Weber defines *authority* as the 'probability that a command with a given specific content will be obeyed by a given group of persons' (1968, p. 53). Commands are most often given in formal settings—for example, in an organization or institution. Therefore, *authority* is an institutionalized and legitimized form of *power.* Duverger (1967) cogitates Political Sociology as the science of power or authority relationships.

The field of Political Sociology is the realm of the state-society relationship. Studies of state-society relationships with a wider perspective, in which historical and comparative developments are traced and specific social-political formations are understood on their own terms, also exist. In the emergence of Political Sociology, one of the chief intellectual issues that had to be resolved was the conflict over the analytic primacy of *society or the state* (Greer and Orleans 1964, p. 810). We can define the *state* as the part of society that has the power, force, and authority to allocate the resources and facilities of a social system.

Political sociologists concentrate on analyzing what ways society affects the state. As Bendix and Lipset say, 'Political Sociology starts with society and examines how it affects the state' (1957, p. 87). This is an inclination supported by tradition and personal interest, not by any definition. To Max Weber, the state is a special kind of institution that successfully possesses a monopoly of the legitimate use of power within a given territory. In practice, however, political sociologists tend to concentrate on 'power behaviour' in so far as it is relevant to understanding the way political systems work. Greer and Orleans (1964, p. 810) observe that Political Sociology is mainly concerned with (i) the structure of the state; (ii) the nature and conditions of legitimacy; (iii) the nature of the monopoly of force and its use of the state; (iv) the nature of the sub-units and their condition with the state. In other words, the discipline is concerned with consensus and legitimacy, participation and representation, and the relation between economic development and political change.

Political Sociology deals with a broad range of questions concerning the organization and exercise of political power, democracy and autocracy, the politics of social classes, social movements and political parties, the diverse historical types of political systems, political change and conflict, nationalism and the formation of new nations, and aspects of global politics in the late twentieth century (Bottomore 1993). Political Sociology has changed and developed a great deal since its institutionalization during the 1950s and early 1960s. While sociologists traditionally assumed that the social order could be analyzed and understood without special reference to the economy (Gouldner 1970, p. 94), the economic structure of society is at the center stage of contemporary sociology. Compared with the political sociologists of the 1950s and early 1960s, contemporary political sociologists are much more concerned with individuals' political beliefs and behavior are shaped by their positions in the economy and how the actions of the state are constrained by the economic structure in which it is embedded (Hedstrom 1986, p. 174). In short, the main explanatory variables of Political Sociology have changed from the cultural/normative realms of society to the economic realms. With the above conceptual understanding, we would like to discourse upon the reflections on specifics of contemporary Indian polity.

Reflections on Specifics of Contemporary Indian Polity

Politics cannot grow in isolation; at the same time, society learns from the changing ethos of the polity. A relatively young discipline, *Political Sociology* tries to seek research excellence, in its process of evolution (Roy 2014). This is a well-established discipline in the Western world, but it is in its infant stage in India. To keep pace with the West, there is a need to develop our thinking for a perceptive understanding of our own society and politics. The original work of indigenous writings is scattered. There is an acute demand for writings in the form of a reference-cum-text books in the field of Political Sociology.

My earlier work on Political Sociology especially *Factionalism, Politics and Social Structure* (1984) is an attempt to go beyond several analytical assumptions of the subject. I have touched upon the most substantive areas of interest to the political sociologists who appeared in my book on Political Sociology (1999) which includes the writings of Jayant Lele, J. S. Gandhi, Dipankar Gupta, Yogendra Singh, K. L. Sharma, V.B. Singh, Jaganath Pathy, S. L Sharma, etc., besides me. These scholars have reviewed various aspects of the specifics of Political Sociology in India as political socialization, political modernization, power elite, factionalism, deprivation and political consciousness, tribal cultural autonomy and national integration, civic modernization, and trade unions in India.

The field of Political Sociology is the realm of the state-society relationship. Studies of state-society relationships with a wider perspective, in which historical and comparative developments are traced and specific social-political formations are understood on their own terms, also exist. However, they do not usually fall within the framework of academic Political Sociology. Jayant Lele concentrates primarily on the discussion of academic Political Sociology. He examines the historical roots of our contemporary thinking since they lie squarely in our colonial heritage. Further, he re-examines the major antecedents and recent transformations of Political Sociology as a behavioral, scientific discipline in India (Nagla 1999). Political Sociology deals with different variables of society that influence various facets of political dynamics. It also analyzes the attitudes and behavioral patterns of the public who act as political actors.

India is a multicultural country, but so far this has not meant a diminution of centripetal sentiments toward the nation-state. Indian experiment becomes analytically significant to understanding Western theories of the nation-state. The credit for the development of Political Sociology in India goes to the leadership of Rajni Kothari, who founded the Centre for the Study of Developing Society, in Delhi. He was also instrumental in encouraging election studies in India across all social sciences. He was the first political scientist in India who pioneered empirical studies among political scientists in India. Though the first elections in Independent India were held in 1952 it was at the time of the fourth general elections in 1967 when the Research Programme Committee of the then Planning Commission sponsored studies of voting behavior in different parts of the country after that election studies became a part of a regular feature in India.

Political Sociology as a specialized field in the teaching departments in Universities in India was introduced in the early sixties as S.C. Dube initiated at the same time the paper on Political Sociology at the Institute of Social Sciences, Agra. Earlier studies done by various scholars such as ethnographers and scholars who did fieldwork among rural and tribal people studied various aspects which can easily be classified as areas of Political Sociology. For instance, some of them studied, such as factionalism, group dynamics, and even leadership issues to provide a holistic picture of the life of these communities.

The first Survey of Research in Sociology and Social Anthropology edited by eminent Sociologists (Srinivas, Rao, and Shah) in 1974 includes a chapter by Baviskar (1974) which has been titled *Sociology of Politics*. This article by Baviskar covered the period from 1900 to 1969. While tracing the history of Political Sociology, Basviskar writes that in 'India one trace the early beginning of the subject in a rudimentary form during early decades of the century' (1974, p. 432). However, the second survey in 1986 contains an article by Ahmad (1986) which has been titled *Political Sociology*. After that, it became a part of the trend report of the Indian Council of Social Science Research. Research in areas of Political Sociology has been discussed in the following sections. In the first section studies of the power structure in India have been highlighted. The second section includes studies on elections, political socialization, and political parties. The next section covers studies on democracy, civil society, and nation-building. Studies on coalition government and communalism have been discussed in the last section.

A Survey of Research in Political Science (Volumes I–III) was brought out by the Indian Council of Social Science Research (ICSSR) in the late seventies. The survey is subdivided into three volumes, titled respectively as Political Systems, Political Dynamics, and Political Process. Volume I (ICSSR 1979) on the 'Political System' includes studies that do not pertain to the 'system' as the term is understood traditionally in sociological parlance. The studies concern more specifically the political system, but also, its dynamic functioning. And it is in this that one can possibly locate the sociological relevance of political studies. Volume II (ICSSR 1980), titled 'Political Process,' primarily relates to the second-level abstraction of the political system, and seeks to examine the influence of macro-systematic features (i.e., features pertaining to the overall socio-cultural and political system). Volume III (ICSSR 1981) is indeed a befitting finale to the three-volume series and is perhaps the most sociological in the overall emphasis. The issues dealt with are all topical and have been examined through surveys which are indeed termed as 'scholarly.'

Some scholars have consciously chosen to eschew purely formal descriptions and analyses of the political system inclusive of constitutions, and political organs like the legislature, parliament, judiciary, etc. Instead, they have chosen to focus on studies on political behavior, political systems, and political processes. However, J.S. Gandhi emphasizes that the compilation does bring out a nature of shift in the orientation of research in political science which also signifies a sociological sensitivity (Nagla 1999). Here, we illustrate major perspectives, issues, and events for our description related to the politics of India as follows:

(i) Some Macro Studies with multiple Perspectives
(ii) Major issues and events.

Some Macro Studies with Multiple Perspectives

The complex socio-cultural context of post-independent India has aroused the intellectual curiosity of several eminent scholars, especially from the West. All of them have been interested in fathoming the nature and extent of change that India has been undergoing, in its manner of working out of the system of democracy. The system of democracy has produced a variety of aberrations both in the model of democratic functioning as well as by way of deflection from the intended constitutional goals. Below, we shall sample a few such accounts.

One of the earliest and perhaps the most celebrated accounts of the said encounter has been Harrison's *India: The Most Dangerous Decade* (1968). Another macro account, *The Government and Politics of India*, by a well-known political scientist, W.H. Morris-Jones, is relatively more systematic. Still, a macro examination that has enjoyed some respectability is *Independent India*, authored by French author Charles Bettelheim (1968). An interesting examination of contemporary India's debacle on the economic policy is given by Francine R. Frankel's India's Political Economy, 1947–1977 published in 1978. In the two volumes on *Dominance and State Power in Modern India*, R. Frankel and M.S.A. Rao (1990) did a useful compilation of the patterns of the socio-cultural stratification system. Another stream of analysis by Rajni Kothari with very strong sociological implications is the one founded upon the premise that Indian polity in the wake of the country's independence, has been undergoing a persistent attrition of its democratic character with a consequent wear and tear of its civic character. Another interesting work in the same genre is a much-mentioned macro analysis with important political-sociological implications, entitled *In Pursuit of Lakshmi* by Lloyd Rudolph and Susanne Rudolph, published in 1987.

The argument implicit in nearly all the works reviewed above seems to be that the social, cultural, and religious composition of the Indian society gives rise to a congregation of expectations and aspirations that cannot be fulfilled within the framework of democratic polity India has (Nagla 1999).

Major Issues and Events

Political Sociology in India has been significantly influenced by events that have taken place in the country. Gupta (1996a, b, 1999) reflects current trends in Political Sociology in India (from the 1980s) in relation to the ground realities in the social and political arena. This study spans the years beginning from the late 1970s to the early years of the 1990s: from the Emergency and its fallout to the Punjab crisis and the recommendations of Mandal Commission. He analyzes the basic issues of ethnic and communal movements to thematize the concept of the nation-state and the government for understanding the tension between local concerns with national issues. In this context, Gupta reviews the contemporary literature on Political Sociology in India under the following themes: (i) Social bases of political Support; (ii) Crisis of institutions; (iii) Ethnic and Communal Politics; and (iv) Farmers' Mobilization. The basis of the groupings is for two reasons: (i) Political events suggest such groupings, ii) political sociologists' writings on these issues. The analysis of these themes reflects the profound concern with political issues among intellectuals nationwide. Questions of dynasty, corruption, and poverty are perennial phenomena. We shall highlight some of the major issues of Political Sociology that need attention based on events in India.

Political sociologists did not take a long-term view of India, but rather that research was influenced by very immediate happenings in the political sphere. In the early 1980s concern was inherited from the previous decade having to do with the short-lived Janata experiment and its consequences on political participation and articulation in the country. The focus of the resulting research was the re-emergence of the Congress (I) led by Indira Gandhi and the nature of governance and viability of Indian democratic institutions. Intellectuals were drawn by the situation to analyze the power that charisma and dynastic authority can play within a democratic Indian society.

As we move on to 1984, a distinctive feature of the 1980s emerges, viz, a bourgeoning interest in the issue of ethnicity and communalism. For example, the rise of Sikh secessionism in Punjab, though this is not the first time that ascriptive politics has made its presence felt in India. The question of secession was never seriously there on the agenda before.

It is true that the majority of Sikhs were not in favour of a Sikh homeland (or *Khalistan*), but the Sikh extremist demand nevertheless figured very centrally in India in all political issues and debates for well over the years. This is probably because Punjab has always been such an integral part of the country that the very demand for *Khalistan* compelled scholars and lay persons in the country to think profoundly about the nature of the nation-state.

There have been other movements in India, both in the early years after Independence in 1947 and later, which were also drawn by ascriptive loyalties, but none of them really questioned the sovereignty of a nation-state. This is why it is necessary to differentiate ascriptive mobilization into ethnic and communal movements and separate one from the other. Ethnic movements are those which thematize the nation-state while communal movements thematize the government. In ethnic uprisings—issues of territory and sovereignty, while in communal movements disputes primarily over the allocation of government resources among communities.

In both cases, the understanding of the 'insider' and 'outsider' or the definition of the community rests on ascriptive factors, such as language, religion, or caste. However, the issues raised by these two categories of ascriptive mobilization are very different. Therefore, it is important to delink ethnic mobilizations from communal ones, because not every inscriptively charged movement is a threat to the nation-state.

Looking back on the trends in contemporary Political Sociology one recognizes how important it is to understand the specifics of the Indian case. Nowhere are these specifics more apparent than studying the issue of ethnicity and its relation to communalism. Besides the concern with the nature of democratic institutions and ascriptive mobilizations (whether communal or ethnic), political sociologists have also concerned themselves with the rise of the farmers' movement in India. Much of the enthusiasm is again inspired by events in the country. Both the Shetkari Sanghthan led by Sharad Joshi in Maharashtra and the Bhartiya Kisan Union (BKU) led by Mahendra Singh Tikait in U.P. received wide publicity. Of the two, Tikait probably got more attention as political sociologists were attracted to Tikait's completely rural persona. The current emphasis on the farmers' movement is also unique in the sense that the attention is now on the so-called beneficiaries of the Green Revolution.

In the end, we must mention that the issues that have been discussed here do not exhaust our interest without knowing varying aspects of society and politics in India. Certainly, there are remarkable areas of social and political inquiry not included in the above analysis, and even those discussed are only briefly introduced because of the limitation of the paper.

We believe that there is a great degree of sensitivity in India regarding the problem of keeping India united. A congregation of interrelated factors has disrupted efforts to achieve goals of equality and social justice as well as building a nation-state. We can see at least three main forces. (i) The diversity of groups that constitute Indian society, (ii) Regional and cultural identities, and (iii) Casteism. In this context, caste, religion, and language play a very significant role in Indian politics, which can be considered as the epitome of more ethnic and religious groups as compared to other countries of the world. They have become a party of identity politics. It is for this reason that there exists a nationwide, near-jingoistic hostility toward any party or individual remotely linked with some kind of secessionist platform. While the cultural critiques do not bring in the issue of secession (say as in the Punjab, Mizoram, or Kashmir), India is facing certain perennial issues due to internal and external factors of the country. For example, terrorism, naxalism, religious violence, regional separatist insurgencies, and caste-related violence are important issues that affect the political environment of the Indian nation. India has unresolved territorial disputes with China which escalated into a war in 1962 and 1967, and with Pakistan which resulted in wars in 1947, 1965, 1971, and 1999.

The above descriptions reflect that political sociologists should investigate relationships between the political system and cultural diversity, the role of religion, ethnicity, and castes in elections, the legitimacy of democracy, and the nation-state itself. In brief, it may be viewed that an area of substantive and analytical concern for the political sociologist is the problem of social order and political conformity which is related to the governance and administration in India and elsewhere. In the foregoing section I, it is stated that *Political Sociology has changed from the cultural/normative realms of society to the economic realms in contemporary society. Compared with political sociologists of the 1950s and early 1960s, contemporary political sociologists are much more concerned with individuals' political beliefs and behaviour shaped by their positions in the economy.* Studying the Political Sociology of contemporary society not only increases theoretical knowledge about actual problems of contemporary politics but also think in an independent and critical manner about contemporary political life and its phenomena in the era of globalization.

Looking back on the developments in modern Political Sociology, one comprehends how significant it is to appreciate the specifics of the Indian case. We must understand that the sub-discipline of Political Sociology in India has not been the job of Indian researchers alone but to recognize the contributions of Western scholars to the subject of Political Sociology in India. In some cases, Western scholars provided ideas and concepts to the Indian scholars, and in some instances, they followed the Indian counterparts though in some cases Indian academics have contested Western paradigmatic influences (Gupta 1999). It is not the question of what has been done by political sociologists in the past, but the issue is what to do now for the development of society in the context of the present situation—the world over in the crisis situation of unrest. Peace and freedom are the paths to any society's development and progress. This is possible when political sociologists analyze the role of political elites who govern the country understanding the bearing of the masses. Moreover, political leaders of different countries are competing with each other moving toward war or war-like situations for their hegemony. This must be a serious concern to political sociologists to explore ways and means for progress and development keeping in view the evolving new culture of freedom and peace.

References

Ahmad I (1986) Political sociology. In: Ferreira JV (ed) Survey of research in sociology and social anthropology, 1969–79, vol 3. Satvahan Publication, New Delhi

Baviskar BS (1974) Sociology of politics. In: Srinivas MN, Rao MSA, Shah AM (eds) Survey of research in sociology and social anthropology, vol 2. Popular Prakashan, Bombay

Bendix R, Lipset SM (1957) Political sociology: an essay and bibliography. Curr Sociol 6(2):79–99. Paris: UNESCO

Bottomore T (1993) Political sociology. Pluto Press, London

Coser L (ed) (1966) Political sociology. Harper and Row, New York

Dahl RA (1963) Modern political analysis. Englewood Cliffs, Prentice-hall

Dahrendorf R (1959) Class and class and conflict in industrial society. Stanford University Press, Stanford

Duverger M (1967) The idea of politics: the uses of powers in society. Methuen, London

Greer S, Orleans P (1964) Political sociology. In: Faris RL (ed) Handbook of modern sociology. Rand McNally, Chicago

Gouldner A (1970) The coming crisis of western sociology. Basic Books, New York

Gupta D (1996a) Political sociology in India: contemporary trends. Orient Blackswan

Gupta D (1996b) Engaging with events: the specifics of political sociology in India. Curr Sociol 44(3):53–69

Gupta D (1999) Engaging with events: the specifics of political sociology in India. In: Nagla BK (ed) Political sociology. Rawat Publications, Jaipur

Hedstrom P (1986) From political sociology to political economy. In: Himmelstrand U (ed) Sociology: from crisis to science? Volume 1: the sociology of structure and action. Sage Publications, London

Indian Council of Social Science Research (ICSSR) (1979) A survey of research in political science (vol 1), political system. Allied Publishers Pvt. Ltd., New Delhi

Indian Council of Social Science Research (ICSSR) (1980) A survey of research in political science (vol 2), political process. Allied Publishers Pvt. Ltd., New Delhi

Indian Council of Social Science Research (ICSSR) (1981) A survey of research in political science (vol 2), political dynamics. Allied Publishers Pvt. Ltd., New Delhi

Lasswell H (1958) Politics: who gets what, when and how. Meridian Books, New York, p 23

Lepawsky A (1964) The politics of epistemology. In: Proceedings of the western political science association (supplement to the Western Political Quarterly, September 17)

Lipset SM (1960) Political man. Anchor Books, Garden City, New York, p 477

Lipset SM (1966) The field of political sociology. In: Coser LA (ed) Political sociology. Harper and Row, New York

Lipset SM, Rokkan S (1967) Cleavage structures, party systems and voter alignments: an introduction. In: Lipset SM, Rokkan S (eds) Party systems and voter alignments: cross-national perspectives. Free Press, New York

Lukes S (1978) Power and authority in bottomore. In: Bottomore T, Nisbet R (eds) A history of sociological analysis. Basic Books, New York, pp 633–676

Nagla BK (1984) Factionalism, politics and social structure. Rawat Publications, Jaipur

Nagla BK (1999) Political sociology. Rawat Publications, Jaipur

Roy S (2014) Society and politics in India: understanding political sociology. PHI Learning Pvt. Ltd., Delhi, 260 pages

Small A (1905) General sociology. University of Chicago Press, Chicago

Weber M (1948) Class, status and party. In: Girth M, Mills CW (eds) From max weber. Routledge and Kegan Paul, London, p 180

Weber M (1968) Economy and society: an outline of interpretative sociology (Roth G, Winch C eds and trans), vol 1. Bedminster Press, New York (Originally published in 1922)

Chapter 10
Digital Sociology: Dawn and Development

Abdul Matin

Abstract The digital revolution has altered the economics, politics, and society since the middle of the twentieth century. When we consider the technology connected to the digital revolution in terms of General Purpose Technology (GPT), it makes more sense. Building an Integrated Circuit (IC) has been made possible by Si-Materials as a GPT. Regarding how technology and society interact, Melvin Kranzberg's law should be taken into consideration. IC technology is governed by Moore's law. An understanding of Metcalf's law is necessary to dissect the network society. In the evolution of si-materials, IC, and nanotechnology technology, digital sociology in its new avatar has been born. With its new concepts and subject matter in the context of technology-society linkages, digital sociology should be used to study changes in the fields of economy, politics, society, and culture.

Keywords Moore's law · Metcalf's law · Network society · Kranzberg's law · General purpose technology (GPT) · Si-Materials

Introduction

The dawn of digital sociology can be attributed to the digital revolution and the ensuing rise in technology's presence in our daily lives. Understanding how digital platforms and social media affect several facets of our lives, such as social interactions, identity formation, and power dynamics, is essential as society grows more dependent on these technologies. The goal of digital sociology is to investigate and examine these phenomena in order to offer useful insights into the quickly changing digital landscape and its effects on people and communities. Fussey and Roth (2020) point out that the term "digital sociology," which was first used in 2009, is gaining popularity and sociologists' focus because digital forms of interaction are permeated throughout all spheres of social life, including families and relationships (finding

A. Matin (✉)
Department of Sociology, University of Science and Technology Meghalaya (USTM), Baridua, Meghalaya, India
e-mail: amatinamu@gmail.com

A. Chauhan et al. (eds.), *Hundred Years of Sociology in India: Evolving Issues, Emerging Trends*, https://doi.org/10.1007/978-981-96-1317-5_10

or betraying partners through dating websites[1] or maintaining relationships through texts, phone calls, video conferences, or social media), including the workplace because of the rise of the gig economy, and general public due to the proliferation of smartphones and social media. Due to the remarkable pace of technological advancement, particularly in the wake of the digital revolution, they have also noted that an extensive definition of "digital" is challenging and transitory (Fussey and Roth 2020, p. 660). This arduous effort is now made easier by the identification of si-materials as a General Purpose Technology (GPT). What factors led to the development and expansion of digital sociology, and how should the discipline be described under this new name? Si-Materials as General Purpose Technology (GPT) have been crucial to the development of the digital age. Later, as a result of technological advancements, the web of social relationships between individuals and institutions has changed. The network of social connections between people and institutions has been changed by technological advancements. The information revolution[2] has significantly improved by ARPA (Advanced Research Projects Agency) and DARPA (Defense Advanced Research Projects Agency) studies on space exploration, with implications for developing virtual interactions and eventual social relationships in network society. It should be noted that the information technology paradigm is evolving toward openness as a multi-edged network rather than closure as a system. Its physicality is strong and imposing, but its historical growth has been flexible and unrestricted. Its defining traits are comprehensiveness, intricacy, and networking (Castells 2010a).

Melvin Kranzberg's (1986) rule on the relationship between technology and society suggests that the societal effects of the information technology revolution will follow it. This law asserts that "technology is neither good nor bad, nor is it neutral (Kranzberg 1986, p. 545)." This is due to the fact that technology is a force that, in accordance with the current technological paradigm, more deeply than ever permeates both life and the human psyche. However, rather than being predetermined, how it is used in the context of conscious social action and the complex web of interactions between the forces of technology that our species has unleashed and the species itself are still subjects of investigation. Sociologists like Manuel Castells (2009), (2010a), (2010b), (2010c), Van Dijk (2012), Felix Stadler (2006), Richard Susskind and Daniel Susskind (2017), and Frank Webster (2006) are interested in informationalism in network society as a result of all of these changes.

The digital revolution has been transforming the economy, politics, and society since the middle of the twentieth century. Zhang (2012) has called attention to several important findings. The discovery of stone dates back to 3.3 million years ago, Bronze to 3300, Iron to 1400, steel to 1900, cement to 1960, and nanomaterials to 2001. The discovery of bronze after stone, iron after bronze, steel and cement after iron and si-material, and steel and cement, took a very long period. However, the gap between discoveries is closing, particularly since the discovery of Si Material. Zhang and Yang (2011) have drawn attention towards the tremendous significance of nanomaterials relevant for digital sociology. Let's review industrial revolutions in order to comprehend the relevance of Si-Material and Nano Materials as GPT. We all know that the then-current structures of the economy, government, and society were destroyed by the Industrial Revolution,[3] which was preceded by the Renaissance and the French

Revolution. The Industrial Revolution changed the economy, the political system, and society in the majority of the world as well as initially in some regions of Europe. Similar changes are being made to institutions and every aspect of daily life not only in Europe and America but also in Asia, Africa, and Latin America on a variety of scales. Fussey and Roth (2020) have noted this shift in the fields of culture, economy, polity, and society after recognizing this tendency. Digital sociology examines the affordances of technologies in various social spheres and how they shape and are shaped by social relations, social interaction, and social structures. In recognizing the features of "digital," they have referred to ICT, CMC, AI, nanotechnology, hardware, software, and infrastructure. Before the advent of the modern "chip-based" (Integrated Circuit or IC) technologies, humans had been using some types of information technology for millennia. Studies on how the advancing chip-based technologies[4] affect how people utilize information technology have found a wide variety of direct implications. These are intertwined with a variety of impacts that are widely dispersed among institutions and human endeavors.

Paradigm Shift with Si-Materials as GPT

When we consider the technology[5] connected to the digital revolution in terms of General Purpose Technology (GPT), it makes more sense. Interesting information on GPT can be found in the works of Basu and Fernald (2008), Bresnahan and Trajtenberg (1995), Cantner and Vanuccini (2012), Helpman (1998), Moser and Nicholas (2004), and Youtie et al. (2008). The features of GPT presented in these literatures can be summed up as being pervasiveness, technological dynamism, and innovational complementarities. These three traits define the techno-economic paradigm, a more comprehensive idea that encompasses the entire economic system as well as the social institutions. But for all of these qualities to exist, a vibrant market economy that is fueled by creative business people looking to make a profit is necessary. The argument that nanotechnology is a GPT is based on patent and patent citation databases, which only record the innovative stage of the technology cycle (important during the frenzy and golden age periods), not the inventive stage, which is crucial throughout the gestation period. The market's pervasiveness results from the diffusion of numerous complementing breakthroughs after the new techno-economic paradigm has already been established. Because they meet all of the aforementioned criteria, computers, smart phones, and the internet[6] can all be considered GPTs. Computers, smart phones, and the internet as GPT and their effects on altering social ties between people and institutions may be one of the topics for digital sociology. The result of technical development known as General Purpose Technology (GPT) was the new subject matter of the classical sociologists.

The Third Industrial Revolution began in 1969, a century after the end of the Second Industrial Revolution. The third revolution gave rise to the development of electronics, telecommunications, and of course computers, which emerged in the latter half of the twentieth century. The third industrial revolution made space exploration,[7] research, and biotechnology possible thanks to the new technologies. Two significant industrial innovations—Programmable Logic Controllers, or PLCs, and robots—helped usher in a period of advanced automation. Industry 4.0 is the fourth Industrial Revolution in the eyes of many, yet there are still many who disagree. If we were to think of Industry 4.0 as a revolution, we would have to acknowledge that it is one that is currently taking place. It is something we encounter every day, but we are not yet aware of its scope. Industry 4.0 began with the one thing that everyone uses every day—the Internet—at the beginning of the third millennium. We can observe the shift from the first industrial revolution, which laid the foundation for technical advancement, to Industry 4.0, which creates virtual reality worlds and enables us to defy the rules of physics. The world is shaped by the four industrial revolutions. They form the foundation of the world economy. Around the globe, programs and projects are being carried out with the goal of assisting people in utilizing the wonders of the fourth revolution in their daily lives. The EU is funding initiatives like the RESTART project, which aims to involve industry in the reform of VET systems in order to address the demand for digital skills in line with technological advancements in industries (iED, 2019).

Network Society and Technology Laws[8]

The phrase "network society" was first used by Jan van Dijk in his 1991 Dutch book De Netwerkmaatschappij (The Network Society) (Van Dijk 2012) and later by Manuel Castells in the opening volume of his trilogy on the information age, *The Rise of the Network Society* (1996/2010a). Early sociologists like German Sociologist Georg Simmel and French Sociologist Émile Durkheim discussed the importance of examining the patterns of connections that link social actors in their writings, which laid the theoretical foundation for social network analysis. Since the early twentieth century, social scientists have used the term "social networks" to refer to intricate webs of connections among individuals in social systems on all scales, from the personal to the global (Freeman 2004). Basic analytical techniques were first introduced in the 1930s by Jacob Moreno and Helen Jennings (Freeman 2004). Bounded groupings (such as tribes, families, and households) and social categories (such as gender and ethnicity) are two ideas that have historically been used by both the general public and social scientists. John Arundel Barnes began using the word systematically to define patterns of relationships in 1954. The application of rigorous social network analysis was advanced by academics like Barry Wellman, Douglas R. White, and Harrison White (Freeman 2004, pp. 121–128). In a clear and concise manner, Stadler (2006) critically analyzed Manuel Castells' notion of the modern network society. Ong (2013) studied the advantages and influence of social media. VanDijk (2006) noted that social network history is a part of the history of humanity. He has read *The Human Web: A Bird's Eye View of World History* by J. R. McNeill and W. H. McNeill, in which five global webs are more thoroughly addressed, to support his position. According to van Dijk, all webs combine cooperation and competition. Social collaboration has generally increased throughout history—both voluntarily and forcibly—driven by the realities of social rivalry, and human webs have a tendency to expand.

The value-governance laws outline the core worth of a network from the viewpoint of people a part of it. These laws outline the possible value to any given network based on the connections between individuals. The following list of laws that regulate social networks and communities is presented in order of increasing significance with reference to the use of social media. According to Sarnoff's Law, a broadcast network's worth is directly equal to the number of viewers. A radio network station might have aired a single message to millions of listeners, for instance. According to Moore's Law, every couple of years, processing power will double while cost remains constant (Moore 1965). It predicts that the number of transistors in an integrated circuit will double every couple of years starting in 1965 and will increase for at least another ten years (Moore, 1965). Moore's prediction of doubling every two years has been used in the semiconductor industry to guide long-term planning and set goals for research and development. It has had a significant impact on developments in digital electronics, such as CPU pricing, memory capacity, sensors, and cameras. Industry experts have not come to an agreement on when Moore's law will stop, however, as of 2018, top semiconductor producers claim to have created mass-produced Integrated Circuit (IC) fabrication techniques that follow Moore's law. Moore's law makes better sense in relation to Metcalfe's law. Metcalfe's Law attaches significance to computer users, not the computer itself (unlike Moore). The utility of a network is equal to the square of the number of users. According to Metcalfe's law, the value of any telecommunications network is inversely correlated with the square of the number of users who are connected to the system. By sending emails to the intended recipients, people might have many conversations going on at once in both directions. According to Reed's law, the size of social networks in particular can grow exponentially as more people join them. When you post a message in a group, community, or social networking site like Twitter (renamed as 'X'), your network grows more effectively than it did for Sarnoff or Metcalfe. In comparison to a network of 10, the impact of a network of 100 people is many times (basically an exceeding large number) more valuable. Subgroup formation and communication are fostered by social networks. Speaking in groups can lead to more effective information filtering, vetting, and emphasis. As a result, the fundamental structure and governing principles of social networks have "tapped" into the immense potential of communities. Information sharing and receiving is greatly facilitated by social networking. It is the combined effect that makes social networks, together with user-generated content and social media, so potent in the eyes of consumers. These highly interconnected social networks are similarly seen as effective in vetting that information. Members of the online community are learning how simple it is to find, learn about, and exchange information that directly aids in making an informed decision (Ong 2013).

Sociology in Its New Avatar

Let's examine the work being done by digital sociologists. I fervently contend that the internet, mobile devices, and computers should be treated as GPT. In light of this backdrop, I'd want to talk about what the Digital Sociologists have been doing and should be doing as follows. In collaboration with the Eastern Sociological Society (ESS), the first Digital Sociology Conference was held as a "mini-conference" in New York, USA, on February 27 and 28, 2015. Tressie McMillan Cottom, Karen Gregory, and Jessie Daniels all worked together to co-organize the conference. The conference was really productive. There were 60 contributions from academics in 11 different countries. Massive literature is springing up on the subject of digital sociology, including works by Castells (2010a, 2010b, 2010c, 2009), Stadler (2006), Tapscott (1996), Van Dijk (2006), and Webster (2006) covering different aspects of digital sociology ranging from digital economy to network society.

Digital sociology has two words: digital and sociology. Digital signals and data are described as series of digits 0 and 1 in the Oxford dictionary, often represented by values of physical quantities like voltage or magnetic polarization. Using or storing data or information in the form of digital signals is also included. It frequently stands in contrast to analog, which is the use of signals or information represented by a physically variable quantity that is continuously changing, such as spatial position, voltage, etc. A phonograph record contains analog data. All of the institutions and web of social relations underwent a transformation as a result of the digital revolution from pre-industrial societies characterized by urbanization and industrialization in a new bureaucratic form, as well reflected in the writings of classical sociologists like Karl Marx and Max Weber, which considered the study of the web of social relationships articulated through social groups, institutions, and organizations. According to Lupton's definition of digital sociology, "it provides a means by which the impact, development, and use of digital technologies and their incorporation into social worlds and concepts of selfhood may be investigated, analyzed, and understood" (2012, p. 4). In its broadest sense, digital sociology examines the issue of reinvention in novel situations where the core of this 'newness' is primarily determined by the digital. Because of this, it is possible to characterize digital sociology from my viewpoint as a complex web of virtual (digital) / real social relationships between stakeholders of man–machine configurations for the purposes of simplification. The necessity of multidisciplinarity in the field of digital scholarship should be highlighted at this point (Lupton 2015).

The social and cultural aspects of digital media technologies have been the subject of interesting research by academics in a number of other fields, and these findings are particularly pertinent to sociologists' concerns. Interdisciplinary fields like science and technology studies, internet studies, and digital cultures also have a lot to offer. Particularly, the fields of mass communication, media studies, cultural geography, and digital anthropology, as well as some branches of computer science research, like those that concentrate on human–computer interactions, have a lot to offer. Separate fields of study, such as software studies, game studies, mobile media studies, and platform studies, have started to emerge that investigate the social, cultural, and political aspects of the digital world.

In an ideal world, researchers in various fields would collaborate and gain from one another's work. Others may have different ideas about what digital sociology entails, but Lupton has created a four-fold typology that can be summed up as follows: Analyze digital technology use by examining the ways in which people's use of digital technologies configures their sense of self, their embodiment, and their social relations, as well as the role of digital media in the creation or reproduction of social institutions and social structure. Professional digital practice by using digital tools as part of the sociological practice: to build networks, construct an online profile, publicize and share research, and instruct students (Lupton, 2015, pp.15–18). For this purpose, the writings on big data (Kitichin 2014), culture (Schiller 1989); sustainable development and empowerment (Bedi, 1999), (Bhatnagar and Schware, eds. 2000); (Daly 1999), (Ernberg 1999a), (Ernberg 1999b), (Heeks 1999), (Mansell and When, eds. 1998), (Sood 2001); digital governance (Matin 2003); digital divide (Schiller 1996), (Matin 2005); digital economy (Tapscott 1996); digital transformation (Siebal 2019); empowerment (Ernberg, 1999a, b); ethics/ethical algorithm (Kearns and Roth 2019); (Stuckelberger 2016); rural extension services (Samarta 1993), (Sharma, 2003); futurology (Sardar and Ravetz, eds., 1996), (Susskind and Susskind 2017), (Zuboff 2019), informationalism (Bell 1979), (Castells 2010a), (Castells 2010b), (Castells 2010c), (Matin 2020); social media (Mayfield 2008), Sinha et al. 2020); social network (Ong 2013), (Van Dijk 2012), (World Bank 2000) and theory (Feenberg 1991), (Stadler 2006), (Webster 2006) and digital policy (Rao et al. 1999) are pioneering, and landmark for future practitioners and researchers on digital sociology.

Conclusion

The mid-twentieth century saw a digital revolution comparable to the industrial revolution of the eighteenth century. The ongoing digital revolution is on the verge of altering current society in all areas of economy, politics, and culture, much like the industrial revolution did for society, politics, and culture. The embeddedness of GPT, which is in charge of the network society, must be taken into consideration in order to comprehend this developing web of social ties. Understanding how the GPT and society interact can be done with the help of Kranzberg's law. Moore's law predicts how IC will evolve in the market. The framework of network society is governed by Metcalfe's law. In terms of how new technology is incorporated into society and how the laws affect the new web of social ties may be understood by re-conceptualizing and re-theorizing in the light of new evolving virtual–real relationships. Sociology in its new avatar has to explore these social relations, social interaction and social structure in big data in pursuit of truth.

Acknowledgements This is a substantially revised version of my Convener's address at the first Digital Sociology RC meeting held at the USTM, Meghalaya, organized by the Indian Sociological Society on 20-22 December 2022. I am thankful to the participants for their feedback.

Notes

1. The extramarital dating app Gleeden, founded in France in 2009, debuted in the Indian market in 2017. According to numerous sources, 20% of the Gleeden's 10 million users—or as many as 2 million—are Indians (Maganjan 2023).
2. It has taken many decades to realize that the new wealth is neither "money" nor "power" but "information" and "knowledge" (Shah 1999, pp. 17–18).
3. Social scientists have demonstrated that the first industrial revolution, which began in the last third of the eighteenth century, was marked by new technologies like the steam engine, the spinning jenny, the Cort's process in metallurgy, and, more broadly, by the replacement of hand-tools by machines. The second, which occurred about 100 years later, was marked by the development of electricity, the internal combustion engine, science-based chemicals, and effective transportation. There are important similarities and distinctions between the two, with the key one being the crucial role that scientific knowledge had in supporting and directing industrial advancement after 1850. The similarities between them may provide invaluable insights into understanding the logic behind technology revolutions precisely because of their contrasts. The Third Industrial Revolution ended in 1969 and the Fourth Industrial Revolution began in 2019 (iED Team, UNIDO 2019).
4. Studies on how the advancing chip-based technologies affect how people utilize information technology have found a wide variety of direct implications. These are intertwined with a variety of impacts that are widely dispersed among institutions and human endeavors. To understand its intricacies and effects on the economy, politics, including governance, and society, a thorough study is necessary. Fast-forward to 1957, when US Army employee Jack Kilby originally suggested the notion of producing tiny ceramic wafers with a single component on each. As the initiative to advance this concept gained momentum, Kilby was motivated to develop a different, even more sophisticated design that became the IC that we are familiar with today. Although Kilby's prototype was outdated by today's standards, it was functional, and after he left the army and began working for Texas Instruments, his invention gained significant traction. Kilby showed the first functional IC on September 12th, 1958, and on February 6th, 1959, he submitted a patent application. The term "integrated circuit" was first used by Kilby to describe the device as a completely integrated electronic circuit. Kilby was awarded the Nobel Prize in 2000 in recognition of his role in creating the first genuine integrated circuit.
5. People have always been reliant on technology throughout history. Each era's technology was undoubtedly interesting to look at, even though it wasn't quite the same as what we have today in terms of size, shape and scale. People would constantly make use of the technology they had at their disposal to assist make their lives easier while also working to advance and improve it. The idea of the industrial revolution was first introduced in this way. We are currently experiencing the fourth industrial revolution, sometimes known as Industry 4.0.
6. In 2022, 66% of the world's population, or about 5.3 billion people are online, according to projections from the International Telecommunication Union (ITU). This marks a 24% growth from 2019 with an expected 1.1 billion individuals using the internet throughout that time. With over 749 million users, India has the second-largest internet population in the world in 2020. Of these, 744 million users used their mobile phones to access the internet. By 2040, it is predicted that this number would have surpassed 1.5 billion. Due to the increased accessibility of affordable smart phones since 2010 and the government of India's enormous investments in its telecommunications sector, as well as the further opening of the market with new telecom

spectrum licenses, mobile internet has been such a positive development in the country's digital progress that in 2019, more than 73 percent of India's total web traffic came from mobile phones.
7. The "Information Revolution" was largely sparked by research conducted by the Advanced Research Projects Agency (ARPA) in 1958, including the conceptual development of the ARPANET, a groundbreaking network for sharing digital resources among computers located in different places. The United States' branch for advanced technologies is called the Defense Advanced Research Projects Agency (DARPA). Defense Department DARPA is working to create a wide range of other capabilities besides artificial intelligence, including but not limited to robots that can repair satellites, technologies for automated mapping of underground spaces, and computers that are powered by biological processes.
8. The integrated circuit (IC) is a collection of transistors assembled on a compact, flat piece of silicon. It revolutionized the electronics sector and contributed to the globalization of cutting-edge electronic devices.

References

Basu S, Fernald JG (2008) Information and communications technology as a general purpose technology: evidence from U.S. industry data, FRBSF economic review
Bedi A (1999) The role of information and communication technologies in economic development: A partial survey. ZEF Discuss Pap Dev Policy. Bonn. [http://www.zef.de/download/zef_dp/zef_dp7-99.pdf].
Bell, Daniel (1979) The social framework of the information society, in Michael . Dertouzous, Joel Moses (eds). Comput Age, Twenty Year View. Cambridge. MA: MIT Press, pp 163–211
Bhatnagar S, Schware R (eds) (2000) Information and communication technology in development: cases from India. Sage Publ, New Delhi
Bresnahan TF, Trajtenberg M (1995) General purpose technologies: engines of growth? J Econ 65(1):83–108
Cantner, Vannuccini (2012) A new view of general purpose technologies. Jena Econ Res Pap, 054
Castells M (2009) The communication power. Oxford University Press, New York
Castells, Manuel (2010a) The information age: economy, society and culture. (Vol.-I). MA: Blackwell
Castells, Manuel (2010b) The information age: economy, society and culture. (Vol.-II). MA: Blackwell
Castells, Manuel (2010c) The information age: economy, society and culture. (Vol.-III). MA: Blackwell
Daly, John (1999) Measuring impacts of the internet in the developing world. IMP: Inf Impacts Mag. May 1999. [http://www.cisp.org/imp/may_99/daly/05_99daly.htm]. 14 November 2000
Ernberg, Johan (1999) Empowering communities in the information society: an international perspective. [http://www.fao.org/WAICENT/FAOINFO/SUSTDEV/CDdirect/CDre0042.htm]. 14 November 2000
Ernberg, Johan (1999) Telecommunications for sustainable development. [http://www.fao.org/WAICENT/FAOINFO/SUSTDEV/CDdirect/CDre0028.htm]. 14 November 2000
Feenberg A (1991) Critical theory of technology. Oxford University Press, New York
Freeman LC (2004) The development of social network analysis: a study In the sociology of science. Empirical Press, Vancouver, BC
Fussey P, Roth S (2020) Digitizing sociology: Continuity and change in the internet Era. Sociol 54(4):659–674
Heeks, Richard (1999) ICTs, poverty and development. Working paper No.5, development informatics working series, institute for development policy and management, University of Manchester, www.man.ac.uk/idpn

Helpman E (ed) (1998) General purpose technologies and economic growth. MIT Press, Cambridge, MA
iED Team (2019) The 4 industrial revolutions, institute of entrepreneurship development (iED). https://ied.eu/project-updates/the-4-industrial-revolutions/ (Accessed on 05/04/2023)
Kearns M, Roth A (2019) The ethical algorithm: the science of socially aware algorithm design. Oxford University Press, London
Kitichin, Rob (2014) Big data, new epistemologies and paradigm shifts. In Big Data Soc, April-June
Kranzberg, Melvin (1986) Technology and history: Kranzberg's Laws. Technol Cult 27:3 (July)
Lupton D (2012) Digital sociology: an Introduction. University of Sydney, Sydney
Lupton D (2015) Digital sociology. Routledge, London
Maganjan, Srishti (2023) Everything to know about Gleeden, the extra-marital dating app where 20% users are Indians, https://www.businessinsider.in/india/news/everything-to-know-about-gleeden-the-extra-marital-dating-app-where-20-users-are-indians/articleshow/97318722.cms (Accessed on May 2, 2023)
Mansell R, When U (eds) (1998) Knowledge societies: information technologies for sustainable development. Oxford University Press. [http://www.susx.ac.uk/spru/ink/knowledge.html]
Matin A (2003) E-Governance in India: genesis and prognosis. In: Alam A (ed) Crisis of Governance. Raj Publications, Delhi, pp 176–197
Matin A (2005) Backward classes, dalits and the digital divides. In: Shabbir M (ed). Ambedkar on law, constitution and social justice: Ambedkar's perspective. Rawat Publications, Jaipur, pp 271–291
Matin, Abdul (2020) Informationalism in Ritzer, George and Chris Rojek (Editors in Chief). Wiley Blackwell Encycl Sociol, 2Nd Ed. (Gillian Kane: Project Manager). London: Wiley
Mayfield, Antony (2008) What is social media? icrossing.co.uk/ebooks
McNeill JR, McNeill WH (2003) The human web: a Bird's-Eye view of world history. Norton WW, New York
Moore, Gordon E (1965) Cramming more components onto integrated circuits. Electron, 38(8)
Moser, Nicholas (2004) Was electricity a general purpose technology? Evidence from historical patent citations. Am Econ Rev, pp 388–394
Ong Jasper (2013) The power and value of social networking http://socialmediaonline.com/the-power-and-value-of-social-networking/. (Accessed on 27 April, 2021)
Rao, Madanmohan, Sanjib Raj Bhandari SM, Iqbal, Anjali Sinha, Wahaj us Siraj (1999) Struggling with the digital divide: internet infrastructure, policies and regulations. Econ Polit Wkly, XXXVI(46 & 47), November 20, pp 3317–3320
Samanta RK (1993) Extension strategy for agricultural development in 21st Century. Mittal Publications, New Delhi
Sardar Z, Ravetz JR (eds) (1996) Cyberfutures: culture and politics on the information superhigway. Pluto Press, London
Schiller H (1989) Culture Inc: The corporate takeover of public expression. Oxford University Press, NY
Schiller H (1996) Information inequality: The Deepening Social Crisis in America. Routledge, NY
Selwyn Neil (2019) What is Digital Sociology? Cambridge, UK: Polity
Shah SL (1999) Information technology. Gyan Publishing House, New Delhi
Sharma VP (2003) Cyber extension: Connecting farmers in India—Some experience, http://www.gisdevelopment.net/proceedings/mapasia/2003/papers/i4d/i4d003.htm
TM (2019) Digital transformation: survive and thrive in an Era of mass extinction. RosettaBooks, New York
Sinha, Ajay, Abdul Matin et al. (2020) Online safety and internetaddiction: a study conducted amongst adolescents in Delhi—NCR. New Delhi: CRY
Sood, Aditya Dev (2001) How to wire rural India: problems and possibilities of digital development. Econ Polit Wkly, October 27.
Stadler F (2006) Manuel castells: the theory of the network society. Polity Press, Cambridge

Stuckelberger, Christoph (2016) Global ethics—scenarios for the future, in christoph stuckelberger (et al.). Global Ethics for Leadership. Globethics.net
Susskind R, Susskind D (2017) The future of the Professions: How Technology will Transform the Work of Human Experts. Oxford University Press, Oxford
Tapscott D (1996) The digital economy: promise and peril in the age of networked intelligence. McGraw-Hill, New York
Van Dijk J (2012) The network society, 3rd edn. Sage Publications, New Delhi
Webster F (2006) Theories of the information society. Routledge, New York
World Bank (2000) The networking revolution: opportunities and challenges for developing countries. infoDev Working Paper. Washington, D.C. [http://www.infodev.org/library/NetworkingRevolution.pdf]
Youtie J, Iacopetta M, Graham S (2008) Assessing the nature of nanotechnology: can we uncover an emerging general purpose technology? J Technology Transfer 33:315–329. https://doi.org/10.1007/s10961-0079030-6
Zhang B (2012) On typical materials acting as the dividing standard of the development stages of human substance civilization. Interdiscip Descr Complex Syst 10(2):114–126
Zhang B, Yang Y (2011) On the substance of civilization in human society entering into the nanomaterials age. Arts Soc Sci J 2011:ASSJ-28
Zuboff S (2019) The age of surveillance capitalism: the fight for a human future at the new frontier of power. Profile Books, London

Chapter 11
Theorising the Information Society: Counting the Havens and the Hazards

Srabanti Choudhuri

Abstract The present paper begins with tracing back to the birth of an information society, better known as the knowledge society. We shall explore the dynamics of this society and its wider implications for post-modern society. The questions that we seek to answer are: What is an information society? How did the various thinkers conceptualise this society altogether? And what is the impact and the challenges that the new society poses for us? As we delve further into the nitty–gritty of the information society, we shall be squatting on the soft terrain of the post-industrial society and try to explain its vicissitudes as if with a magical hoop. What sounds even more interesting is that every time we turn our magical box upside down to show how hard we are for new emergent theories, we are suddenly encountered with a new jet of meanings concerning the digital age and its undercurrents. We never run short of meanings evolving constantly to explain the tide of change in fits and starts. Probably, one strong reason why this paper was written was to appraise us not only of the recent developments in the domain of the information age but also to understand the volatility and malleability that life suddenly poses for us. I shall be explaining the various dimensions of the information society and the risks contained at its various stages. My aim in this paper is not to deter the pace of digitisation but to understand the hazards it entails itself. It shall be difficult to contain the momentum of digitisation, but of course, knowing its perils may help us combat its menace and pitfalls.

Keywords Information society · Sociology · Knowledge society · Digital · Risks

---

S. Choudhuri (✉)
Professor in Sociology, School of Social Sciences, Netaji Subhas Open University, Salt Lake City, Kolkata 700064, West Bengal, India
e-mail: srabantichoudhuri@gmail.com

A. Chauhan et al. (eds.), *Hundred Years of Sociology in India: Evolving Issues, Emerging Trends*, https://doi.org/10.1007/978-981-96-1317-5_11

Introduction

Media and communication policy had emerged as a prominent field within the wider context of Western media and communication analysis in the 1950s. During this period, there was not only a trend towards studying interrelationships between media but there was a felt urge to question the forms of ensuing social and economic development, mostly at the national level. There was a gradual shift in the 1960s and the 1970s when the post-colonial backdrop had instigated the comparative studies and the policy implications of the unequal global North and South. From the 1980s onward there was a surging awareness that media and communication programmes must be understood from the transnational standpoint. It must be interpreted at a stage of rigorous policy debate where the role of the non-government stakeholders must be taken into consideration. Therefore, we find that there was the coexistence of the 'global' media and the communication both of which gathered momentum with the twin processes of technological and geopolitical change. The 1990s witnessed a spree of heated discussions to include the local or the native problems within a fast-globalising information society (Raboy 2011).

Information Society: A Close Focus

There are certain technological, economic, occupational, spatial and cultural aspects of the information society that have been distinguished from the rest (Webster 1995). These dimensions are important for it is thought that these will beset the system with a jet of social change not witnessed before. Of these dimensions, the most important is the technological conceptions of the information society that signalled an array of innovative measures since the late 1970s. New technological changes have been the most visible indicators of the new era descending over modern society. The coming of the information society was profusely evident through the massive use of cable and satellite television, computer-to-computer communications, personal computers, new office technologies etc. This iota of technological change by all measures was monumental in reconstituting and impacting the social world (Webster 1995). These changes crept in from the late 1970s to the early 1980s and revolutionised our ways of life.

Alvin Toffler had felt that a new civilisation had been emerging in our lives and this new civilisation is here with its nucleus of exploding changes. For Toffler, it is a central event worth understanding to foresee the world ahead. It is as eventful as the first Wave of change unlocked by the agrarian society. It perhaps may be more unshackling than the second wave of change unfettered by the industrial revolution. However, he asserts we are the offspring of the next boom, the third wave of the Information Age (Toffler 1981). The fervour to grapple with this changing discourse was pervasive. This had come out in the different choice of terms used by the scholars to allude to this era. For Zbigniew Brzezinski, it was the technetronic age when the entire globe was in closer reach than a middle-sized European power probably was to its own capital, say fifty years ago. The technetronic society is gradually shaped culturally, psychologically, socially and economically by the impact of technology and electronics, especially the impact of computers and communications which has been mind-boggling.

Brzezinski asserts that the digital process instead of its industrial paraphernalia is the crucial determinant of social change metamorphosing the mores, values and most importantly, the social structure (Brzezinski 1971). Norbert Wiener coined the term, Cybernetics which was derived from the Greek word, *kubernetes* or 'steersman', the same Greek word from which the word governor is derived (Wiener 1989). There was no dearth of appellations for a bunch of sociologists who came forward with different coinages.

Daniel Bell's Post-Industrial Society

Daniel Bell preferred the term 'post-industrial' over those of knowledge or the information society. The famous work, *The End of Ideology* (Bell 1960) emphasised the role of decision-making, especially technical decision making which was far more calculating and instrumental, than say, an ideology that instead was emotional and expressive. Bell signalled towards exhaustion of old political passions to give prior importance to technocratic thought in relation to politics. With this Bell was probably inviting us to a sectorial shift from a goods-producing to a service society with an augmented emphasis on the intellectual technology that was to become the determinant of post-industrial society. He was however not sure whether this historical change in the social relations signalled a departure from the propertied elites and was bound to stay. Though he was certain about the robust character of the capitalist civilisation from the mid of eighteenth to mid-twentieth century, Bell only made conjectures about the interstitial time he inhabited (Bell 1973).

Daniel Bell seemed to be the most important theorist of a 'post-industrial' society (1973). This is a term often synonymous with the 'information society' and is often used in Bell's works. The work focussed on the sustained patterns of change in the occupational structure over time. This has found a tendency towards a decline in the manufacturing sector and a concomitant rise in the service sector of the economy. There was an ongoing interpretation that given the havoc loss of jobs, there was a simultaneous replacement with the white-collar workers. It was presumed that since the staple of any non-labour production is information, therefore, an increasing growth in such quantum of information acquired can lead to the inauguration of the much sought-after information society.

The account becomes more evident from the fact that almost seventy per cent of the workforce in Western Europe, Japan and North America are in the service sector of the booming economy and white-collar workers are now the most predominant part of the working population. Taking these facts together, we might argue that we are inhabiting an information society since the majority of the workforce is constituted of information workers (Bell 1976).

It was Daniel Bell who showed that mere technology itself does not usher a new society, what matters is the concomitant change in the occupational sector. A close focus on occupational change will surely signal the revolutionary power of information and communication technology which perhaps bypasses mere technology. Agricultural and industrial revolutions too spoke of technological innovation but there was no question of communication and informational prowess. For the first time, we understood that information society rose owing to the collaboration between information and technology and once you decouple one from the other, the soul of this new society would dissipate. Such is the charisma of the information and communication media that is encapsulated in people through their ways of life and living. The current façade stresses that mere technology is not sufficient to take that giant step which can only be facilitated through wide-scale use of information and circulation of knowledge. This however was one thing which distinguished the bygone epochs from the current tide of change.

Bell had already asserted that the information society had presumed a massive change in the occupational front in society. Therefore, what transpired was that information was nothing but something that was reproduced in occupations or enmeshed in people through their education and their rich experiences. This way of defining information undoubtedly was significant for it showed how information society changed the very nature of occupation and its filaments. More than technology, what stood out was information and its paraphernalia that set before us an unknown terrain waiting to be navigated.

Leadbeater's Concept of the Information Age

Charles Leadbeater (1999) says that the challenge that we are about to face in the information age is often precarious and quite deadly. However, we must be steeled enough to venture into this unknown terrain because retreat can never be an alternative here. Giving up is almost similar to being confronted with a gridlock that refuses stubbornly to unlock before us. The grand institutions of social and political spheres might stop functioning for they are taken aback by the mighty knowledge economy and may get sapped of their momentum. But we shouldn't lose hope as we see our familiar structures around us getting enfeebled day in and out by the dynamics of the information society and getting outstripped by their usual capacities of response and resilience. This is sure to happen in a society where suddenly the contours of familiar predicaments have been replaced by economies of uncertainty and peril.

This modern economy's most impressive marker is its capacity to produce a flow of new products and services. This is the outcome of the skyrocketing growth of organised science that has accelerated the pace of technological change. This led to the spurt of new ideas which eventually got translated into commercial products. The astronomical growth in the second half of the present century in certain sectors of the economy like travel, communication, medicine, pharmaceuticals, robotics, information, and generic engineering are signposts of a massive revolution in the knowledge economy. It points out the huge importance of human intelligence and its aptly made commercial applications in the occupational terrain to build up a robust knowledge industry.

Now the question which we are asking is very tenable here. Shall it be possible to keep up with this kind of undaunting competition into which people are thrust suddenly without any sort of protection from the larger umbrella organisation? Is it at all possible to keep ourselves afloat in this fast-changing society without any shield from the parent structures? At times it may feel like we are living in a blissful world that is replete with its prolificity and resourcefulness and one that is pervaded with an unprecedented rate of creativity and production. Science and technological innovation ensnarl us and we are generating new products every day with vast ranging possibilities. So what we see is that the storehouse of knowledge is what is driving us forward. We sustain our economy through the thin air that envelops us. We must think carefully to understand that we produce things that can neither be weighed, touched, or easily measured. We produce subtle but abstract things which often remain invisible before us.

The Hazards of the Thin Economy

Interestingly, the outcome that we produce is often imperceptible for it may transcend substantive production. Think for a moment, the knowledge economy yields fruits that are not tangible merchandise and wares. They are not stockpiled at harbours, stored in warehouses or shipped in railway cars (Leadbeater 1999). Most of the people who work for the economy today are experts in their own field but they produce things that are hardly visible to the common eye. It is as if something is dangling from the thin air beyond our common senses. Think of the multiple ways we sustain our living today. These range across a wide spectrum such as working for a telephone call centre, a lawyer's office, a governmental department or even a chemical laboratory. This also implies that since our economy is explicitly a knowledge-based economy centred around the people who contribute to the knowledge capital. It should have been more humane and possibly contain the traits of being tender-hearted and beneficent. This humane economy should have more free air for our children to breathe in. This is possibly because our children will be freed from the drudgery of toiling in smoke-billowing dark factories, squatting into dense and grungy pits or smothering mills or axe wood into finished products. We should have been possibly happy that our children will live a genteel life away from the smutty and sooty factories. They will perhaps lead a decent life away from the hazards of manufacturing units where perils are uncountable. What is more pleasing is, that our children should do all those aesthetic things that our high culture idealises such as creativity, imagination, and soulful thinking.

However, to our stunning dismay, we find that just the contrasting outcomes are superseding us and instead of appeasing our minds with harmony and concord, we are suddenly filled with distaste and fear. It is the undaunting fear of losing your job, feeling more insecure and enfeebled such that you are no longer in a position to control your life. What is even more surprising is as we plunge forward in this bandwagon of development, we find sharp and knotty contrasts that are difficult to disentangle. There are massive developments on various vistas such as scientific rationality, uproarious technological developments, and emerging transnational corporations, but alongside at the homestead, we find massive inequality, pressing poverty, and dripping standards of life.

When it comes to the welfare state's capacity to roll out pensions, it hobbles. Doling out basic services like housing, education, and sanitation seems an unnerving task for the state despite its brilliant achievements in other domains of public welfare. Churning out dollars from Sensex-driven global financial firms seems easier than, say, improving a lot of its own citizens. Despite the unprecedented pace of development of the information society, people still feel baulked at the sinister ideas of down-sizing, re-engineering, restructuring, and down-scaling. Jobs and careers are closeted on a bumpy roller-coaster ride which can bring fear and melancholy to people. This can be disturbing for those who had thought the new economy will be far more placid and steady. Such fitful and jerky rides are preordained for those at the rear end of the fat global economy which gets creamier at the cost of these men on the edge. While some benefit from the premium earned by a fast-expanding global financial corporation, others face no considerable change. Even when such corporations fight crises, those at the brim may be the first to get knocked out.

Conclusion

It is interesting to note that not just Leadbeater, but a spree of thinkers in the second half of the last century thought likewise and had eventually stressed on an information-fed economy that is all set to rejig the society and its dispensations. We might start from Robert Reich (1991) to Peter Drucker (1993) to Manuell Castells (1996–98) to envision an emerging form of economy that manoeuvres information (Leadbeater 1999). They have undoubtedly used several different terms to identify this new genre of connoisseurs that dabbled with knowledge, its manufacture and mediation. However, what is important is, that we now have a burgeoning army of knowledge experts whose work is to create and use information in ways they find relevant for society. However, the question is how safe are these people? Do their creativity and imagination pay off? Or are they laid off in the name of economic downsizing and refurbishing at the quickest instance? What is the use of such massive technological change, if it could not ensure a peaceful cosmos or a canopy to these men who serve the economy?

Now, it is already understood that we are undergoing a revolutionary transformation that shall turn our polity and economics upside down in the upcoming centuries.

Rather the process has already started and there is no stopping here. We soon shall have no national commodities or technologies, nor shall we have any national corporations and industries. In that sense there shall be no such idea of a national economy for what we only possess is a national border and the people enshrined within it who actually constitute a nation. A nation's assets are its citizens and the skills and acumen which they have managed to hone. The global economy seemed all set to decide the binding forces that mobilised the economy with no regard for its men. It does not bother how its men live their lives.

The global economy is all garnered to hierarchise in its layers to empower those citizens with the most profound level of skill and insight. It discriminates against those with diminutive flair or finesse. The standard of living will vary likewise based on the axis of knowledge and information that each section of its citizens display. As this happens the information society becomes even more problematized especially with national borders becoming more porous enabling osmosis across nations. With national borders becoming blurred and transnational corporations emerging, societies will no longer provide the soft cushion to their workers that they once offered. The parent organisations and structures which had supported us so far had stopped functioning. Traditional support structures like trade unions and government bodies no longer work in our favour. The bureaucracy seems even more intimidating than before. In short, the knowledge economy with its grand institutional paraphernalia is more a threat than a succour or palliation for its men around. Therefore, any inquisitive reflection on the information society is important. It not only signals these changes in occupations and skills developed but also questions the huge challenges that the new age throws. The paper counts on both the havens and the hazards of the information society which must be noted instead of letting the heroes of the new age beguile us by the razzmatazz of the new eon.

References

Bell D (1960) The end of ideology: on the exhaustion of political ideas in the fifties. Harvard University Press, Cambridge
Bell D (1973) The coming of post industrial society. Basic Books, New York
Bell D (1976) The cultural contradictions of capitalism. Basic Books, New York
Brzezinski Z (1971) Between the Two ages. The Viking Press, New York
Castells M (2000) The rise of the network society (2nd ed). Blackwell
Dahrendorf R (1959) Class and class conflict in industrial society. Routledge and Kegan Paul, London
Drucker PF (1993) Post-Capitalist society. HarperCollins
Gleick J (2011) The information: a history, a theory, a flood. Random House
Leadbeater C (1999) Living on thin air: new economy. Viking, London
Raboy RM (2011) The handbook of global media and communication policy. In Raboy RM. The Handbook of Global Media and Communication Policy (p 589). USA: Wiley Blackwell
Reich RB (1991) The work of nations: preparing ourselves for 21st century capitalism. Random House
Toffler A (1981) The third wave. United States: Bantam

Webster F (1995) Theories of the information society. Routledge, USA
Wiener N (1989) The human use of human beings: cybernetics and society. Free Association Books, London

Part III
Sociology from Margins: Caste, Religion and Gender

Chapter 12
Dalit Movement in Odisha: 'Castes in Caste' and the Politics of Partisan

Bibhuti Bhushan Malik and Vijay Laxmi Mall

Abstract Dalits are unassertive because of the feudalistic social framework, rigid caste system, and dogmas. The nation-state governance is behind their backwardness, lack of consciousness, and non-mobilisation, which is the fact-based reality of present-day Odisha. An autonomous nation-state of expeditious and inelastic socio-historical moorings of enormous covert and grinding value organisations championed by higher or upper-caste hegemony have succeeded and disorganised them and their mobilisation. The paper makes an apparent effort to analyse the pertinent problems and queries regarding the Dalits of Odisha, such as why a significant Dalit movement has not yet materialised there and how a class of interest came together for mobilisation and assertion in contrast to divided Dalits.

Keywords Dalit movement · Assertion · Odisha · Caste · Class

Introduction

Odisha is caught inseparably by vicissitudes of multi-layer problems and ambiguities. The manner and process by which the state and society are valiantly replicated due to historical-social moorings make it clear that a significant portion of Odisha's population, especially Dalit-Adivasi, is far behind current-day globalism, culture, and civilisation. Without interruption and alternative, the state and society have been ruled and hijacked by high or dominant castes who intensify hierarchy, stratification, and religious dogmas to subjugate, exploit and marginalise the Scheduled Castes — untouchable Dalits. A leading social scientist, Manoranjan Mohanty, stated this situation:

B. B. Malik (✉)
Department of Sociology, Babasaheb Bhimrao Ambedkar University, Lucknow, Uttar Pradesh, India
e-mail: bbmalik57@gmail.com

V. L. Mall
Department of Sociology, YBN University, Ranchi, Jharkhand, India

A. Chauhan et al. (eds.), *Hundred Years of Sociology in India: Evolving Issues, Emerging Trends*, https://doi.org/10.1007/978-981-96-1317-5_12

> Odisha presents a crisis of democracy with upper caste, patriarchal domination that has been consolidated through the formation and expansion of a middle class, which provides services to the capitalist extractive economy, while vast sections of the population, especially adivasis, Dalits, and agricultural workers, remain marginalised. This process has been accentuated during the recent decades of neo-liberal policies, during which the scale and magnitude of mining-based industries and their implementation through a massive deployment of security forces have hugely grown (Mohanty 2014, p. 46).

The *Dalit* movement occurs due to a rise in education, awareness, and mobilisation against the caste system, untouchability, and marginalisation in a society among other socio-political factors, where 'religious nexus with caste system defines the rule of law'. However, in present-day Odisha, these communities who suffered during earlier societies are more acutely marginalised. Without minimum rights and justice, these people face every adverse situation, condition and challenge to raise their voice, resistance and protest against the authoritarian state and the upper caste hegemony. The Dalit identity vis-a-vis solidarity is always used and manufactured by ritually so-called high caste people in different forms, categories, and planks like belief, dogma, and superstition suited to their needs. Oligarchy, the gimmick of welfare and the monopolistic manoeuvring state have always divided the Dalit unity without igniting. In this context, the paper unambiguously attempts to analyse the pertinent issues and questions about the Dalits of Odisha, including why a substantive Dalit movement has yet to emerge in Odisha and how a class of interest unified vis-à-vis divided untouchable Dalits and touchable Dalits for mobilisation and assertion.

Dalits in Odisha: Caste and Class

Caste identity-based social and economic marginalisation is strongly ingrained in Indian society. South Asia as a whole and Indian society alike share the defining characteristic of caste. Even today's Muslim-dominated communities in Pakistan and Bangladesh still uphold untouchability and caste-based social marginalisation as essential components of caste identity (Wessler 2020). The Brahmins and higher castes enjoy numerous privileges and dominate Odia society. The Dalits are unable to exercise certain fundamental rights. The aristocratic upper caste groups have turned to exploitation and tyranny as the norm. The caste system's relationship with the religion and Dharmasastra has severely restricted non-caste Hindus (Malik 2018, p. 6). The biggest challenge for the Dalits in the state is that the upper caste still forbids them from entering several temples despite their numerous problems with caste and untouchability. Despite innumerable atrocities and denying Dalit rights, dignity, and self-respect, Odisha is one of India's most backward states. Dalit movements in Odisha have not been successful since the precolonial era. In the past, the state has seen a few small, dispersed Dalit protests that have proclaimed Dalits' freedom, rights, and dignity in opposition to the caste system and untouchability. However, these movements remained restricted to literature and religion for various reasons.

The historiography of Odisha is undoubtedly supra-distinct, and the deep-rooted caste hierarchy of ideal–typical pursuits prevalent in the macro social structure of the state always predetermines Dalits' existence and overall conditions. However, the narration below substantiates the situation that has not yet changed over the years:

> F G Bailey, the renowned British social anthropologist, conducted fieldwork in Bisipara in the highlands of Orissa in the 1950s to examine the ways in which the state, democracy and new forms of economy were changing the traditional organisation and apprehension of power and status. At the time, and following the Temple Entry Act, the former untouchables of the village attempted to gain entry to the Shiva temple. On that occasion, and as Bailey recounts, they were unsuccessful. A new fieldwork conducted in 2013 in the same location presents an update of the continuing drama surrounding the Shiva temple, against a backdrop of the changing polity and economy of the village, and as a manifestation of contested postcolonial identity politics (Otten and Simpson 2016, p. 5)

When the priority of nation-state imbroglio still bemuses many minds with ethnonationalism, off-late, globalism has not benefitted most people either. The paradigm of development is fractured and absent in the empirical-structural sense. Because the state's economy is in a doldrums situation as poverty, inequality (not mere inequality) is rampantly rising among most people. Only selected people, not all, representing a particular caste community from selected areas have had access to education and mobility. Vast traces of arable lands and human-social capital have remained unutilised, leading to brain drain and backwardness. Oddly not enough to be surprised, Odia nation's so-called proud socio-cultural milieu is forcefully guided by aggrandised tradition-driven values and continuous single caste-class nexus hegemony controlling power structure, governance machinery and other essential spheres of socio-cultural life and activities. Odisha being almost static and with no change remnants, many a people belonging to low, untouchable Dalit-Adivasi vis-a-vis poor class are often strategically exploited, marginalised and excluded almost in all walks of their adapted life.

In Odisha, caste is class, and vice versa, wherein only upper castes represent the upper class, and the pattern of class-caste domination persists. Caste and class are reciprocally moulded according to time, space and situation in an actual and potential sense. In Odisha, most people or communities who enjoy a high status, privilege, power and authority are not only hailed from a solid economic background but equally superior ritually. Accordingly, the commanding position of a person, caste and community is determined based on the estates that managers and labourers broadly serve. So, Odisha's political economy and social structure are beset with both explicit power structure and implicit value organisations between the upper caste power and powerlessness of the Dalit-Adivasi. Likewise, modernity myth and global mesmerisation adequately divided the Dalits of the dithering nation-state to the greatest extent sans minimum equality and justice. Negation of negation wilfully aggravated Dalit pauperisation and alienation, giving rise to numerous problems in the lives of many poor people who remained victims of caste atrocities and stereotypes. Caste resilience contributed enough cleavages among the upper and low castes, wherein the latter, to date, are even organised nowhere. The caste hegemony bereft of a cohesive Dalit ideology and consciousness perpetrated and stigmatically generated by high caste trials regularly forbids radical mobilisation among the Dalits and Adivasis in Odisha.

The Eastern Versus Western Odisha

The caste system, another manifestation of the dreadful situation, exemplifies Odisha's predicament. As stated by Biswamoy Pati, "The vision of the 'Odia' is confined to the coastal, upper caste/class urban and feudal sections, where the coastal Dalits are part of the vision. The pre-existing gap between the coastal tract and the western interior was heavily reinforced by colonisation" (2001, p. 48). In the Eastern part of Odisha, the Dalits are better educated and more advanced than those in western part of the state. In the western and eastern parts of Odisha, Dalits live their way of life very differently regarding language and culture.

In contrast to the coastal and eastern regions, which have been uncommon throughout the colonial era, missionary efforts and conversion are more prevalent in western Odisha. Some factors limiting Dalit activities against the dominant culture and system are the upper castes' divisive caste politics, the Dalits' great devotion to and confidence in the religion, shastras, caste structure, and notably in the religious tradition. The Dalits are compelled to embrace the Brahminical system because of its superstructural power, which the Dharmashastras and Puranas legitimised. The Dalits attribute it to a lack of awareness and education. Due to an unreasonable conviction in ignorance or fear, Dalits in Odisha still adhere to the caste system. They uphold it in the name of "Tradition" and do not wish to alter it because God has approved it through the Dharmasastras. According to Chad Bauman, those who purposefully politicised and communalised local tensions contributed to the violence in Orissa by portraying communal identities as rigid, exclusive, and particular on both the local and national levels. These causes include how a tribal state like Odisha became Hinduised, Brahminisation and feudalism formed the state, and a tribal state like Odisha became Hindu (2010, p. 264).

Dalits and Identity

Our sense of identity can significantly influence the strength and warmth of relationships with others, such as neighbours, people from the same community, fellow citizens, or members of the same neighbourhood. Our attention to individual identities can deepen our relationships, inspire us to do many things for one another and help us move past our self-centred lifestyles. A sense of belonging to a community is, thus, viewed as a resource like capital in the recent literature on "social capital," which has been persuasively explored by Robert Putnam and others. The literature convincingly shows how an identity with others in the same social community can improve the lives of all in that community. While acknowledging this fact is crucial, it is also necessary to recognise that a sense of identity can both firmly exclude many people and warmly embrace others. It is possible to make the hardship of exclusion coexist with the blessings of inclusion.

The location of Odisha and its social history, in its entirety, is not distinctly different from other states of India. Since its inception, the state apparatus's social structure and political economy were equally blended with the same or similar elements that were also seen as prevalent in other states. Likewise, archaic Odisha's simple economy, polity and socio-cultural institutions were allied with other Indian states. Facts and figures, drawn from folk and mores and empirical and theoretical studies, delineate that Odisha, earlier having different nomenclatures of *Udra, Kalinga* and *Utkal*, was primarily divided into many pockets or areas, and a high caste king ruled each of those areas. Kings and emperors undertook warfare and fought for the annexation and expansion of their respective territories. So, in a structural sense, primaeval Odisha was similar to other societies and remained ultimately under feudalism and a kingly model in rule and governance. Possibly, amidst Odisha's level of overt similarity in its geopolitical condition with other states, the state's population profile, consisting of castes and tribes (Dalit-Adivasi), ethnic blocs and religious communities, is an admixture of complexities with phenomenal contradictions and especially in case of the Dalits, issues, crises and problems are always endless and fathomless in nature, character and structure. Before separating Odisha from Bihar and West Bengal, the conditions of low-caste Dalits and tribal counterparts were equally on the wrong feet and worse. Surprisingly, unlike other Indian states, harmony, mutual reciprocity and co-sharing were never found nor noticed between the majority Adivasi abode with a relatively small number of Dalits habitation.

On the contrary, the two communities were at almost every intra and inter-fight on very petite issues and matters. Rich ethnography, archival and anthropo-sociological literature adequately reveal that most people belonged to these communities. High castes openly used Dalit-Adivasi of the state to meet their necessity and personal benefit. The high or upper castes depended upon the Dalit-Adivasi but kept them separated. Ascribing them Harijan and Adivasi according to the mythologies and religious texts, the upper caste manipulated them the way they like. Though it's tough to precisely understand the fundamental motif of the upper caste behind the perpetration of orthodoxy against untouchable Dalit-Adivasi, one thing above doubt is that in Odisha, both the Dalit-Adivasi are victims of religious harassment. Because in Odisha, only a single dominant caste has had non-interrupted prominence and monopoly for a long time. Simultaneously, the development of the Jagannath cult from the personification of a tribal deity and name of some untouchable Dalit saints and devotees like Sriya Chandaluni, Dasia Bauri, Bhaktakabi Balaram Das, and Bhima Bhoi mesmerised the majority of Dalit to accept and abide by high caste hegemony and prescriptions. To keep the Dalit-Adivasi from attaining consciousness and raising protest, resistance and rebellion, the ritually higher caste groups injected fear psychosis of God and Goddess and *karma* and *dharma* dogmas into the mind of the downtrodden Dalit-Adivasi. Such persistence of rigid caste hierarchies and feudalistic social structures keep Dalits and Adivasis imprisoned, disunited, and unassailable in all walks of life.

According to Amartya Sen, the "illusion" of fixed and single identities contributes to the perception that conflict between many communities is inevitable (2006, pp. 2–4). The presumption of fixed and solitary identities helps those who support Hindutva ideology and aim to exclude and divide others. For them, the claim that Christianity is a "foreign" religion (and therefore necessarily subversive) is connected to the claim that Hinduism is an indigenous and eternally Indian religion that is static and undivided, even though rigorous historical analysis reveals that this claim is also problematic (Kesavan 2001 p. 45; Needham and Rajan 2007; Sarkar 2002 pp. 122–23; Van der Veer 1994:1). Sen claims that a choice-related component is always present in both individual and social identity (p. xiii p. 4). The options are limited but still available, especially regarding how important an individual or group attaches to different aspects of its identity (pp. 5, 34). For example, individuals or a group of people can decide at any time to emphasise their economic, political, linguistic, or religious identities.

There is also the fact that for many centuries, Adivasi groups that underwent a gradual process of assimilation, sanskritization, or, to put it more provocatively, conversion to Hinduism, have become assimilated into the more economically developed and powerful Hindu community to access its wealth and social power (Hardiman 2014; Robinson and Clarke 2003, pp. 10–11; Pati 2003, pp. 11–16). The rhetoric of 'force, fraud, and inducement' is that people choose their religion based on material calculations alone. As Viswanathan (2007 p. 337) has noted, the presumption is particularly pronounced when the subjects are underprivileged Dalits and Adivasis who are assumed to be crude, gullible, and stupid. Although there are many theories of conversion, the 'interest' idea in its different manifestations continues to dominate the sociological analysis of religious transformation.

Dalit: 'Castes in Caste'

As a particular culture-space boundary, territorial zone, and nation-state, Odisha is a bastion of open feudalism and maintains ambiguity and profound perplexities. The old-fashioned question of having a special culture-space, many planks of dubious questions undoubtedly get revisited into its structure. Much after the creation of Odisha as a separate state and in its post-independent period with abundant policies, programmes, packages, and schemes, it is pretty astonishing to see that not a single powerful Dalit-Adivasi joint protest and movement is found among them till now. The state is rich in natural resources, human capital, and its educated people's high global mobility rate; the nation-state remains static. A sizeable population of Odisha, or most people represented by Adivasi-Dalit, are squarely caught by poverty, illiteracy and backwardness.

However, one may still twistedly say that they are responsible for the Dalit backwardness, lack of consciousness and non-mobilisation more than nation-state governance. Indeed, the concrete, fact-based reality is that the present Odisha as an autonomous nation-state of expeditious and inelastic socio-historical moorings of enormous covert and grinding value organisations which are directly championed by high or upper-caste hegemony succeeded and disorganised the Dalit-Adivasi. The present political culture of massive manipulation and partisan self-interest relegated dream-need of politics of benevolence. This trend is alarmingly high as there is an unholy nexus between bureaucratic officialdom and hierarchical power structure upholding patrician politicians. Due to the hegemony of the so-called upper castes, the low-caste Dalit-Adivasi has remained embryonically static without voice, mobilisation, and assertion. Nonetheless, retaining these rigid values and organisations, the powerful upper castes relentlessly continue segregation between the untouchable and touchable Dalit castes, bringing sizeable gulfs and rupture in their plausible emerging solidarity. Hence, the dichotomy between 'powerful' upper castes and 'powerlessness' Dalit-Adivasi is sharply intensified as the former can promote, patronise and create 'castes in caste' and 'exclusions in exclusion' for the latter, weakening them.

Present-day Odisha is a hierarchical, problematic, and contentious state inconsolable of qualitative vis-a-vis structural transformation from its earlier days. Nevertheless, many people innocently believe that the economy has undergone an upsurge in recent times, and a sea change has occurred in the life of the people and the allied fields. However, ordinary people, irrespective of social stratification and occupational gradations, are still reeling with the vicious circle of poverty, old, perennial sufferings and side by side stationed at the receiving end. The successive governments argue that their pro-people policies and programmes announced and implemented have far-reaching consequences that benefit the state's people immensely. Suppose the government's welfare measures have come to the deserving people and brought desirable change among them; why have both Dalit-Adivasi spread over the nation-state not achieved minimum status mobility in a positive direction? Did the government and state machinery ever show interest and come forward to understand and address the multiple chronic problems of the untouchable Dalit-Adivasi people? Behind these peoples' subservient economic conditions, the role of the upper caste is direct as they quickly inject ascription and religious dogma into their minds. In Odisha, the doctrine of God and Goddess discretion and duty allocation for different people varies according to their birth in the caste hierarchical structure. It has pushed them into the oblivion of darkness and danger. People belonging to the low caste groups and segmentation typically presume the words uttered and advice from upper castes as righteous and virtuous since they represent nobility as per the directive of God and Goddess. So, ordinary people from poor castes are misled by upper-caste people in the name of God, affecting the possibility of their awakening of consciousness and identity.

Besides the above and as practically witnessed and pragmatically evaluated, the government's most drives and packages announced long before are yet to reach the needy and desired sections of people. In the true sense, neither the rural poverty declined nor even minimum employable avenues are generated to engage the educated middle class, who are forced to migrate to urban centres searching for work and jobs. Contemporary Odisha suffers from exploitation, torture, exclusion, and large-scale atrocities against the Dalit-Adivasi on experimental and statistical parameters.

Conclusion

Odisha is amply reckoned with the high trajectory of mass-scale exploitation, exclusion and marginalisation of the Dalit people in almost all sectors of their lives. In this way, it is evident that the rigid dogma and feudal social structure orchestrated and upheld by a single caste hegemony denied the minimum right, duty, and existence to the Dalit people in Odisha, whose number and strength are much higher than the other high caste groups. 'Castes in caste' and 'exclusions in the exclusion' mantra of modern political culture segmented, frightened and denied everything to the Dalits. Further, it is solely due to their poverty and lowest position in the caste hierarchy. The politics of partisan and convenience have, therefore, overridden the politics of benevolence and welfare in a much-hyped and global era of rapid transformation, wherein a mere chance of Dalit upheavals is yet to be occurred or invited by the highly disorganised and traumatised Dalit-Adivasi of Odisha.

References

Bauman C (2010) Identity, conversion and violence: Dalits, adivasis and the 2007–08 riots in Orissa. In: Robinson R, Kujur JM (ed) Margins of faith: Dalit and tribal Christianity in India. Sage, pp 263–90

Hardiman D (2014) Dalit and adivasi assertion. In: Sarkar S, Sarkar T (ed) Caste in modern India. Permanent Black, pp 403–428

Kesavan M (2001) Secular common sense. Penguin, New Delhi

Malik SK (2018) Social exclusion and the mindscapes of caste: a study of Kendrapara district of Odisha. In: Bhattacharyya A, Basu S (ed) Marginalities in India: themes and perspectives. Springer, Singapore, pp 35–49

Malik SK (2021) Genesis, historicity and persistence of Dalit protest literature and movements in Odisha. Contemp Voice Dalit 13(1):81–94

Malik BB, Kumar A (2022) Basic amenity and the caste Conundrum: a study of the Dalit communities in East Uttar Pradesh. Contemporary Vice of Dalit Sage Publications, pp 1–16. https://doi.org/10.1177/2455328X211066189

Mohanty M (2014) Persisting dominance crisis of democracy in a resource-rich region. Economic and Political Weekly XLIX(14):39–47

Needham AD, Sunder Rajan R (eds) (2007) The crisis of secularism in India. Duke University Press, Durham

Otten T, Simpson E (2016) FG Bailey's Bisipara revisited. Economic and Political Weekly 51(26–27):25–32

Pati B (2001) Situating social history: Orissa (1800–1997), Orient Longman, New Delhi, p 48

Pati B (2003) Identity, hegemony, resistance. Three Essays Collective, Delhi

Robinson R, Clarke S (eds) (2003) Religious conversion in India. Oxford University Press, Delhi

Sarkar T (2002) Missionaries, converts, and the state in colonial India. Stud Hist (n.s.) 18(1):121–133.

Sen A (2006). Identity and violence: the illusion of destiny. W. W. Norton, New York City
Van der Veer P (1994) Religious nationalism: Hindus and Muslims in India. University of California Press, Berkeley
Viswanathan G (2007) Literacy and conversion in the discourse of Hindu nationalism. In: Needham AD, Rajan RS (eds) The crisis of secularism in India. Duke University Press, Durham, pp 333–355
Wessler H (2020) From marginalisation to rediscovery of identity: Dalit and Adivasi voices in Hindi literature. Stud Neophilol 92(2):159–174

Chapter 13
Decoding the Contemporary Dynamics of Communalism: A Critical Examination of Emerging Trends and Patterns

Arvinder A. Ansari

Abstract The paper critically analyzes and examines the sociological dimensions of communalism within the Indian context. It aims to shed light on the social, cultural, and political factors that contribute to the growth and sustenance of communal tensions and conflicts. By delving into the underlying structural causes and group dynamics, this paper seeks to uncover the complexities of communal identities, power relations, and intergroup dynamics. Furthermore, it aims to explore the social implications of communalism, such as its impact on social cohesion, and intergroup relations, particularly between the Hindus and the Muslims, and marginalized communities. The ultimate goal is to provide a comprehensive sociological understanding of communalism in India and offer insights for addressing this phenomenon, promoting communal harmony, and fostering a more inclusive and equitable society. The paper also focuses on the State's role in perpetuating communalism, highlighting that it has often been a willing participant in inflaming religious tensions. The paper argues that the institutionalization of communalism infiltrates various aspects of society, including the educational and cultural sectors, thereby eroding the secular spaces.

Keywords Communalism · Nationalism · Secularism · Minorities · Media · Muslim identity

Introduction

Communalism in India serves as both a reflection and a catalyst of deeply ingrained social cleavages, challenging the constitutional principles of secularism and religious pluralism. It refers to the allegiance to one's own religious community at the expense of the wider social good, manifesting in inter-community conflicts, most commonly between Hindus and Muslims. Communalism is not merely an ideological stance

A. A. Ansari (✉)
Department of Sociology, Jamia Millia Islamia, New Delhi, India
e-mail: arvinder2009@gmail.com

A. Chauhan et al. (eds.), *Hundred Years of Sociology in India: Evolving Issues, Emerging Trends*, https://doi.org/10.1007/978-981-96-1317-5_13

but a pervasive social and political phenomenon that drives exclusionary practices, thereby disadvantaging minority communities like Muslims, Dalits, and Christians. In the current context, communalism has escalated into a majoritarian political tool, exacerbated by political manoeuvring and identity-based populism. The ideology has evolved from localized manifestations to institutionalized forms, amplified by political decisions, and has increasingly marginalized minority communities both socially and politically. The role of political parties and leaders in fomenting communalism cannot be overlooked. Some political parties and leaders have been known to exploit communal sentiments for electoral gains, further deepening the divisions between communities. This short-sighted approach to politics has long-term consequences for social harmony and national unity (Pai and Kumar 2018; Raheman 2016, 2018).

Communalism in India also has significant implications for the country's social fabric. It undermines the principles of secularism and religious tolerance enshrined in the Indian Constitution, which are essential for maintaining a diverse and pluralistic society. Communal tensions often lead to social exclusion and discrimination, as members of minority communities may be marginalised and denied equal opportunities (Singh 2018; Kothari 1989; Kumar 1990; Shaban 2012). The rising trend of communalism and the accompanying violence has created a feeling of insecurity among religious minorities and ethnic groups. In India, communalism primarily centers around tensions between Hindus and Muslims. Muslims in particular fear discrimination and confrontation after the Gujarat 2002 riots and more recently due to the rise in majoritarian Communalism in post-2014 India. The rising tide of Hindutva has threatened and marginalized minorities beyond imagination particularly Muslims, Dalits, and Christians.

The paper aims to shed light on the social, cultural, and political factors that contribute to the growth and sustenance of communal tensions and conflicts. By delving into the underlying structural causes and group dynamics, the paper seeks to uncover the complexities of communal identities, power relations, and intergroup dynamics. Furthermore, it aims to explore the social implications of communalism, such as its impact on social cohesion, intergroup relations, and marginalized communities. The ultimate goal is to provide a comprehensive sociological understanding of communalism in India and offer insights for addressing this phenomenon, promoting communal harmony, and fostering a more inclusive and equitable society.

In this context the paper also focuses on the State's role in perpetuating communalism, highlighting that it has often been a willing participant in inflaming religious tensions. This institutionalization of communalism is alarming, as it infiltrates various aspects of society, including the educational and cultural sectors, thereby eroding the secular spaces within the country.

Communalism has been a subject of extensive study across multiple disciplines, each contributing diverse perspectives and insights. The research is informed by the works of Kothari (1989) and Kohli (1990), Engineer (1991), Panikar (1993), Brass (2003), Hasan (1998), and Ahmad (1969) who have notably explored the politicization of religion and the criminalization of politics in India in the 1980s. These scholars have been instrumental in shaping our understanding of the new phase of communalism, illuminating its historical roots, social intricacies, and its influence on Indian democracy. This study further aims to enrich the existing literature on communalism in India. Scholars such as Sudhir Kakkar have explored the psychological underpinnings of ethnic conflict, while economists like Sen (1987) and Bagchi (1984) have offered economic viewpoints. Political scientists including Paul Brass (2003), Vanaik (1997), Pai and Kumar (2018) have dissected the intricate relationship between communalism and politics in a contemporary context. Furthermore, intellectuals like Nandy (1997) have incited discussions about the complex relationship between communalism and secularism. This multidisciplinary dialogue indicates the interconnectedness of secularism, democracy, nationalism, and minorities when examining the phenomenon of communalism.

Recent years have witnessed intense debates on the changing ideological landscape of India, largely attributed to the electoral ascendancy of the Bharatiya Janata Party (BJP). This has had a profound impact on the academic discourse, including contributions from Western scholars like Jaffrelot (2019), and van der Veer (2015). This study recognizes these valuable contributions while aiming to provide a comprehensive analysis of how communalism has been institutionalized within various facets of Indian society. By situating the issue of communalism within a multidimensional framework, the paper asserts that understanding this issue is not just an academic exercise but also a social and political imperative. This includes grassroots social programs to foster inter-community dialogue and understanding, as well as the implementation of stricter laws to deter hate speech and other provocations that incite communal discord.

The Peril of Communal Politics

Communalism operates at different levels ranging from individual relations and interests to the local institutional and national politics and to communal riots. There is a whole range of social relations and politics over which communalism pervades today and this spread of communalism involves two interrelated central issues. The first is the state of consciousness in society. The second is communalism as an instrument of power, not purely for capturing state power but for operating in political, social, and economic domains and at almost all levels of social organization (Brass 1996; Raheel and Michael 2012; Jha 2014; Berenschot 2012; Singh 2018).

Religious identity is a core part of our societal consciousness and is often used for communal mobilization. Certain political parties manipulate this for power, with communal parties being overt and others, like the Congress, using subtler means. To counteract its dwindling electoral support, the Congress started appealing to the religious sentiments of the majority community in the 1980s. Their reliance shifted from the charisma of Jawaharlal Nehru and national movement nostalgia to other strategies after his passing.

Indira Gandhi resorted to populist slogans and measures like bank nationalism, the abolition of privy purses, and 'garibi hatao'. But the appeal of these slogans and programs was short-lived. Faced with political upheaval after the Bangladesh war, and the failure of the family planning program, Indira Gandhi lost her electoral base among minorities, especially Muslims. In the post-emergency period when Congress came back to power in 1980 with a greatly reduced majority, the Muslims did not vote for it during this election. Therefore, faced with an electoral debacle, the Congress sought to overcome the crisis by manipulating Hindu religious sentiments to its advantage. Mrs. Gandhi's policy underwent a major change as she became unsure of the Muslim votes and tried to woo the middle-class Hindus. The first major manifestation of this trend was the Hindu Kalash Yatra. By openly blessing and supporting the Yatra, Indira Gandhi tried to identify herself with Hinduism. Ektamatayagna and Ektamata Yatra was organized by the Vishwa Hindu Parishad soon after some poor Hindus of Meenakshipuram in 1981 were converted to Islam and both the BJP and the VHP raised a hue and cry over it. This raised the temperature of Hindu communalism in the country. The VHP jumped into the fray and launched an aggressive campaign against the conversion (Ansari 2012).

The Indian political arena underwent a notable transformation, increasingly veering towards communal lines, signaling the rise of Hindu nationalism. The electoral machinery started capitalizing on religious emotions to gain traction. This drift was palpable in regions like Punjab and Jammu and Kashmir, with the Congress party frequently implicated. The 1984 anti-Sikh riots estranged the Sikh minority, while a series of communal riots in the 1980s, such as those in Meerut, Assam, and Bhagalpur, served to erode the Muslim community's trust in the Congress.

Meanwhile, the government's proposal to implement a common civil code—sparked by a Supreme Court verdict supporting maintenance for a divorced woman, Shah Bano—faced severe backlash from the Muslim community, viewing it as an infringement on Shariah law. Despite initial support, the government wavered on the code, largely for electoral gains, ultimately choosing to retain Muslim personal law. This indecision fueled communal debates, sidelining secular perspectives. The BJP capitalized on this, presenting it as Muslim appeasement, and gained support from the Hindu middle class for a uniform civil code. Consequently, the issue became central to the Hindutva agenda. In a subsequent move, Rajiv Gandhi's government, after passing the Muslim women's bill, acquiesced to Hindu fundamentalists, leading to the reopening of the previously sealed Babri Masjid due to an earlier dispute (Ansari and Ansari 2016).

The reopening of the Babri Masjid was hailed as a victory by Hindus, escalating tensions between communities. In 1984, the Ramjanaki rath procession across North India highlighted the Ram Janam Bhoomi Andolan's push for Lord Rama's "liberation" from Muslim control. The Congress leaned more on religion for electoral benefits, inadvertently fueling Hindu communalism. Nehru had warned at an All India Congress Committee session in New Delhi in May 1958, that the "communalism of the majority is far more dangerous than the communalism of the minority," primarily because it often masquerades as nationalism (Noorani 2015). The BJP, sensing an opportunity, aimed to capitalize on this sentiment to become a dominant political force. It focused on cementing its influence among middle-class Hindus, believing that Hindu nationalism resonated widely and continually nurtured this ideology.

The Ramjanam Bhoomi movement was primarily political. Its intensification, marked by the Rath Yatra, led to numerous communal riots, especially after the Babri Masjid demolition on December 6, 1992. This event triggered violence in major cities. This tragedy, often viewed as a BJP strategy to gain parliamentary seats, resulted in significant loss of life. Consequently, what started as Congress's tactic to recover electoral favor evolved into a wide-reaching communal agenda, impacting national governance, institutions, and societal harmony, and prompting a reevaluation of Nehruvian secularism. The incorporation of communal ideologies within state mechanism is a key factor in the diminishing of secular domains and the growing communal divide in Indian society.

Crisis of Secularism and the Politics of Appeasement

Nehru believed that genuine secularism was crucial for a harmonious modern India. At its core, secularism promotes universal well-being and requires the state to be impartial towards personal beliefs, ensuring religious freedom. India's secularism emphasizes "Sarva dharma samabhav", signifying equal respect for all faiths. This principle, deeply ingrained in the Indian ethos, forbids discrimination on religious, racial, or gender grounds. Gandhi too dreamt of an India marked by religious harmony.

However, over time, Nehru's secular vision was labelled as "pseudo-secularism" and seen as overly accommodating to Muslims (Engineer 2002). A letter from Prime Minister Nehru on October 15, 1947, meant for chief ministers, shows how this debate was noticeable in the early days of India's independence. Nehru writes, "I know there is a perception in the nation that the Central government has been weak and appeasing Muslims" (Thakur 1993). These accusations gained more credibility in post-independence due to Prime Ministers Indira Gandhi and Rajiv Gandhi's attempts to establish "vote banks" along sectarian lines. A series of laws, decisions, and policies cumulatively imposed secularism on the majority community while granting the Muslim minority the right to live by their personal laws. Allowing, for example, Muslim men to practice polygamy feeds the Hindu chauvinists' narrative that Muslims will eventually conquer India (ibid).

The Shah Bano case and the Ayodhya movement serve as critical litmus tests for India's secularism. In 1985, Shah Bano, a 62-year-old Muslim woman, won her Supreme Court case for alimony under Section 125 of the Criminal Procedure Code, triggering outrage among Muslim organizations like AIMPLB (Mody 1987). To quell this, the Rajiv Gandhi government excluded divorced Muslim women from this secular law, garnering accusations of "Muslim appeasement" for electoral gain (Noorani 2015). Concurrently, the government decided to reopen the Babri Masjid in Ayodhya for Hindu worship in 1986, in a bid to appease Hindu sentiments. This move alienated both Muslim and Hindu communities and handed political ammunition to the BJP. Party leader L.K. Advani declared the Shah Bano case a "turning point" for the party (Thakur 1993).

The BJP capitalized on this disaffection, propelling themselves to electoral prominence. Advani's 1990 Ratha Yatra, covering 10,000 kilometers, galvanized Hindu sentiment for the BJP (Engineer 1991; Thakur 1993). The subsequent destruction of Babri Masjid and the ensuing riots compromised secularism's standing in India (Valenta 2018). Claims of "Muslim appeasement" surged following the Sachar report, painting any remedial actions for Muslim backwardness as mere "vote-bank politics" (Ahmed 2019). Despite these manoeuvres, the Muslim community saw no socio-economic upliftment although unsubstantiated, these allegations have significantly eroded India's secular fabric and heightened vulnerabilities and prejudices against Muslims.

The Politics of Majoritarian Communalism: Muslim Marginalisation and Exclusion

Initially perceived primarily as an urban concern, communal ideologies underwent a transformative revelation during the Gujarat riots. These events highlighted the extensive reach of Hindutva forces into rural India. This ideological shift institutionalized through politics, education, media, and state actions, has bolstered communal consciousness (Singh 2018). The demolition of the Babri Masjid in 1992 and the Gujarat pogrom of 2002 serve as salient markers of this escalating bias. Subsequent instances of a series of communal violence, such as the Muzaffarnagar riots in 2013 and the communal violence in North East Delhi in 2020, further corroborate the existence of an alarming pattern. This majoritarianism communalism has drastically influenced India's socio-political landscape, creating rifts between religious communities and making it challenging to foster an inclusive democracy.

Dutch anthropologist Berenschot (2012) contends that these instances, once termed 'riots,' now exhibit the characteristics of 'pogroms.' This semantic shift underscores the premeditated nature of these events and the involvement of extensive and varied networks, ranging from politicians and local criminals to Hindu nationalist activists and even law enforcement agencies. These networks, rather than emerging spontaneously, appear to be pre-existing structures that enable a specific form of violence. This is manifest in instances where political figures, like the BJP leader who openly incited violence during the Delhi communal unrest in 2020, faced no reprimand from the authorities, thus illuminating institutional complicity. This points to an institutional infrastructure that enables, rather than mitigates, communal violence. Consequently, these patterns draw attention to critical vulnerabilities in India's democratic framework, raising questions about the efficacy of the state's mechanisms to protect its diverse citizenry.

It will be illuminating to examine Indian democracy's representational claims by concentrating on the ongoing under-representation of Indian Muslims in the political domain in modern India, in the context of the BJP's electoral and ideological supremacy. As a result of long-term changes in Indian politics, democracy in India has taken a majoritarian turn (Farooqui 2020). The issue of Muslim under-representation, based on the 2014 Parliamentary election and the 2017 UP Assembly election, has become a matter of grave concern (Wolfe et al. 2019; Hasan 2022). In the 2014 election, not a single Member of Parliament (MP) from the Muslim community was elected from India's largest state, Uttar Pradesh, which elects eighty MPs to Lok Sabha. In this election ticket distribution policy in Uttar Pradesh, the deliberate exclusion of Muslims is aimed at denying them from becoming part of the political power structure and policy-making processes, emphasizing Hindutva reasoning and the exclusion of Muslims from the polity.

The message from the 2017 UP assembly election was clear that the Muslim vote does not matter, signaling the absolute marginalization and electoral exclusion of Muslims from the political sphere. Coming back of the BJP with a thumping majority in 2019 has expanded the political space for the Hindutva regime and expedited the Muslim community's political exit, denying them spaces in decision-making and governance; and shrinking the political space for Muslims.

In this environment of majoritarian communalism, Muslims live in a state of constant anxiety and apprehension. While some Muslim-centric media outlets endeavor to bring these issues to the forefront, mainstream media often exhibits a concerning neglect. This oversight has perpetuated a rising tide of Islamophobia, resulting in the social marginalization of Muslims and an encroachment on their socio-economic opportunities. This prevailing atmosphere not only emphasizes the widening divide between religious communities but also calls into question the viability of maintaining a genuinely inclusive and democratic society in India. Events like the Dharam Sansads in Haridwar in December 2021 which target and vilify Muslims, have catalyzed organized attacks against Muslim neighborhoods. These attacks showcase patterns of social exclusion and display pronounced anti-Muslim rhetoric. The constant targeting of Muslims in recurrent sectarian riots, paralleled by their socio-economic marginalization, has eroded the very fabric of coexistence.

Muslim Ghettoization and Spatial Segregation in Post-Gujarat Riot India

The proliferation of the BJP and its Hindutva ideology has precipitated a marked geographical separation between Hindu and Muslim communities, intensified by persistent threats and attacks against Muslims. This has driven many to seek refuge in Muslim-dominant areas, while Hindus in those regions have migrated to Hindu-dominant neighborhoods (Jaffrelot and Gayer 2012). This segregation extends beyond areas that have experienced communal riots; it's a widespread phenomenon. The ideological aftermath of communal violence intensifies mutual distrust and fear between communities, leading to long-lasting and pervasive effects. Such repercussions perpetuate stereotypes and fuel longstanding prejudices, reinforcing a cycle of suspicion and animosity that persists.

This intensification of rifts between Hindus and Muslims has led to abrupt spatial segregation, in stark contrast to previous generations of harmonious coexistence. Muslims increasingly find solace in ethnic enclaves, creating "cities within cities," commonly referred to as "Muslim ghettos" by academics, media, and politicians (Sengupta 2005; Ramachandran 2020; Anand 2016). This self-imposed isolation, far from being spontaneous, has been expedited by recurrent communal violence and a pervasive sense of "othering," resulting in consistent social ostracization and reinforcing a trajectory of self-segregation among Muslims. Our own Study on Muslim ghettos in Delhi and Meerut has reaffirmed this trajectory, illustrating that while some Muslims have chosen to reside in safer neighborhoods, others have been compelled due to an inability to rent or purchase property in mixed communities. The resultant migration has steered them towards Muslim-majority regions, which unfortunately lack homogeneity in socio-economic dynamics.

State-sponsored violence, historical biases, and pressing security concerns have collectively nudged the Muslim minority toward urban segregation. The Sachar Committee report candidly highlights the increasing phenomenon of Muslims seeking refuge in ghettos, especially in cities with recurrent communal incidents. This ghettoization, despite providing an ephemeral sense of safety, has had a plethora of adverse implications like inadequate infrastructure, diminishing inter-community interactions, and restricted economic opportunities (SCR 2006). The Pew Research Centre (2022) report highlighted Hindutva politics' impact on India's societal norms, indicating a form of religious tolerance that avoids inter-faith interactions. This is evident when Muslims face property restrictions in non-Muslim areas. Hansen's 2022 study on Ahmedabad's ghettoization notes that while previous differences were cultural, today's divides stem from fear and distrust.

This transformation has redefined the geographical contours of caste and community in ways that are without historical parallel, crystallizing political allegiances along territorial lines more sharply than ever before. In addition, socio-religious divisions have restructured daily routines and preferences, affecting everything from leisure activities to consumer habits and general mobility within urban spaces. As Nandy (1997) insightfully observes, the rise of religiously segregated housing not only impedes India's comprehensive growth but also marks the erosion of a once-intimate and organically integrated socio-cultural fabric.

Media and Cultural Imperialism: Process of Othering and Demonization

Cultural imperialism marginalizes minority groups, rendering them as the "Other" and subjecting them to stereotypes (Young 1990). The BJP's rise and its Hindu-majoritarian stance have intensified the public demonization of Muslims, aligning with their agenda of a Hindu Rashtra (Sikander 2020). Post-2014 sectarian rifts birthed the notion of an 'abstract Muslim,' a stereotyped target for zealous Hindus.

Victims, like alleged beef-carrying drivers or skull cap wearers, face hostility fueled by a desire for nationalistic validation on social media platforms popular among Hindu nationalists (Featherstone et al. 2019).

Recent nationwide trends have seen increased attacks on Muslims, with these acts often celebrated and justified as a form of assertive Hinduism. Ghassem-Fachandi (2012) discussed the era of "perverse permission" after events like the 2002 Gujarat pogrom, where rumors and manipulated images of sectarian strife spread rapidly, magnifying their repercussions. Tambiah (1996) noted that localized events could now incite unrest on a national scale due to the reach of social media.

RSS organisations such as the Bharatiya Gau Raksha Dal, have been actively promoting and instigating violence, targeting Muslims and Dalits over beef consumption and cow slaughter. The ABVP, associated with the RSS, engages in student altercations, with Hindutva proponents employing platforms like WhatsApp to spread hatred and misinformation. A study by Soma Basu on pro-BJP WhatsApp groups, inclusive of BJP assembly and IT cell members, disclosed 25% of the content as anti-Muslim (Saha et al. 2021).

Obtaining reliable hate crime data is increasingly difficult. Previous media monitoring has ceased, and the National Crime Records Bureau (NCRB) excluded minority and dissident data in its 2017 report (Schultz 2019). However, Basu (2021) provided credible evidence of a rise in religious hate crimes following the BJP's 2014 electoral win. Utilizing data from the Citizen's Religious Hate Crime Watch and the Election Commission, Basu found a 76% increase in such crimes from 2009–2013 to 2014–2018. While crimes against Christians and Sikhs declined, those against Muslims escalated from 36 to 83%. This trend was most prevalent in states where the BJP had significant electoral success, potentially due to lax law enforcement by BJP-led governments (Basu 2021)

Hindu communal ideologies effectively perpetuate this negative image incidents of mob lynching, threats from the CAA and the NRC, communal violence, and conspiracy theories like "Corona jihad" and "love jihad" have contributed to a sense of alienation (Mohammad-Arif et al. 2020). The height of communalism in our society was intense during the COVID-19 pandemic introduced new dimensions of social exclusion. The Tablighi Jamaat was unfairly charged with spreading the virus, while conspiracy theories like "Corona Jihad" circulated widely. Calls for a social and economic boycott of Muslims using hashtags like #QuranVirus and #IslamicVirus further exacerbated the situation (Sikandar 2020). The international community condemned India for repressing such negative forces during a vulnerable time. Key policy decisions, such as the abrogation of Article 370, the introduction of the NRC and CAA, the criminalization of Triple Talaq, and the construction of the Ayodhya temple, have targeted Indian Muslims, leaving them feeling humiliated and abandoned (Biswas 2020).

Beyond politics, Muslim clothing and food habits have also been stigmatized. Politicians have used clothing to stereotype individuals, further polarizing communities (Kumar 2019). Election rallies have become platforms for demonizing the Muslim community, with references to "Babur's sons" and appeals to Hindutva nationalism. Dog whistle politics and "Politics of distance and deniability" are employed to advance the BJP's agenda (Mahmudabad 2020). The BJP's saffronization efforts, including promoting the concept of Love Jihad, Ghar Wapsi, and reforming Muslims, threaten to deepen divisions within society. The continuous stigmatization and stereotyping of Muslims have alienated a significant portion of the population. Experts warn that this alienation could lead to increased conservatism and radicalization, which is not in India's best interest (Biswas 2020). This situation calls for serious examination, as it questions India's commitment to inclusive democracy. The consistent marginalization of Muslims in social, political, and economic areas challenges the core values of Indian democracy.

Dismantling Communalism: Confronting the Normalization of Violence

Scholars and secular intellectuals have increasingly expressed concerns about the societal normalization of violence, particularly in relation to how prevailing systems perpetuate and enable aggression. In India, the everyday acceptance of Hindu nationalist violence warrants close scrutiny. Hannah Arendt's seminal work on the banality of evil offers a framework for understanding how bureaucratic structures can dehumanize individuals, making heinous acts seem routine and even obligatory. Scholars like Gyanendra Pandey and Zygmunt Bauman have extended this concept to modern nation-states. Populist demagogues and religious nationalists, especially right-wing Hindu extremists, have excelled at normalizing violence. They depict the majority community as victims, thus framing retaliatory violence as morally justifiable, a tactic that obscures the aggressors' responsibility (Pandey 2006).

This manipulation has been notably active in Hindutva politics, which has revamped its anti-Muslim agenda to vilify every aspect of Muslim life in India as incompatible with Hindu norms and national identity. The tactics include accusing Muslims of eating beef as anti-Hindu and anti-national, claiming Muslim men practice 'love-jihad' to convert Hindu girls, and the assertion that they offer namaz on streets to transform public areas into mosque domains (Ahmed 2019) and even suggesting that Muslim couples aim to out-populate Hindus. These narratives lead to real-world violence against Muslims, including pogroms, lynching, and online harassment, compromising Indian secularism and escalating communal tension. This climate of dissonance and violence allows for a culture of impunity, supported by various legal, political, and religious frameworks.

Legal theorist Julia Eckert's (2006) discourse on the imbrication of India's laws with preconceived notions of violence offers a crucial perspective. She contends that there exists an inherent double standard that criminalizes Muslim violence as premeditated fanaticism while recasting Hindu violence as a 'natural reaction.' This inherent bias lays bare the tacit acceptance and naturalization of Hindu majoritarian anger. Such institutionalization has multi-faceted implications. It not only enforces upper-caste Hindu hegemony but also reframes Hindu nationalism as synonymous with Indian nationalism.

It is evident that communalism is a product of a more entrenched ideology; it is destructive and pervasive, separating communities and fostering polarisations based on primordial identities, caste, religion, and race. The persistent stereotyping and stigmatization of India's Muslim community have resulted in their marginalization and exclusion, aiding the BJP's cultural nationalism agenda. However, alienating such a substantial population carries risks of increased radicalism. It is essential to address this issue to prevent further division in Indian society. The narrative of "Us vs. Them" must be replaced with a more inclusive approach to ensure the well-being and unity of the nation.

The concept of institutional communalism sheds light on both the widespread influence of Hindu dominance across various institutions and the depth of Hindu domination within these institutions (Singh 2018). It underscores the profound inequality in power relations between the majority Hindu community and religious minorities. Sometimes, this perspective goes even further, suggesting that majority Hindu communalism is merely a reaction to minority communalism. However, a key flaw in this argument is its failure to acknowledge the substantial power imbalance between the majority and the minority.

Regardless of whether it emerges from majority or minority communities, communalism stands in stark contrast to the foundational tenets of secularism and equal citizenship, central to the design of pluralistic democracies. Majority communalism, in particular, carries a distinct weight. By virtue of representing a larger segment of the population, its potential to incite tensions is amplified, endangering harmonious coexistence with minority groups. Such a trajectory imperils the commitment to religious and cultural pluralism, thus underscoring the imperative of safeguarding democratic values to ensure a more inclusive and cohesive future.

This requires borrowing from best practices globally, such as equal opportunity initiatives that have proven effective in mitigating racism and sexism. By forcing us to look beyond superficial acts of discrimination to the systemic structures that enable them, it provides the tools not just for critique but for meaningful, and enduring change.

Further combating majoritarian communalism in authoritarian contexts requires a multi-pronged approach that goes beyond typical political and legal avenues. Singh (2018) and Pandya (2010) have emphasized the proactive role civil society can play in fostering social harmony. Being proactive means not just responding to instances of communal flare-ups but continually working to build a culture of tolerance and inclusion through serving as a bridge between governments and citizens' Interfaith Initiatives. This proactive approach supports Habermas's (1991) notion of the public sphere, where civil society is instrumental in shaping collective opinions, values, and social norms.

India stands as a distinguished epitome of a syncretic culture, wherein esteemed luminaries such as Gandhi, Buddha, Nanak, Dara Shikoh, and Kabir have bequeathed a profound intellectual heritage, extolling values of social harmony, compassion, and unity. Amidst a backdrop of escalating social discord, these iconic figures present a moral compass, steering society towards a more inclusive paradigm.

The teachings of Gandhi, emphasizing non-violence, Buddha's philosophy rooted in compassion, Nanak's relentless advocacy for egalitarianism, and Kabir's poetic verses championing unity collectively serve as poignant reminders of our shared human essence. Dara Shikoh, a visionary of his time, aspired to cultivate a syncretic society by fostering open dialogues and mutual respect among diverse religions. His seminal work, "Majma Ul Bahrain (The Mingling of Two Oceans)," assumes paramount importance as a guide for interfaith harmony. His dialogical approach, prioritizing spirituality over ritualistic practices, cultivated an environment of trust and coexistence, leaving an indelible legacy in advocating religious inclusivity within the Indian context.

To recalibrate its societal compass to value religious diversity as an asset rather than a divisive liability, India must adopt a sustained, integrative approach. By integrating principles of diversity and harmony into education, discourse, and policy, India has the potential to reclaim its heritage as a symbol of social harmony and drive meaningful societal transformation. This aspiration is urgent and promising, offering a pathway to overcome societal divisions.

References

Ahmad I (1969) Secularism and communalism. Econ Polit Weekly *4*(28/30):1137–1158. http://www.jstor.org/stable/40739868

Ahmed H (2019) Siyasi Muslim: a story of political islams in India. Penguin Viking, India

Anand D (2016) Hindu nationalism in India and the politics of fear. Springer

Ansari AA (2012) Communalisation of Indian society: a sociological analysis. Aakar Publications

Ansari AA, Ansari IA (2016) Being a minority in India: issues and challenges. AlterNotes Press

Bagchi AK (1984) Towards a political economy of planning in India. Contrib Polit Econ 3(1):15–38

Basu D (2021) Majoritarian politics and hate crimes against religious minorities: evidence from India, 2009–2018. World Dev 146:105540

Berenschot W (2012) The spatial distribution of riots: Patronage and the instigation of communal violence in Gujarat, India. *World Development* 39(2): 221–230

Biswas S (2020) "Babri Mosque: India's Muslims feel more abandoned than ever. The BBC online, September 30. https://www.bbc.com/news/amp/world-asia-india-54356713. Accessed 4 Oct 2020

Brass PR (1996) Introduction: discourses of ethnicity, communalism, and violence. Riots and pogroms. Palgrave Macmillan, London, UK, pp 1–55

Brass PR (2003) The Production of Hindu-Muslim violence in Contemporary India. University of Washington Press, Seattle, WA

Pew Research Centre (2022) Religion in India: tolerance and segregation, March 3. https://www.pewforum.org/2021/06/29/religion-in-india-tolerance-and-segregation/. Accessed 13 Mar 2022

Raheel D, Michael B (2012) The political logic of ethnic violence: the Muslim pogrom in Gujarat, 2002 ANI. Polit Soc 40(4):483–516

Eckert J (2006) From subjects to citizens: legalism from below and the homogenisation of the legal sphere. J Legal Pluralism Unofficial Law 38(53–54):45–75

Engineer AA (1991) The bloody trail: Ramjanmabhoomi and communal violence in UP. Econ Polit Weekly 26(4):155–159. http://www.jstor.org/stable/4397237

Engineer AA (2002) Gujarat riots in the light of the history of communal violence. Econ Polit Weekly 37(50):5047–5054. http://www.jstor.org/stable/4412966

Farooqui A (2020) Political representation of a minority: Muslim representation in contemporary India. India Rev 19(2):153–175

Featherstone D, Björkdahl A, Chatterjee I, Jazeel T, Williams P (2019) Everyday peace? Politics, citizenship and Muslim lives in India, Philippa Williams, Wiley Blackwell, RGS-IBG Book Series

Ghassem-Fachandi P (2012) Pogrom in Gujarat: Hindu nationalism and anti-Muslim violence in India. Princeton University Press

Habermas J (1991) The structural transformation of the public sphere: an inquiry into a category of bourgeois society. MIT Press

Hasan M (1998) Memories of a fragmented nation: rewriting the histories of India's partition. Econ Polit Weekly 33(41):2662–2668. http://www.jstor.org/stable/4407270

Hasan Z (2022) Majoritarian politics and the representation of India's Muslims. In: Politics of representation: historically disadvantaged groups in India's democracy. Springer Nature Singapore, Singapore, pp 143–159

Jaffrelot C (2019) The fate of secularism in India—the BJP in power: Indian democracy and Religious Nationalism. https://carnegieendowment.org/2019/04/04/fate-of-secularism-in-india-pub-78689. Accessed 23 Jan 2022

Jaffrelot C, Gayer L (2012) Muslims in Indian cities: trajectories of marginalisation. Columbia University Press, p 320

Jha S (2014) 'Unfinished business': historic complementarities, political competition and ethnic violence in Gujarat. J Econ Behav Organ 104:18–36

Kohli A (1990) Democracy and discontent: India's growing crisis of governability. Cambridge University Press

Kothari R (1989) Cultural context of communalism in India. Econ Polit Weekly 81–85

Kumar M (2019) 'Can See Who's Violent by Their Clothes': PM on citizenship act protests. NDTV, December 15. https://www.ndtv.com/india-news/pm-modi-says-congratulate-brothers-and-sisters-of-assam-for-keeping-away-from-violence-theyre-making-2149157. Accessed 17 Aug 2020

Kumar R (ed) (1990) Problem of communalism in India. Mittal Publications

Mahmudabad A (2020) Indian Muslims and the anti-CAA protests: from marginalization towards exclusion, December 15. https://journals.openedition.org/samaj/6701?lang=fr. Accessed 28 Feb 2022

Mody NB (1987) The press in India: the Shah Bano judgment and its aftermath. Asian Surv 27(8):935–953. https://doi.org/10.2307/2644865

Mohammad-Arif A, Naudet J, Jaoul N (2020) The Hindutva turn: authoritarianism and resistance in India. South Asia Multidisc Acad J (24/25)

Nandy A (1997) The twilight of certitudes: Secularism, Hindu nationalism, and other masks of deculturation. Alternatives 22(2):157–176

Noorani AG (2015) Shah Bano & ayodhya, 11–15. Frontline. https://frontline.thehindu.com/the-nation/shah-bano-amp-ayodhya/article7912320.ece

Pai S, Kumar S (2018) Everyday communalism: riots in contemporary Uttar Pradesh

Pandey G (2006) Routine violence: nations, fragments, histories. Stanford University Press

Pandya A (2010) Muslim Indians: struggle for inclusion. The Henry L. Stimson Center, Washington, DC, pp 1–63

Panikar KN (1993) Culture and communalism. Soc Sci 24–31

Ramachandran S (2020) Hindutva violence in India: trends and Implications. Counter Terrorist Trends Analyses 12(4):15–20. https://www.jstor.org/stable/26918077

Rehman M (2016) Communalism in postcolonial India: changing contours. Routledge, New Delhi

Rehman M (2018) Rise of Saffron power: reflections in Indian Politics. Routledge, New Delhi

Saha P, Mathew B, Garimella K, Mukherjee A (2021) "Short is the Road that Leads from Fear to Hate": fear speech in Indian WhatsApp Groups. In: Proceedings of the web conference 2021, pp 1110–1121

Schultz K (2019) Murders of religious minorities in India go unpunished, report finds. The New York Times. Published on 18 February

SCR (2006) Implementation of Sachar committee recommendations (status ... https://minorityaffairs.gov.in/sites/default/files/Follow-up-Sachar.pdf. Accessed 1 Mar 2022

Sen A (1987) Gender and cooperative conflicts

Sengupta R (2005) Communal violence in India: perspectives on causative factors. Econ Polit Weekly 40(20):2046–2050. http://www.jstor.org/stable/4416640

Shaban A (2012) Lives of Muslims in India. Routledge, New Delhi

Sikander Z (2020) Indian media is waging a holy war against Muslims. It acts like Hyenas, April 13. https://theprint.in/opinion/indian-media-waging-holy-war-against-muslims-hyenas/400407/. Accessed 10 Feb 2022

Singh P (2018) Institutional communalism in India. In: Communalism in postcolonial India. Routledge India, pp 78–100

Tambiah SJ (1996) Leveling crowds: ethnonationalist conflicts and collective violence in South Asia, vol 10. University of California Press

Thakur R (1993) Ayodhya and the politics of India's secularism: a double-standards discourse. Asian Surv 33(7):645–664. https://doi.org/10.2307/2645353

Valenta M (2018) The Muslims as victim, the Muslims as agent: on Islam as a category of analysis. In: 1802898942 1269264204 Shaban A (Author), Lives of Muslims in India: politics, exclusion and violence. Routledge, New Delhi, India, pp 35–65

Van der Veer P (2015) Communalism. In: International encyclopedia of the social & behavioral sciences, 2nd edn

Vanaik A (1997) The furies of Indian communalism: religion, modernity, and secularization. Verso

Wolfe D, Kopf D, Thaker A (2019) Why is Muslim political representation declining in India?, June 3. https://qz.com/india/1617067/indian-election-2019-why-few-muslims-make-it-to-the-lok-sabha/. Accessed 20 Feb 2022

Young IM (1990) Five faces of oppression. In: Rethinking power, pp 174–195

Chapter 14
The Conundrum of Being a Feminist Pedagogue in a Gender Studies Classroom

Leena Pujari

Abstract Based on a classroom ethnography of teaching Sociology of Gender over a decade and a half, this paper explores the troubled relationship between feminism and gender. It documents the conflicts and dilemmas that confront a feminist pedagogue and asks why being a feminist sociologist in a gender studies classroom or even a sociology classroom is fraught with all kinds of risks. It is not easy being a feminist teacher. Why are we so apologetic about disseminating feminist messages? Why do we bend over backwards to justify that we are 'kind' feminists? That we mean good, we are family-oriented.

Keywords Feminism · Pedagogy · Intersectionality · Classroom · Reflexivity

Introduction

It has been one hundred years of doing Sociology in India and this offers an opportune moment for us, as pedagogues to reflect on how we have been practicing our craft. This paper emanates from a classroom ethnography of having taught gender studies not just to students of sociology but also to students across disciplines, over two decades and I draw significantly from my conversations with students, colleagues, and academic mentors. As pedagogues, we come from different social locations and we cater to a diverse student community, thus, our approaches to knowledge-making are bound to be different. (Haraway 1988). What I write here, comes from my specific location of being a feminist sociologist in a South Mumbai college and my experiences of teaching both undergraduate and postgraduate students of Sociology. This is a work in progress as I navigate new terrains in my academic journey.

One question that we as sociologists, have not engaged with enough, is our relationship with the discipline. For instance, how do we relate to our disciplines? What are the points of convergence and discontents? How are the discontents channelized

L. Pujari (✉)
Department of Sociology, KC College, HSNC University, Mumbai, Maharashtra, India
e-mail: leena.pujari@kccollege.edu.in

A. Chauhan et al. (eds.), *Hundred Years of Sociology in India: Evolving Issues, Emerging Trends*, https://doi.org/10.1007/978-981-96-1317-5_14

into newer perspectives and innovative pedagogic practices? After all, teaching is an embodied process and we bring our whole selves into classrooms (hooks 1994 and Smith 1987). Self-reflexive journeys, therefore, are necessary, though the educational structures that we inhabit today, driven primarily by a neo-liberal logic, would have us uphold a mind/body split, a disconnect between our public and private lives.

Sociology and the Margins

The discipline of Sociology has been critiqued for privileging a 'view from above' (Xaxa 1999; Oommen 2013; Kumar 2016) and its inability to draw significantly from the margins. Scholars and academics have spoken about the silences, absences, and omissions in the way sociological knowledge has been constructed and I think this is something unique to our discipline, that it enables a process of reflection and course correction. Feminist sociologists too have mounted a strong critique of the patriarchal nature of the discipline with calls for a reconceptualization of the dominant theories and paradigms from a feminist perspective. They sought to mainstream gender concerns in the methodologies, epistemologies, and pedagogical practices within sociology (Chaudhuri 2002; Poonacha 2003 Rege 2003; Chadha 2018; Pujari 2018).

In due course, this critique extended to the heteronormative bias within sociology and the absences and silences on marginalized genders, and the lack of an intersectional focus within sociology (Kumar 2014; Pujari 2019). As Cressida Heyes (2003, p. 2) writes, 'feminist politics needs to speak to many more subjects than just men and women'. While we do speak to many more subjects other than gender, like the subaltern groups of Dalits and tribals and the lower classes, we have not adequately represented the concerns of those in gender-marginal locations. Even when we do, we see them simply as a monolith without attempting to locate interpenetrating axes of oppression within them. For instance, what does it mean to be Dalit, gay, and poor or to be a Muslim and a hijra? What explains these silences and omissions? Can they be located in the largely positivist, functionalist framework that continues to inform our classroom teaching and research methodologies?

The Self and the Discipline

When I started teaching, I was perhaps one of those teachers who used a positivist, functionalist framework in my classrooms. A descriptive, monologic, pedagogy, based on facts drawn from books and what we would refer to as valid sources of knowledge. Over some time, I experienced a sense of discomfort and unease about what I was doing and wondered, whether what I taught connected with the lived realities of my students. I began to notice the gaps in sociological knowledge and asked myself a series of questions, primary among them being, why am I teaching? Every time I enter a classroom, I ask myself 'what am I supposed to do as a pedagogue and how am I supposed to do that? Is my job simply to disseminate the received knowledge or is it also about constructing a non–normative discourse that not only sensitizes students to multiple axes of marginalization and discrimination but also encourages them to raise questions, even when that produces some discomfort. As Freire (1970) asks, is teaching simply about knowledge dissemination, or is it about creating the possibilities of production or construction of knowledge? The classroom and campuses must be enabling and empowering spaces that propel students to re-think and re-imagine the 'standard, the norm, and the given' and construct a transformative vision of the world (Freire 1970; hooks 1994). Driven by this compelling desire to teach for praxis, I began to explore pedagogies that would enable this transformation.

I found myself drawn to feminism and feminist pedagogical practices. Built around the idea of collaborative classroom spaces, use of an intersectional lens in theorizing, disrupting the hierarchy between teacher and students, co-production of knowledge, reflexivity and interrogation of privileges and the need for praxis, feminist pedagogies make for emancipatory and safe classrooms (Shrewsbury 1987; hooks 1994; Chari Wagh 2023). Feminist classrooms are truly invigorating. They open up various possibilities and inaugurate 'new ways of knowing'. Feminist epistemologies with their emphasis on lived experiences, critical dialogue, and an ethics of care and empathy have been very enriching. For instance, my understanding of trans identities and the exclusions and silences of queer spaces in our curriculum, pedagogies, and campuses were brought home to me by my students. While this mode of engagement with the curriculum and the students has produced an enriching classroom environment, it has not been without challenges. I often find myself asking difficult questions for which there are no easy answers.

If feminism is about reflection and self-introspection, do I mark my privileges when I enter a classroom? Am I conscious of my positionality as a savarna, able-bodied and cisgender woman? Even as I speak about praxis and action, do I understand that each one's struggle is different and there cannot be a 'one size fits all' approach? Can I be a feminist pedagogue or teach feminism without being a feminist in my everyday life? What does it mean to be a feminist teacher within the larger institutional framework that may not be overtly anti-feminist but certainly harbors skepticism about feminism and its practices? Very often our institutional norms run contrary to our feminist ideals. How do I challenge everyday sexism including academic misogyny?

Doing gender studies is fraught with all kinds of risks. As a gender studies practitioner, am I not supposed to invoke feminism in the classroom? How else does one teach gender? The mere inclusion of gender-related topics in the curriculum would not by itself generate a feminist consciousness. What is also required are the necessary pedagogic shifts. I soon realized that it was not easy being a feminist and the self-disclosure certainly did not ease matters. I have been told a couple of times, especially while addressing students and teachers from certain constituencies that I should avoid using the word 'feminist' or avoid talking too much about feminism while speaking on gender issues. I have been quite appalled. How does one do that? Is it safer being a gender studies teacher than being a feminist teacher? Perhaps safer to talk about gender equality than feminism. Sometimes though not often, I find myself self-censoring, hence the 'conundrum' that I refer to above.

Greene (as cited in hooks 1984, p. 22) finds it curious that many women who believe in everything that proud feminists believe in, dismiss the term 'feminist' as something unpleasant; something they do not wish to be associated with, even when they acknowledge that they have benefited from feminist-generated reform measures which have improved their lives.

It is indeed paradoxical that a liberatory and progressive ideology is perceived as intimidating. Is it because, as Barbara Smith (1983) says, feminism asks difficult questions about how we live, and how we treat each other, and questions the most intimate of all relations, that between a man and a woman? According to bell hooks (1984, p. 29), the statement 'I am a feminist' suggests a kind of absolutism and preconceived notions of identity, role, and behavior. On the other hand, if we say 'I advocate feminism' the response is usually 'What is feminism?' and is more accepting. These troubling questions triggered a deeper engagement with feminism and an understanding of commonsensical assumptions around feminism especially among students. Besides teaching Sociology of Gender, I also offer a certificate course in Gender Studies at the department which is open to students across all disciplines. Conceptualized in 2014, in response to a felt need for a critical engagement with gender issues on campus and aimed at raising a critical feminist perspective, this course has offered penetrating insights into students' perceptions of feminism. What I discuss below is an attempt to comprehend this 'conundrum', the anxieties and confusions about feminisms.

Commonsense Perceptions of Feminism and the Politics of Naming

Feminism as a term is mired in all kinds of conflicting interpretations and often invites cynicism. I begin my classes on feminism by asking students about their perceptions of feminism. The responses are diverse ranging from 'feminism is too radical' 'against men and family' 'is only about women', 'is about trashing men' to 'equality between men and women but more importance is given to women' and about 'gender equality'. The question 'Would you call yourself a feminist' elicits an interesting array of responses. The responses range from 'I believe in everything that feminism stands for but would not label myself a feminist because I do not want to be trolled, or referred to as a feminazi, or perceived to be too liberating and against familial ideals' or 'I believe in humanism, not feminism,' or 'I am a feminist but not of the extreme kind.' Of all the responses the last one intrigues me a lot.

How does one explain the negative connotations that underpin an understanding of not just a rich and varied body of thought but also a way of life? hooks (2000) writes that this happens because most of the knowledge about feminism comes not from a reading of feminist texts or association with feminist academics but from media. This is so true of the times we live in. Most of the noise around feminism emanates from an uninformed, motivated understanding propelled by parts of social media. A recent study by Agarwal et al. (2022) pointed out how an anti-feminist movement is on X (earlier twitter) the popular social media platform. Arnav, one of the mass media student participants of the gender course 2022 put it aptly.

> *Before taking up this course all my knowledge on the topic came from social media, and while it is a great medium for education and awareness, it also houses half-knowledge and half-baked opinions. Having live sessions with people on the frontlines: activists, educators, and lawyers, was something else.*

hooks also blames the early feminists for the anti-men sentiment and for not being inclusive of diverse identities. She refers to early feminism as 'lifestyle feminism' (1984, p. 27) which was more of an individual and class-based movement than a critical political consciousness based on certain beliefs and ideas. Perhaps we need to travel back in time to find an answer to this vexed question of why feminism is perceived as anti-men. After all, concepts and theories arise in a certain context, a specific historical location. They are not static; they evolve and therefore we must be mindful of how they travel through time and settle into our syllabi (Chaudhuri 2022). For instance, feminism of the nineteenth and twentieth centuries was very different from the way we understand feminism today. It has travelled a great distance since the Seneca Falls Convention of 1848 which marked the beginnings of the women's movement. Over the years it has been enriched by a diversity of voices and positions. But we hear less of this evolution and reflexivity characteristic of feminisms and feminist movements and more of the 'anti-men' sentiment. As one of the students from the course said:

During the sessions, many students expressed immense hatred towards men, because of obvious reasons. And as much as their rage is justified, demeaning the other gender, expressing that the term 'men' should not exist at all is entirely against what feminism stands for.

It is a fact that the early women's movement was about 'women' alone and there was a certain context to this. Born out of a certain marginalization within the anti-slavery convention of 1840, where women were not allowed to speak and were asked to be mute spectators, Elizabeth Cady Stanton and Lucretia Mott who were active in the abolitionist movement in America, decided to keep men out of conversations around advancing the cause of women. In 1848, they organized a women's convention in Seneca Falls, New York, and campaigned for rights, including the vote, for women and blacks (Davis 1981). But somewhere along the way, feminism became an exclusionary movement, centered around the concerns of white middle-class women in the West. It failed to extend its boundaries to all women on equal terms. Black, working-class, lesbian, trans and bisexual, disabled, Western, and non-Christian women have often been shut out of what theorist Brazilian scholar Heleith Saffioti (1967) has termed 'bourgeoisie feminism' (as cited in hooks 1984, p.20).

However, feminism as an ideology and a movement has been open to these criticisms and has attempted to course-correct. The efforts of black women/women of colour to challenge and deconstruct the category "woman," the insistence on recognition that gender is not the sole factor determining the construction of femaleness was a critical intervention that led to a profound revolution in feminist thought, one that truly interrogated and disrupted the hegemonic feminist theory produced primarily by academic women, most of whom were white.

Many Feminisms

If we believe that the resistance to feminism stems from a flawed understanding of feminism, then we need to pitch the idea of many feminisms and not just one. Feminism speaks with many voices and there is a diversity of feminist positions. This enriches the movement and should not be seen as a weakness of the movement. Feminism has been understood and theorized by several scholars and feminist writers over the years, but one that has stayed with me and I believe is profound, is that of black feminist scholar, writer, and activist bell hooks. This is the feminism that I use in my classrooms. In her book 'Feminism is for Everybody' (2000, p. vii, viii) hooks asks why feminism is so unpopular. It is certainly not what people imagine it to be. 'A bunch of angry women who want to be like men' or 'a group of man-hating lesbians'. For her, feminism is a movement to end sexism, sexist exploitation, and control (institutionalized sexism). hooks debunked the idea of common oppressions based on a biological identity. It was certainly not a movement of women against men for according to her, we all can be patriarchal and can be active or passive participants in perpetuating sexism. Instead, hooks believed that feminism is a fight against patriarchy and systemic biases.

For hooks, feminism meant an understanding of the interconnected nature of oppressions. She imagined a world of peace and possibility, free from all forms of hegemony. She firmly believed that a feminist revolution alone would not create this world. We need to end imperialism, classism, racism, and if I may stretch this further casteism and ableism as well. She was critical of the idea of women's liberation or gender equality. Feminism was certainly not about 'becoming like men' or asking for social and political rights for women equal to those of men. Black women in America and Dalit women in India forcefully argued against equating women with men when men themselves are oppressed by the scourge of racism or casteism.

Similarly, for Menon (2013) feminism is not about women but about recognizing how modern discourses of gender produce human beings as exclusively men or women. It is not about gender alone but about understanding how gender is complicated by our social location be they caste, class, race, ableism, queer politics. Both hooks and Menon emphasize intersectional feminism.

Another text that is particularly useful in feminist classrooms is Sara Ahmed's 'Living a Feminist Life' (2017). She asks what it means to be a feminist. Unlike other theories, feminism is something that one lives. It is personal and involves a politicized understanding of one's lived realities. It raises questions about how to live better in an unjust and unequal world, how to create relationships with others that are equal; how to find ways to support those who are not supported or are less supported by social systems. Intersectionality is a starting point, the point from which we must proceed if we are to offer an account of how power works. Feminism will be intersectional "or it will be bullshit," to borrow from the eloquence of Flavia Dzodan (as cited in Ahmed 2017). She further argues that feminism has a critical political consciousness that seeks to change society and is easily co-opted if it is not rooted in a political commitment to a mass-based feminist movement. Feminism is necessary because of what has not ended: sexism, sexual exploitation, and sexual oppression. (Ahmed 2017). However, these versions of feminism do not enter our classrooms as much as the works of early feminists do.

The Gendered Sociological Canon

I am quite flummoxed by the tensions and contradictions inherent in the syllabi and pedagogies of sociology courses. While I am expected to use a gender lens in teaching Sociology of Gender, to use a similar lens in other courses say for instance Social Theory or Research Methodology invites skepticism. An interrogation of epistemic frameworks is especially unwelcome. What is resisted is a radical reconceptualization of our gendered canons. For instance, the sociological canon is full of misogyny. Auguste Comte, one of the early founders and a positivist believed that a woman is inferior and should be naturally subservient to men as this was good for social stability. Interestingly he also opined that since a woman is the epitome of humanity, her mission was to humanize modern men. Women, as wives and mothers, provide the essential basis for the rejuvenation of a society plagued with alienated, morally and sexually unstable men. He makes a comparison to the animal kingdom and says just as among animals, among humans too, men are superior to women intellectually, physically, and practically.

Similarly, for Emile Durkheim, the evolutionary scale is characterized by increasing differentiation between men and women. While men move close to civilization, women lag behind. Men and women are both body and soul, corporeal and embodied, and have the social (read society) embedded in them. While men can overcome this tussle between senses and morals which is essentially social, women are unable to overcome or resist the pull of the senses. Hence women lag behind in the civilizational discourse. Durkheim assumes, and builds his theory on, the veracity of accounts of absolute sexual difference drawn from such 'sciences' as craniometry, as well as biological accounts of 'drives' and 'instincts.' (Witz and Marshall 2004).

As a feminist teacher am I not supposed to interrogate the gendered canon? To not do so would amount to what Gordon (2006, p. 591) calls 'disciplinary decadence' and Rabaka (2010, p. 13) refers to as 'epistemic closure', where we reify our discipline and leave no room for a re-imagination of our disciplinary canon based on insights drawn from outside our disciplines. The absences and silences in our syllabi are too glaring to be missed. Where are the women sociologists in early sociological thought? Harriet Martineau, Marianna Weber, Ida B Wells among others are missing in undergraduate sociology courses in Maharashtra. Even in Indian Sociological Thought, there is an erasure of early women sociologists and their contributions. (Chadha and Joseph 2018). Our research classes especially at the undergraduate level are devoid of feminist research frameworks and epistemologies.

A feminist re-imagination can be extended to a series of themes that are routinely addressed in sociology classrooms from socialization, marriage, and family to migration, displacement, laws, and many more. This might appear to be a daunting task given the new challenges that we face in current times. The neo-liberal logic that drives our education system has pitched the idea about gender equality in ways that have caught the popular imagination but it has been stripped of its radical re-imagination. For instance, a feminist re-imagination of institutions like 'marriage' and 'family' is difficult today given the increasing propensity to glorify and celebrate the patriarchal basis of these institutions. A case in point is the debate on same-sex marriage.

Conclusion

How does one respond to those who harbour misgivings about feminism? It needs a lot of work, sustained and patience to be able to unravel layers of misinformation and distortions. It is not just the classroom where we as pedagogues encounter resistance to feminist ideas but also in spaces outside the classroom, among our colleagues and staff members. At the core of this skepticism and surveillance of feminist ideologies, is the fear that feminism is out to destroy our time-honoured institutions. The act of calling out sexism is in many ways a threat to established social norms. It is an act of feminist policing (Ahmed 2017).

I come back to the question that I raised at the beginning of this essay about the need for self-reflexive essays or auto-ethnographies, where we as pedagogues critically interrogate our 'selves' in relation to our discipline. Such essays detailing classroom experiences across Universities and campuses would make for enriching and engaging sociologies, bringing to the fore new challenges and newer perspectives. Contrary to the popular perception of feminism being a Western construct, most of us find our feminisms through a politicized understanding of our complex social realities. Feminist pedagogies have an emancipatory and revolutionary potential, one that could radically alter the Sociology classrooms and re-invigorate the subject.

References

Agarwal S, Patel U, Pal J (2022) The Indian anti-feminist movement on Twitter
Ahmed S (2017) Living a feminist life. Duke University Press

Chadha G, Joseph MT (2018) Introduction: mapping and marking feminist sociologies in India. In: Re-imagining sociology in India: feminist perspectives, Chadha G, Joseph MT (eds). Routledge, India, pp 1–29
Chari Wagh A (2023) Interrogating privilege: An autoethnographic pedagogical exercise. Sociol Bull 72(3):294–312. Sage Publishers
Chaudhuri M (2002) Learning through teaching the 'sociology of gender. Indian J Gend Stud 9(247):245–261
Chaudhuri M (2022) Concepts and sociology: some reflections. Doing Sociol
Davis A (1981) Women, race, and class. Random House
Freire P (1970) Pedagogy of the oppressed. Continuum International Publishing Group Ltd.
Gordon LR (1995) Bad faith and anti-black racism. Humanities Press
Gordon LR (2006) Africana thought and African-diasporic studies. In: Gordon LR, Gordon JA (eds) A companion to African-American studies. Blackwell, pp 591–598
Haraway D (1988) Situated knowledges: the science question in feminism and the privilege of partial perspective. Femin Stud 14(3):575–599. http://www.jstor.org/stable/3178066
Heyes C (2003) Feminist solidarity after queer theory: the case of transgender. Signs 28(4):1093–1120. https://doi.org/10.1086/343132
hooks B (1984) Feminist theory from margin to centre. South End Press, Boston
hooks B (1994) Teaching to transgress: education as the practice of freedom. Routledge, Milton Park
hooks B (2000) Feminism is for everybody. South End Press, Boston
Kumar P (2014) Queering Indian sociology: a critical engagement. In: CAS working paper series, Centre for the Study of Social Systems, Jawaharlal Nehru University, New Delhi, May 2014 CAS/WP/14–7
Kumar V (2016) How Egalitarian is Indian sociology. Econ Polit Weekly 51(25):33–39
Menon N (2013) Seeing like a feminist. Zubaan, New Delhi
Oommen TK (2013) Knowledge and society: situating sociology and social anthropology. OUP
Poonacha V (2003) Women's studies in Indian universities: Current concerns. Econ Pol Wkly 38(26):2653–2658
Pujari L (2018) Transforming the sociology classroom: integrating a critical feminist perspective. In: Chadha G, Joseph MT (eds) Re-imagining sociology in India: feminist perspectives. Routledge, India, pp 148–172
Pujari L (2019) Disrupting the gender binary: queering feminist pedagogy. In: Anu Aneja's women's and gender studies: crossings. Routledge, pp 292–304
Rabaka R (2010) W.E.B Du Bois and the disciplinary decadence of sociology. Against epistemic apartheid. Blackwell
Rege S (2003) Feminist challenge to sociology: disenchanting sociology or for sociology In: Rege S (ed) Sociology of gender: the challenge of feminist sociological knowledge. Sage Publications, pp 1–49
Shrewsbury C (1987) What is feminist pedagogy?, Women's Stud Quart 15(3/4):6–14. http://www.jstor.org/stable/40003432
Smith B (1983) Introduction to home girls: a black feminist anthology. Women of Colour Press
Smith D (1987) The everyday world as problematic: a feminist sociology. North Eastern University Press
Witz A, Marshall B (2004) Introduction: feminist encounters with sociological theory. In: Witz A, Marshall B (eds) Engendering the social: feminist encounters with sociological theory. Oxford University Press, New York
Xaxa. (1999) Tribes as indigenous people of India. Econ Pol Wkly 34(51):3589–3595

Chapter 15
Drug Addiction: Exploring the Trials and Tribulations of the Kashmiri Youth

Pirzada Athar Hussain

Abstract The paper brings out the impact of conflict on the mindset of people in Kashmir Valley, particularly of the youth, by examining the most unfortunate circumstances in the post-conflict situation. It focuses on the current situation in South-to-North Kashmir, highlighting the significant involvement of youth in various miserable activities, including drug addiction. The influence of conflict in Kashmir has led to an alarming increase in drug addiction among the youth. The paper draws on in-depth interviews and narratives with young people who took to drug addiction and now have overcome it. It sheds light on how the bodies of young adults, collected from the apple orchards, have become a significant point of contention in society. The paper concludes by highlighting the increasing importance of Kashmir Valley since 2008 and the emergence of a new form of conflict from 2016–23.

Keywords Conflict · Kashmir · Drug addiction · Family · Escape

Introduction

According to Merriam-Webster dictionary,[1] conflict is explained; as a clashing or sharp disagreement (as between ideas, interests, or purposes): mental struggle resulting from needs, drives, wishes, or demands that are in opposition or are not compatible. This 'sharp disagreement' has been considered an important research aspect that further explains here how the eruption of conflict first starts within an individual and gradually affects and involves the larger family (which narrates the life history of an individual from the movement of first-time taking drugs until his death/redemption). The present work attempts to understand the post-conflict scenario of Kashmir Valley by examining drug addiction among the youth of Kashmir. The issue

[1] Merriam-Webster.com Dictionary, s.v. "conflict," accessed July 18 2023, https://www.merriam-webster.com/dictionary/conflict.

P. A. Hussain (✉)
Department of Sociology, University of Ladakh, Kargil Campus (Ladakh), Leh, India
e-mail: atharsociology@gmail.com

A. Chauhan et al. (eds.), *Hundred Years of Sociology in India: Evolving Issues, Emerging Trends*, https://doi.org/10.1007/978-981-96-1317-5_15

of substance/drug abuse has become a global problem influenced by various factors, including social, economic, political, and psychosocial. Combined cases of drug abuse and related psychological issues also increased from more than 14,500 cases in 2014 to 33,222 in 2016, a staggering 130% increase in two years. Till April 2023 alone, this number reached 13,352.[2]

The problem is not limited to an individual or community but involves interaction between the triad, which may refer to the individual, drug, and environment or society (Ortiz 1990, p. 47). The complexity of the problem arises due to the interrelatedness of multiple factors associated with drug abuse. The study assesses the socio-demographic profile of substance/drug abusers admitted at the Drug De-addiction Centre of the Police Hospital in Srinagar. It also discusses the familial inheritance and hereditary factors in developing drug disorders. *Drug abuse* is a complex problem involving multiple interconnected factors that can influence each other (Ray 2007).

In India, traditional drugs like opium, Charas, bhang, and ganja were used for recreation or religious purposes. At the same time, nicotine, caffeine, and ethanol are the most commonly used drugs in other societies. The use of these drugs has changed over the past few decades, and drug abuse has become a serious problem in certain regions, including Jammu and Kashmir (Medina-Mora et al. 1990, p. 09). The heritability of drug abuse and the genetic factors significantly influence the transition from drug use to abuse. The use of newer opioids, like heroin, cannabis, marijuana, amphetamines, and ecstasy, is on the rise, and drug use can lead to physiological changes and observable withdrawal symptoms. The drug situation in the country has changed rapidly over the past few decades. According to Home Department data, between October 2014 and 2016, more than 3800 people were treated for de-addiction in Jammu, Srinagar, Anantnag, and Baramulla. The highest number of cases came from Srinagar (2,260), followed by Jammu (610), Anantnag (603), and Baramulla (391).

The family structure of Kashmir Valley is overly closed in practice, even after the decline of the joint family system. In all families, children are grown up with some cultural standards; if a child does not get a job, parents will not compel them, and many youngsters, both married and unmarried, are living financially dependent on their parents. Job anxiety is not the only question for skillful youngsters. Some additional issues, like late marriages, family worries, deficient dreams, and living in insecure and conflicting situations, have also impacted the young population. Normally, parents believe that investing money and effort in their children's education will ensure their children's future, but when confronted with reality, they get perplexed. The reality is the lack of work opportunities in the present times. Therefore, understanding the social issues these young Kashmiris face could be an attempt to explain why youngsters are becoming drug addicts. There have been changes in the availability of drugs, the choice of psychoactive drugs, and the socio-demographic characteristics of drug users (Sharma 2005, p. 200). The situation is moving towards uncertainty, particularly concerning the youth of Jammu and Kashmir, where heroin abuse has

[2] India News, India News Live and Breaking News Today (hindustantimes.com).

become a serious problem. The socio-political upheaval is challenging the drug abuse scenario. The formulation and delivery of effective interventions depend on the knowledge of the trends and patterns of drug abuse (Singh 1992). This paper discusses the issue of substance abuse in Kashmir, particularly the increase in opiate abuse, including heroin. Media reports reveal the large-scale cultivation of cannabis in southern Kashmir and the terrifying seizures of large capacities of opioids, mostly heroin, in northern edge areas (Margoob and Dutta 1988, p. 254).

Additionally, unlawful sale stores of alcohol are becoming common in the city of Srinagar and the adjoining areas. The situation will likely worsen if sufficient measures are not taken to identify and help vulnerable groups (Margoo et al., 2004, p. 15). The study by Thacore et al. (1971, p. 58) found that various individuals are abusing methaqualone, often introduced to the drug by doctors who are friends. The drug is taken for euphoric and pleasurable effects and can be used regularly or irregularly. It is also found to be an effective tranquilizer and may help with alcohol withdrawal symptoms but with the risk of substitution. The side effects are mainly subjective, and overdose can interfere with normal mental functioning but does not cause psychotic symptoms.

Parents do their duties while being strong on their responsibilities and with consciousness; in other words, they (parents) do hard work, make adjustments, and rely on their children unconditionally. Addiction to drugs among youth describes the various reasons individuals begin to use drugs, including medical reasons, depression, trauma, relationship issues, and peer pressure. This voluntary initiation into the world of addictive drugs has strongly influenced society's view of drug abuse and drug addiction and their treatment. It highlights the importance of understanding the factors contributing to drug abuse and addiction (Bhat and Imtiaz 2017, p. 19). Moreover, as my field data suggests, parents are unaware of their children's hidden desires; and their passive involvement in drug addiction or links with other prohibited activities. At this initial stage, youngsters join drug gangs as suppliers to make themselves financially sufficient. However, how they changed their opinion of earning to investing (using toxic substances), they said they do not know. The common man's thinking about the current situation in Kashmir is as follows:

> Married couples are currently experiencing divorce while unmarried couples are fighting to stay married. Children hurry to grow up; adults are looking to return to their childhood, and youngsters are dissatisfied with their job prospects. Unemployed people are anxious about their jobs, while the poor are striving to become wealthy, and the rich are seeking peace. The average person is dying to be famous, and the famous keep their face away from the masses. We are all struggling through a period of misery. The continuous and ongoing conflict in Kashmir has only exacerbated the problem.

Drug Addiction and the Impact of Conflict

Kashmir is renowned for its natural beauty as well as for the conflict. In other words, Kashmir is famous as 'Paradise on Earth', which manifests the beauty of its natural landscape, but it has become 'Hell on Earth', due to conflict in the region. The everyday situation in Kashmir, an important aspect of understanding social life, has been depicted as an appearance of uncertainty, anxiety, and turmoil. For a long period, Kashmiri-speaking people have faced huge discrimination and oppression. It includes militant attacks, military force strikes, and foreign attacks. Nearly 48,000 people have been killed in the last decade, according to information from the South Asia Terrorism Portal.[3]

The long-standing conflict in Kashmir since the late 1980s has led to many problems, like mistrust and tension between the people and the government. This conflict has also unintentionally made the issue of drug addiction worse in the region. The violence and instability caused by the conflict have created an environment where drugs are easily available, and many people turn to them to cope with their difficult lives. Due to situations like disturbance, there aren't enough good programs to help people with addiction. So, dealing with the problems in Kashmir is not only important for bringing peace but also for helping to reduce the drug addiction that has become a big issue. In the context of Kashmir, where the government lacks popular legitimacy, the military forces have emphasized the importance of winning the hearts and minds of Kashmiris.

This consciousness has involved a campaign to combat substance/drug abuse, which has fused military, medical, and humanitarian aims. The campaign has included establishing multiple treatment centers, such as the Drug De-Addiction Center (DDC), which employs medical-penitentiary techniques to transform substance/drug users and psychologically win their hearts and minds (Junaid 2013, p. 96). In the meantime, people from Kashmir began to openly discuss the issues they believed were wrong for them. The armed forces seized stone pelters, which created long-run confusion and resulted in the closing of educational institutions and witnessed damage to public property in some locations. In fact, all these activities done by armed forces were found compulsory for bringing stability to society, particularly during conflict situations.

A few studies describe the situation in Jammu and Kashmir, where the military forces have been accused of certain human rights violations and lack popular legitimacy. The police's substance abuse campaign, which includes establishing multiple treatment centers, is part of a hearts and minds campaign to win over the Kashmiri population. The Army provides basic drug de-addiction services and organizes activities against drug abuse among youth. However, many Kashmiris see the Indian state as 'uncaring', shaped by their personal experiences with the violence of the security state (Kaul 2011, p. 195). On a wider scale in society, people withdrew from finalising dates for marriage ceremonies. People who faced economic crises, particularly workers who were employed daily, were supported by their relatives and neighbours as they accessed essential items for survival. Thus, taking such actions without a reason, a few psychologists consider this a sign of discontent. Democratically speaking, a person who is a bit pressurized may react. The person is neither involved nor engaged in politics or conflicts, but he does this, only to find himself or being brutally attacked and seek out an answer that will give satisfaction. In this

[3] The History of Kashmir Conflict and Its Various Phases (outlookindia.com).

scenario, suggestions are merely accepted without being checked for their potential harm or benefit for the future.

Understanding Drug Addiction and the Escape from Reality

Year-long conflicts, marked by gunfights, bomb blasts, and massive encounters, have obscured one of Kashmir's most pressing problems: the growing problem of drug addiction in Kashmir's youth. Srinagar's SMHS Hospital, one of the largest in the Union Territory, has data that show an 85% rise in drug and substance abuse cases. It went from 410 in 2014 to 759 in 2016.[4] Since 2008, the police in Jammu and Kashmir have been heavily involved in addressing the issue of substance abuse, which is a separate but related problem to the region's widespread psychological trauma and other conflict-related illnesses. The Drug De-addiction Centre (DDC), established by the police, uses medical and penitentiary techniques to treat addiction, including group therapy sessions where patients tell recovery narratives and express gratitude towards the clinic staff. However, patients also privately demonstrate ongoing commitments to intoxication, which they view as a worthwhile experience, defying biomedical injunctions to forget their pasts (Matloff and Nickelsberg 2009). There are many reasons for substance addiction as stated by the respondents. One reason is that people have friends who might have addictive habits and spend their daily lives with them. It is especially true when there are no tasks to complete with such people. Another reason is that people with greater financial resources may be more inclined towards toxic substances as they have money to buy drugs.

There is also a problem of unemployment, particularly for educated people. It is a risk factor that can determine how high the saturation levels are. Qualified youth, particularly when we talk about the northern portion of Kashmir, has been found uninterestedly engaged in earning at a large level of nonhierarchical positions (a Ph. D holder is working as a LIC agent, an MTech degree holder is working as a shopkeeper) in their locality and outside. They do not feel satisfied with their job, and after they have completed their education, the gifted youths are not able to find employment based on their academic qualifications. This substance/drug abuse epidemic is distinct from but related to the area's widespread psychological trauma and other conflict-related illnesses. Gradually, participation in sports and other activities is declining.

Many problems are faced by Kashmir's youth today. Considering the present situation of Kashmiri youth (who are unemployed), they are confused about whether they should pursue higher education because their future is in jeopardy. Therefore, we have discussed only a few problems, but numerous circumstances have existed over time. These conditions cause anger and suspicion among young people. They also have an underlying sense of concern when they contemplate how their parents

[4] The problem of growing drug addiction among Kashmiri youths missing focus in years of Valley's conflict | Latest News India—Hindustan Times.

work each day in these difficult conditions. They (the youth) initially try to support their parents actively; however, because of the absence of job opportunities, they believe that whatever they receive is better than nothing during this job crisis. One study of 20 months of fieldwork in Kashmir (Varma 2016, p. 53) explains the three areas of anthropological concern: violence and military humanitarianism, the relation between narrative and recovery in mental health and substance/drug abuse treatment, and the relations among emotion, ethics, and love in South Asia. It explores how patients at a drug de-addiction Centre in Kashmir use reveries of romantic love to understand their drug use and pasts in different ways from the clinicians. The article sheds light on the therapeutic function of language and the imaginative resources that patients draw on to revisit their histories of intoxication and recast them in a positive light.

In such a challenging situation where people are emotionally getting involved with their everyday life survival challenges, they feel miserable despite all efforts. So, most people, especially the younger generation, feel they are failing after repeatedly struggling against the circumstances and simultaneously getting frustrated with being dedicated and showing honesty towards searching for comfort for their parents and themselves. They also identify shortcuts to satisfy their needs for luxurious survival without considering the potential consequences and long-term solutions. Drug dealer gangs are active in colleges, universities, and rural areas. They (drug sellers) are looking for students willing to share their heartbreaking tales while they (drug suppliers) demonstrate interest and compassion in helping them discover immediate solutions. This drug-gang strategy is the passive phase of life for young people. Similarly, on the other hand, there is the active phase of the daily life of youngsters, which is completely different. Their daily routine is normal as they consciously and gradually learn to maintain themselves as normal with their parents and siblings. Nevertheless, in reality, they are becoming accustomed to taking harmful substances/drugs. They hide their actual face until an unexpected event occurs before their parents.

Consequences of Drug Addiction: Some Narratives

Drug abuse is becoming widespread in Kashmir Valley, and mass media broadcast visuals of this major accelerating problem. Furthermore, everyone is living with the question of how Kashmiri people are losing peace of mind. In several instances, dead bodies have been discovered in unintentional locations. Local police and media authorities are investigating to discover the reasons for these incidents. Postmortem reports have attributed several deaths to overdoses caused by taking harmful substances/drugs. In this way, the parents of the deceased persons are stunned at the realization of the causes of their children's deaths. As long as they wait for the postmortem report, the parents hesitate to accept that their children's deaths are murder or a natural occurrence.

However, until the parents faced reality on the surface, they were not aware of the reason. Nevertheless, some addicts were persuaded to reveal the reasons that led them to their addiction. It took some time, but eventually, they (redeemed) cooperated with researchers to share the stories behind their involvement in taking toxic substances. In this stage of continuous drug use, some individuals may even exceed the boundaries of what is considered religiously and socially unacceptable, even when facing a cash shortage.

For over three decades, scholars have perceived Kashmir as a precarious and menacing region. From 2008 to 2016, a dangerous trend emerged where Kashmiri youth, holding stones in their hands and facing bullets, exhibited a willingness to risk their lives–a manifestation of profound frustration. This phenomenon raises a pertinent question: Could anyone living a comfortable life with a stable job readily embrace such perilous circumstances? As a result, concerned Kashmiri respondents have articulated that the enduring political tension in the region has inflicted severe hardships on the general populace. Initially, this predicament was confined to a narrow group of individuals; however, over time, its grip has extended to encompass a more comprehensive cross-section of the community. This expansion vividly underscores the intensifying aftermath of the ongoing crisis. This crisis is not confined solely to drug addiction; rather, it encompasses far-reaching ramifications, such as the disturbing rise in suicide attempts among young individuals in public spaces—a distressing trend observed prominently at various bridges spanning the Jhelum River from southern to northern Kashmir. The scope of the crisis's impact goes beyond this single facet, with a multitude of other repercussions casting a long shadow as well. To protect themselves from potential threats in modern society, people invest in technology such as CCTV cameras in luxurious housing colonies and frequently use bullet-proof cars and other modern techniques for safety. Nevertheless, the living threat is why the youth of Kashmir currently use drugs, which is, in my opinion, 'calling for death' and formerly openly facing the bullet with a stone.

Haroon (name changed) mentioned that "I, as well as my friends, had a habit of committing fraud against our parents. We convinced them by stating that we'd have a night out at the homes of other friends. However, as per the plan we flew on, we used to look for motorbikes and cars that had been parked along the roadside in some isolated areas within the town's old part. According to our plan, our group used to remove the tyres from both motorcycles and cars and then sell them for money and purchase drugs with the money".

Parents may be shocked to see their children not doing what is expected of them, as in such situations, they could be more skeptical than if they were watching their children go to the grave. Even if they are aware that it is against morality, they persist. Honour and dignity are the rewards you receive after a long life. In society, children are often judged based on their parents' status. Thus, displaying strong 'sharp disagreement' is considered an important aspect of our research which further explains how conflict begins within an individual before it gradually impacts and influences his wider family (which recounts the life story of an individual beginning with the first time he took drugs, until his death/redemption).

Mahraj Ahmad (name changed) recounted, "During my second year of study in 2016, all the colleges and universities were shut down for nearly one year. In this period of the peak of the conflict in Kashmir, throughout the day, I would spend time with my fellow youths from the villages around my home. Some of them were familiar to me, but we did not have any relationship with one another. I played cricket with them, and slowly we became friends with one another. Every day at 3:00 pm, we began playing cricket in an open area about two and a half km from my home. In the evenings, we would gossip with one another, and they were all smokers. They initially gave me a smoking deal, but I refused. However, due to family issues, I decided to start smoking. I felt more relaxed after having my first smoke, and then I began purchasing with the money I had saved. After two years, I met one of my university acquaintances who offered me 'Charas'. This was the first time I tried the toxic substance, and, on this day, after about four hours, I woke up and felt like I was feeling at peace. As time passed, I became addicted to toxic injections and began to take other drugs and substances until I was shifted for treatment at a rehabilitation center in Srinagar".

This crucial phase of drug addiction has given rise to several new threats in Kashmiri society. At the same time, the researcher talked with the common people (neighbours of these drug addicts) who expressed that they face stigma, uncertainty, and threat. There was a time when both parents of males, and females, searched for a life partner for their children who should be well educated, with a job and belonging to a respectable family. However, the situation has changed now. Parents prefer to let their children remain unmarried rather than marrying them to the wrong person. There are many hidden cases where most husbands are drug addicts, and in a few cases, wives are addicted to drugs. Moreover, in the context of female drug addiction, they were well-educated and had a good time studying in other parts of the country. A United Nations International Drug Control Programme survey in 2008 estimated 70,000 drug addicts in Kashmir, out of which 4,000 were women. Therefore, as a consequence, late marriage is becoming common which later on has other problems like; infertility and adjustment problems after getting married.

Conclusion

To truly understand the people of Kashmir, one must first comprehend Kashmir as a society and its complex social structure. Furthermore, it entails comprehending how individuals interact and coexist with one another. However, gaining an indepth understanding of the social structure of Kashmiri society necessitates more than a fleeting visit. Spending a considerable amount of time with the locals is essential to understand their customs, traditions, and way of life.

Prior to the 1990s, Kashmir was well-known for its communal harmony. However, in the present day, the situation in Kashmir is worsening day by day, particularly for the youth. The escalating drug addiction problem is one of the many issues plaguing Kashmiri society. Drug addiction has destroyed the normalcy of daily life and as shown through the narratives of Kashmiri youth, posed a significant challenge for parents and caretakers in maintaining social stability within the family. Such a situation has increased deviant behaviour and crime in Kashmir, including looting religious sites such as *Dargahs* and *Khanqahs*.

The decline of etiquette in Kashmiri culture is rapidly accelerating, and drug overdoses have caused many individuals to leave their families or even resort to suicide. Despite this, many people still recall the golden era of Kashmir, where individuals lived with courage and vigour, and the Kashmiri Pandits and Muslims inspired and supported each other. There is hope that the situation will return to normal if the Pandits return to Kashmir. However, with the current state of affairs, many individuals are unsure and uncertain of their return. Similarly, with the current state of instability and the escalating problem of drug addiction among the youth, the future of Kashmir remains uncertain.

References

Bhat SA, Imtiaz N (2017) Drug addiction in Kashmir: Issues and challenges. J Drug Abuse 3(3):19

Junaid M (2013) Death and life under occupation: space, violence, and memory in Kashmir. In: Visweswaran K (ed) Everyday occupations: experiencing militarism in South Asia and the Middle East. University of Pennsylvania Press, Philadelphia, pp 90–158

Kaul S (2011) 'An' you will fight, till the death of it': past and present in the challenge of Kashmir. Soc Res 78(1):173–202

Magroob MA, Majid A, Hussain A, Wani ZA, Yousf A, Malik YA, Mushtaq H (2004) Changing sociodemographic and clinical profile of substance use disorder patients in Kashmir valley. JK Pract 11(1):14–16

Margoob MA, Dutta KS (1988) 10-15 years retrospective study of 50 patients of mdp for seasonal variations. Indian J Psychiatry 30(3):253–256

Matloff J, Nickelsberg R (2009) Beyond the breaking point, Dart Center for Journalism and Trauma website, April 9. Accessed 23 Sept 2013

Medina-Mora ME, Tapia CR, Rascón ML, Solache G, Otero BR, Lazcano F, Mariño MC (1990) Epidemiologic status of drug abuse in Mexico. Bull Pan Am Health Organ 24(1):1–11

Ortiz A (1990) Development of a system for registry of information on drug use in Mexico. Bull Pan Am Health Organ 24(1):46–52

Ray R (2007) National Drug Dependence Treatment Centre, AIIMS. New Delhi (IN): WHO Biennium Project

Sharma HK (2005) Substance abuse in India–a socio-cultural perspective. In: Paul MC (ed) Drugs and substance abuse problems, interdisciplinary studies of cause, consequences and preventions. Mittal Publication, New Delhi (IN), pp 193–208

Singh H (1992) 'Drug abuse': a book comprising the summaries of research studies sponsored by the Ministry of Welfare, Govt. of India. National Institute of Social Defence, New Delhi (IN)

Thacore V, Saxena R, Kumar R (1971) Epidemiology of drug abuse in Lucknow with special reference to methaqualone. Indian J Pharmacol 3(1):58

Varma S (2016) Love in the time of occupation: reveries, longing, and intoxication in Kashmir. Am Ethnol 43(1):50–62

Part IV
Sociology of Care

Chapter 16
Sociology of Care: Understanding Existing Social System in the Face of Social Transformations

Samita Manna and Soumyajit Patra

Abstract Sociological reflections on care usually start with a conventional psychoanalysis of a concern for 'others', (which, in fact, lies at the core of the idea of care itself), and ends with an exploration of its impact on other domains of life, especially on the relationships between individuals and groups. This concern for 'others' develops a kind of confraternity by sublimating the 'self' for the cause of the 'other', and places an element of altruism at the core of the notion of 'care'. Individuals, as social beings, collectively construct their own life-worlds; and the manifestations of 'care' (both as an action and as an attitude) as a category can be found in every social relationship and every social formation with varying degrees and intensities. It is, in this sense, processual and associative. This paper would try to examine the inherent dynamics of care from a sociological point of view.

Keywords Care · Trust · Self · Dialectic · Motherhood

The Prologue

The notion of care has been the focus of many sociological and policy-related researches during the last few decades. Though ubiquitous and pervasive, 'care' as a category was almost overlooked by early sociologists and social anthropologists. This is also true of the social scientists of our country. Much has been said about the significance of primary relations or 'irreducible functions of family', but there was a conspicuous absence of the term 'care' in social science discourses and theorisations. In earlier simple societies, care was given within the family with the help of its own limited physical or cultural resources. In many cases, it took the

S. Manna (✉)
Department of Sociology, University of Kalyani, West Bengal, Kalyani, India
e-mail: samita.manna@gmail.com

S. Patra
Department of Sociology, SKB University, Purulia, West Bengal, India
e-mail: soumyajit-patra@skbu.ac.in

A. Chauhan et al. (eds.), *Hundred Years of Sociology in India: Evolving Issues, Emerging Trends*, https://doi.org/10.1007/978-981-96-1317-5_16

help of the community/neighbours as one of its (concerned family's) 'trusted agencies'. As 'trust' and 'intimacy' remained key attributes in the care-giving process, family, in simple societies, stood (and even today stands) as the prime institution in providing individual-level care. With varying degrees, we all need care at times, as, in a sense, everyone is vulnerable. Dependency and vulnerability, irrespective of age, sex and physical capabilities, are the basic conditions of human existence. These core assumptions of care and care ethics (Gilligan 1982; Tronto 1994) alter the epistemological (and to some extent ontological) understanding of care. The recent Covid-19-induced pandemic has been a fatal-proof of the importance of vulnerability and importance of care during the time of crisis. The pandemic itself has opened a new dimension to the study of care, and pointed to its underlying psycho-relational dynamics. Simultaneously, the pandemic has brought the role of the government and the importance of bureaucracy in the care-system to the fore. Therefore, the study of care should include all these agencies in order to address the sociological significance of care in a holistic way.

Sociological reflections on care usually start with a conventional psycho-analysis of a concern for 'others', (which, in fact, lies at the core of the idea of care itself), and ends with an exploration of its impact on other domains of life, especially on the relationships between individuals and groups. This concern for 'others' develops a kind of confraternity by sublimating the self for the cause of the 'other', and places an element of altruism at the core of the notion of 'care'. The recent pandemic, which shattered the entire world in a sense, has divulged new significance of care. The prescription of confinement, to contain the Covid-19-caused pandemic, not only has led to what Ulrich Beck (1992) calls 'individualization' (not individualism), but also has broken the chains of signification of the term 'care', and concomitantly created an aporia or a philosophical conundrum in understanding the concept. The *Différance*, in the Derridean sense, in the signification started, as an inevitable corollary, when the care-givers were identified as 'Covid-warriors'. The process of 'otherisation' took a nuanced turn on the epitaph 'confraternity-confinement' dilemma. And an all-pervasive 'fear' reminded us of the primacy of self. There was really a paradigm shift in the notion of care during this devastating pandemic that teaches us to value what Zizek (2020) has termed as 'corporeal distancing'. This shift in the focus from 'other' to 'self' in care giving process can also be noticed in the case of the professionalisation of care-services. When, for example, care is provided by some professionals (like nurses etc.) this transformation in the form and content of care can be noticed.

We need care to protect our family, our environment, and our natural resources for our survival. But the term 'care' is not defined uniformly. As time and space change, the conceptualisation and application of care differ. Within the same society, the connotations of care may appear differently, as they are both relation-specific and culture-specific. Similarly, with the structural transformation of society (Cooley 1915; Spencer 1908; Sumner 1906; Tonnies, 1887) care is interpreted differently. Even the Sustainable Development Goal 4—2030 takes 'care of our future generations' by adopting a few developmental policies to protect the people; otherwise, they would face serious threats to our survival.[1] Stewardship, conservation, maintenance and repair or healing–these are the fundamental forms of care that take different meanings in different contexts.

The foregoing arguments point to the fact that whether formal or not, the term 'care' in its most commonsensical connotations, means 'to be concerned about or interested in someone or something', and accordingly to do something in its favour. It is, in this sense, processual and associative. Processual, as the action of taking care starts with something and produces certain consequences–subjective or objective. Objective consequences are visible, as the change or improvement after carework can be realised. In fact, in most cases, care-services are required by those who are vulnerable, and are in crisis.

Subjective consequences, on the other hand, are mental satisfaction or feelings of dependence as being cared. In its simplest form, the sociology of care tries to analyse the impact of care-giving and care-receiving in shaping and re-shaping inter-human relationships at the micro level, and its impact on the social institutions at the macro level. The implied assumptions in such analysis start from considering the care-givers as adult, powerful, strong, resourceful and healthy in comparison to those who are receiving care. Starting from the study of Malinowski of the culture of the Trobriand islanders to the abstract formulation of the 'irreducible functions' of family by Talcott Parsons, we have seen this tendency. The role of the young children as the care-receivers is usually undervalued or ignored in the discourses of care, which has erroneously considered 'care-giving' as an adult's responsibility.

Care and the Underlying Dialectics

In simple societies, religion, in the form of beliefs, rituals and practices, is believed to make the constituent communities more cohesive and, in a sense, care-efficient (Malinowski 1954). Radcliffe-Brown also visualised a 'stable system of groupings determining and regulating the relation of those individuals to one another… to make possible an ordered social life' (Evans-Pritchard 1962:55) which is indicative of the in-built mechanism of care collectively nurtured by the adult members of these societies. When care work is done in a family, it is then filled with emotions and love. When mothers, for example, take care of their children or when young people take care of the elders, sick and physically challenged in the setting of a family, care becomes synonymous with affection; and its emotive components outweigh its technical dimensions. Does care-giving require specialised training at all? The dialectic between 'informal-cathectic care' and 'formal-instrumental care' brings the question to the fore.

Besides these, everyday components of home-management including cooking, food-serving, cleaning, sewing etc. can also be considered as ancillaries of care

[1] https://www.un.org/development/desa/dpad/publication/world-economic-situation-and-prospects-as-of-mid-2023/

work. The history of human societies reveals that with some exceptions the division of work has mostly been based on sex (Durkheim 1984). There are scholars who believe that the peculiar brain-lateralisation is responsible for the soft-qualities and emotive attributes of women. Care-giving, from this point of view, is the biological virtue of the women (Pal 2021). It is to be noted that people establish a network of agencies of care, and women play a decisive role in the dynamics of this network. In simple forest-based societies also this network works, while men are engaged in hunting and women manage home without asking for any role-reversals (Durkheim, 1984; Parsons 1951; Spencer 1908). Interestingly, this arrangement is 'insensitive to the risk faced by women' in rendering the services (Yu et al. 2018, p.2).

In course of time, as the role structures got diversified, the aforesaid network of care is shifted to a different set of institutions, for example, from families to hospitals etc. Technology has increasingly started supplementing human-deficiencies, and new systems set the pace and directions of behavioural transformations and negotiations related to care-giving and care-receiving. The foundation of these behavioural transformations and concomitant expectations again lies on the parallelism between 'informal-cathectic care' that is provided at the individual pane and 'formal-instrumental care' which is supported by complex institutional arrangements. The epistemological foundation of 'care' gets changed, as we raise the question 'Is care an obligation?' or alternatively, 'Is it simply a commodity, a by-product of capitalism?' A critical understanding of care, in some of its contemporary forms, is full of such unresolved-ambiguities. Some of the classical thinkers, with their strong inclinations towards what is known as the 'positive' philosophy, tried to understand the significance of 'care' (they have not used the term in a straightforward way, but implicit in their understanding of various forms of social relationships was a notion of care) in a way different from that of the perspectives of the contemporary theorists (Derrida 1967; Foucault 2001; Baudrillard, 1988).

A fresh understanding of the nuances of care not only helps reveal its multilayered dimensions but also leads to identifying the 'ethical' issues involved in care-giving and care-receiving. We have already pointed out the dynamics of 'self' and 'other' in the process of taking care of those, who are in crisis. The recent Covid-19 pandemic had put this dynamics even within the family, as an all-round fear overshadowed the entire process of care-giving and care-receiving. In other contexts, the distinction between 'self' and 'other' in the said process is manifested in different ways according to gender, power differentials and class differences. For this reason, issues like obligations and responsibilities, hesitations and obligations often enter into the care-dynamics making the whole process a bit nuanced. Even sometimes these issues determine the nature and extent of care to be received or to be given.

Motherhood: The Niche of Care?

Societies have different outlooks and strategies to deal with care. Developed country's visions (and missions) are quite heterogeneous, but one thing has always been the baseline in perceiving 'care' as a right. This is the primacy of women/mothers as care-givers. Whether it is a developed country or a developing one, the imageries of women is defined in almost similar terms, which have inevitably been questioned by the feminist critiques. These issues, which are related to human development as such, and gender justice in particular, cannot be ignored. Especially since 1970s or so, when the feminists started raising their voices for getting equal status with their male counterparts, the cultural practices to attach such attributes as softness, sincerity, affection, motherliness etc. to women were also questioned. And, accordingly, the perception that women are the best care-givers came under severe intellectual attacks. Two-thirds of the domestic work are done by the women, and often this is justified by the norms of patriarchy. Most of the time women care-givers are metaphorically bracketed with 'mothers', and they seem overburdened with their 'culturally' prescribed responsibilities that reflect subversive patriarchal definitions. The word 'mother' evokes a kind of emotional arousal among many of us, as 'motherhood' is identified with certain attributes like love and affection, dependence and trust, honesty and chastity. Others, considering the feelings and emotions the word 'mother' evokes in the mind of women, have come to the conclusion that despite the cultural variations in the role and position of women in families and communities, 'motherhood' is seen as the 'highest of human achievements' almost in every part of the world (Allen 2005, p. 2).

Motherhood usually entails care at the 'individual' level mostly within the framework of institutions like family. The role performances of the mothers are sometimes considered as pivotal in the foundation of a social system that depends, in Parsonian view, on the 'goal attainment' (Parsons 1951) outside this (family) institutional domain. Motherhood corresponds to care, and care corresponds to institutional well-being at the end of the analysis. Mothers' love for their children is sometimes portrayed as divine and exemplified as the epitome of spontaneity and devotion. But this line of argument is challenged by the thinkers like Ann Oakley (1974) or Bruno Bettelheim (1969) who have put counter-examples, and concluded that the role of mothers and the meanings attached to it are culture-specific, and they vary from one group to another. They tried to unveil the politics of patriarchy that underlies the gradual process of relegating the women towards what is known as the 'private domain'.

A trifold set of stages helps us explain any socially constructed notion: creation, confusion, and deconstruction. These cognitive processes take place cyclically. Creation always involves absorbing new sorts of excitement creating new categories of relationships. It is often a fleeting stage of accomplishment and transcendence. Within the process of creation, the seeds of deconstruction lie. As a result, every creation is not fully or completely original or subjectively absolute. It always contains old and contradictory elements, which give birth to new ones. The next important stage is confusion. Society becomes stereotypical and straight-jacketed. To negotiate with this, individual agencies and creative ingenuities start redefining the socially constructed concepts and ideas leading to the stage of deconstruction. It is rightly said that:

> Deconstruction is the active antithesis of everything that criticism ought to be if one accepts its traditional values and concepts.... Some of Jacques Derrida's most powerful essays are devoted to the task of dismantling a concept of 'structure' that serves to immobilize the play of meaning in a text and reduce it to a manageable compass (Norris 2002).

In this stage, we actively try to find out new meanings and connotations counter-poising the things and constructs we previously believed or perceived. Thus, deconstruction goes on, and this helps us reorient our rational/logical everyday understanding of reality. Sociology of care tries to find out the manner in which the notion of care gets colonised under the buffets of patriarchy, and simultaneously focuses on its hidden shades of meanings. It is not difficult to trace the line of evolution that 'care' as a category took. For example, with the passage of time, institutional care, which has deliberately been commodified, is rapidly replacing individual-level informal care, whether through health care systems or through 'old age home' facilities.

Care work reinforces not only gender inequalities, but also generates inequalities of age and class. For example, often the care taken by the children is not considered as 'taking care' at all; hence it is undermined. In many cases, unpaid care work takes place in larger contexts, which directly or otherwise reproduces the gendered nature of care work, and points to the untenable social support systems for ensuring care during the hours of need. There are also market-based options for care that can be availed by affluent classes only (Meyer 2000; Daly 2001). In many metropolitan set ups paid care seems to be replacing informal and non-technical (as it is often said) care. Scholars have opined that paid and unpaid care-givers may work together to negotiate successful strategies for care institutions as such (Abel & Nelson 1990; Ungerson 1997). A thorough analysis of the nature of the commodification of 'care' is important to understand the underlying intricacies between paid and unpaid care. Paid care workers sometimes take a 'matter of fact' attitude, and 'care' itself becomes 'professionalised'. But to the care-receivers the emotive components of care are equally important to its technical-professional aspects (Foner 1994).

In this connection, we would like to refer to the work of Meyer, who has said that 'care is not simply a natural and uncomplicated response to those in need but actually hard physical, mental, and emotional work, which is often unequally distributed through society' (Meyer 2000). Society depends on care. And care starts with the family and community, and gradually becomes commercialised along with the changes in inter-personal relationships, which finally lead to transformations in social systems.

Final Remarks

Care work is deeply embedded in normative structures, with narratives depicting such work as examples of personal commitments, selflessness, altruism on the part of workers who ideally should possess a particular 'caring disposition' (Daly and Fisher 2023). Sociology of care examines the impact of these attributes in interpersonal relationships and institutional arrangements. Sociology of care also focuses on three other features: (i) the marketisation and commodification of care and care work (Esping-Andersen 1990), (ii) the trans-nationalisation of care (care has transformed from individual-informal responsibilities to institutionalised-global systems) and (iii) care in this transformed form have sought for new forms of governance and institutional practices (Aulenbacher et. al. 2018). Sociology of care thus covers a vast arena of care that has individual, local and global implications.

The important thing to remember is that the form of care is oriented towards institutional facts (which are conventions) and structural changes (which are adaptive). So, perspectives on 'care' are not absolute rather they are temporal and context-specific. The following things are important in this regard:

(i) Communication: Communications in general and inter-human interactions in particular are important in the process of construction and reconstruction of the nature of care;
(ii) Communication is constitutive, and every action that is directed to change the 'existing situation' of the care-receivers is consequential;
(iii) Meanings attached to a particular 'care-action' have wider implications on inter-personal relationships at the individual level, and on institutional credibility at the politico-administrative level. This is important as meanings are collectively constructed and collectively decoded (Berger and Luckman 1966).

In general, 'care' implies a concern for others, and revolves around the primacy of well-being. At the individual-informal pane, it aims to do something for betterment and wellbeing. It is relational, and its foundation stands on a system of trust, which is buttressed by the 'agencies' of individuals and support of the institutions. Individuals, as social beings, collectively construct their own life-worlds; and the manifestations of 'care' (both as an action and as an attitude) as a category can be found in every social relationship and every social formation with varying degrees and intensities. In a sense, it has both objective and subjective dimensions, which are basically prerequisites for human existence as such. And Indian sociology has rightly extended its horizon to include them within its domain.

References

Abel EK, Nelson MK (1990) Circles of care: work and identity in women's lives. State University of New York Press, Albany

Allen AT (2005) Feminism and motherhood in western Europe 1890–1970. Palgrave Macmillan, New York
Aulenbacher B, Lutz H, Riegraf B (2018) Introduction: towards a global sociology of care and care work. Curr Sociol 66(4):495–502
Baudrillard J (1998) The consumer society: myths and structures. Sage Publications Ltd., US
Beck U (1992) Risk society: towards a new modernity. Sage Publications, London
Berger PL, Luckmann T (1966) The social construction of reality. Knopf Doubleday Publishing Group, New York
Bettelheim B (1969) The children of the dream. Thames and Hudson, London
Cooley CH (1915) Social organization. Scribner, New York
Daly M (ed) (2001) Care work: the quest for security. International Labor Office, Geneva
Daly M, Fisher D (2023) The job and work orientations of workers in English care homes, Department of Social Policy and Intervention. University of Oxford, UK
Derrida J (1967) Of Grammatology. Johns Hopkin University Press, Baltimore
Durkheim E (1984) The division of labour in society. The Macmillian Press Ltd., London
Esping-Andersen G (1990) The three worlds of welfare capitalism. Polity Press, Cambridge
Evans-Pritchard EE (1962) Social anthropology and other essays. The Crowell-Collier Publishing Company, New York
Foner N (1994) The caregiving dilemma: work in the American nursing home. University of California Press, Berkeley
Foucault M (2001) Power. New Press, France
Gilligan C, Langdale S, Lyons N, Murphy J (1982) The contribution of women's thought to developmental theory: the elimination of sex bias in moral developmental research and education. Final Report to the National Institute of Education. Cambridge, Mass: Harvard University Press.
Malinowski B (1954) Magic, science and religion. Ingram, India
Meyer MH (2000) Care work: gender, class, and the welfare state. New York
Norris C (2002) Deconstruction. Routledge, New York
Oakley A (1974) Housewife. Allen Lane, London
Pal R (2021) Women in mathematics: a reverse pyramid of time. Indian Science Cruiser 35(4)
Parsons T (1951) The social system. Free Press, Glencoe, III
Patra S, Paul B (2018) Maa and Maa Manasa. In: Manna S, Patra S, Roy S (eds) Sociology of motherhood and beyond: roots and rejuvenation. Levant Books, Kolkata
Spencer H (1908) The principle of sociology, vol 1. Apleton, New York
Sumner WG (1906) Folkways. University of Michigan, Michigan
Tonnies F (1887) Community and association. Michigan State University Press, Michigan
Tronto J (1994) Moral boundaries: a political argument for an ethic of care. Routledge, New York
Ungerson C (1997) Social politics and the commodification of care. Soc Polit 4(3):362 81
Yu SW, Rubby C, Kühner S (2018) Defamilisation and familisation risks, adult worker models, and pro-employment/decommodification measures for women: The case of Hong Kong. J Int Comparat Soc Policy 35(2):194–210
Zizek S (2020) Pandemic! covid-19 shakes the World. OR Books, New Work

Chapter 17
Bridging Generations: Intergenerational Solidarity for Healthy Ageing

Tattwamasi Paltasingh

Abstract Family relationships become the foundation of social and emotional bonding as people get older. Intergenerational relationships are nurtured through positive reciprocity throughout a person's life. The Potential advantages of intergenerational relationships for the bonding of two or more generations are being recognised. Recent studies have revealed that the contributions of grandparenting to grandchildren are associated with reduced adjustment difficulties and more positive consequences among children and adults. From a solidarity perspective, positive family relationships can facilitate interactions between members of different generations and contribute to the progressive development of each member. Due to the increased life expectancy and better health provisions, grandparents have a significant influence on grandchildren's lives. However, due to the ongoing processes like urbanisation, industrialisation, and migration; both structural and functional changes in the family are clearly noticed. Against this backdrop, the paper highlights the importance of intergenerational relationships. The subsequent section focuses on the factors that influence the bonding between generations with a framework of intergenerational solidarity for healthy ageing. Relevant suggestions for bridging generational differences and promoting intergenerational perspectives in policy and practice are outlined in the Indian context.

Keywords Older adults · Intergenerational solidarity · Grandparenting · Healthy ageing · India

Background and Context

Life expectancy has increased significantly over the last century, accompanied by a demographic growth in the senior population worldwide (Paltasingh and Tyagi 2015). India, a developing country, is likewise witnessing this demographic change. According to the 2011 Census, India has approximately 103.8 million persons over

T. Paltasingh (✉)
Department of Sociology, Sambalpur University, Sambalpur, Odisha, India
e-mail: tpaltasingh@gmail.com

A. Chauhan et al. (eds.), *Hundred Years of Sociology in India: Evolving Issues, Emerging Trends*, https://doi.org/10.1007/978-981-96-1317-5_17

the age of 60 years. The proportion of older adults has increased from 5.6–8.6% between 1961 and 2011 (Ministry of Statistics and Programme Implementation [MOSPI] 2021). As per predictions, India's ageing population might reach 300 million by 2050 (Bhandari and Paswan 2021). This accelerated ageing population, combined with socio-economic changes, is a matter of concern about altered family values, living arrangements, health, well-being, and lifestyles. During later years, older people rely heavily on their families and children for care and support. However, in the current scenario, the traditional familial relationship in India is deteriorating (Paltasingh and Jena 2021). The demographic transitions have posed significant challenges to family structures and intergenerational relationships. Most of the research studies highlight that rapid economic development in recent decades, a large drift towards urbanisation, migration, an unprecedented modernisation process, and the spread of western ideology can eventually lead to the loss of preferred as well as functional roles of older members of the family (Sudha et al. 2007). The declining conventional caregiver support system in this changing environment has drawn the attention of researchers, members of civil society organisations (CSOs), and policymakers to think over the intergenerational relationship issues within the family. The emotional connection of the grandparent–grandchild relationship may persist till old age, which can have a further positive impact on the next generation.

Generational interactions are recognised as reciprocal support among people, in which both younger and older generations influence one another. The quality of life of older family members is correlated with this reciprocity of relationship. Strong and good intergenerational solidarity entails numerous benefits, such as the enhancement of human capital and life skills; the transfer of values and culture; the preservation of multi-generational cohesion; and the reduction of age-based discrimination, and so on (Tabuchi and Miura 2015). Evidences from the literature suggest that family relationships and support may have a positive influence on older people's health. The bond between grandparents and grandchildren is an important component of the older adults' social support network. The health of the older adults is linked to social relationships. Lower level of social support results in higher mortality rates among older generations. Apart from that, taking care of grandchildren can encourage grandparents to stay active, which is linked to better health and well-being as well as a reduction in anxiety and depressive symptoms among older people. However, there seems to be little research on this issue, especially in India. So, emphasis must be given to intergenerational solidarity, which may contribute to the resolution of social issues arising from the changing balance between older adults and young people. In this context, the paper provides an overview of the notion of intergenerational relationships and the factors that influence the bonding between generations. The subsequent section has shed light on the significance of intergenerational solidarity for the health and well-being of older people along with the framework of intergenerational solidarity. The paper also recommends approaches for bridging generational differences and promoting intergenerational perspectives into policy design in order to foster a healthy community living with multiple generations.

Intergenerational Solidarity and Healthy Ageing: A Sociological Approach

Healthy intergenerational relations are important for both older adults and younger individuals. Positive relationships with their children or grandchildren may provide older individuals a feeling of belonging, and emotional support as they age. From a sociological perspective, these connections offer an opportunity to pass on cultural knowledge and practices from one generation to the next, fostering continuity and stability in society. Enabling people to reach their full potential for physical, social, and mental well-being as well as to engage in social life even in their later years of life is the purpose of active and healthy ageing. The availability of a network of support, security, and care is essential throughout the lifetime of older people. The sociological perspectives underline the value of intergenerational relationships further. The successful and positive ageing process can make older people feel less lonely and isolated, which may help them sustain their physical and mental health. People may lose friends and family members as they age due to death or relocation, which results in a lack of social relationships. However, developing strong relationships with people from the younger generation might assist resolve this problem by offering companionship and emotional support (Rossi et al. 2014; Shi 2017).

The importance of intergenerational relationships in forming social structures is explained by several sociological theories. From a functionalist viewpoint, the emphasis is on the need to preserve social order and coherence through generations by upholding common values and norms. Another viewpoint is conflict, which contends that power imbalances between age groups can cause conflict and inequality. The modernization theory contends that as a result of industrialization, traditional values are replaced by rationality and efficiency, which has an impact on family structures and relationships. Increasing pressure to conform to shifting cultural standards or economic expectations may result from this tendency, affecting intergenerational relationships (Antonucci and Jackson 2007; Thomas 2019).

Family and Intergenerational Relations

The family has been identified as the socio-economic foundation of the nation as it constitutes the fundamental and universal social structure of human society. Strong family values are upheld in Asian nations, including India, where many people live near one another in extended family households to meet their psychological, social, and physical needs (Paltasingh and Tyagi 2012; Patel 2005). Family members have consolidated their assets to assist one another during illness or emergencies. Relationships between generations are valued and sustained through families. Several intergenerational studies, usually framed within the context of "family studies," investigate how people of different generations perceive and interact with one another.

Relations between two or more generations are referred to as intergenerational relations. In traditional Indian society, older people lived in a multigenerational extended family, which could include one or more adults, children, grandchildren, and other kin. In these families, the older adults were accorded an unparalleled sense of honour, legitimate authority within the family or community, as well as decision-making duties in the family's economic, political, social, and religious affairs. Evidence from the literature suggests that grandparents have a positive influence on the functioning of intergenerational families. Grandparents are referred to as "family resources" and "family guards" in multigenerational families across cultures. The older family members, such as grandparents, are often the ones who pass on their wisdom and are admired for their role in protecting the values and culture of the younger members of the family. In both traditional and modern societies, intergenerational learning refers to the systematic transfer of knowledge, abilities, and competencies between generations. Making connections between the present and the past keeps the younger generation interested in their culture through this method of information dissemination. Apart from that, the intergenerational theory facilitates the inquiry of intergenerational interactions in a multicultural society. It reinforces the interaction of two people at different stages of development in a variety of situations and environments (Paltasingh and Tyagi 2017).

The Indian family is currently seen as existing in a continuum with tradition and modernity as its two extremes. Traditional social structures are disintegrating, leading to a shift in the social value system. The family has been under some strain and the ties of kinship are weaker and less unified than they used to be. People are moving more swiftly toward modernity because of the associated limitations of living in a joint family. The family is growing vertically, but it is constricting horizontally, according to demographic change. In other words, as the average lifespan rises, more families with three or four generations are formed, but fewer family members are left to assist in caring for older adults (Batra and Bhaumik 2007).

Factors Influencing Intergenerational Bonding

Numerous factors influence intergenerational relationships. The family, the primary care provider, has undergone significant structural and functional change as a result of some developmental processes such as-modernisation, and globalisation. Further advances in science and technology resulted in the transfer of power from the older patriarch to a member of the younger generation who could deal with contemporary institutions. The reliance of young people on older adults for guidance has decreased, and in fact, a role reversal is being seen. A result of this is that the family is becoming more fragmented (Batra and Bhaumik 2007). Figure 17.1 highlights some of the influencing factors such as—growing nuclear families, caregivers' migration to mega cities, modern lifestyles and over-dependence on technology, changing values and ethos that affect the intergenerational solidarity between generations.

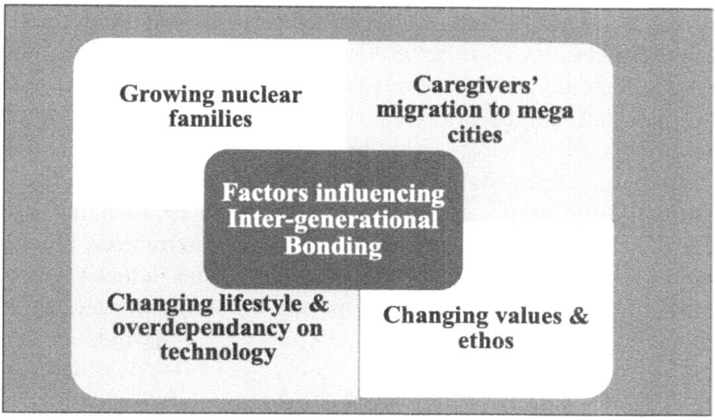

Fig. 17.1 Factors influencing integrational solidarity (*Source* Author's compilation)

Growing Nuclear Families

The older adults' living arrangements are regarded as a form of the family structure in which the leadership they value and the people they live with. The notion of a joint family system has begun to deteriorate recently, and families are choosing to have a nuclear household. As a result of unprecedented urbanisation and industrialization, multigenerational co-residence is declining. In India, a new type of household is emerging where the sons of two or more brothers may live in different households. Nevertheless, they consider themselves a single family. Older adults are particularly vulnerable because they live alone at older ages due to the rising prevalence of nuclear families. In nuclear families, the affective connection is essentially absent (Srivastava et al. 2022). In India, a new kind of living arrangement is becoming a common choice in which married adult children prefer to live nearby to their aging parents rather than cohabiting with them. Living arrangements consequently have an enormous impact on the aging population. Age-related problems, chronic illnesses, and functional limitations are more likely to affect older people who live alone (Paltasingh and Jena 2022; Kumar and Kumar 2019).

Caregivers' Migration to Mega Cities

The conventional extended family structure in India has changed as a result of factors like international trade and migration from rural to urban areas. The young's pursuit of education and higher aspirations led them to leave their hometowns and move to large cities or nations, leaving the older adults (first generation) to fend for themselves with the minimal necessities of life. The Indian joint family's structural changes therefore inevitably led to functional modification. Apart from that, young adults are increasingly relocating to urban areas in search of employment, despite the fact that a sizable portion of the population is concentrated in rural areas. This trend has some positive effects on the economy, but it also has some negative effects, such as being attributed to the nuclearization of families and leaving older parents and grandparents alone in rural areas. This has resulted in a variety of effects on the lives of older adults. Older adults, who are frail, vulnerable and in need of socio-emotional support, receive less attention and care from their family members (Kaplan and Chadha 2007). In addition, currently, there are fewer options for day-care for ageing parents as a result of the large number of younger women who frequently look after older adults' family members entering the workforce (Rajan and Sudhir 2020).

Changing Lifestyle and Over-dependence on Technology

The large ideological gap that exists, particularly between young adults and older adults, is profoundly worrisome for the well-being of the ageing population. The consumerist society was formed as a result of modernization and industrialization. Relationships gradually change as a result of modernity's productivity and content. In the current scenario, the dynamics of interpersonal relationships are rapidly changing. The modern family system now largely revolves around concerns for individual freedom and individuality. In contrast to the "family self," the "individual self" seems to be a relatively new social phenomenon (Khan 2015). The primary areas of contention between younger and older generations are those related to education, marriage, lifestyles, general behaviours, and values. Recent technological advancements, shifting ideologies, and lifestyle changes have altered India's social landscape (Paltasingh and Tyagi 2015).

The lack of support from their family, frequent verbal and physical abuse, neglect, and disrespect from their children force the older adults to move into an old age home. In addition, technology has had a significant impact on the family. According to the literature, there is a generation disparity when it comes to incorporating digital services. The older generation's hesitation to embrace the most recent online services has been met with annoyance from the younger generation. A new generation gap is considered to exist when discomfort is expressed across generations. It is deemed to be a generational shift (Khan 2015). As a result of increasing rates of technological innovation and the spread of information and communication technologies (ICT), we are currently witnessing the digitalization of daily life (Seifert and Cotton 2020). ICT usage was higher among the younger generation than the older generation. Younger generations' excessive reliance on technology has caused them to spend less time with older members of their families, which isolates older people.

Changing Values and Ethos

In Indian society, older people have always played a significant role in the institution of family. Their position and autonomy were upheld in earlier times, and family members used to view them as assets. All of the ancient literature, including the Veda and various epics, highly values parents. As a result, young people used to show respect for senior citizens (Paltasingh and Jena 2021). The obligation of children to support their ageing parents is considered as one aspect of the larger concept of caregiving norms. The acknowledged obligations and responsibilities that define the social role of adult children with regard to their ageing parents are part of the larger concept of familism morals. Gans and Silverstein (2006) highlight the fact that, over the past few decades, there has been a significant change in adult children's familial responsibilities to their ageing parents. The ability of families to provide support is eroding which was once seen as the senior population's primary caregiver. As a result, more older adults are living alone or merely with their spouse, which puts them at risk for financial hardship and a lack of support systems; both of which can have a negative impact on their health (Turagabeci et al. 2007).

Significance of Intergenerational Solidarity

In accordance with legal obligations, children are expected to look after and assist their aged parents. However, intergenerational solidarity in families also includes other social interactions that help to strengthen family ties and encourage adult children to assist and care for their aged parents. The definition of intergenerational solidarity is the cohesiveness between generations or the intergenerational cohesion between parents and children once the children have grown up and started their own families (Kuligina and Dobelniece 2022). It has long been acknowledged that social support between generations affects older parents' physiological, financial, and psychological health. Relationship reciprocity is positively associated with the quality of life for older family members; as they age, the more involved they are in the family, the happier they are with their lives. This contentment is positively co-related with younger generations and vice versa. However, understanding the relevance and shaping of relationships through intergenerational solidarity is crucial.

Intergenerational Solidarity Framework

The framework of intergenerational solidarity was developed by sociologists and psychologists Bengtson and Roberts (1991) to provide the means of understanding these relationships. The model was put to the test empirically, and in 1994 it underwent modifications and was used as a model construction to study intergenerational solidarity in families. The intergenerational solidarity model developed by Bengtson and Roberts has served as a major source of inspiration for studies on family ties and family solidarity. Most researchers who examine intergenerational solidarity in families place an emphasis on one or more dimensional representations of intergenerational solidarity in order to identify the pertinent elements, and manifestations that might influence how adult children and their parents interact. The six components of "solidarity" include: affectual, associational, consensual, normative, structural, and functional.

- ***Affectual solidarity*** describes the reciprocity and feelings of closeness among family members. Mutual affection and the manifestation of emotional closeness can serve as indicators of affectional solidarity (Hogerbrugge and Komter 2012).
- ***Associational solidarity*** describes various forms and patterns of conversation and communication among family members. It can be seen through shared activities and how frequently people interact (Evan-Zohar 2011).
- The agreement of views, principles, and convictions among relatives is referred to as ***consensual solidarity***. It can be seen by the shared sense of family identity, the perception of having similar morals and beliefs, or by shared political and civic pledges (Hogerbrugge and Komter 2012).
- The concept of ***normative solidarity*** refers to expectations of parental and filial duties, as well as the sense of obligation connected to a person's position within the family and adherence to family norms and values. It shows up in behaviours that are family-focused, reverence for filial piety and familial hierarchy, and the sense of responsibility to take care of family members (Chen and Silverstein 2000).
- ***Structural solidarity*** describes prospects for intergenerational interaction made possible by geographical proximity. It is evident when family members share a home or are in close proximity to one another (Kuligina and Dobelniece 2022).
- ***Functional solidarity*** describes intergenerational assistance that may be instrumental (such as cooking, doing chores around the house, or getting groceries) or affective (e.g., listening considerately, articulating compassion, appreciating the other person). It can be seen in the way that support is given and received or in the amount of time that family members spend with one another (Duflos and Giraudeau 2022).

According to studies on support networks for older adults in India, structural characteristics of the network, such as its size, composition, and functional features—such as the degree of instrumental support and care—maintain or enhance the psychological and physical well-being of older people. It has been discovered that emotional support is a significant predictor of favourable physical and psychological outcomes in older parents (Chen and Silverstein 2000).

Bridging Generations for Healthy Ageing

WHO (2018) states that the idea of healthy and active ageing is a continuous process that spans the entire life course. It describes the method of enhancing and retaining an aged person's physiological, psychological, and functional capability. Life expectancy is significantly impacted by health. Older people contribute more to society if their extra years are complemented by a healthy environment and good health. So, long-term care is required to address the socioeconomic and health-related issues that the ageing population is experiencing. The family plays a crucial role in providing both social and medical care for the older adults. Nevertheless, the rising older population, increased life expectancy, and migration poses a challenge to the next generation of adult children as they strive to recognise their potential while adhering to family cultural traditions related to care and assistance provided to their parents.

In the coming years, intergenerational interactions will likely become more challenging. As a result, special emphasis must be placed on some strategies for successful family (intergenerational) interactions, with a particular emphasis on geriatric care. Reciprocal intergenerational interactions are linked by moral responsibility and emotional support. Therefore, educational interventions, such as individual and family-based intervention programs, must be designed in order to foster favourable perceptions toward older adults (Jamuna 2007).

Linking Generation through Digital Inclusion

The development of science and technology has many positive impacts on society, at the same time, a large segment of the older population is alienated due to lack of exposure and access, and there is less scope for healthy inter-generational relations. The basis of digital inclusivity is that it is an instantaneous, virtual form of communication. Digital inclusion among older people, through telephone communication, provides expressive and instrumental forms of support. The digital participation of older individuals enhances intergenerational group cohesion in ways that both complement and replace more traditional means of communication, which require more time and coordination. Digital inclusion can help to bridge the intergenerational gap by providing opportunities for younger and older generations to interact, learn from each other, and share experiences. Peng et al. (2018) found that older adults who use the internet often and are digitally involved may be more likely to interact with family members and communities online, which may strengthen social connections between generations. Beyond the family, the use of digital technology would be advantageous in a variety of contexts, such as healthcare, and recreation, all of which support older adults' quality of life and autonomy.

Need for Intergenerational Programmes

The concept of creating intergenerational activities and programmes through proper planning could manifest in a variety of ways. Initiatives that promote cooperation, interaction, or exchange between younger and older generations are referred to as intergenerational programmes. The focus is on formal initiatives established in setups like residential facilities, community centres, and education institutions. Intergenerational programme frameworks have historically been divided into three categories. Firstly, initiatives that involve bringing in senior citizens to help with personal development (educational, psychosocial, career development, and so on) Secondly, initiatives in which young participants assist senior citizens in some way. Thirdly, initiatives in which participants of all ages collaborate to achieve a common objective. While the intergenerational intervention model in the majority of western nations tends to be oriented towards fostering relationships and support networks between non-relatives, the emphasis is more heavily placed on familial ties in India and other Asian countries as well. Older adults in India take on the role of cultural watchdogs through their participation in inter-generational initiatives. The older generation is thought to be more effective as advisors, educators, and supporters if they have emotional bonds with older adults (Kaplan and Chadha 2007). Intergenerational programmes must therefore be emphasised and promoted.

Awareness Building in Educational Institutions

Concerns about intergenerational issues must be viewed from the perspectives of both young people and older adults. The gap could indeed be successfully managed if school-age children were made more aware of senior citizens' needs and expectations of their families. The intergenerational relationship could be strengthened simply by including it in children's education. This can further have an easy transition to the institutions of higher learning. Additionally, older adults need to redefine their expectations considering the shifting realities of family life. It is important to envision healthy ageing from a holistic approach. Every child must be raised with strong values that promote caring for older adults (Khan 2015).

Policy Initiatives

Ageing policies are at the centre of the response to the radical change in the demographic structure. The kind of society that will be formed as a result of changes in demographic structure remains not comprehended by policy planners and programme developers at various levels. To enhance the quality of life and well-being of all generations, the government, civil society, other stakeholders, and family members must strengthen much closer relationships across all generations. The mainstay of individual and societal security, and consequently of stronger human bonds, continues to be intergenerational solidarity. The interconnectedness of the generations must be strengthened by policies and programmes. In order to increase intergenerational solidarity, societies must encourage interpersonal interaction.

Concluding Remark

It is important to emphasise the effects of intergenerational conflict in a country where families are largely in charge of the social and economic well-being of older citizens. Throughout a person's life, the appearance, absence, and nature of their social connections have an impact on their psychological and overall well-being. Older adults who connect with children and young people appear to maintain their own health to a greater extent. The consideration that young people receive from other devoted adults contributes to their development as well. An effective intervention that can benefit both the young and the old must be implemented for bridging the generations. Therefore, the challenge is to find strategies for bringing generations together to enhance relationships and better foster collaboration in order to address family, community, and societal issues, thereby promoting overall and sustained development. It is necessary to improve counselling services in order to reduce inter-family tension. Strengthening family care is necessary to encourage dyadic interaction and healthy ageing. In addition, older adults can maintain better health with the support of intergenerational health and wellness programmes. Intergenerational programmes must be promoted because they provide the connections required to promote healthy ageing, a pathway that starts early in life.

References

Antonucci TC, Jackson JS (2007) Intergenerational relations: theory, research and policy. J Soc Issues 63(4):679–693

Batra S, Bhaumik K (2007) Intergenerational relationships—a study of three generations. In: Sharma KL (ed) Studies in gerontology-intergenerational perspectives. Rawat Publications, Jaipur

Bengtson VL, Roberts REL (1991) Intergenerational solidarity in aging families: an example of formal theory construction. J Marriage Fam 53(4):856–870. https://doi.org/10.2307/352993

Bhandari P, Paswan B (2021) Life style behaviour & mental health outcomes of elderly: modification of socio-economic & physical health effects. Ageing Int 46:35–69

Census (2011) Elderly in India-profile and programmes, 2021. Retrieved from https://www.mospi.gov.in/documents/213904/301563/Elderly%20in%20India%2020211627985144626.pdf/a4647f03-bca1-1ae2-6c0f-9fc459dad64c

Chen X, Silverstein M (2000) Intergenerational social support and the psychological well-being of older parents in China. Res Aging 22(1):43–65

Duflos M, Giraudeau C (2022) Using the intergenerational solidarity framework to understand the grandparent-grandchild relationship: a scoping review. Eur J Ageing 19:233–262. https://doi.org/10.1007/s10433-021-00626-6

Evan-Zohar A (2011) Intergenerational solidarity between adult grandchildren and their grandparents with different levels of functional ability. J Intergenerational Relat 9:128–145. https://doi.org/10.1080/15350770.2011.567915

Gans D, Silverstein M (2006) Norms of filial responsibility for aging parents across time and generations. J Marriage Fam 68:961–976

Hogerbrugge MJA, Komter AE (2012) Solidarity and ambivalence: comparing two perspectives on intergenerational relations using longitudinal panel data. J Gerontol B Psychol Sci Soc Sci 67(3):372–383. https://doi.org/10.1093/geronb/gbr157

Jamuna D (2007) Intergenerational issues in elder care. In: Sharma LL (ed) Studies in gerontology-intergenerational perspectives. Rawat Publications, Jaipur

Kaplan M, Chadha NK (2007) Intergenerational programme and practices—a conceptual framework and an Indian context. In: Sharma KL (ed) Studies in gerontology-intergenerational perspectives. Rawat Publications, Jaipur

Khan AM (2015) Bridging inter-generational gap through school education. In Paltasingh T, Tyagi R (eds) Caring for the elderly: social gerontology in the Indian context. SAGE, pp 226–244

Kuligina N, Dobelniece S (2022) Intergenerational solidarity in family influencing factors. SHS Web Conf 131. https://doi.org/10.1051/shsconf/202213101002

Kumar S, Kumar KA (2019) Living arrangement and economic dependency among the elderly in India: a comparative analysis of EAG & non EAG states. Ageing Int 44:352–370

Ministry of Statistics and Programme Implementation. Ministry of statistics & programme implementation (MOSPI) (2021) Elderly in India: profile & programmes. Central Statistical Organization, New Delhi. Retrieved from https://www.mospi.gov.in/documents/213904/301563/Elderly%20in%20India%202021l627985144626.pdf/a4647f03-bca1-1ae2-6c0f-9fc459dad64c

Paltasingh T, Jena B (2022) Toward healthy aging: emerging geriatric health care issues in India. In Rajan SI (eds) Handbook of aging, health and public policy. Springer, Singapore. https://doi.org/10.1007/978-981-16-1914-4_189-1

Paltasingh T, Jena B (2021) Life at sunset years: health and health care need among Indian elderly. In: Shankardass MK (ed) Ageing issues in India: practices, perspectives and policies, vol 32, 1st edn. Springer, pp347–360. https://doi.org/10.1007/978-981-16-5827-3_20

Paltasingh T, Tyagi R (2012) Demographic transition and population ageing: building an inclusive culture. Soc Change 42(3):391–409

Paltasingh T, Tyagi R (2015) Caring for the elderly: social gerontology in the Indian context, 1st edn. SAGE

Paltasingh T, Tyagi R (2017) Situating elderly role in family decision-making: Indian scenario. Ind J Gerontol 31(1):43–57

Patel T (2005) The family in India: structure and practice. SAGE Publication, Delhi

Peng S, Silverstein M, Suitor JJ, Gilligan M, Hwang W, Nam S, Routh B (2018) Use of communication technology to maintain intergenerational contact: toward an understanding of "Digital Solidarity". In: Barbara BN, Cláudia C (eds) Connecting families? information & communication technologies, generations, and the life course, pp 159–180. https://doi.org/10.1332/policypress/9781447339946.003.0009

Rajan S, Sudhir. (2020) Home away from home: profile of old age home and its inmates. Ind J Gerontol 34(2):170–176

Rossi G, Boccacin L, Bramanti D, Meda SG (2014) Active ageing: intergenerational relationships and social generativity. Stud Health Technol Inf 203:57–68. https://doi.org/10.3233/978-1-61499-425-1-57

Shi J (2017) The evolvement of family intergenerational relationship in transition: mechanism, logic and tension. J Chin Sociol 4(20):1–21. https://doi.org/10.1186/s40711-017-0068-z

Seifert A, Cotton SR (2020) In care and digital savvy? modern ICT use in long-term care institution. Educ Gerontol 46(8):473–485. https://doi.org/10.1080/03601277.2020.1776911

Srivastava S, Chauhan S, Patel S, Kumar P, Purkayastha N, Singh SK (2022) Does change in family structure affect the household headship among older adults in India? a gendered perspective. Ageing Int 47:1–19. https://doi.org/10.1007/s12126-020-09401-x

Sudha S, Rajan SI, Sarma PS (2007) Intergenerational family support for older men and women in South India. In: Sharma KL (ed) Studies in gerontology-intergenerational perspectives. Rawat Publications, Jaipur

Thomas MH (2019) Ageing and modernization theory. Asian Rev 32(2):53–62

Tabuchi M, Miura A (2015) Young people's reactions change elderly people's generativity and narratives: the effects of intergenerational interaction on the elderly. J Intergenerational Relat 13(2):118–133

Turagabeci AR, Nakamura K, Kizuki M, Takano T (2007) Family structure and health, how companionship acts as a buffer against ill health. Health Qual Life Outcomes 5(61):2–9

World Health Organisation (WHO) (2018) Ageing & health. Retrieved from https://www.who.int/news-room/fact-sheets/detail/ageing-and-health

Chapter 18
Intricacies and Exigencies of Gerontological Care in India

Anagha Tendulkar Patil

Abstract This paper reviews aspects of ageing in India. However, by virtue of its subject matter, this paper is also concerned with the ageing issues of India. It attempts to review the dimensions and efficacy of gerontological care in Indian society. The study addresses the pertinent but hugely neglected domain of the complex care system and comments on the impact of the processes of modernisation and industrialisation on the status of the aged. It examines the current socio-cultural scenario within which the Indian gerontological care system is nested, highlighting certain major concerns and apprehensions about the well-being of the ageing population in India.

Keywords Ageing · Population ageing · Care · Caregiving · India

An Ageing World

Ageing is an inevitable and normal phase in the life of living beings. Old age is an organic culmination of ageing, which subsequently results in the death of a living organism. This linear understanding of age, using the life-course perspective, has prompted scholars to portray (and rightly so) old age as a benign and natural termination of existence. Hence, for a long time, old age did not merit attention from academicians and scholars. The work of Maddox and Wiley (1976) cites Russell Ward as noting, 'Perception of old age as a social problem had emerged by the 1930s and there was a growing recognition of the need for collective action on behalf of the aged' (Ward 1979). However, even up until the 1950s and 1960s, the study of ageing was not mainstreamed in research. The White House Conferences on Ageing, in 1961, and again in 1971, called attention to the problem of ageing.

As industry-centric processes gripped the globe and medical sciences began to improve, an increasing number of people started living longer lives. In parallel to 'individual ageing', a slow and steady 'population ageing' was evolving. Population ageing, also known as demographic ageing, implies an increase in the total number

A. T. Patil (✉)
Sophia College for Women, Mumbai, Maharashtra, India
e-mail: anaghatendulkar@gmail.com

A. Chauhan et al. (eds.), *Hundred Years of Sociology in India: Evolving Issues, Emerging Trends*, https://doi.org/10.1007/978-981-96-1317-5_18

Table 18.1 Population of the aged across the world, 1995–2050

Year	Population (billion)	Percentage of population aged 60+
2000	6	10
2030	8.5	16.4
2050	9.7	22
2100	10.4	29.8

Source United Nations, 1998. World population projections in 2050. Department of Economic and Social Affairs, Population Division

of elderly in the community. This phenomenon was first discussed in 1982, when the United Nations organised the first-ever world assembly on ageing in Vienna (UN 1982).

Population ageing is a complex process. Although demographic variables such as birth rate, death rate, total fertility, and dependency ratio play a decisive role in shaping the style, pace and spread of the process, it is not solely demographic in nature. It has social and economic implications as well. To comprehend it effectively, it is important to understand it in the socio-cultural and economic context in which it occurs.

Ageing is common across the globe, but its manifestations are varied. The population of the world in 1995 was 5.7 billion; it was 7 billion as per the 2011 record and is expected to reach 9.4 billion by 2050 (UN 1996). The percentage of elderly in the world population in 1995 was 9.5; it was 9.9% in 2000. It is estimated to reach 14.6% in 2025 and 20.7% in 2050 (UN 1998) (see Table 18.1).

South-East and East Asian countries have begun to experience the initial tremors of population ageing but remain largely unaware of the gravity of the grey explosion. The UN report 'Lifelong Preparation for Old Age in Asia and the Pacific' (1996) notes that population ageing is much faster in Asia than in Europe or North America. The pace at which many countries in Asia are ageing is a matter of great concern because of its anticipated social, economic and political implications.

India is also ageing. The population of 60+ individuals in India is slated to rise from 103 million in 2011 to 319 million by 2050, a three-fold increase (LASI 2020). These numbers reflect the slow and steady (and almost unnoticed) grey evolution of India. The issues concerning population ageing are seriously understated. The sporadic and scattered mention of it in sociological discourse is far from noting the gravity of the phenomenon.

This paper unearths the complicated social texture of gerontological care and demands serious attention to the emerging gaps in the care system in India. It looks at existing data and literature to ascertain the position of the elderly in society at large and the care infrastructure in India specifically. It examines the concept of care, establishing the oft-missed distinction between gerontological and geriatric care. It analyses the role of the aged as both receivers and givers of care. The paper also attempts to highlight important questions to consider addressing data gaps regarding gerontological care in India.

The Position of the Elderly in Society

Population ageing cannot and should not be studied in a vacuum. The process is assimilative, incorporating the socio-cultural trends, values and beliefs prevalent in a given society. The community in which an individual age is instrumental in providing the frame through which 'old age' is viewed and managed. The phenomenon of care for the elderly emerges from this reference point because of the dialectical connection between group/community ageing and the demand to manage the bulk dependence in society.

Prior to the emergence of population ageing, when life expectancies were shorter, the question of care did not really arise because people rarely lived long enough to become inactive or dependent on others for extended periods of time. Any care needed was then provided by family or community.

Historically, three factors seemed to determine a community's attitude towards its elderly: the mode of economy, the demographic structure of the community and the consequent value system. These three exercised their influence in the same order, with the economy having the most decisive power. The mode of economy implied the most prominent kind of economic system followed, whether food gathering and hunting or horticultural or agricultural. The demographic structure of a community specifically implied the dependency ratio between the productive and non-productive populations. The dependency ratio is important because it has a serious bearing on the allocation of resources in a given community. Last, but not least, the values held by the community played a crucial role in shaping the attitude of the community towards the elderly and consequently, the treatment given to them. One can find several historical references provided by the scholars to substantiate the point.

'Extreme poverty leads to improvidence: the present is all-important, and the future is sacrificed to it. Where the climate is severe, the environment harsh and resources inadequate, human old age often resembles that of animals' (de Beauvoir, 1970, p. 54).

In certain communities, there was an inbuilt mechanism whereby the young and the strong customarily got rid of the old. The elderly were socially conditioned to accept their fate. It was considered inappropriate if the elderly thought otherwise. 'Among the Amassalik Eskimo in Greenland, elders could select an appropriate evening and make a sort of public confession before heading out in Kayak, never to return. In other cases, the failing old person might enjoy a feast, smoke a pipe of peace, sing, dance, and—while the dancing continued—fall from a blow by a relative designated for the duty' (Orlock 1995, p. 7).

When tribes and clans chose to settle down, which implies that they moved from the hunting and gathering mode to horticultural, agricultural modes of production, customs and practices changed accordingly. The concept of the community gathered a more established dimension, thereby making the positions of different age categories clearer and more crystallised. The status of the elderly changed. This is not to suggest that such communities suddenly started believing in 'old is gold', but that the utility value of the old in terms of accumulated wisdom and gathered experiences was acknowledged and was put to use wherever possible. Light economic tasks were entrusted to them. These were not lucrative but supplemented the main economic activity. 'The position of aged was not based solely on charity, however. The aged assumed positions of social significance because of abilities useful to the society and the control over valued resources' (Ward 1979, p. 72). So, the position of the aged did not necessarily improve in settled economies, but at least, they were no longer discarded by the community in a socially sanctioned manner.

In the twenty-first century, it seems more pertinent to consider the modernisation theory explored by Donald Cowgill and Lowell Holmes in 1972. This theory rests on the assumption that modernisation results in a status inversion, lowering the position of the elderly in society.

Cowgill (1986) presented four notable features of modernisation as having a serious bearing on the status of the elderly. First is the use of scientific technology that is generally youth-friendly, widening the gap between young and old. Older occupations become redundant and the elderly are marginalised in modern society. The second is health technology, which implies a longer life expectancy. With a higher number of old people around, the burden on the productive working group increases. Another inevitable feature of industrialisation is urbanisation. Young people are attracted towards urban areas, resulting in changes in the family structure, residential segregation and increased social distance between generations. Lastly, modern education for younger people seems to result in a lower position for parents. The process of modernisation, therefore, automatically pushes the elderly out of the mainstream.

This theory, with its obvious macro implications, was very well received initially. However, in modern society, a great deal of evidence has been put forth against several of the generalisations drawn by Cowgill. The theory does not account for differences in gender, class, ethnic backgrounds, etc. Besides, Cowgill's comment that the status of the elderly has declined in modernised societies has been questioned by many, citing the comprehensive pension schemes, effective health care systems, etc. available for the elderly in modern societies. There is a lot of empirical evidence to refute the theory of modernisation. However, the theory is deemed as a significant milestone in understanding the status of the elderly population in industrialising and modernising society. So, what is the reality of the aged, especially in India? Has a modernising India pushed its aged population to the side lines? How does India care for or neglect to care for its aged?

Care for the Aged in India

In human society, care is embedded in the very idea of coexistence and caring is intrinsic to human nature. Such care has a broad canvas; it goes beyond the medical and includes physical, emotional, financial and psychological care that aims at general well-being and not a mere cure for a disease or relief from pain.

Caring is a universal tendency. Human society thrives on interdependence and care. It can be viewed as an integral part of human existence. The written testimony of former first lady Rosalynn Carter mentions, 'There are only four kinds of people in the world. Those who have been caregivers. Those who are currently caregivers. Those who will be caregivers, and those who will need a caregiver' (Written Testimony of former First Lady 2011).

A Lack of Understanding of the Types of Care

Humans are probably the only species that care for their young as long as they do. Interestingly, similar emotions are not displayed for the aged. Based on the cultural assumption of care being organic to human society, childcare and old-age care should have almost parallel trajectories in society, which it does not. This paradox is just the beginning of the complexities of the care system.

For this reason, I prefer to use the expression 'care system' rather than the word 'care'. In India, while paediatric care seems to be rich with conventional and modern remedies and solutions, geriatric care has never been given much attention as a special body of knowledge. Our knowledge about gerontological care is rudimentary or almost non-existent. Moreover, it is insensitive and compassionless. The very fact that we cannot appreciate the distinction between gerontological and geriatric care implies that we do not deliver care as practice but care as work.

Geriatric care refers to healthcare, maybe even specialised medical care, while gerontological care refers to the social support that elderly people need. Not all senior citizens need geriatric or medical care as soon as they turn 60. In fact, good gerontological care can reduce the load on geriatric care.

Although India has specialisations in paediatric, prenatal and natal care, geriatric care as a specialisation has no value. It is not even a subset of adult medical care. Very few hospitals maintain and run separate geriatric wards. Geriatric medicines are clubbed with medicines for adults. We have a simplistic understanding of old age care. We constantly use the parameter of chronological age and assume that care is offered as a remedy to health-related pathological conditions. Even within geriatric care, we seem to not recognise the varieties of care, like palliative, hospice, curative and supportive care. The only positive aspect of geriatric care, when compared with gerontological care is that it is definite and empirically tested. This means that geriatric morbidity and comorbidities are documented and exist with definite solutions. Though mere treatment (even if accurate) cannot be called 'care', old people are treated for their empirically tested problems and age-related disabilities, if reported in time.

Eldercare is a unique combination of assistance and supervision conditioned by the characteristics of older persons who are receiving care from his/her caregiver (Jamuna & Ramamurti 2000). Caring has both qualitative and quantitative aspects. Quantity refers to the amount of time and effort spent in care giving while quality refers to the nature of caregiving (affection, succour, concern etc.). Quality of caregiving involves relationships or services in various aspects. Dimensions such as psychological interdependence, motivating factors like attachment, obligation, altruistic behaviour and desire to extend care determine dyadic interactions (Jamuna and Ramamurti 1999).

Gerontological care is broader in scope than geriatric care but has not been documented satisfactorily. In India, there is complete invisibility and ambivalence about gerontological care.

Lack of Diversity in Care

Another concern is about a uniform formula of care. Studies in the ageing have proved that different factors affect how we age: class, caste, gender, marital status, having or not having children, living situations, literacy level, job profile and professional accomplishment. If one can age in such diverse ways, then how can we arrive at a uniform formula for care? Even the category of old age is not monolithic; there are several classifications of this group. Many scholars have accepted a three-fold grouping of senior citizens asserting that every subcategory is distinct, and therefore, their needs for care would differ. The three subcategories are 'young old' (60–69), 'middle old' (70–79) and 'old old' (80+).

In addition, the phenomenon of Ageing of aged complicates the scenario. As pointed out by Chakraborti (2004), if the age of 60 years and above introduces social and economic complications, the ageing of the older population will aggravate the problem. Rapid ageing will produce a group of an extremely aged population in demand of yet different types of care. Moreover, an old person is different in every stage of his/her old age. Capacity does not always decline in a linear fashion in old age. It varies from person to person.

Caregivers

Nel Noddings, an American philosopher, highlighted the relationship between the 'one-caring' and the 'cared-for', which means at least two people who may come to develop a reciprocal commitment to each other's wellbeing (Noddings 2013).

Christina Victor has cited the contribution of Parker (1981) where the distinction is drawn between 'caring about' and 'caring for' based on the criterion of tasks and functions undertaken by carers. 'Caring about' is conceptualised as being concerned about an individual and could include such tasks as providing emotional support, while 'caring for' is usually taken as being concerned with more direct hands-on help and can also be conceptualised as tending (Victor 2005).

If the ethics of care (also known as care ethics) is applied to the realm of gerontological care, several concerns emerge about the quality of care provided to old people.

Firstly, in a society like India, old people rarely speak out. They are culturally trained to be less vocal and silent about their problems. The communication channel necessary between the one-caring and the cared-for is not encouraged. It invariably results in the one-caring delivering care as a response to their perception of the needs of the cared-for. This may not always match the actual needs of the cared-for.

Secondly, the profile of caregivers is changing. Typically, care is provided by agencies like family, community (which includes institutional arrangements like old age homes, senior citizens' associations, day care centres, etc.), non-governmental organisations, and the State itself. The institution of family has undergone unprecedented changes in modern Indian society. Forces of modernisation, industrialisation and the altered status of women have revised the identity of the family and contested one of its important functions, which is care giving. There is an ambivalence and ambiguity about the position of the primary caregiver. The notion of family as a care-giving agency is challenged by multiple structural factors like the shrinking size of the family, fragile intergenerational bonds, migration for lucrative options, socialisation of children, changed domestic role of working women, and ideas of individualism and self-sufficiency.

Since family care is no longer easy and available, the community seems to be gradually extending its role. Old Age Homes (OAH) and assisted care homes have certainly increased in number. However, the quality of care they provide is not tracked or assessed on a regular basis. There are two types of OAHs: aided ones, funded by the government and private unaided ones operated by their management. Since OAHs are residential institutions, they technically provide an alternative to home care. Senior Citizens Associations (SCAs) make provisions for the elderly population to spend a few hours in the company of other old people. SCAs have mushroomed in India. Although their number is quite impressive and they undertake many activities, the kind of activities and programmes they conduct are almost random and often unregulated. Day Care Centres (DCCs) are the need of the hour in the Indian society, but there are few professionally operated DCCs for the aged in India. The proportion of OAHs, SCAs and DCCs to the respective target groups of old people is worrying. Besides the paucity of these community associations, the attitude of society towards these associations is discouraging. The senior citizens who avail of the facilities provided by community-run associations are looked at with pity or their family is labelled as irresponsible and cruel.

Thirdly, the lack of data about the gerontological care system is an impediment. Despite the profound work being done by the community for the aged, when it comes to measuring the success of voluntary activism for old people, information is scarce. Poor documentation hinders awareness and hampers the reach and scope of community care.

The government, particularly state governments, must be allotted greater responsibility and power to provide resources and legislate for the well-being of old people. However, to do so, they must have a sound database, reliable experts and a strong political will to utilise these resources to help and protect senior citizens. In the absence of meaningful dialogue, between the government and other stakeholders, to understand the needs and problems of senior citizens, the State as a caregiver falls short of expectations. While care receivers should be educated to articulate and communicate the issues they face, dialogues with caregivers are necessary to create the necessary infrastructure to provide better care for the elderly and to ensure support for caregivers. Care is multi-layered and typically involves multiple stakeholders. The components of a care system must operate in tandem with a common paradigm. There should not be competition or hostility among caregivers but correspondence.

The Feminisation of Ageing and Care Giving

Traditionally, women have played the role of active caregivers in families. Their work as unpaid caregivers is invisible and undocumented. The feminisation of ageing, whereby there are more old women than old men, since women live longer than men, has raised tricky questions. Though women live longer, are they fit enough to look after others? Since women typically are not encouraged to make independent decisions, can they make smart decisions in situations where they need to? Who looks after old women, who have probably been caregivers, when they need care? As reliable caregivers, are they careful care seekers as well when need be? What does caregiving mean for the health of female caregivers as they age? These are all important questions that must be addressed and require, as in the case of many sociological concerns, a gender-disaggregated approach to both data and solutions.

The Elderly as Caregivers

The phenomenon of the ageing of the aged has altered the care system quite significantly. Participation in the care process can be studied with the 'etic' and 'emic' perspectives to care. Application of these perspectives, originally from the discipline of Anthropology to gerontological care would imply that the etic view is an outsider's view and hence is less appreciative of the actual need for care. The emic perspective is an insider's perspective, it emerges from within the framework/culture and hence is likely to be meaningful and beneficial. We must not ignore or discredit the multi-layered care system in India. In the network of care, the primary caregiver/manager must be known. In several cases, old people themselves are caregivers to their partners. A lot of them have the added responsibility of their grandchildren in the family.

Conclusion

Indian society is both typical and unique. India is a poor country, so it is important to understand who is responsible for the care of its citizens aged 60 and above. The first impact of the demographic transition is a significant change in the dependency ratio. Demographically a poor dependency ratio implies a considerable burden on the working population. To illustrate this further, typically a middle-aged couple will have two pairs of senior citizens to look after. In addition, their child/children will have to be supported. With limited resources at their disposal, the quality of care for senior citizens is automatically short-changed.

Population ageing implies that an increasing number of people are living longer. However, it does not mean they are living healthy, pathology-free lives. In fact, in a developing country like India, the quality of life in an increased lifespan cannot be vouched for. To support the aged who have depleted money and resources, a strong and professional caregiving agency is needed.

Caregiving, however noble, is not free. While the rich might be able to afford care from outside the family even when they are no longer active members of the workforce, the poor cannot. Unpaid care is increasingly unavailable due to changes in the institution of family. Paid care, particularly in India, is unregulated and often inaccessible. State-sponsored care is inadequate. And for developing nations, that seems to be greying fast; solutions, unfortunately, are still few and far between.

In considering aspects of care for the elderly, this paper has been limited by data and time and has only been able to examine a largely urban, typically heterosexual population. What about single persons, especially women, without families? What about LGBTQIA+ people? What about those with disabilities? What about the urban poor and what about rural India? And in India, in particular, one must also consider the element of caste. These are all aspects of the issue that merit closer study. In fact, another aspect of old-age care in India that is troubling is the lack of multi-faceted studies on its various concerns.

Care for the elderly should be a comprehensive phenomenon. Governmental care and societal care cannot be treated as contending parties but as complementary wings to ensure the well-being of the elderly population. Ensuring the blend of etic and emic perspectives to care will augment society's capacity to provide care to its senior citizens. Curating care connections is the need of the hour. The older people should be asked about their needs and should be made partners in engineering gerontological care. They cannot be placed on the periphery. To design and implement an effective, inclusive, and sustainable gerontological care system, it is important to map needs, strategize services, pool resources, and ensure flexibility.

References

de Beauvoir S (1970) Old age. Penguin Books Ltd., United Kingdom, London

Chakraborti RD (2004) The greying of India population ageing in the context of Asia. Sage Publication Ltd., New Delhi
Cowgill DO, Holmes LD (eds) (1972) Ageing and modernization. Appleton-Century-Crofts, New York
Cowgill DO (1986) Ageing around the world. Wadsworth Inc., Belmont CA
International Institute for Population Studies (IIPS), National Programme for Health Care of Elderly (NPHCE), MoHFW, Harvard T. H. Chan School of Public Health (HSPH) and the University of Southern California (USC). Longitudinal Ageing Study in India (LASI) Wave, 2017–18, Executive Summary, International Institute for Population Studies, Mumba, 2020
Jamuna D, Ramamurti PV (1999) Contributions to good caregiving: an analysis of dyadic relationships. Social change: issues and perspectives. J Counc Soc Dev 29(1 & 2):138–144
Jamuna D, Ramamurti PV (2000) Burnout among the caregivers of disabled elderly: effect of intervention. Psychol Stud 45(3):150–155
Maddox G, Wiley J (1976) Scope, concepts and methods in the study of ageing. In: Binstock R, Shanas E (eds) Handbook of aging and the social sciences. Van Nostrand Reinhold, New York
Noddings N (2013) Caring a relational approach to ethics and moral education. University of California Press, California
Orlock C (1995) The end of aging. How medical science is changing our concept of old age. Birch Lane Pr., USA
Parker GR (1981) Teaching and social policy. In: Goldberg GM with Hatch S (eds) A new look at the personal social service. Policy Studies Institute, London
United Nations (1982) Report of the world assembly on ageing. Vienna 26 July to 6 August, 1982. New York
United Nations: Economic and Social Commission for Asia and The Pacific (1996) Lifelong preparation for old age in Asia and the pacific. New York
United Nations: Dept. for Economic and Social Information and policy analysis (1998) Ageing. In: Proceedings of the united nations international conference on ageing populations
Victor C (2005) The social context of ageing a textbook of gerontology. Routledge, London and New York
Ward RA (1979) The ageing experience. An introduction to social gerontology. J.B. Lippincott Company, USA
Written testimony of former First Lady Rosalynn Carter before the Senate Special Committee on Ageing (26 May 2011)

Part V
Employment, Education and Environment: Emerging Trends

Chapter 19
Agency Regained: Low-End Job Gulf Migrants, Middle Class and the Kerala Model

Antony Palackal and N. B. Lekha

Abstract The paper seeks to construct a narrative of the low-end job among Malayalee Gulf migrants with a view to situate their transformative sojourn in the developmental map of the state of Kerala. Within the framework of a narrative paradigm, it examines qualitative empirical evidences to establish the role of the Gulf migration of the lower-class Malayalees in the making of the middle class as a predominant category in the social development of the state in the post-colonial era. The paper opens up a discussion on the agency played out by the lower-class Gulf migrants in the making of the much-debated "Kerala Model of Development" and tries to ascertain their agency in the emergence of Kerala society. It argues that the history of the post-independent modernity of the State and its developmental trajectory is intertwined with the pangs and perils of the lower-class Gulf migrants.

Keywords Migration · Gulf migration · Low-end Job migrants · Kerala · Kerala Model of Development · Middle class

Introduction

The paper opens up a discussion on the agency played out by the lower-class Gulf migrants in the making of the much-debated 'Kerala Model of Development'. The state of Kerala is acclaimed in the tourist map as 'God's own country'. However, from the vantage point of development, Kerala is a region in the developing world with a unique pattern of development, known as the 'Kerala Model' that exhibited a trajectory with high social achievements on a weak economic base (George

A. Palackal (✉)
Department of Sociology, University of Kerala, Thiruvananthapuram, Kerala, India
e-mail: antonypalackal@gmail.com

N. B. Lekha
Department of Sociology, Sree Narayana College, Chempazhanthy, Thiruvananthapuram, Kerala, India
e-mail: vaishnavy@gmail.com

A. Chauhan et al. (eds.), *Hundred Years of Sociology in India: Evolving Issues, Emerging Trends*, https://doi.org/10.1007/978-981-96-1317-5_19

1993; Oommen 1992, 1999; Ramachandran 1996). The most obvious component of the Kerala Model is the set of statistical quality of social indicators putting Kerala closer to high-income developed countries than to its counterparts in the low-income world. In the demographic indicators like life expectancy, birth rate, death rate, infant mortality, maternal mortality, and population growth rates Kerala stands at a higher level and well above the all-India average. Kerala Model, thus showcased to the world how a poor region in a developing country could achieve remarkable progress in matters of literacy, public health, education, longevity, death and birth rates, population growth, sex ratio and mortality rates without sufficient economic growth. The Nobel laureate Amartya Sen wrote: 'Kerala, despite its low-income level, has achieved more than even some of the most admired high-growth economies such as South Korea' (Sen 1997, p. 7). Hence, Kerala holds a distinctive position in the developmental map of the world and continues to be the focus of attention for both Indian and international scholarship.

In the light of the much-debated Kerala Model of Development, the paper proposes to unearth the participation of the low-end job migrants to the Gulf as a critical category in the development of modern Kerala of the neo-liberal era. To this effect, the paper examines the process by which the low-end job migrants were able to transform themselves into the middle class. It argues that the developmental trajectory of modern Kerala and thereby the history of post-independent modernity of the State since its formation, is intertwined with the pangs and perils of the lower class Gulf migrants and the transformations there off both at the micro- and macro-levels.

Marginal and Excluded

The paper is set in the context of three fundamental questions concerning the nature and approach of the vast array of diaspora studies in general and studies on the Kerala diaspora in the Gulf in particular. First and foremost is the question regarding the specific subjects who formed the focus of those studies. The Malayali[1] migrants to the Gulf, in fact, constitute a heterogeneous and diverse group in terms of their occupation, income status, education, region, religion, and gender. However, these groups are classified differently in different studies (Zachariah et al. 2006; Zacharia and Rajan 2015, 2012; Prakash 2000). Notwithstanding, it is important to note that the category of 'Other workers', who are in low-end jobs that are unspecified (Prakash 2000), constitute the highest group of Gulf migrants. They mainly include construction workers, both skilled and unskilled, such as masons, carpenters, plumbers, electricians, helpers, and domestic workers, manual labourers in factories and bakeries. This category of Gulf migrants always had to struggle through a 'casual' and marginal existence, in most cases, both before going to the Gulf and even while they were in Gulf as migrant labourers.

---

[1] People of Kerala are known as 'Malayalees' after their regional language 'Malayalam'.

Interestingly, the empirical data that is analyzed later in this paper reveal the fact that these low-end job migrants who lived on the fringes of society, indeed participated actively in the socio-cultural and economic programmes and activities of both the host country as well as the home State. Paradoxically, there exists a serious dearth of studies that take cognizance of the predicament of this category of 'other workers' who were into low-end jobs. Consequently, their contribution to the making of the much-celebrated Kerala Model of Development was ignored and thus their agency in the history of modern Kerala is unrecognized.

The second question pertains to the epistemological frame in which diasporic studies are commonly pursued. It has been found that there prevailed an epistemological bias towards objectivism mostly resorting to macro studies that quantitatively assessed the impact of outmigration and remittances (Zachariah et al. 2006; Prakash 2000; Pushpangadan 2003; Rajan and Narayana 2010; Zacharia and Rajan 2012, 2015; Basu 2016; Muckerjee 2017). First, these studies treated migrants as solely economic actors. Second, they generally examined economic indices such as the cost of emigration, trends of return emigration, causes of return and profile of return emigrants, economic consequences to the host region in terms of fall in remittance and economic recession, and so on. Hence, they tend to neglect a micro-level understanding, exploring the subjective and local ramifications of the non-economic aspects of the migration.

The third question flows from the above two questions. It concerns the concept of 'agency' of the 'Kerala Model' of development. Studies on the Kerala Model of Development tend to ignore the contribution of the lower-class population who migrated to the Gulf and engaged actively in the socio-economic, political, religious, and cultural growth of the State (Zachariah et al. 2006; Prakash 2000; Pushpangadan 2003; Rajan and Narayana 2010; Zacharia and Rajan 2012, 2015). This paper intends to address these fundamental issues and seeks to ascertain the 'agency' of the lower-class Gulf migrants in the developmental map of the Kerala Model. The discussion on these questions, however, is integrally linked to the debate on the evolution of Kerala Society as primarily comprised of the middle class and the process of middle-classisation of the low-end job Gulf migrants. A disjunction, thus seems to prevail in the migration studies in general, and the studies on the dynamics of the transformative processes of the low-end migrants in particular that grossly neglected the socio-cultural dimensions of their lives. Given this context, the paper embarks on a journey through the lives of the low-end job Gulf migrants with a view to decipher the subjective and objective transformations that occurred on account of their Gulf migration. More specifically, it navigates through the milestones of the tangible changes in the life of a low-end job migrant and thereby unravelling the dynamics of the processes of transformation at the personal, familial, community and societal levels.

Methodology

The study employed a qualitative approach to data collection and its empirical basis is founded on narratives based on the qualitative data. It is designed as longitudinal in terms of the time span that ran through three generations at the same time. The three generations included: (1) the Generation of the parents of the migrant, (2) the Migrant's generation and (3) the Generation of the migrant's children. Male migrants from Kerala who engaged in low-end jobs for a minimum of ten years in the Gulf, who either have returned or still working in the Gulf, constituted the subjects of the study. Ten years of working in the Gulf was fixed in order to ensure a reasonable time period for perceivable changes to be noticed in the socio-economic profile and life styles of their family and the resultant transformation it brought to Kerala society.

We engaged in face-to-face conversations with twenty-five low-end job migrants across the state from 2017 December to 2018 March. As part of the ethnographic engagement, we have spent on an average two hours with each respondent, in addition to spending a day with the family of a few respondents in their place of residence. Further, we also walked through some villages, which are densely populated by return migrants. Twenty-five male respondents were identified from the three zones of the State, namely, South, Central and North spread through four districts—Thiruvananthapuram, Quilon, Pathanamthitta and Malappuram, which have the largest number of migrants in the state, according to the statistics of the Economic Survey (2016). The study included only the male migrants for two reasons (1) males constituted the higher percentage of Gulf migrants engaged in low-end jobs (Prakash 2000; Raja and Narayana 2010), and (2) to understand the situation of females left behind, when the male member/s in the family go to the Gulf to make a living. The names of the subjects of the study are changed in the narratives so as to maintain anonymity and confidentiality. For the sake of brevity, we limit the narratives in the analysis to a minimum.

Penury to Prosperity

The migrants belonged to the lower class in terms of their class position as they grew up in an environment of penury and hardships. Here is a sample of several such narratives on the everyday predicaments of the lives of the migrants. It reveals the following:

> In my childhood, life was really difficult. I was living in utter poverty and we didn't even have a cent of land in our name... When I was about two years old, my father abandoned my mother (...), and my mother and I were left to fend for ourselves and in order to survive I used to do many odd jobs and earn very little doing so (Muhammed, Malappuram, 2019).

Most of the parents of the migrants could engage only in menial and low-end jobs. They had to struggle to make both ends meet as the following narratives reveal.

Several of the migrants had to help out their parents in their struggle to find some means of livelihood before they left for the Gulf.

The migrants in the study seem to have more or less fulfilled their bridled aspirations, namely, to acquire the entitlements for a decent existence back home. They longed for a life that rendered all their basic needs such as good food, housing, education, and health care, with reasonable household utensils, gadgets and other goods. Sebastian from Pathanamthitta who worked in the Gulf for more than twenty years vouchsafed thus: *Now we have everything—we have microwave, fridge, washing machine, TV, laptop and what not.*

The sojourn to the Gulf did increase their purchasing power so as to translate their aspirations into reality to a great extent. As a result, the aspirations of the migrants enhanced dramatically, which in turn propelled their consumer propensities, whetting out their desire to buy and possess things. Before their Gulf migration, this was a near impossibility, because of their low purchasing capability. Consequently, they seemed to buy and possess consumables such as clothes, sandals, cosmetics, vehicles, household gadgets, media and communication equipment and so on that the market threw before a voracious consumer. In sum, there occurred a huge transformation in the lives of the low-end job Gulf migrants from a state of penury to a state of prosperity, which ultimately led to their entry into the middle-class camp in Kerala.

Housing, Health and Education

The aspirational accomplishments of the low-end job migrants, consequent to Gulf migration, were most conspicuously manifested in three areas, namely, housing, health care and education. When the migrants started their journey to the Gulf in search of work and money, the only capital they possessed was the confidence that they could do any work and face any challenge, and the most cherished aspiration to build a house of their own back home. 'I need to make some money and come back to build a new house of my own', was their priority and challenge that gave them the strength to face any adverse conditions in the Gulf. Thus, building a house seemed to be the most basic requisite for every migrant. Koya from Malappuram who slogged in Abu Dhabi for twenty-two years, testified:

> Now there aren't any thatched roof houses that I can show you; back in the day it had been thatched roof upon four legs of wood and that's where we all stayed. (....) I remember my mother saying that when it rained the water flowed into the house; so if a baby was on the floor she would keep him or her on the other side where there was no water and keep doing that to avoid the baby from getting wet (Koya, Malappuram, 2019)

In the final analysis, it was the Gulf migration that enabled the migrants to build a house of their own, thus translating their long-cherished dream into a reality. To this effect, some of them invested whatever they could earn and save in the Gulf. Further, for several of the migrants, the house is regarded as the major asset they possess as a result of their working in the Gulf. The possession of a house, in a way, elevated them to a higher status from their earlier lower position. In other words, the house remained as a symbol par excellence, of the shift in the class position of the lower class migrants and exemplified their upward mobility in the socio-economic hierarchy of Kerala society.

Similarly, in the wake of acquiring heightened purchasing power, unprecedented transformations occurred in the attitude and practice of health care of the low-end migrants. After their migration to the Gulf, they began to pay more attention to their health and treatment, an area that was either neglected or given the least priority. Here is a testimony about the situation of health care before and after their sojourn:

> In the olden days we either used to go to the 'vaidyar' (traditional medical practitioner) or to a government hospital; now we go to private hospitals not only because they provide better service but also because going to a particular private hospital displays our wealth and status. But people like that are less here (Muhammed, Malappuram, 2019).

With respect to health care and medical treatment, one finds a substantial transformation from generation one to generation three. The transformation was visible in the attitude and approach to health care, medical treatment, the type of health care centres visited, and the health care policies obtained.

Education was another important arena in which, they invested their earning from the Gulf. Realizing the importance of education, especially in a market-driven society, all of them invested a good portion of their hard-earned Gulf income in providing quality education to their children. Our empirical data revealed unambiguously that progressive and conspicuous change in the educational profile occurred from generation one to three. The majority of the children of the migrants, both boys and girls alike have acquired higher educational degrees that fetched them high value in the job market. Given the conventional practice of the Muslim community, even if the girls were married off at a younger age, the basic education that they gained brought them bridegrooms with good educational qualifications and thus good jobs. It appears that housing and education seemed to be the key areas in which the lower-class Gulf emigrants have invested their earnings from the Gulf. Correspondingly, while housing vested them with social capital with high prestige and honour, education bestowed them symbolic capital that could accrue them rich dividends in the future.

Making of the Middle Class

The term 'middle class' has generally been employed to refer to that section of a capitalist society, that lies between the capitalist and the working classes. However, it is comprised of a heterogeneous historical bloc with differential access to relations of production, status and political power. What constituted them as middle class were their aspirations for upward mobility and modernity through consumerism (Palackal 2012a, b). It has been rightly noted that the new economic policies enabled the middle class to consume goods that had been treated as luxury items, such as household appliances, toiletries, packaged foods, and other consumer goods but were now perceived as crucial indices of upward mobility (Mankekar 1999). In this way, the demographic expansion of the middle class was reinforced by its cultural constitution.

The plethora of consumer-world is the privileged stage where the contestations and negotiations of identities occur in contemporary society (Palackal 2011). The increase in purchasing power has enabled the migrants' entry into the consumer market and provided them with the required entitlements, although in varied degrees, to become dynamic players in the market. In other words, on account of Gulf migration, lower-class migrants could occupy a specific space of their own in the public sphere, hitherto unavailable to them. This new spatial position has enhanced their social status and prestige, which enabled them to redefine their identity. Thus, the whetting of the aspirations sparkled by going to the Gulf, acted as an asset that elevated their position in the class ladder of the State and reconstructed their identity from that of the earlier one. In other words, possession of goods and commodities served as markers of renewed social status, position and identity for the migrants in society. As a result, the low-end job Gulf migrants began to increasingly adopt middle-class mores and attitudes.

However, the consumer culture of these migrants contained two distinctive features, namely, frugality in spending and modesty in lifestyle. While they were in the Gulf, the majority of them pursued the singular motive of sending the 'maximum' back home, and almost all of them used to send home 'whatever that was left' after their simple and meagre existence in the Gulf. For instance, here is a testimony,

> (...) I really save my money. I don't spend it unwantedly. Because when I started in the Gulf I had this dream of buying some land and building a house of my own. Now also I save the money I earn. After I started working in this company only did I start to buy things priced Rs.1000/- and more, but still I don't want to...
>
> (Sasi, Thiruvananthapuram, 2018).

The migrants, by and large, with their increased entitlements, were not only able to translate their aspirations for a decent living, but have also initiated a new culture of philanthropy and social service that improved the lot of the vulnerable members of their respective communities. Moreover, it contributed to the progress of the socio-economic and cultural spheres of the society at large.

The triumphs at the subjective front, in turn, had their objective consequences on the community and societal fronts too. The hard-earned Gulf triumphs of the migrants did not end with the personal and familial transformations alone. As an unintended positive consequence, it also had its transformative impact on the wider society. Thus, we have an emphatic stand-alone claim:

> Every inch of development in Malappuram is due to the hard work of the Pravasi. Not just Malappuram, I would say all the development seen in Kerala is due to the pravasi. But dominating would be those from the Malabar region for sure (Abdhu, Malappuram, 2019).

It appears that the Gulf migration of the lower class population in Kerala has contributed not only to the making of a distinctive genre of the middle class, mostly of the lower and middle levels, but also to the making of the State of Kerala with its distinctive character of development. Their risky sojourn in the Gulf has definitely contributed to the growth and sustainability of various sectors such as market economy, business, commerce and banking, construction, health care, education and so on, in short, to the socio-economic development of the State. Therefore, the lower-class migrants who attained middle-class status because of their Gulf migration seem to positively contribute to the development of Kerala society. Undoubtedly, therefore, one can say that they have written a unique chapter in the history of the development of modern Kerala—a distinctively separate one at that, from the rest of the chapters that the mainstream authors and various socio-political agencies claim to have written.

Gulf Returnee—A New Identity Outfit

A key figure in the debates exploring the cultural process linked to consumption and consumer culture is the French Semiologist, Baudrillard (1988). In a post-liberalized world, Baudrillard sees the entire society as organized around the consumption and display of commodities, with its accompanied forms of gift giving, philanthropic and social service activities, through which individuals gain identity and prestige. He observed that consumption plays a critical role in defining people's identities and consciousness, so that styles of consumption are held to have superseded the old class-consciousness.

Baudrillard's work (1988) is valuable in that he draws attention to the increasingly fundamental role of signs and images in a consumer society. The new forms of consumption and the renewed market relations that they were able to establish in the wake of their sojourn in the Gulf, enabled them to realize their compelling aspirations to a great extent. This process, in fact, gave birth to a new section of the middle class in Kerala, who are christened as *Gulf Returnees* that conferred them with a unique identity. This new identity outfit, which they have obtained through their struggle-ridden sojourn in the Gulf bestowed them a distinctive locus in Kerala society. Neither any other category nor any agency can take credit for its origin and growth, the middle-class status, prestige and honour that the low-end class Gulf migrants thus achieved.

In sum, the processes of the dynamics of the transformative trajectory from a lower class predicament to a middle class gave them entry to a new passage—the passage to the consumer market. That was the road they entered from their penury to prosperity with power, ability and entitlements. It is important to note that it was the heightened purchasing power, and the renewed consumption behaviour whetting out the long cherished aspirations in the wake of their migration to the Gulf that has elevated the lower class migrants and bestowed them with the identity of the middle class. Hence, the Gulf migration of the lower class has contributed in a special way to the making of the middle class in Kerala.

Notwithstanding, the lower-class Gulf migrants, upon their elevation to the middle class, remain a separate genre altogether. The middle-class standard of living that was made possible on account of their Gulf migration did not lead them to a life of *westoxication* (Gupta 2000) that exhibited unbridled propensities for consumption at any cost with a display of extravagance and wasteful affluence. Not only they did not seem to indulge in conspicuous and unscrupulous consumption, typical of the Indian middle class, but they have initiated a new culture of philanthropy and social service in the State. In fact, several of them consciously experimented with a life of simplicity and modesty. In this sense, the emergence of the lower-class Gulf migrants as a middle class, by and large stands out as a distinctive cultural category, who do not fit neatly into the generic universe of the Indian middle class who are prone to display consumption patterns that resemble the cosmopolitan cultural forms in other parts of the world (Kemper 1993; Appadurai 1996).

Conclusion: Kerala Model Under Scrutiny

The study thus points to the need for a revisit of the prevailing discourses on the 'Kerala Model of Development', acclaimed as a unique pattern of development. As stated in the beginning, the State, a developing region in the Indian subcontinent with its distinctive socio-economic and demographic characteristics, has been compared with developed nations with respect to its developmental experience (Ramachandran 1996; Oommen 1992, 1999, Vol. 1 and 2). A composite index of quality of life, taking into account the various factors, placed Kerala far above the general social condition that existed not only in India but also in most parts of the Third World (Parameswaran 2000). The explanatory discourses while looking at the causative factors of this developmental experience have focused on the role of 'agency' in paving the way for the 'Kerala Model' (Sen 1997; Tharamangalam 1998; Kannan and Pillai 2004; Desai 2005). Nonetheless, these discourses, both academic as well as public, seem to have neglected the 'agency' played out by the low-end migrants in the making of the 'Kerala Model'.

The study has highlighted that, this emergent segment of the middle class—*Gulf returnees*–shaped their destiny from that of their earlier miserable predicament, basically on their own. They seem to have received little support or assistance of any kind from any Government or agencies in the State, irrespective of ideological or religious affiliations. At the same time, this segment seemingly contributed heavily to the economic, social, political, religious and cultural sustenance and growth of the State. This points to the need to underline the 'agency' of these hitherto invisible players in the making of the 'Kerala Model' and the developmental trajectory of the State to situate their untold contributions in the very making of it. Therefore, it is important to locate the growth of the low-end job of Gulf migrants as middle class and their role and contribution to the developmental trajectory of the State, as a critical economic factor which sustained Kerala's economy from mid-seventies (Jeffrey 1992). In this context, the struggle-filled sojourn of the lower-class Gulf migrants and the resultant transformations at the personal and societal terrains need to be mapped as a distinctive locus in the development scenario of modern Kerala. It necessarily calls for a revisit of the 'Kerala Model'.

References

Appadurai A (1996) Playing with modernity. In: Breckenridge CA (ed) Consuming modernity—public culture in contemporary India. Oxford University Press, Delhi

Baudrillard J (1988) Selected writings (Ed Poster M). Stanford University, Stanford

Basu S (2016) Diasporas transforming homelands nuancing 'collective remittance practices in Rural Gujarat. Econ Polit Wkly 51(41):54–61

Desai M (2005) Indirect British rule, state formation and welfarism in Kerala, India, 1860–1957. Soc Sci Hist 29(3):457–488

Economic Survey (2016) Government of India. Government Press, New Delhi

George KK (1993) Limits to Kerala model of development: an analysis of fiscal crisis and its implications. Centre for Development Studies, Trivandrum

Gupta D (2000) Mistaken identity—India between worlds. HarperCollins, New Delhi

Jeffrey R (1992) Politics, women, and well being: how Kerala became a model. Palgrave Macmillan, UK

Kannan KP, Pillai VN (2004) Development as a right to freedom—an interpretation of the Kerala model. Working paper 361. Centre for Development Studies, Thiruvananthapuram

Kemper S (1993) The nation consumed—buying and believing in Sri Lanka. Publ Cult 5(3):377–393

Mankekar P (1999) Screening culture, viewing politics: an ethnography of television, womanhood, and nation in postcolonial India. Duke University Press, Durham and London

Muckerjee A (2017) Gulf migration and the flows of social remittances: a study of Barkas in Hyderabad. Sociol Bull 66(1):91–103

Oommen MA (ed) (1999) Kerala's development experience, vol 1 and 11. Concept Publishers, New Delhi

Oommen MA (ed) (1992) The Kerala economy, vol 1 and 2. Oxford and IBH, New Delhi

Palackal A (2012a) Globalization and Kerala society—a cultural analysis. In: Vilanilam JV, Palackal A, Luke S (eds) Introduction to Kerala studies. International Institute for Scientific and Academic Collaboration (IISAC), New Jersey, pp 571–584

Palackal A (2012b) Kerala model of development—legacy and paradox. In: Vilanilam JV, Palackal A, Luke S (eds) Introduction to Kerala studies. International Institute for Scientific and Academic Collaboration (IISAC), New Jersey, pp 993–1002

Palackal A (2011) Globalization, consumer culture and identity—middle class in a postmodern society. Rawat Publications, New Delhi, Jaipur

Parameswaran MP (2000) What does the Kerala model signify? Towards a possible 'Fourth World'. In: Parayil G (ed) Kerala: the development experience. Zed Books, London

Prakash BA (2000) Exodus of gulf emigrants: return emigrants of Varkala town in Kerala

Pushpangadan K (2003) Remittances, consumption and economic growth in Kerala: 1980–2000. Working paper 343. Centre for Development Studies, Thiruvananthapuram

Ramachandran VK (1996) On Kerala's development achievements. In: Derze J, Sen A (eds) Indian development: selected regional perspectives. Oxford University Press, Delhi, pp 205–356

Rajan SI, Narayana D (2010) The financial crisis in the gulf and its impact on south Asian migrant workers. Working paper 436. Centre for Development Studies, Thiruvananthapuram

Sen A (1997) Economies and the family. In: Oberoi P (ed) Family, kinship and marriage in India. Oxford University Press, Delhi

Tharamangalam J (1998) Perils of social development without economic growth: the development debacle of Kerala. Bull Concerned Asian Sch 30(1):23–34

Zacharia KC, Rajan I (2012) Kerala's gulf connection, 1998–2011—economic and social impact of migration. Orient Blackswan, New Delhi
Zacharia KC, Rajan I (2015) Dynamics of emigration and remittances in Kerala: survey 2014. Working paper 463. Centre for Development Studies, Thiruvananthapuram
Zachariah KC, Gopinath N, Rajan SI (2006) Return emigrant in Kerala: welfare, rehabilitation and development. Manohar Publications, New Delhi

Chapter 20
The Condition of Nagaon and Cachar Paper Mills in Assam: The Present and Future Trajectories

Pranjal Sarma

Abstract The trajectories of the closure of mills in India over the last hundred years or more have become a social phenomenon. The trend of such occurrences is a worldwide sociological issue leading to several causes of shutdown/closure. It has many adverse social consequences like joblessness, increase in unemployment, affecting the lives of employees in terms of economic status, lifestyle, medical treatments, education of children, displacement and poverty. The closure of mills is a process of deindustrialization that generates a decrease in economic production and entails job and income loss, with job strain and increased exploitation. In this paper, the author has tried to analyse the condition of the Nagaon Paper Mill (NPM) and Cachar Paper Mill (CPM) in Assam, owned by Hindustan Paper Corporation Ltd. The mills were liquidated in March, 2017 and October, 2015 respectively. Suppliers have not got their money; employees have suffered a lot and have not received their salaries for more than 56 months. Four persons committed suicide and about 115 died so far due to ill health, lack of proper treatment etc. because of the financial crisis. Students are suffering due to poor financial condition preventing them from higher studies. Many of the workers are working as daily labourers and producing vegetables for the market. Some of them are doing small business or joining private jobs. Finally, the Chief Minister of Assam distributed a relief package of Rs. 810.02 Crore for the benefit of the employees.

Keywords Paper mills · Liquidation · Trajectory · Workers · Deindustrialization · Social assistance

P. Sarma (✉)
Department of Sociology, Dibrugarh University, Dibrugarh, Assam, India
e-mail: pranjalsarma@dibru.ac.in

RC-16, Work, Labour and Organisation, Indian Sociological Society (ISS), New Delhi, India

A. Chauhan et al. (eds.), *Hundred Years of Sociology in India: Evolving Issues, Emerging Trends*, https://doi.org/10.1007/978-981-96-1317-5_20

A Brief Background of Hindustan Paper Corporation Ltd.

Hindustan Paper Corporation LTD (HPC) was incorporated in 1970 which was a government undertaking. HPC is one of the largest paper manufacturers in the country. It is involved in the manufacturing of premium writing and printing paper based on bamboo. HPC functions directly under the Department of Heavy Industries (DHI). Figure 20.1 shows the product and raw material share in India, given by the Central Pulp and Paper Research Institute (CPPRI).

HPC has two (2) units/plants, namely Nagaon Paper Mill (NPM) and Cachar Paper Mill (CPM). It has subsidiary companies like Hindustan Newsprint Limited, Jagdishpur Paper Mills Ltd, and Tuli Paper Mill.

Nagaon Paper Mill (NPM) was established at Jagiroad, Assam and commenced its commercial production in 1985. It is situated on the National Highway 37 at a distance of 60 km from Guwahati. The yard is located at around 2 km from the Jagiroad Railway Station where there is a large covered railway unloading yard in the mill for unloading of the different inputs for the mill. On the other hand, Cachar Paper Mill was established in Panchgram, Assam and commenced its commercial production in 1988. It is situated on the National Highway 37 at a distance of 25 km from Silchar. The yard is located at about 2 km from the Panchgram Railway Station

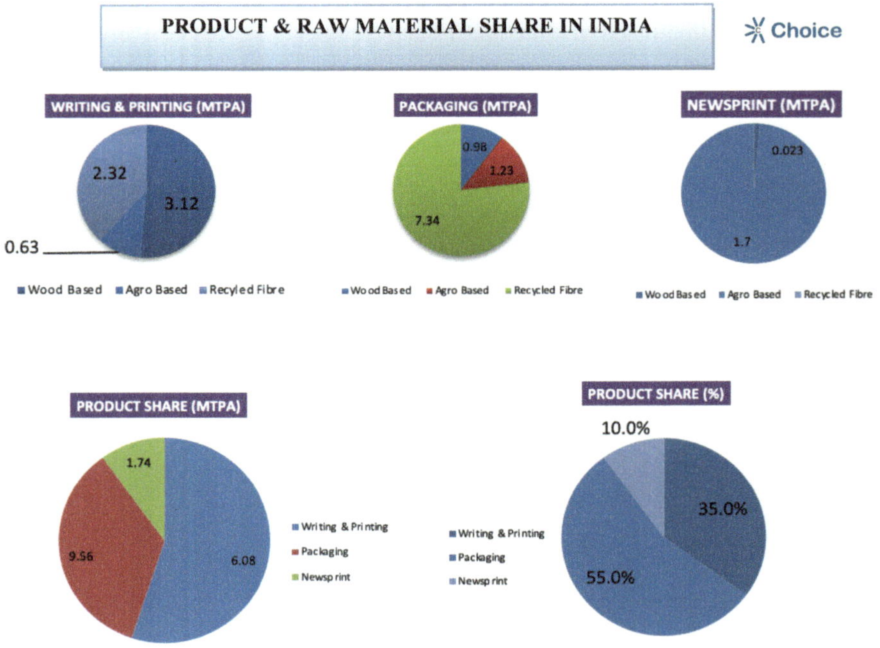

Fig. 20.1 Product and raw material share in India (CPPRI: Central Pulp and Paper Research Institute). *Source* CPPRI data base and Choice Research

Raw Material- Bamboo Availability

Choice

BAMBOO AVAILABILITY IN NORTH EASTERN STATES	
STATE AREA	IN SQ. KMS
Assam	7557
Mizoram	7091
Tripura	2397
Arunachal Pradesh	8681
Manipur	5825
Nagaland	4345
Meghalaya	3031

BAMBOO DISTRIEUTION IN ASSAM	
DISTRICT	IN SQ. KMS
Karbi Anglong	5758.00
North Cachar Hills Cachar & Karimganj	831.45
Kamrup	491.91
Goalpara	280.00
Nagaon	196.00
Total	7557.36

Fig. 20.2 Raw material—bamboo availability in north-eastern states (*Source* Hindustan Paper Corporation Ltd.)

where there is a large covered railway unloading yard in the mill for unloading of its different inputs. The raw material availability in both mills is highlighted in Fig. 20.2.

In the paper manufacturing process (Fig. 20.3), Bamboo is fed manually in a Bamboo yard comprising 6 flumes of 150 m of Length in the chipper house. Thereby, flowing water washes and transports bamboos up to the Conveyor Belts. The Conveyor Belts carries the bamboo to Bamboo Chippers where the bamboo is washed and cut into chips of desired size. Next, screening of fines (Dust) and large pieces is done. After the screening process, dust is sold or used in boilers with coal or making briquettes, and the larger chips are taken back for chipping at the Re Chipper. The final screened chips are stored in 2 chip silos. Finally, chips are removed with the help of two Para Screws in controlled flow where the chips pass through the Chip Washing Screen for further cleaning and washing, ultimately leading up to the digester (Fig. 20.4).

Process of paper production:

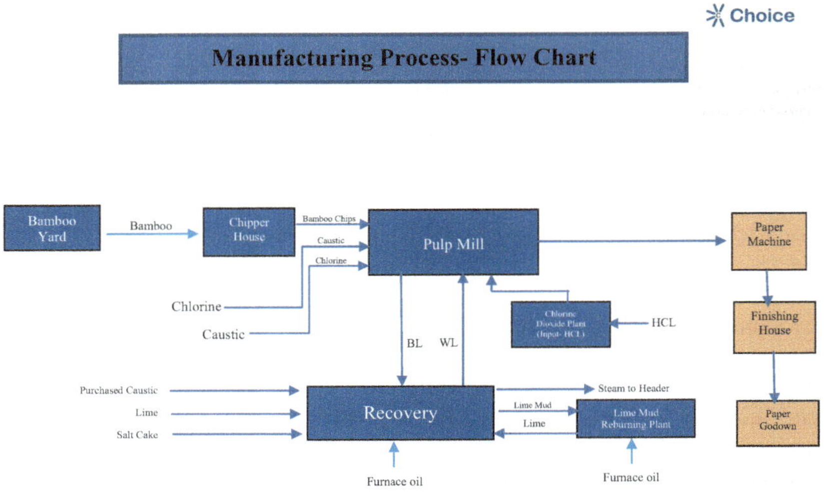

Both NPM & CPM have identical manufacturing process. However the following points are to be noted:		
Points	NPM	CPM
Caustic & Chlorine Supply	Proposed to be supplied using Membrane Technology to Pulp Mill and Recovery Sections in modernization plan	
AFBC Boiler	Commissioned and was running till March 2017	Coal firing trial was taken in March 2015. Commissioning was planned during winter but could not be completed prior to shutdown
Lime mud reburning plant	Commissioned	Yet to be Commissioned
Mills also have Utility plant with Boilers and TGs, Effluent Treatment plant and Water treatment/ supply plant		

Fig. 20.3 Paper production process (*Source* Hindustan Paper Corporation Ltd.)

This is followed by the pulp mill process where washed and screened chips are passed onto the cooking plant from the chipper house. The pulp mill process is supported by a Chlorine Dioxide Plant, Lime Mud Reburning Plant, and a Chemical Recovery Plant that is designed to recover the cooking chemicals and heat. Spent cooking liquor and the pulp wash water are combined to form weak black liquor which is converted into a white liquor and sent back to the digester system.

Both the mills described above have a production capacity of 1,00,000 (1 Lakh) metric tonnes per annum (MTPA). We have already initiated that the main raw material for the integrated pulp and paper unit is bamboo and the pulping process followed is sulphate cooling. The raw material is bamboo in both mills which has an integrated pulping process (Kraft Process) to produce 100% bamboo Kraft pulp. In the cooking plant, the pulping process is done with the Kraft Process which is carried out in continuous cooking mode. A flow chart of the same is shown in Fig. 20.5.

The CPM and NPM have a 30 MW capacity capture power generation facility and also a caustic soda and chlorine plant of capacity 50–60 MT. In the mills, machines were installed with a pneumatic and analogue system. Subsequently, the systems were converted to Distributed Control System (DCS) and Quality Control System (QCS) for Qualities Parameter Control. QCS automatically controls the base weight, moisture, caliper, and ash on the paper. The mills have their own Broad Gauge (BG)

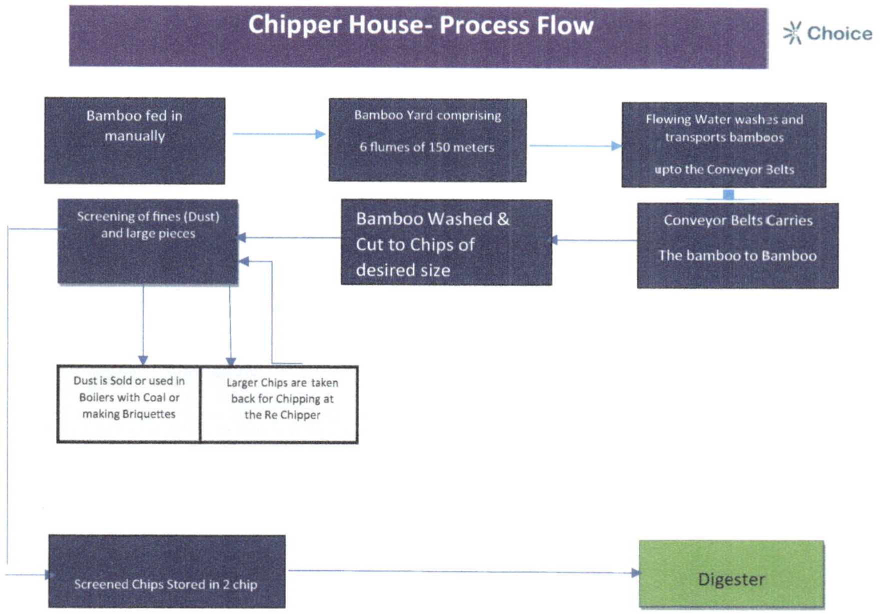

Fig. 20.4 Chipper house process flow in paper production process (*Source* Hindustan Paper Corporation Ltd.)

yard inside its compound where paper can be directly loaded in the rail from the product warehouse.

The Indian paper industry contributes approximately 3% of the world's paper production and has a turnover of INR 50,000 Crore (USD 8Bn). The industry provides direct employment to about 5 Lakh employees and indirect employment to about 15 lakh people. The per capita paper consumption in India is over 13 kg, in comparison to the global average of 57 kg. Organised sector had an installed capacity of 4.1 metric tonnes per annum (MTPA) in the financial year 2015–16 and was running at capacity utilization of 90%. 70% of the total installed capacity is spread across the states of Gujarat, West Bengal, Odisha, Andhra Pradesh, Karnataka and Maharashtra. (Choice Research, https://www.hindpaper.in).

Literature Review

Eleen and Bernardine (1971) in their work, 'Shutdown: The impact of plant shutdown, extensive employment terminations and layoffs on the workers and the community' clearly explain that factories shutdown were caused by the depressed economic situation, poor management, and inefficiency and inferior end-products, domestic as well as foreign competitions, and lack of restrictions on foreign goods. They also

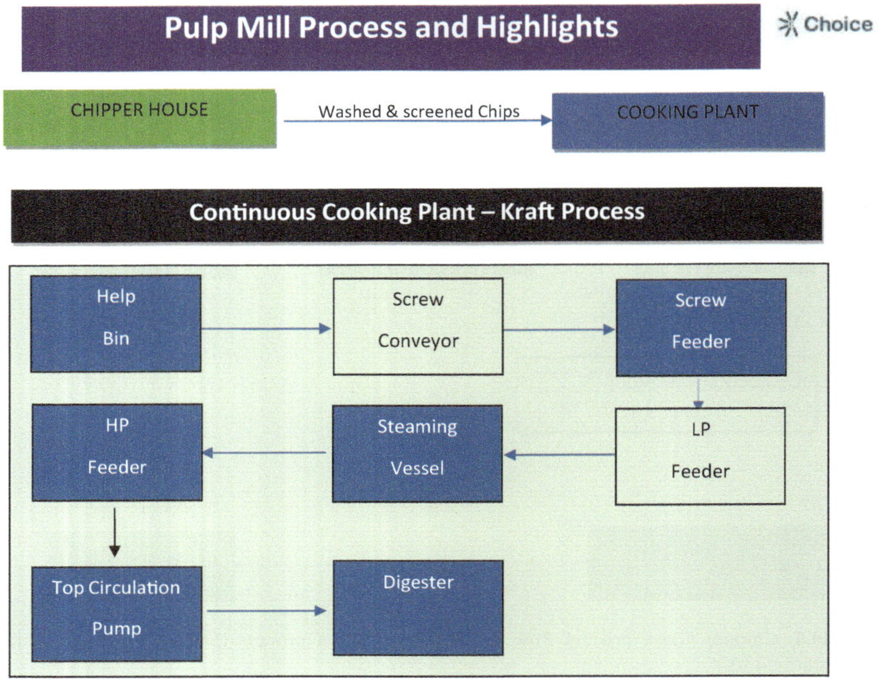

Fig. 20.5 Pulp mill process flow in paper production process (*Source* Hindustan Paper Corporation Ltd.)

expressed that youth wanting to enter the labour force and being rejected through no fault of their own, face a traumatic experience and this can have a lasting effect on their attitude. The shutdown of factories can create unemployment and massive human misery and distress. In this work, they also discussed the psychological impact of factory shutdown on the workers, particularly, the less skilled and those at the bottom of the income scale.

In the work, 'Consequences of plant closure', discusses about the economic impact of plant closure on the income of workers exercising different vocational choices. The study explains that the semiskilled workers and unskilled production workers will suffer a long-run reduction in earnings because of plant closure unless they have interplant transfer rights. The study finds that younger and better-educated unskilled workers will suffer smaller reductions in income than their older and less-educated counterparts. This study also shows that experienced production workers faced a permanent reduction in earnings after the closedown of industry and were bound to compete in the labour market again.

In his paper titled, 'The closure of factory and its impact on health', Grayson (1985), concentrates on the consequences of the shutdown of factory on employees. The study was based on one of Sweden's foremost corporations namely, SKF. The closure of SKF Canada Ltd. was devastating for the employees as well as their families as it impacted their health creating stress and ill health due to economic hardship. Nance et al. (1994) in their article, 'Studying the Social Impact of the Texas Shrimp Closure' discuss the decision of the Gulf of Mexico Fishery Management Council to close the shrimp fisheries in federal waters off the coast of Texas for several weeks duration. They found that the shrimper's opinions on closure differed considerably in relation to ethnicity, geographic areas and vessel type.

Bhagat and Dixit (2000) discussed in their study, 'Impact on workers of closure/relocation of industrial units in Delhi', about the impact of the closure of factories on the workers. This study explains the impact on the workers after the Supreme Court judgment on 8th July, 1996 regarding the closure/relocation of hazardous units in Delhi. Factories shut down can resulted in agitation by the workers as it affected their economic status, food habits, medical treatments, and education of their children. Workers felt helpless and ashamed of their status of being jobless persons. This study also explains that changed employment status has an impact on the existing relationships both with and outside their families.

Haney and Shkaratan (2003) in their work, 'Mine Closure and its Impact on the Community: Five Years after Mine Closure in Romania, Russia, and Ukraine' explore the impact of mine closure on communities in which large-scale downsizing of the mining workforce began in 1997. Mine closure had its impact on employment and labour migration, municipal and social services, environment and community cohesiveness.

Chakrabarti (2007) in his work, 'Labour and Closure of a Mill: Lives of Workers of a Closed Factory in Kanpur' explains the causes and impact of the closure of a factory in Kanpur, India named J.K. Cotton Spinning and Weaving Mills. Due to the closure of the factory, many workers lost their livelihood and because of that, they experienced problems related to medical, educational and economic status. Workers and their agitations come across as 'powerless' and 'ineffective' in this case.

Chapain and Murie (2008) discuss in their work, 'The impact of factory closure on local communities and economies: the case of MG Rover long bridge closure in Birmingham' that the closure of this industry was regarded as presenting a crisis for the government and the local community. The closure of the MG Rover works in Birmingham created an image of jobless, a sudden increase in unemployment and an immediate shock impact on households and local communities. Marais and Cloete (2013) in their article, 'Labour Migration, Settlement and Mine Closure in South Africa' explore the impacts of mine closure in the Free State goldfields. They argue that mine closure leads to considerable economic decline and poverty. It emerged not only among the workers but also in the locality from where the migrant labour came from. This also leads to the massive decline of house prices in the nearby area of the mine. The closure of the mine also had an impact on the economic status of municipalities.

Arman (2014) in the work 'Death Metaphors and factory closure' provides a systematic attempt to analyse the metaphorical underpinnings of organizational members' enactments of the closure of a factory. The study findings explain three root-metaphors of different kinds of closure of factories that change over time.

Firstly, it is the managers who are considered by the employees to be responsible for the closure of the factory and the decisions are illegitimate and deliberate. Secondly, managers and others have described the decision of closure as strategic and inevitable. The third metaphor offered a contextualized, process-oriented and gentic understanding of the closure. Here the closure was described as being bound to happen.

In the work, 'The Closure of the Sugar Mills Narrated by the Workers', Estrada (2017) discusses the closure of more than half the existing sugar mills in Cuba between the last decade of the twentieth century and the end of the first decade of the twenty-first century. The older generations were emotionally attached to the sugar mills so they were disappointed with the decision of the government. Some workers mentioned that it is a strategic mistake of the government to close down the industry upon which the economy of the country rests.

Huynh et al. (2017) in their work, 'Industry shutdown rates and permanent layoffs: evidence from firm-worker matched data', discuss that firm or factory shutdown creates a conflict situation for workers as it leads directly to layoffs for the workers. The study finds that an increase in industry shutdown rates increases the probability of permanent unemployment situation and displacement of employees and decreases earnings growth for workers at continuing firms

In their article, 'We Were the Ones Really Doing Something About It: Gender and Mobilisation against Factory Closure', Robertson and Clark (2019) discuss the understanding of female workers against factory closure. They also discussed the gendered challenges encountered by women workers. Chatterjee (2019) in her thesis "Chawls, Malls and High Rises: Rethinking Gentrification in the Textile Mill Lands of Mumbai" highlighted the process of deindustrialization in Mumbai city which led to the closure of the textile mills from 1980 onwards. The large and small mill structures, small-scale industries, and hundred-year-old chawls contrast with the emerging gated communities, high-rise buildings and chawl redevelopment buildings bringing heterogeneity to the area. The new infrastructure caters to the wealthier counterparts of the society changing the existence of the textile mill compounds into unique and different spaces.

Scheiring and King (2023) said that Deindustrialization is a major burden on workers' health in many countries. They conceptualize industry as a social institution, whose disintegration has widespread implications on the social fabric. Combining Durkheimian and Marxian categories, they show that deindustrialization slows down economic production, which entails job and income loss, an increase in exploitation, social inequality, and the loss of services.

Similarly, many paper mills were closed/shut down in different parts of the world, particularly in India due to deindustrialization.

Table 20.1 Respondents of the Study

Sl. No.	Category	Number	Percentage (%)
1	Officials and staff of Nagaon and Cachar paper mill	20	50
2	Union leaders of Nagaon and Cachar paper mill	05	12.5
3	Senior citizen of the locality	10	25
4	Officers of Assam government of the locality	05	12.5
Total		40	100

Methodology

Indeed, it is very difficult to write academically something on a crucial matter related to the closure of the two largest paper mills of Asia located in Assam, namely the Nagaon Paper Mill (NPM) at Jagiroad and the Cachar Paper Mill (CPM) at Panchgram. They have remained non-functional from March 2017 and October 2015 respectively. The case related to these two mills is still subjugated in Delhi High Court with the Government of India and liquidator Kuldeep Verma as party. It was filed by Cachar Paper Project Workers Union on August 26, 2021. The case comes under the purview of the Delhi High Court as the head office of Hindustan Paper Corporation is in Delhi. Moreover, the Appellate Tribunal National Company Law Tribunal (NCLAT) is involved in this case.

In this paper, the author has taken into account both primary and secondary sources of data. The official and the staff of the mentioned mills, union leaders and senior citizens of the locality as well as the local leaders, and officers of Assam Government of the locality where the mills are situated, were interviewed personally and telephonically. A sample size of 40 numbers of respondents was selected purposively. Twenty (20) officials and staff of both Nagaon and Cachar paper mills of Assam, five (05) union leaders and ten (10) senior citizens of the locality, as well as five (05) officers of Assam Government were interviewed personally and telephonically. The secondary sources of data included journals, official documents, magazines, books, newspapers and internet sources (Table 20.1).

Analysis and Discussion

The organization of Hindustan Corporation Ltd (HPCL) was established by the Government of India through a decision passed by the parliament on 29th May 1970. The main aim of HPCL was to achieve self–reliance in paper production in order to reduce the import of paper and to create employment as well as to bring economic development in the industrially less developed states of the North-eastern region. As a result of that, two heavy paper industries came into existence of which Nagaon paper mill started commercial production w.e.f. 1st April 1985 and Cachar paper mill started its commercial production with effect from 1st April 1988. These industries undoubtedly play a vital role in providing large-scale employment in the state of Assam and help in the upliftment of the socio-economic status of the state. Also, it is a fact that during the 1970s–1980s there was serious social turmoil and social movement in Assam and the problem of extremism existed in north-east India. Looking into all these circumstances, the government of Assam strategically decided to provide large-scale employment to the unemployed youths and installed two heavy paper industries in the state. In the course of time, HPCL achieved tremendous success in the industrial scenario of the state as well as in north- east India and was established as a dividend paying profit-making organizations that paid dividends to the Government of India till 2008–2009 and has been marked as scheduled "A" and Mini Ratna status by the Government of Assam.

According to the opinion of thirty-five numbers (87.5%) of respondents, the performance of these two industries, along with the Tuli paper mill or Nagaland Pulp and Paper Company Limited (NPPCL), started to deteriorate due to various reasons. Some of the prominent reasons were Gregarious Bamboo Flowering causing a raw material crisis in the north–east, particularly in Mizoram in 2007, the imposition of Blanket restriction on coal mining in April 2014 by the National Green Tribunal (NGT), and the ban on transportation of coal from Meghalaya along with non-availability of broad gauge railway connectivity in Barak valley in earlier days. Moreover, corruption, the unprofessional attitude of management and inefficient administration and so on have imposed serious obstacles on the way of production of the Cachar paper mill as well as the Nagaon paper mill. The Tüli paper mill or Nagaland Pulp and Paper Company Limited (NPPCL), was first conceptualized in 1971 for the socio-economic upliftment of the people of Nagaland. It was a joint venture between Hindustan Paper Corporation Limited (HPCL), a Government of India (GOI) Enterprise and the Government of Nagaland; which is now defunct, and had stopped its operations from the month of October 1992.

Twenty-five numbers (62.5%) of the respondents opined that the Government of India had discontinued the grant of transport subsidy, which was earlier available for Cachar Paper Mill with effect from April 2016. This resulted in the complete destabilization of the financial structure and functioning of the industries. Finally the production of both the industries, that is, Nagaon and Cacher Paper Mills was suspended with effect from March, 2017 and October 2015 respectively on the plea of dearth of working Capital.

Five (12.5%) Union leaders of the mentioned two industries opined that these two mills were closed in order to extend benefits to Private paper industries and the private paper industries are trying to increase the price of the paper monopolistically in the domestic market. They said HPCL is selling paper per ton at the rate of 49,000 and the private owner is now selling paper at 95,000 to 1,20,000 per MT after closing the production of paper by HPCL Paper Mills of Assam. Also, India is importing paper from China, Indonesia and Bangladesh to fulfill its domestic requirements. It makes India *Bidesh Nirvar Bharat* (Foreign Dependent India) instead of *Atmanirbhar Bharat* (Self-Sufficient India).

In addition, some other factors for the closure of the two mills were highlighted by the respondents. Four (10%) respondents blamed the lack of technological upgradation as cause for closure; six (15%) opined that hike in the rise of price of raw material, i.e. bamboo; nine (22.5%) blamed the location of paper units in remote areas, situated far away from the cities; three (7.5%) put the blame on shortage of raw material, thirteen (32.5%) believed the competition from foreign imports to be the reason, five (12.5%) believed that due to Covid 19 pandemic, there was a decline in demand for paper products, five (12.5%) opined that the decline in the profitability of the mills is responsible for closure, four (10%) believed the reason to be the hike in price of raw material, and occupational hazards, and ten (25%) believed that it was due to environmental regulations and it could be corrected by using alternative raw material to produce high quality paper by adopting eco-friendly manufacturing processes. Twenty (50%) of the respondents reflected that they have demanded an inquiry about why the production of paper at the two HPCL Mills was stopped, but there was no such Inquiry by the government.

In the meanwhile, the Government of India has enacted a new law named as 'Insolvency and Bankruptcy Code 2016'. In view of the new law, a vendor of HPCL Nagaon Paper Mill went to the National Company Law Tribunal, New Delhi Bench and claimed ninety-eight lakhs (Rs. 98 lakhs) which he was supposed to get from HPCL. The present Government of India failed to settle the claims of rupees ninety-eight lakhs and in turn, the National Company Law Tribunal (NCLT) ordered the liquidation of the entire Organization of HPCL. It affected the livelihood of two lakh people for this reason who were directly or indirectly dependent on these two paper mills of Assam. On the other hand, five (12.5%) trade union leaders opined that they have challenged the order of NCLT at the appellate Tribunal of NCLT and the NCLT ordered to ensure that the company remains a growing concern vide order dated 29-05-2019.

Surprisingly, 5 (12.5%) union leaders of the two mills informed that in an Indian Parliamentary reply on 9-07-2019, Minister of Heavy Industries and Public Enterprises, Sri Arabind Ganpat Sawant said that the Government of India has already invested rupees 4141 crores in HPCL within the accounting year 2014–15 to 2017–18. However, 20 (50%) respondents of the study reflected that during this period both the mills remained inoperative and they questioned the investment of rupees 4141 crores in these mills.

Also, it is interesting to mention that, a commitment was made by the BJP government before the huge rally where the Prime Minister of India, Narendra Modi, on 27/03/2016 at Kalinagar near Cachar Paper Mill and on 08/04/2016 at Roha near Nagaon Paper Mill declared that they will revive both the paper mills of Assam. However, the revival process has not been taken up by the government till date.

It is a fact, as reported by the respondents that from 2015 and 2017 onwards, employees of both the mills of Assam have suffered a lot and have not got their salaries for more than 72 months. Suppliers and contractors have not got their money. Four (04) persons from the mills committed suicide and about 115 employees died so far due to ill health. They did not undergo proper treatment because of the financial crisis. Students are suffering due to the poor financial conditions of their parents preventing them from higher studies. Many of the workers are working as daily labourers and some are producing vegetables for the market. A small number of them are doing small business like running small shops, driving auto rickshaws and joining private jobs. The condition of lower-grade workers of these two mills are more vulnerable and feel difficulties in day-to-day living.

All 40 (100%) respondents of the study opined that there are four different types of quarters namely type A, B, C and D for the employees. Around 1200 quarters are there in both the paper mills of Assam. Type A and type B are for the workers. Type C and type D are for supervisors and others respectively. It was reported that 28 (70%) employees do not have their own houses and they stay in the allotted quarters given by the industry. HPC's liquidator Kuldeep Verma issued a notice on September 3, 2021, asking the employees of the two paper mills in Assam to vacate their residential quarters within 15 days. Then the employees of two defunct paper mills in Assam have decided unanimously not to vacate their quarters/accommodation without receiving their due salaries of 56 months.

The Joint Action Committee of Recognized Unions (JACRU) of Cachar and Nagaon Paper Mills of Assam under the banner of the HPC revival committee has been performing relentless struggle in both Barak and Brahmaputra Valley for the last 7–8 years. They with the cooperation of the citizens of Assam are doing agitations like Rail *Rokho*, Barak *Bandha*, National Highway Blockage, Religious Candle March, Hunger Strikes, and many other ways to legitimate their demands.

JACRU's Prime issues are as follows:

1. The JACRU demands immediate revival of Nagaon and Cachar Paper Mills keeping Central Public Sector Enterprise (CPSE) Public Sector Undertaking (PSU) status intact and opposes any form of privatization.
2. Start recruitment of local unemployed youth to fill up vacancies.
3. Initiate in-depth independent inquiring to find out the intention behind the suspension of production of Nagaon and Cachar Paper Mills which resulted in direct benefits to private paper industries and import lobbies along with abnormal enhancement of the price of paper and imposed monopolies control over paper market.
4. JACRU demands the release of a White Paper on investment of Rs. 4141 Crores declared in the Parliament and where the huge investment has gone.
5. JACRU reaffirms its continuous struggle till the industries are revived and all the legitimate dues are released for full settlement.

Ultimately, the Chief Minister of Assam, Dr. Himanta Biswa Sarma distributed a relief package of Rs. 810.02 Crore, and it benefited 2751 employees of both mills including 2003 regular employees and 748 contractual workers. The Assam Government has credited a trust of Rs. 25 Crores for medical benefits, educational support, social assistance etc. of the ex-employee and workmen. Also, the Government of Assam initiated steps for providing employment to 84 eligible ex-employees. Now the Assam Government is planning to revive the Cachar paper mill, and the land of the Nagaon paper mill will be utilised for the expansion of the Capital region. This shows that the Government of Assam, to some extent, goes for deindustrialization and does not have any interest in the revival of the Nagaon Paper Mill as such. On the contrary, they have a plan to expand the state capital till Jagiroad and utilize the mill area for expansion of the state capital.

After getting the package from the government, the employees vacated their quarters in both the paper mill of Assam. But 30 (75%) respondents reported that the Assam Chief Minister has only given a relief package for the rescue of the dying employees. It does not include 72 months' salaries, provident fund, gratuity, pension and other benefits. Though the Government of Assam also declared that they would provide 100 employment opportunities for the employees, only sixty-six (66) of the young people from both mills joined and the rest did not. It is because, if one joins the given government job in Assam, the person is not going to get the relief package, and also only the young employees will benefit, the older employees who do not have many years of service left will have to join in the initial level which is not beneficial for them. Hence the older employees did not join this scheme offered by Assam Government.

Moreover, 35 (87.5%) respondents informed that the Assam Government acquired the Hindustan Paper Corporation defunct mill for Rs. 375 crores only, where Assam Industrial Development Corporation (AIDC) was declared as the successful bidder on behalf of the Government of Assam. The total land areas of both mills are about 1550 acres and it includes other assets like machinery, residential quarters, oil reserves and a huge amount of inventory such as coal, unslaked lime, bamboo and limestone went under the hammer. So Rs. 375 crores in their mind is very less as compared to the value of the whole properties of the two mills of Assam. In addition to that Assam Government has to pay around 65 crores for the registration of land. So, the relief package of Rupees. 810.02 crores will be in reality turn into only Rupees 810.02 crores minus Rupees 375 crores plus Rupees 65 Crores. Therefore, it will be only Rupees 370.02 Crores.

Fifteen numbers (37.5%), of the respondents of the study also opined that though the Government of Assam has given the above-mentioned package, at the same time the case is still subjugated in Delhi high court as the Cachar Paper Project Workers Union on August 26, 2021 have filed it in the Delhi high court and they are optimistic for a successful result.

Conclusion

To conclude one can say that the phenomenon of deindustrialization is visible in India, particularly in Assam. Although the Government of Assam has given a relief package to the dying employee of Nagaon and Cachar Paper Mills of Assam, it is not complete in itself; because the salaries of 56 months (now it becomes 72 months), provident fund, gratuity, pension and other benefit are not inclusive. In this globalised world, liberalization and privatization are the main components of the capitalist global economy, but at the same time, the need of the hour is to sustain the local government institutions and industries in order to protect the backward regions of the North-Eastern States by giving ample opportunities for government jobs in such industries and institutions. So, the government should take initiatives for industrial development in North East India.

The ideology and policy of neo-liberalism emphasize the value of free market competition and favours the transfer of control of the economy from the public to private sectors. It limits government spending, government regulation, and public ownership. India after LPG reforms in 1991 opened the country to the world for free trade and commerce. Several mills and industries in India have closed down. The reasons for closure include many factors like financial problems, increasing production cost, obsolete machineries, stiff competition, insufficient cash flow, corruption, inadequate working capital, stressed assets and so on. These industries across the country faced many significant challenges; millions of skilled, unskilled and contractual Indian workers were rendered jobless. The employees went on strike and other types of agitational activities in order to fulfil their demands to revive those industries. The situation of the two paper mills of Assam, the Nagaon and Cachar Paper Mills are also not the exception.

Declaration of Conflicting Interests The author declared no potential conflicts of interest with respect to the research, authorship and/or publication of this article.

Funding The author received no financial support for the research, authorship and/or publication of this article.

Notes An earlier version of this paper was presented in the 47th All India Sociological Conference held at University of Science and Technology Meghalaya, from 20th to 22nd December, 2022 in the session of Research Committee 16: Work, Labour and Organisation of Indian Sociological Society, New Delhi.

References

Arman R (2014) Death metaphors and factory closure. Cult Organ 20(01):23–39

Bhagat M, Dixit R (2000) Impact on workers of closure/relocation of industrial units in Delhi. Ind J Ind Relat (IJIR) 36(02):125–140

Chakrabarti M (2007) Labour and closure of a mill: lives of workers of a closed factory in Kanpur. Econ Pol Wkly 42(21):1942–1950

Chapain C, Murie A (2008) The impact of factory closure on local communities and economies: the case of the MG Rover Longbridge closure in Birmingham. Policy Stud 29(03):305–317

Chatterjee D (2019) Chawls, Malls and High Rises: rethinking gentrification in the Textile mill lands of Mumbai, dissertation. Humanities & Social Science Department: Indian Institute of Technology Bombay, India

Department, policy research working paper, no 3083, World Bank

Eleen JW, Bernardine AG (1971) Shutdown: the impact of plant shutdown, extensive employment terminations and layoffs on the workers and the community, Ontario Federation of Labour

Estrada AV (2017) The closure of the sugar mills narrated by the workers. Oral Hist 45(2):60–70

Geography 98(2):77–84

Grayson JP (1985) The closure of a factory and its impact on health. Int J Health Serv 15(1):69–93

Haney M, Shkaratan M (2003) Mine closure and its impact on the community: five years after mine closure in Romania, Russia and Ukraine. Social Development, Washington D.C

Huynh KP, Ostrovsky Y, Petrunia RJ, Voia MC (2017) Industry shutdown rates and permanent layoffs: evidence from firm-worker matched data. IZA J Labor Econ 6(7):01–31
Marais L, Cloete J (2013) Labour migration, settlement and mine closure in South Africa
Nance JM, Garfield NH, Paredes AJ (1994) Studying the social impact of the Texas shrimp closure. Hum Organ 53(1):88–92
Robertson M, Clark A (2019) 'We were the ones really doing something about it': gender and mobilisation against factory closure. Work Employ Soc 33(2):336–344
Scheiring G, King L (2023) Theory Soc 52:145–178. https://www.researchgate.net/publication/359221134_Deindustrialization_social_disintegration_and_health_a_neoclassical_sociological_approach. Accessed 22nd January 2023
Stern JL (1972) Consequences of plant closure. J Hum Resour 7(1):3–25

Newspapers

The Assam Tribune—Centre mulling plan for revival of Cachar, Nagaon paper mills (2010)
The Assam Tribune—Centre may privatise Nagaon, Cachar paper mills (2010)
The Assam Tribune—Employee of defunct Assam paper mills dies failing pay for treatment (2022)
The Assam Tribune—Future of Nagaon, Cachar paper mills bleak (2010)
The Assam Tribune—one more Cachar paper mill employee passes away, death tally rises to 144 (2023)
The Economic Times—Assam Cabinet Sanctions Rs 375 Crores to bid for taking over assets of closed HPCL units (2022)
The Economic Times—Assam govt. distributes relief package to ex-employees of Nagaon paper mill and Cachar paper mill (2022)
The Economic Times—Assam govt. to acquire Hindustan Paper assets, Provide Rs 570 Cr package to employees (2021)
The Economic Times—Assam Industrial Development Corporation takes over assets of Hindustan Paper Corporation, Cachar paper mill (2022)
The Economic Times—Assam to setup a welfare fund for the workers of Hindustan Paper Corporation Ltd. (2021)
The Economic Times—HPC under liquidation on direction of NCLT, NCLAT: Govt. (2021)
The Economic Times—Union urge HPCL liquidator to disclose valuation of oil reserves in defunct Cachar paper mills and area (2021)

Internet Sources

Employment trends in textiles and apparel, 1973–2005. https://www.bls.govt.mir. Accessed 16th January 2023
Great Bamboo textile strike—Wikipedia. https://en.m.wikipedia.org. Accessed 22 January 2023
Hindustan Paper Corporation Limited. https://www.hindpaper.in. Accessed on 22 January 2023
https://www.toppr.com questions-why cotton mills have been closed down in Karnataka recently?—Toppr. Accessed 4 February 2023
https://m.thewire.in article labour why Ahmedabad Mills are closed?—were closed down because they faced tough completion from power 100ms in the 1980's and 1990's. Accessed 4 February 2023
https://www.bbc.co.uk textiles b...Nation on Film—Decline of the cotton industry—BBC why Mumbai Mills Shut down? Accessed 5 February 2023

Chapter 21
Changing Patterns of Work in the Gig Economy: A Sociological Analysis

M. T. Joseph

Abstract Sociology of work maps the structural and phenomenological aspects of work. One of the most significant developments in the world of work in neoliberal times has been the emergence of gig work. The neoliberal logic associated with it lays emphasis on notions of autonomy, flexibility, and entrepreneurship. Reviewing a few empirical studies on work in the gig economy, this paper argues that the claims of autonomy, flexibility and entrepreneurship hide the varying forms of precarity involved in gig work. The paper proceeds to develop the argument by referring to the issues connected with the platform economy and algorithmic control. It also analyses the response of the workers and the state reflected in unionisation as well as the welfare measures.

Keywords Gig · Gig work · Gig economy · Platform economy · Aggregator business · Precarity

Introduction

The changing patterns of work and employment in the formal and informal sectors have been a major area of research in Sociology, particularly in the sub-disciplines of Sociology of Work, Industrial Sociology and Sociology of Organizations. Terms and conditions of work are mediated by transnational agencies, the policies of nation-states and the various organizational cultures of particular corporations and companies. Sociologists have concentrated their gaze on the changing nature of work since the very foundation of the discipline since modernity and its related developments have been the mainstay of sociological understanding in its initial phase. Changing patterns of work and employment have been pivotal to the analysis of class by Karl Marx. Max Weber's explanation of the iron cage of modernity and the shift from

M. T. Joseph (✉)
Research Committee 06 – Sociology of Religion of the Indian Sociological Society (ISS), Teaches Sociology at the Department of Sociology, University of Mumbai, Mumbai, Maharashtra, India
e-mail: dr.josephmt@sociology.mu.ac.in

A. Chauhan et al. (eds.), *Hundred Years of Sociology in India: Evolving Issues, Emerging Trends*, https://doi.org/10.1007/978-981-96-1317-5_21

mechanical to organic solidarity propounded by Emile Durkheim have also a close connection to the changing forms of work and employment.

Sociology of Work engages with the world of work in multiple ways; particularly giving emphasis to the changing structural arrangements, the collective mobilization of workers and the issues related to the everyday life of the workers themselves. The structural aspects are integrally connected with the ideologies of economic development negotiated and adopted at the global level exerting their decisive imprint on policy-making and planning by the nation states. The global parameters set in motion by the transnational institutions and conglomerates such as the International Monetary Fund, the World Bank and other allied agencies frame the agenda for the nation-states to follow. The broad roadmap of policies and the direction of economic development mandated by the global agencies and the national governments have a determining impact on the nature and organization of work. The Bretton-Woods Agreement and the Washington Consensus ushered in a neoliberal framework of economic development for the world with far-reaching repercussions for the structure and conditions of work in the various sectors of the national economies. For instance, Knowledge Process Outsourcing (KPO) and Business Process Outsourcing (BPO) formed a major theme of analysis for the sociology of work in the last three decades.

In line with the aforementioned developments in the Sociology of Work, this chapter is an analysis of a very recent change in the domain of work and employment, namely the emergence and spread of gig work. The neoliberal logic of development has given rise to novel structures and patterns of work. Platform economy and algorithmic organization of work are two significant developments in the transformation of work and employment in recent times. This paper is an attempt to map the extent to which both of these new developments have influenced the nature of work, the living conditions of the workers, and how workers are forging their own pathways of coping with and responding to the changing nature of work.

Gig work has emerged as a significant form of employment in recent times. In the Sociology of work, informalization of labour[1] and feminization of labour[2] emerged as terms that captured rapid and significant changes in the form and nature of work in neoliberal times. Gig work is a progression from those modalities in the sense that gig work is rooted in the structures that neoliberalism has given rise to. One of the major avenues in which gig work has taken shape is the growth of platform-based aggregator businesses. Aggregator business has spread its dominance in many sectors of economic life and has turned out to be one of the most visible forms of entrepreneurship and business models of today. Particularly, aggregators are not small-time players or lone wolf investors or entrepreneurs. They are funded and run by big capital under the banner of multinational corporations. The behemoths who trigger aggregator mode of business in any sector make the rules, the terms

[1] Korreck (2020) analyses the new forms of informality in the gig economy.

[2] Studies have focused on the skewed nature of gig work in terms of the number of men and women who make up the workforce in various sectors. Hunt (2019), Kasliwal (2020) and Ansari (2022) explain the various aspects of women's work in the gig economy.

of employment and the modes of consumer contact. The earlier days of aggregator businesses witnessed the blitzkrieg of marketing that these firms engaged in with depictions of individuals who have made it big by working in the aggregator industry.[3]

Business models based on the aggregators gave unprecedented fillip to what is known as gig work. The marketing strategy of the aggregators projected gig work as a specific part of work related to a whole chain of products and services which one undertook at one's own choosing of time frame with one's own capital and assets facilitated by the marketing strategy and the mammoth reach of the aggregator. Gig work was given the aura of work at one's choosing distinguished from the older kinds of employment where one worked as per the whims and fancies of the management. The advantage of gig work for flexibility is touted as its uniqueness compared to other forms of work. A study by Lehdonvirta (2018) based on interviews with gig workers concluded that, "...online pieceworkers enjoyed considerable formal freedom in scheduling their work, and valued this freedom as a means to satisfy individual needs and combine work with other activities" (Lehdonvirta 2018, p. 25). Economies, where aggregator business and gig work were gradually taking shape, were inuncated with strategized 'success stories' of individuals who made it big due to gig work.

However as aggregator business expanded in its reach and scope, gig work evolved into the most visible form of employment. The predatory character of aggregator business ensured that it grew at the expense of other forms of business. Other players in the economy had the viable option of joining the bandwagon as providers and sellers all under the overarching umbrella of aggregators. Under these circumstances, the business enterprises with access to huge chunks of capital withstood the onslaught of aggregators. All others were left by the wayside or got absorbed into the many arms of aggregators. Aggregators connected manufacturers, sellers, sales executives, delivery agents, valets and consumers on a hitherto unimaginable scale.[4]

This paper seeks to analyse the nature and characteristics of work in the gig economy. Beginning with a brief overview of the gig economy and its scope in the world today, the paper proceeds to assess the various facets of work in the gig economy. It concludes with a section on the consumers in the gig economy and a review of some developments in the field of gig work and gig workers in India.

---

[3] In a review article Vallas and Schor trace the growth of platform economy in two ways. One, it initially grew as part of the traditional economy with the spread of mini computer and the internet. The second stage of its growth was outside the traditional economy with the exponential growth of e-commerce platforms, capital platforms, service labour platforms and video streaming and content platforms (Vallas and Schor 2020, p. 274–275).

[4] Prof. Juliet Schor, Professor of Sociology at Boston College explained the predatory undercurrents of platform-based aggregators and the degrees of precarity among gig workers in a lecture titled *Gig economy: Predatory platforms, precarious work* at School of History and Sociology, Georgia Tech Ivan Allen College of Liberal Arts on 03 April 2023. https://www.youtube.com/watch?v=K0iPP1aU1e8. Accessed on August 31, 2023.

Gig Economy

One of the earlier references to work in the gig economy is 'crowdsourcing.'[5] It refers to platforms that create a digital interface between workers and clients for specific tasks some of which are completely online, and others are carried out in offline situations. The term owes its origin to the term 'gig'[6] which both describes the nature and scale of work involved and acts as a metaphor of sorts standing for and facilitating flexibility, convenience, and autonomy of decision-making at the hands of the person who does the 'gig.' In other words, work is divided into tasks or gigs which are then offered as single transactions through platforms circumventing the entire gamut of relations, protocols and structures of employment that existed in older forms of work. Arguments in favour of crowdsourcing or gig work are centred on the range of flexibility[7] it offers the worker and the range of choices that it offers the customer. People who argue in favour of the merits of gig work state that algorithm-based metrics keep at bay the socio-cultural biases associated with traditional modes of work, making the process of work relatively immune to the pressures and fissures typical of human relations and ethnic identities. The argument is also made that breaking down the processes of work into tiny 'gigs' opens the possibilities for a greater number of people to join the workforce. It is also contended that the logic of crowdsourcing redistributes income from wages more equally across sectors and countries.

The gig economy is derivative of the term platform economy.[8] Platforms are novel digital business models that act as aggregators between the seller/service provider and the customer. The new segment of aggregation has emerged as a pathbreaking business model for investment and profit maximization. The platform economy in a way has given rise to gig economy as contingent, short term work arrangements brokered by the platforms.

---

[5] "The term *crowdsourcing* dates to 2006, when two editors of *Wired* magazine, Jeff Howe and Mark Robinson, coined the phrase to describe the use of the internet to spawn and connect ideas". https://www.britannica.com/money/topic/crowdsourcing. Accessed on August 31, 2023.

[6] "Gig work…finds its roots in the music industry. In the past, musicians would refer to their performances as 'gigs.' They would play at concerts, bars, events, or any venue where they were hired for a specific time frame. This term eventually expanded its meaning to encompass any temporary job or project." https://www.ncesc.com/why-is-it-called-gig-work/. Accessed on August 31, 2023.

[7] However, the much publicized 'flexibility' is severely constrained by what is termed as 'gamification' of work with techniques such as incentives, ratings, and algorithmic manipulation (Sekharan 2022).

[8] Platform economy "…is any type of digital platform that uses the internet to connect dispersed networks of individuals to facilitate digital interactions between people. Within the platform economy there is a triangular relationship between three parties (1) the platform (2) the worker and (3) the customer. It is the job of the platform to connect people with demand (the customer) to people that provide supply (the worker)". https://www2.deloitte.com/content/dam/Deloitte/nl/Documents/humancapital/deloitte-nl-hc-the-rise-of-the-platform-economy-report.pdf. Accessed on August 31, 2023.

True to the logic of neoliberal economics that runs the roost in the world today, gig economy has clear cut division between the classes, particularly of investors, managers, and the workers. Gig economy has a band of investors in financial capital for whom opportunities of investment are created through innovative and completely novel ideas, mechanisms and structures of production, distribution, and consumption. For the uninitiated, it would be interesting to note that there has arisen a variety of terminologies to just name the investors alone such as pre-seed investors, seed investors, angel investors, incubators, accelerators, series investors (venture capital and corporate venture capital), institutional investors and exit investors.

The Scope of Gig Economy

A phenomenal upsurge in innovation and commercial application of automation and robotics has given rise to a new form of work generally named 'work in the gig economy.' Gig economy is characterised by the ever-growing sector of aggregation of products and services with humungous levels of the infusion of capital into the sector by venture capitalists and other investors. This has transformed the nature of work for the large army of workers who have entered the workforce as gig workers based on the twin principles of voluntarism and automation. Globally, one estimates that in projects by 2025, one third of all transaction of work will be in the gig economy (Graham and Anwar 2019, cited in Ness 2023, p.1).

On the one hand, work in the gig economy is touted as offering workers the kind of flexibility that they never had since the industrial revolution. Gig economy enables a worker to log in and log off at will and offer tailor made products and services at the time and space of one's choosing. However, the very character of gig economy is entwined with automation, robotics, and surveillance. Coupled with these machine-based intrusive technologies and the scope and range of products and services decided and facilitated by automation, we have reached a transformed stage of work where the worker in the gig economy is at the throes of a kind of precarity never imagined before.[9]

Gig economy is the product of the current evolution of global neo-liberal capitalism. It facilitates the infusion of global financial capital in technological platforms prompting the swell of billionaires and the rising control and influence of the managerial class. On the other side, it triggers hitherto unseen degrees of inequality of wealth, erosion of wages and labour standards and increased precarity of women, people of colour, the underclass, and the migrant labour.

At the heart of work in the gig economy are digital labour platforms. International Labour Organization divides these generally into two categories; (a) online labour

[9] This paper employs the term 'precarity' as explained by Guy Standing in his work *The Precariat: The New and Dangerous Class*. According to him, the precariat has class characteristics and status position. They have a specific place in relations of production, relations of distribution, and relations to the state (Standing 2014, pp. 10–12).

platforms, and (b) location-based labour platforms (Rani and Gobel 2023, p. 15). In both cases, technology is used to outsource tasks through web-based platforms and work is mediated through app-based platforms.

Work in the Gig Economy

In terms of the nature of work, work in the gig economy can be categorised as (a) freelance work,[10] (b) microtasks[11] and (c) app-based aggregation.[12]

The gig economy has given rise to novel arrangements of work such as short-term, temporary, hourly, or zero-hour contracts. The possibilities of technology-mediated work have given rise to independent contractors and algorithmic management of work. In the process, the worker today generates the assets and the equipment; bears the operational costs, and absorbs the risks associated with the entire process. The nomenclature of 'self-employed' and 'independent contractor' gets attached to the worker in the gig economy, foreclosing the possibility of invoking the benefits and rights of 'workers' per se.

Based on their research on gig workers, Rani and Gabel (2023) have particularly focussed on (a) terms of service agreements of the platforms, (b) the algorithmic management practices and (c) design features as distinctive aspects of work in the gig economy.

Terms of Agreement

Terms of the agreement are unilaterally drafted by the platforms naming the workers in idioms and jargons (such as 'driver partner,' 'self-employed,' 'independent seller') robbing them of workplace protections and entitlements accruing to workers. The service agreements entail commission pre-determined by the platforms which also dictate the required etiquette for the workers. The platforms shift the responsibility of capital investment as well as operational expenses to the workers. The platforms exercise control over the conditions of work. For instance, as per a survey conducted by ILO, 37% of taxi drivers reported that they faced repercussions when they rejected a ride. Workers in the gig economy who are at the receiving end of many of its ill-effects are then left with no choice as the platform-based aggregators would have by then decimated other avenues of employment. In other words, platform-based aggregator mode of business is predatory in its business model and practices.

Platforms function on 'dual labour market' with a tiny core work force as their 'employees' and a large swathe of workers out there who are not defined as workers.

[10] Platforms such as 'freelancer,' 'PeoplePerHour,' 'Upwork,' 'Toptal' etc.

[11] Clickworker, Amazon MTurk, Microworkers, Appen, Survey Junkie etc.

[12] Uber, Ola, Porter, Zomato, Swiggy, Airbnb, TaskRabbit etc.

As mentioned in the previous paragraph, they are given highly exaggerated nomenclatures but turn out to be people robbed off their status as workers, pushed to the ever-increasing degrees of informality and precarity. Thus, the social protection of work and workers which have evolved over time[13] as well as the rights of workers including collective bargaining and unionising are given short shrift in the very conception of work in the gig economy.

Freelance and microtask platforms offer opportunities for highly skilled and educated people. However, many of them are relegated to doing mechanical routine kind of work unrelated to their qualification and education. For instance, a survey by ILO revealed that on freelance platforms, one-third of the workers reported that they had more skills than required for the work that they do. Only 60% of the workers trained in Information Technology got to do work in their specialization. On microtask platforms, it was reported that around 57% of the workers with skills in STEM (Science, Technology, Engineering and Medicine) perform lower-end, repetitive, mind-numbing jobs. (Rani and Gobel 2023, p. 20).

Algorithmic Management Practices

The feedback system has evolved into an algorithmically determined system of control. The determinants of such feedback mechanisms are opaque. But the feedback generated by the metrics of the algorithm is considered as the most objective and reliable way of measuring excellence and compliance on the part of the worker. Algorithmic monitoring of work and compliance has unleashed forms of intrusive surveillance on the workers. App-based aggregators use a combination of bonuses, incentives, and subsidies to build up a network of workers and customers. It is commonplace now to observe gig workers in any sector making impassioned pleas to the customers to make sure that they rate their service without fail or delay. The platform sends reminders to the customers time and again to rate the gig work and the worker in terms of punctuality, promptness, politeness, standard of the work done and so on.

Algorithmic surveillance track workers location, generate data about worker behaviour and assign work. This happens as part of a multi-modal surveillance which includes also managerial and customer surveillance (Newlands 2023, p. 64). Such surveillance accelerates the nature of control experienced by the workers coupled with issues of worker privacy. For those workers negotiating distances, digital cartography is singularly longitudinal and does not consider the complex routes a worker needs to negotiate.

[13] These include health insurance, provision to address work related injury, unemployment insurance, old age pensions and so on.

Platform Design

Platform design features segregate the nature of work and the worker in terms of location, gender, and other specificities. Researchers have unearthed a correlation between design and the way work, with better pay prospects getting accrued to workers from developed countries.

Empirical studies of workers in the gig economy have pointed out the promise of autonomy and flexibility built into the logic of gig work as an attraction. However, it has also been pointed out that such a promise is not seen as fulfilled in the lives of the gig workers. As Gayatri Nair points out, though the façade of autonomy and flexibility has certain value for the workers, in the final analysis they experience precarity of work like earlier forms of informalization mainly due to algorithmic control, surveillance and spread of informality (Nair 2022).

Unionisation

Gig economy presents the worker with many difficulties when it comes to the question of forming workers collectives and unions. The principles that guide gig economy leads to the atomisation of the gig worker. Lack of human contact and dispersal of workers across a wide geographic area is one of the challenges. The gig economy runs on the logic of individual rights and not collective bargaining. Attempts at unionising are taking place at the grassroots level far from the formal structures of trade unions. One such example is that of the Independent Workers Union of Great Britain (Zahn and Busby 2023, p. 153).

Nevertheless, scholars such as Maccarrone and Tassinari (2023) have documented clear trends towards collectivism and unionising among some sectors. Employing Labour Process Theory, they explain the emergence of solidarity and unionising among gig workers. They point to the inherent contradiction in the gig economy that leads to solidarity among the workers. General insecurity, reduced remuneration, and increased working hours act as triggers for collectivism. Further, the opaque mechanisms of management also act as a trigger. Strikes and protests by workers in the location-based gig economy (food delivery and ride-hailing platforms) have been the most visible signs of protest. They have resorted to mass logging out from apps, physical public protests in front of offices, and 'shitstorming'[14] on social media platforms. There have also been worker-led cooperative platforms in a few countries.

---

[14] 'Shitstorming' refers to outrageous or exciting reactions from a significant number of people in response to posts, comments, and statements. https://socialmediaagency.one/shitstorm-what-does-it-mean-prominent-example/. Accessed on August 31, 2023.

Consumers in the Gig Economy

The consumer is literally the supreme player in the range of options, standards, and conveniences that the gig economy offers. In a way, the consumer then becomes an axis for understanding the transformation of work in the gig economy. The popularization of the term 'ethical consumption' has widened itself to involve labelling and product placement with clear-cut benchmarks for the ethical treatment of the workers.[15] Consumers have begun to engage the economy through involvement in platform markets, interactions with gig workers, and contact with wider regulatory processes. In terms of the decision that consumers make to access products and services from the gig economy or not or when making a choice between the available gig platforms, the idea of the 'socially conscious consumer' is invoked. Advertising of 'worker-friendly' approaches and 'fair work practices' have gained traction in recent times. Tipping the gig worker can also be a consumer-directed action in favour of the workers.

On the other hand, instances of consumer bias on the ethnic, national, religious, racial or caste-based identity of the gig worker have cropped up in different parts of the world. In India for instance there have been reported cases of customers refusing to accept a ride in aggregator cab or receive the order of a particular aggregator if the valet or the gig worker delivering the service is from an ethnicity/identity that is perceived as inimical to the ideology, identity, interests or even the whims and fancies of the customer.

Gig Work in India

In India, policy makers, associations of industries and political leaders generally look at gig economy as generators of employment for the large mass of unemployed. "India is the largest supplier of digital freelancing work on global platforms: in 2020, India alone accounted for 30% of the global supply of crowd workers" (Duvisac 2023, p. 362). In India the rise of gig work is to be seen in the context of increased informalization of labour and the gradual weakening of the provisions for labour rights. It is often claimed that the nature of gig work makes it more convenient for women to enter that sector. However, the available statistics on this matter remains inconclusive.

The newly implemented Code of Social Security (2020) has for the first time legally named gig workers, stipulating work-related benefits. However, the legislation separates gig work from platform work by not extending the same benefits to workers who are named by the industry as self-employed. The Code fails to pin accountability with gig platforms other than the mandatory contribution to the social security board of the gig workers. Since the other extant labour codes do not include gig workers, the provisions towards decent work, occupational safety and minimum

[15] For a discussion on 'ethical consumerism' in India during Covid-19 pandemic, see Gupta (2023).

wage don't apply to them. To remedy this situation, a paper in India Development Review argued for the inclusion of gig workers in the Urban Employment Guarantee Schemes which are active in a few states such as Odisha, Himachal Pradesh and Kerala. The review has specific suggestions on how the provisions of UEG can be extended to gig workers. Gig workers can be enlisted as part of the UEG to address the on-demand service needs of public institutions and recognised employers. Flexibility in the way work is understood to enlarge its gambit to part-time and mostly unpaid caregiving jobs is proposed. To ensure that gig workers come under the stipulations of daily minimum wages under UEG, Jean Dreze argues for worker collectives to be placement agencies.[16]

There have arisen trends of unionization among gig workers in different parts of India, where they have adopted conventional tactics of unionization and collective bargaining. Pan India unions such as All India Gig Workers Union, Indian Federation of App-based Transport Workers, Telangana Gig and Platform workers union, and Rajasthan App *Adharit Shramik* Union are a few examples. Addressing the issues faced by gig workers Rajasthan has emerged as one of the first states in India to enact legislation for the welfare of workers in the gig economy titled "Gig Workers Welfare Act" announced in the state budget of 2023–24.[17]

Conclusion

Neoliberal economics has given rise to multiple forms of employment for managers and workers at various levels of the economies worldwide. Agencies like Oxfam has over the years documented the steep rise in inequality of income between different classes. While the capitalist class at the top bracket has increased wealth multiple times over, the top echelons of the managerial class has reaped significant benefits. For the rest of the people in various levels of the economy, the real levels of income has decreased. Neoliberal economics has spawned newer forms of employment and arrangements of work. Initially the terms informalization of work and outsourcing gained traction in Sociology of Work to document and discuss the rapid changes from formal employment to informal work environments and to document the ways in which the entire process of work was then divided into multiple potions and outsourced to overseas locations. The division of a process of manufacture or delivery of a service in multiple roles and parts came to be later called as 'gigs'. Gigs gained traction as one of the promises of neoliberalism which claimed to provide with workers with better flexibility in terms of employment and autonomy in decision making in some cases. However, platform based aggregation powered by algorithms and big data turned out to be the Frankenstein that determined all matters with regard

---

[16] Dreze (2020). An Indian DUET for Urban Jobs. https://www.bqprime.com/opinion/an-indian-duet-for-urban-jobs. Accessed on August 31, 2023.

[17] https://theprint.in/feature/indias-gig-workers-score-A-big-win-rajasthan-first-to-budget-rs-200-cr-for-protection/1365190/. Accessed on August 19, 2023.

to gig economy. The effects of technology having such enormous control over human predicament in gig work has now given way to collective action by the gig workers to demand better terms of employment and greater humanization of the entire edifice. As is evident from recent legislations in different parts of the globe, states are taking note of the issues and problems faced by the large mass of gig workers and are addressing these through welfare-oriented policies and regulations.[18] Gig work has grown enormously over the years and in times to come more and more people will be absorbed in to the orbit of work in gig economy.

References

Ansari HC (2022) Analysing women's labour in India's gig economy. Feminism in India. https://feminisminindia.com/2022/01/25/india-gig-economy-women-work-zomato-urban-company/. Accessed 31 August 2023

Dreze (2020) An Indian DUET for Urban Jobs. https://www.bqprime.com/opinion/an-indian-duet-for-urban-jobsAccessed on August 31, 2023.

Duvisac S (2023) The unfulfilled promise of gig work: Unpacking informality and gig work in India. In: Ness I (ed) The Routledge handbook of the gig economy. Routledge, London & New York, pp 361–373

Gupta B (2023) Ethical consumerism: Gig economy's road ahead. In: Arora P, Raman U, Konig R (eds) Feminist futures of work: reimagining labour in the digital economy. Amsterdam University Press, pp 207–215

Graham M, Anwar MA (2019) The global gig economy: towards a planetary labour market? First Monday 24(4). https://doi.org/10.5210/fm.v24i4.9913

Hunt A et al (2019) Report: women in the gig economy: Paid work, care and flexibility in Kenya and South Africa. Data-Pop Alliance. https://cdn.odi.org/media/documents/women_in_the_gig_economy_final_digital.pdf. Accessed 31 August 2023

Kasliwal R (2020) Gender and the gig economy: a qualitative study of gig platforms for women workers. ORF Issue Brief 359:1–13

Korreck S (2020) Raisina debates: the future of work: Embracing informality. https://www.orfonline.org/expert-speak/the-future-of-work-embracing-informality-60680/. Accessed 30 July 2023

Lehdonvirta V (2018) Flexibility in the gig economy: managing time on three online piecework platforms. N Technol Work Employ 33(1):13–29

Maccarrone V, Tassinari A (2023) Worker solidarity among gig and precarious workers. In: Ness I (ed) The Routledge handbook of the gig economy. Routledge, London & New York, pp 193–204

Nair G (2022) New Terrains of precarity—gig work in India. Contemp S Asia 30(3):388–401

Ness I (2023) Introduction. In: Ness I (ed) The Routledge handbook of the gig economy. Routledge, London & New York, pp 1–12

Newland G (2023) The algorithmic surveillance of gig workers: mechanisms and consequences. In: Ness I (ed) The Routledge handbook of the gig economy. Routledge, London & New York, pp 64–73

[18] Stewart and Stanford (2017) offer certain concrete suggestions to nation states on the laws and regulations that can be put in place. They propose five major options: "…enforcement of existing laws; clarifying or expanding definitions of 'employment'; creating a new category of 'independent worker'; creating rights for 'workers', not employees; and reconsidering the concept of an 'employer'" (Stewart and Stanford (2017), p. 420).

Rani U, Gobel N (2023) Job instability, precarity, informality and inequality: labour in the gig economy. In: Ness I (ed) The Routledge handbook of the gig economy. Routledge, London & New York, pp 15–32

Sekharan A (2022) India's gig workers: overworked and underpaid. India Dev Rev. https://idronline.org/article/livelihoods/indias-gig-workers-overworked-and-underpaid/. Accessed 04 April 2023

Standing G (2014) The precariat. Contexts 13(4):10–12

Stewart A, Stanford J (2017) Regulating work in the gig economy: what are the options? The Economic and Labour Relations Review 28(3): 420-437 https://doi.org/10.1177/1035304617722461

Vallas S, Schor JB (2020) What do platforms do? Understanding the gig economy. Ann Rev Sociol 46:273–294

Zahn R, Busby N (2023) Trade unions, women's labour and the gig economy. In: Ness I (ed) The Routledge handbook of the gig economy. Routledge, London & New York, pp 145–157

Chapter 22
Hundred Years of Sociology in India: The Way Forward for Sociology of Sports at Home and the World

Sanjay Tewari

Abstract Considering the development of sociology in India over the last hundred years, this study zeroes in on the state of sports sociology in India, a country with a 1.42 billion-strong population and a sports culture that seems to share some characteristics but has received little attention from scholars. Academics from India and other nations may find a multitude of possibilities presented here to conduct additional research. In order to better understand the Indian environment, this research draws on the theoretical work of scholars from Europe and other parts of Asia. One of the many unanswered questions is how parents feel about their children's participation in athletic activities, both as a recreational activity and prospective career path. Public schools in the United States put a lot more emphasis on academics than on physical education, therefore, examining their role in sports is important. This is yet another issue that requires closer examination. In light of this challenge, this study aims to draw attention to potential objectives for a research agenda in sports sociology in India. The insular nature of Indian sports culture, together with the aforementioned issues, discourages youth from engaging in sports and other forms of physical activity. Given this context, the goal of this paper is to shed light on the sociological factors that can significantly impact the growth of our nation's young and physical culture, as well as the advancement of these fields.

Keywords India · Sociology · Sports · Youth · Development · Integration

S. Tewari (✉)
Hony Professor, Russian Academy for Social & Fundamental Sciences, Moscow, Russia
e-mail: sanjay.tewari@yahoo.co.in

Convener, Research Committee on Sociology of Sports & Managing Committee Member (2018-23), Indian Sociological Society, New Delhi, India

A. Chauhan et al. (eds.), *Hundred Years of Sociology in India: Evolving Issues, Emerging Trends*, https://doi.org/10.1007/978-981-96-1317-5_22

Introduction

Over the past decade, national governments, non-governmental organizations (NGOs), international sports federations, and United Nations (UN) agencies have all used sport as a vehicle for development. In specific contexts, research has demonstrated that sports has positive effects on physical health, including disease prevention, reduced risk of engaging in harmful behaviors (like drug use and unsafe sexual practices), the capacity to encourage social integration, as well as the inclusion of women, girls, and individuals with disabilities in society. Sports also has positive effects on self-esteem, which in turn contributes to society as a whole (United Nations 2015; Coalter 2010a, b). There has been a shift in thinking about how a country's level of development is determined, moving away from an economic focus on the industrial, agricultural, and service sectors. The nation is now being assessed differently as a result of this change. In the context of the UN Declaration on the Right to Development, the idea that a nation's success is mainly tied to its economic growth was challenged (1986):

"Development is an all-encompassing social, cultural, political, and economic process with the overarching goal of enhancing the standard of living for all people everywhere through ensuring that everyone has an equal opportunity to take part in and benefit from development efforts" (United Nations 1986, p. 1).

Since my goal is to delve into "the sociological perspective of sport—the potential formation mechanism—it would be beneficial" to have a broader understanding of the term. This field focuses on describing and explaining the connections between various parts of society and sports. Another feature of the sociological perspective on sport that differentiates it from the psychological one is the increased focus on sport's function as an element of social organization (Edwards 1973). Three pillars support the sociological view of sports: first, that sports merits sociological study; second, that sports reflects and reinforces society's most important philosophy because they are a microcosm of society at large; and third, that due to the interconnected nature of sports and other social institutions, changes in one sphere almost always affect other parts of society (Coakley 2009).

Because of the methodological concerns that have been considered, Bourdieu and Giddens see the present research as a social practice discursive creation. Many have recognized the value of Bourdieu's social approach to sports studies, the field of sports sociology, and the opportunities it presents to those interested in the societal aspects of PE and sports (Clement 1995; Jarvie & McGuire 1994; De France 1995). His sociology has inspired many publications on 'sport studies' (Clement 1995). Clement (1995) thinks that Bourdieu's approach is appealing because it highlights the importance of attitude—the physiological aspects of sport. It would be more precise to state that he offers an analytical framework for the study of culture and society derived from sociology, as opposed to a social code of ethics. Specifically, his concept of habitus provides a framework for comprehending the ways in which regular practice, athletic competition, and other forms of organized physical activity, function as a symbol for the complex interplay of gender, class, and culture (Bourdieu 1978).

It is human activity that Giddens defines as agency. Although not all agents are humans, being human does imply being an agent. Giddens argues that agency has the potential to bring about societal reform as well as reproduction (Giddens 1984). Within the setting of the paradoxical relationship between structure and agency, practices are developed (Stones 2005a, b) and do not solely stem from their own doing. The practices are the building blocks of social structures, and those structures can influence the way most Indians think, especially the youth, strengthening the collective development and unity of the nation.

This paper will provide academics with fresh insights and chances for further research on the subject of the Sociology of Sports by analyzing existing literature in this area. With any luck, this is indicative of a more robust research culture in many countries, and we're crossing our fingers that it will be incredibly helpful to Indian academics, especially "Sports Sociologists." The Asian area that has a longer tradition of social science research on sports, is the Far West (Coakley 2009). Our current goal is to attract the attention of scholars in the greater Asia-Europe region who are interested in the economic, political, and social effects of sports. This study is based on research into the sociology of sports in India and new developments within the field. Two Indian states provide the groundwork for this investigation, which aims to entice academics from the EU and other parts of Asia.

Importance of the Study and Objectives

"In most developing nations today, young people make up the largest segment of the population—in some cases more than 50% (United Nations 2020). This means that countries will be facing noteworthy fiscal pressures to fund secondary education" (World Bank, 2018). A tremendous potential is presented by the big youth population. With a youthful workforce on the rise and a smaller population overall, there are fewer people to care for, such as the elderly and children. Governments can then reallocate those funds to sectors with a high return on investment (ROI) for development, such as human capital (World Bank, 2018). The World Bank has recognized five aspects of youth development or transitions that significantly influence the protection, development, and utilization of human capital for every young person (World Bank, 2018):

- Starting a family;
- Developing a healthy lifestyle;
- Beginning to work;
- Beginning to learn;
- Being an active citizen.

Given the growing global attention to youth development over the past few years, its relevance may be readily assessed. Especially in the previous two decades, this importance has been rising at a steady rate (United Nations 2020). The following is a list of key commitments that are among them:

- "Every child has the right to play and leisure, according to the 1959 United Nations Declaration of the Rights of the Child"(United Nations 1959).
- "The United Nations Educational, Scientific, and Cultural Organization (UNESCO) General Conference at its twentieth session in Paris, 1978, adopted the International Charter of Physical Education and Sport, which reaffirmed the importance of sports and physical education as universal human rights"(UNESCO 1978).
- "Following the report of the UN Inter-Agency Task Force on Sport for Development and Peace in 2003, the UN General Assembly passed a series of resolutions entitled Sport as a Means to Promote Education, Health, Development and Peace in 2003, 2004, and 2006" (United Nations 2006).
- "In 2005, the UN declared 2005 the International Year for Sport and Physical Education (IYSPE) and urged leaders to unite in supporting sports, physical education, and sport-based development" (United Nations 2005).

Many nations have come to the realization that being able to compete at a high level in athletics is a sign of a strong and intelligent nation. Countries that have consistently maintained their status as sporting nations include the US, China, Canada, Australia, and the UK. These nations are shown to us as examples (Coalter 2010a, b). Although India has been a part of several sports programs throughout the years, it has never been able to match the total success of these other nations. The Indian government has made some past efforts to determine what went wrong with the country's performance (Ministry of Youth Affairs and Sports 2014).

However, one of the most important issues that need to be investigated is the sports culture in two states in India, namely Bihar and Uttar Pradesh (more particularly, the districts of Patna, Darbhanga, Kanpur, and Unnao). Among the many problems that require fixing is the societal perspective of parents on sports, which sees them mostly as a form of entertainment and seldom as a means to an end (professional advancement). Another issue that requires investigation is the school curriculum, which prioritizes academics above athletics (Kumar 2019). The dynamics between parents and their offspring warrant a great deal of study. The reason is that kids' motivation to keep doing sports might be influenced by their parent's behavior and outlook (Bailey 2006). Based on this information, it is expected that this research will help us understand the sociological factors that can promote sports, youth development, and national progress.

The United Nations designated 2005 as the International Year of Sport and Physical Education, which greatly expanded the worldwide examination of the relationship between sport and the development of children and youth. "Additionally, they made significant strides in promoting sports as a medium to achieve certain global development objectives, such as the Millennium Development Goals (Van Eekeren 2006). Although much of the literature reviewed in this document uses definitions, concepts, and evidence from high-income countries, a great deal of international attention is being paid to the potential utility of sport for child and youth development in Lower Middle-Income Countries (LMICs) (Beutler 2008). Scholars have recently argued for the necessity of conducting prolonged and empirical analyses of the utility of sport for child and youth development in low- and middle-income countries (LMICs). However, this literature is only now emerging, and evidence of the success (or failure) of sport and child/youth development interventions in LMICs is scarce at this time (Darnell & Hayhurst 2011)".

In the context of India, there is a dearth of research on the social metrics associated with youth and children's development through athletics. When it comes to sociological assessments, this is particularly the case (Kumar 2019). Therefore, the complex nature of the relationship between youth sports and their personal growth cannot be captured by using just one kind of data or one set of statistics. A large number of studies necessitate commentary, in addition to evidence-based research.

"*Panchayat Yuva Krida Aur Khel Abhiyan* scheme document states, Sports and physical education play a crucial role in the all-round development of children, adolescents, and youth, hereafter referred to as youth in general". In addition to making up about 70% of the population, our youth also form our greatest asset in terms of human resources, giving us a distinct edge over other industrialized nations, like China, that are experiencing an aging population. A common theme throughout the Indian prime minister's statements is this (Ministry of Youth Affairs and Sports 2008, p. 2).

According to Peter Donnelly & Simon Darnell, University of Toronto, and Jay Coakley from the University of Colorado in their report on "The Use of Sport to Foster Child and Youth Development and Education" (2007):

Rather than being a direct result of playing a sport, the apparent advantages seem to be a byproduct of the social interaction and setting that is possible in sports. This holds true for all the other advantages of participating in sports that have been documented in scientific studies. In light of the results shown above, two main areas necessitate further research.

1. Studies to further our understanding of the specific conditions in which sports may have a good impact on gender relations, inclusion of people with disabilities, "youth development, mental health, peace, and conflict resolution".
2. The leadership style, as well as the expertise and experience of those in charge, have been named time and time again as critical factors in the success of programs designed to encourage healthy lifestyle choices among youth (Donnelly, Darnell, & Coakley 2007, p. 15).

Feren Takacs (1988a, b), in his report on "The Development and Theoretical Background of Sport Sociology in Hungary", published by the International Review for the Sociology of Sport, narrates:

In contrast, the leading professional and sociological research on the topic of physical education in Hungarian secondary schools was carried out by Ferenc Kemeny, who was a friend of Coubertin's and a founding member of the International Olympic Committee. Questions like, "What impact do physical activities have on (a) the moral views of young people?" are representative of the standard questions asked by conventional sociologists. b) In terms of physical maturity, how far along are they? c) personality types? How can parents and society at large impact the realm of physical education? Given that, what then?"(Takacs 1988a, b, pp. 287–303).

In their article "Sport and Development: An Overview, Critique and Reconstruction" published in the Journal of Sport and Social Issues, Douglas Hartmann and Christina Kwauk examine social initiatives that are centered around sports (2011), state:

"Development" has turned into a buzzword and a topic of interest in the world of sports. The authors employ critical theory and their own research on sport-based social programs to try to clarify the relationship between sport and development. There is a dominant vision that sees sport as a means to perpetuate existing social relations, and an interventionist approach that sees sport as a tool to bring about more systemic change. (Hartmann & Kwauk 2011, pp. 284–305).

Donnelly and Harvey (1996) and Houlihan (2008a, b) "outline the structural barriers to participation in sport and physical activity, which they classify as":

1. "Infrastructural barriers—associated with the material means of access (e.g., cost, available transportation, time, etc.)";
2. "Superstructural barriers—associated with ideas about access (e.g., policies, knowledge, prejudice, etc.); and"
3. "Procedural barriers—associated with the course of action available to individuals to attain access (e.g., social support, citizens' rights, organizational structure, and management style) (Houlihan, 2008a, b; Donnelly & Harvey 1996)".

Donnelly (1993) described the second as "a fully democratized sport and leisure environment [which] includes both the right to participate, regardless of one's particular set of social characteristics, and the right to be involved in the determination of the forms, circumstances, and meanings of participation"(Donnelly, 1993, p. 417).

Richard Light (2001), from the University of Melbourne, finds:

"Among prominent sociologists, Bourdieu stands out for his preoccupation with the body and the conceptual tools he employs, which provide a potent framework for studying the societal aspects of sports and PE"(Light 2001, p. 12). Bourdieu's key analytic concepts might be applied to the analysis of the relationships between the body, culture, class, and gender in sport and physical education (Clement 1995; Jarvie & McGuire 1994).

In order to do a literature review, the writer must first seek for a basis for their study or, more precisely, try to summarize the prior studies. It is necessary to critically evaluate this corpus of literature because the United States has imagined and studied the importance of sports critically, yet most of the focus has been on economically developed states (United Nations 2015). Reviewing the *Panchayat Yuva Krida Khel* Scheme gives a somewhat clearer picture (Ministry of Youth Affairs and Sports 2008). "The benefits of sports, according to Peter Donnelly, Simon Darnell, and Jay Coakley" research, are a byproduct of the positive interactions that take place during athletic events. The advantages may be further ascertained with the help of this study. (Donnelly et al. 2007). Feren Takacs, while studying the Hungarian Sport Sociological approach, finds the benefits of exercise and other physical activities on the upgrading of the moral attitude of society, and this literature will add to the present study (Takacs 1988a, b). Within the context of this study, the interventionist method that Douglas Hartmann and Christina Kwauk have taken has made a contribution in the sense that sport is capable of transforming (Hartmann & Kwauk 2011). Similarly, Donnelly and Harvey have contributed to this study by examining the impact of infrastructural barriers, including geographical locations and access to sport facilities (Donnelly & Harvey 1996; Houlihan 2008a, b). Richard Light, through Bourdieu, attempts to analyze the social dimensions of sports, and this analysis, in turn, tries to further the sociological impact on sports (Light 2001).

Research Methodology

Many researchers and politicians have taken an interest in the variables that influence people's decision to participate in athletic activities as of late. To find out what makes people interested in sports or not, I've decided to use a constructive and exploratory study approach. As everyone knows, fewer individuals participate in athletic activities as they get older. This trend is most noticeable between the ages of 16 and 23, when most people complete their full-time education. When this time frame ends, participation rates keep going down, but they're going down more slowly (Roberts and Brodie 1992).

Five hundred people from the two big states of Bihar and Uttar Pradesh (U.P.) in India were involved in the simultaneous collection of data utilized in this study. While 150 interviews were conducted in Bihar, 350 were conducted in Uttar Pradesh. We selected Patna, Darbhanga, Kanpur, and Unnao districts for our interviews based on their geographical location. All districts, both powerful and weak, were considered when these districts were selected from the two states. The geographical classification technique was used to ensure that the sample was balanced. The criteria for selecting empowered and underpowered persons were established after considering the regions' Human Resource Management, Health Services, and Logistics management. I made sure to consider urban, semi-urban, and rural areas to make my research more useful and meaningful. Splitting the questionnaire in half was an absolute must for every single interview. Part one of the survey was for the kids' parents, and part two was for the students themselves, and part three was for the students only. The students who were polled were in the age bracket of twenty-five to twenty-four. The parents were asked a series of questions regarding their occupations, socioeconomic backgrounds, and whether or not they come from a sporting culture. If they did, then we wanted to know if they have tried to give their children opportunities in this area. We also wanted to know their thoughts on national and international sporting events, how they feel about sports as a social tool for their children's development and growth, how they feel about sports as a hobby, as a career goal, as a sense of patriotism, and what role the government should play in promoting sports. On top of that, other interviews were recorded. A score between zero and one hundred was assigned to each question, with scores falling into three groups: zero to ten, ten to twenty, and twenty to thirty. Because of this, the data could be quantitatively categorized. The next thing that was considered was the distribution of frequencies.

It was with the help of renowned figures in the sports industry that the fifty-question survey was designed. Among these esteemed individuals were the Secretary and Joint Secretary of the Athletics Federation of India, a number of Kabaddi and cricket trainers, and more. We went ahead and did this since we thought it would be useful in coming up with the best questions to ask. A Pre-testing was carried out on four or five groups of parents and kids to gain a better grasp of the program's strengths, weaknesses, costs, and timing, among other things. Also, I made sure to include the changes into the interview schedule. The great distances between the two sites meant that it took eighteen months, from 2016's start to 2017's start, to complete the task.

Major Findings

This sociological research sought to examine the major impacts of a number of impending elements on the development aspect. Below are the statistics summary tables for several levels, along with brief explanations of each (Table 22.1).

Parents' inclination to enroll their children in athletic activities is declining (i.e., 27 and 24% in the group of 1–1.25 lac) in both states, according to a study that takes socio-economic status into consideration. In the 0.75 to 1 lac category, there was a little 1% growth, or 29% in the state of Uttar Pradesh. On the other hand, the disinclination was shown by a decline in the same category in Bihar. Given that one's habitus and cultural capital interact to determine one's level of engagement and success in a "field," the more culturally capitalious organizations may be able to "dictate the legitimate means of entry. The victims are the working class".

From a socio-cultural perspective, things are different, and there are some good things about it. The parents were informed about their children's social and cultural

Table 22.1 "The Socio-economic backgrounds of parent's vis-à-vis inclination towards sports"

Income Bracket Annually (INR)	State of UP	State of Bihar	Inclination/Sports UP Bihar In %
38,000–49,999	73	23	21 16
50,000–75,000	174	69	28 27
75,001–1,00,000	58	33	29 25
1,00,001–1,25,000	45	25	27 24
Total	350	150	

*According to the most recent index available from the Planning Commission of the Government of India, which was published in 2012, the yearly income of the typical Indian is 36,500 Indian Rupees. This was the fundamental criterion that led to the establishment of a beginning salary bracket of 38,000 Indian Rupees

origins through conversations about their involvement in sports and other extracurricular activities. An individual's inclination to engage in cultural and athletic pursuits is positively correlated with their economic level, as demonstrated in Table 22.2. Sports are "a social field (Bourdieu, 1990), a structured space of positions that impose specific determinations on those who enter it and this has been tested (Table 22.3)."

Participant from the study suggest that people's attitudes are shaped in large part by their geographical region. Nevertheless, we have noticed an increase in both the percentage and participation in the state of Bihar, even if it has a lower percentile compared to Uttar Pradesh. What this means is that where you live may affect your sense of social consciousness and belonging in the context of sports, at least to a certain degree. It is critical that the Indian government use its power fairly to ensure that the sports development programs accomplish their purpose, so that they can benefit the public, especially since these policies have not yet produced any results (Table 22.4).

Positive results were seen in relation to the participation of both sexes. Across all of the shown income brackets, the proportion of women in the top one percent grows as one moves up the income ladder. It should come as no surprise that they were able to take advantage of more opportunities as their income level rose. Having a basic education is crucial for getting into the sports industry and thinking about social neoliberalism. One way to look at sports (and the organizations that play in them) is as a means of creating different kinds of capital (Bourdieu 1986). From this

Table 22.2 In terms of their proclivity toward sports, the socio-cultural backgrounds of parents are taken into consideration

Income Bracket Annually (INR)	State of UP	State of Bihar	Inclination/Sports UP Bihar In %
38,000–49,999	73	23	19 14
50,000–75,000	174	69	32 25
75,001–1,00,000	58	33	34 23
1,00,001–1,25,000	45	25	35 25
Total	350	150	

Table 22.3 Impact of geographical location

Income Bracket Annually (INR)	State of UP	State of Bihar	Inclination/Sports UP Bihar In %
38,000–49,999	73	23	36 11
50,000–75,000	174	69	39 13
75,001–1,00,000	58	33	41 14
1,00,001–1,25,000	45	25	46 17
Total	350	150	

Table 22.4 One of the factors that influences sports is female involvement

Income Bracket Annually (INR)	State of UP	State of Bihar	Inclination/Sports UP Bihar In %
38,000–49,999	73	23	29 22
50,000–75,000	174	69	36 25
75,001–1,00,000	58	33	41 29
1,00,001–1,25,000	45	25	53 31
Total	350	150	

capital, certain advantages may be received, which in turn enable social agents to better or retain their social status.

Limitations

Some limitations are associated with this investigation. To be more specific, I was unable to address the following constraints owing to a lack of time, energy, and money; these constraints were both internal and external to my control:-

1. Western industrialized nations typically decide on the validity of data regarding underdevelopment and development, and as a result, the indicators for "development" are typically set by these nations. This is because development statistics are typically analyzed in relation to the concept of a developed country. However, the details of the sites have been well considered.
2. The reader should be cautious not to draw generalizing conclusions based on this investigation's results because of the exploratory character of the study and the small sample size.
3. In totality, the terminology sports is being investigated, and research into the disciplines is wide open.
4. There was no way to include students and youngsters in the age bracket of 9 to 14. The reasoning behind choosing an age bracket of 15–24 was that participation rates start to decline beyond that age; thus, research done between those two decades would be suitable. There is a breadth of research in this area that includes people of all ages.

Expected Contribution of the Research

Potentially helpful opportunities exist in the field of sports for people with radically divergent worldviews. Chances to promote trust, responsibilities, redistribution, and love of sport in a more socially conscious and humanitarian environment may provide the basis for these views. Questions regarding social transformation can occasionally raise the most substantial intellectual and practical concerns, despite the importance of explaining and understanding the physiological, economic, sociological, historical, psychological, and countless other aspects of what sport may do for society (Jarvie 2007).

A broader discussion relates to the capacity of sociology to address multiple publics (Burawoy 2005). All university researchers and faculty, but especially those with an interest in the social sciences, should take this matter into consideration, as it is relevant not only to the work of sociologists of sport but also to other sociologists. Rising interest in and demand for sports sociology and studies can be attributed to several interrelated factors, including India's young population, the country's promising sporting future, recent developments in Indian sociology, the country's booming economy, and other factors. The importance of sports and the strength of Bourdieu's theory are both brought to light in this expanded analysis.

Rather than focusing on sports per se, this study highlights the significance of people involved in sports. My intended contributions to educationalists and policymakers are the following:

1. This study will identify the factors that may help children and youth gather resources for sports practices, with the goal of addressing their usage and inculcating a habit of engaging in physical activities.
2. Sports developmental patterns in families are undervalued due to the socio-political context of the states of U.P. and Bihar. Future research can incorporate more social perspectives.
3. "The primary reason why this work is vital is because it will help awaken and cultivate a sociological imagination" in Indian society, which is a humanistic approach to sports-related matters. Additionally, it will help formulate future hypotheses that can be utilized in more advanced empirical studies.
4. The "physical culture—society" will focus on the social aspects of physical culture, including its adaptations and transformations, the historical factors that have influenced and shaped these changes, and the fundamental developmental tendencies that stem from the social nature of this culture, such as the norms and value systems that govern human behavior within it.
5. Keeping a strong database of statistics and sports news is prioritized so that scholars may access it in the future.
6. According to Wang (2006), "National reputation is one clear indication of a nation's power strength" (p. 91), and it both reflects and impacts the status of the country in the global arena, as pointed out by Mercer (1996). Indian national pride and strength will increase as the country's young get more involved in sports. A sociological imagination is necessary for this, which can then be combined and used for future studies.
7. The predicted change in perspective will assist the government in formulating a Sports for All strategy since involvement in sports will go from being seen as unusual to being seen as normal and even normative.

8. To wrap things up, our research project aims to provide a foundation for future work in sports sociology that will systematically examine ideas of social movements in India and throughout the world.

Opportunities to learn new things, work in different settings, and show confidence exist despite the fact that language hurdles, financial limitations, and cultural disparities are everywhere. Scientists from Europe who are interested in the sociology of sports can find a safer and more appropriate setting to conduct their studies in India. Moving to a new country gives early-career researchers a chance to learn about other cultures and get a fresh perspective on science. Research suggests that sports may play an important role in promoting sustainability, community building, and societal transformation". So, even if most of these assertions are based on anecdotal evidence and follow the principles of the new neoliberal ideology, using sport in this way has yielded a plethora of positive outcomes. The question of directionality, namely whether or if sport aids social development, whether or not sociological development aids sport, and whether or not there is reciprocity, remains unsolved. The two states also illustrate an issue that has been identified through a review of the literature. Past research has highlighted the following problems with government-based initiatives or involvements: they are top-down, they fail to address the specific issues in the targeted communities, they squander human resources, they are ideologically motivated, and they exacerbate social inequalities (i.e., perpetuate the status quo). There is zero relationship between these kinds of programs and the people they claim to be helping. Although ideology is also fundamental to this new approach, it offers a strong case against conventional state welfare policies and initiatives.

References

Journals

Bailey R (2006) Physical education and sport in schools: A review of benefits and outcomes. J Sch Health 76(8):397–401

Beutler I (2008) Sport serving development and peace: Achieving the goals of the United Nations through sport. Sport in Society 11(4):359–369

Bourdieu P (1978) Sport and social class. Soc Sci Inf 17(6):819–840

Buroway, Michael (2005) For Public Sociology. Am Sociol Rev, 70(1) pp 4–28

Clement Jean-Paul (1995) Contributions of the sociology of pierre bourdieu to the sociology of sport. Sociol Sport J, 12(2) pp 147–157

Clement J (1995) Sport sociology in France: A review. Int Rev Sociol Sport 30(3–4):335–349

Coalter F (2010a) Sport-for-development: Going beyond the boundary? Sport in Society 13(9):1374–1391

Coalter F (2010b) The politics of sport-for-development: Limited focus programmes and broad gauge problems? Int Rev Sociol Sport 45(3):295–314

Darnell SC, Hayhurst LMC (2011) Sport for decolonization: Exploring a new praxis of sport for development. Prog Dev Stud 11(3):183–196

Donnelly P, Darnell S, Wells S, Coakley J (2007) The use of sport to foster child and youth development and education. In Sport for Development and Peace, International Working Group (SDP/

IWG): Literature reviews on Sport for Development and Peace (pp. 7–47). Toronto, Ontario, Canada: University of Toronto, Faculty of Physical Education and Health
Donnelly P (1993) Democratization revisited: Seven theses on the democratization of sport and active leisure. Soc Leis 16(2):413–434
Donnelly P, Harvey J (1996) Overcoming bureaucratic barriers to the democratization of sport. Soc Leis 19(1):23–36
Eakereneng Van, Frank (2006) Sport and Development: Challenges in a new arena. Sport and Development. In: Vanden Auweele Y, Malcolm C, Meulders B (Eds). (pp 19–34). Leuven: Lannoo Campus
Georgakis S, Light R (2009) Visual data collection methods for research on the affective dimensions of children's personal experiences of PE. ACHPER Healthy Lifestyles, 56(¾) pp 23–27
Hartmann D, Kwauk C (2011) Sport and development: An overview, critique, and reconstruction. J Sport Soc Issues 35(3):284–305
Harvey J, Houle F (1994) 'Sport, World Economy, Global Culture, and the NewSocialMovements. Sociol Sport J, 11(4), pp 337–355
Houlihan, Barrie (2008) 'Sport and Society' Sage Publications, p 608
https://megsports.gov.in/documents/PYKKA.pdf, Page 1
https://www.aare.edu.au/data/publications/2001/lig01450.pdf, (pp 1–15)
Jarvie, Grant (2007) Sport, social change and the public intellectual. Int Rev Sociol Sport, 42(4), pp 411–424
Kumar N (2019) Sociology of sports in India: Issues and challenges. Sociol Bull 68(2):215–231
Light, Richard L (2010) 'Children's social and personal development through sports: a case study of an Australian Swimming Club. J Sport Soc Issues, 34(4), pp 379–395
Mercer, Neil (1996) The quality of talk in children's collaborative activity in the classroom. Sci Direct—Learn Instr, 6(4), pp 359–377
Roberts K, Brodie DA (1992) Sports Participation: How much does it cost? Taylor & Francis, 11(1), pp 19–29
Sage GH (2011) Physical Education, Sociology, and Sociology of Sport: Points of Intersection. Sociol Sport J,. 14(4), pp 317–339
Takacs F (1988a) The development and theoretical background of sport sociology in Hungary. Int Rev Sociol Sport 23(4):287–303
Takacs, Feren (1988) The development and theoretical background of sport-sociology in hungary. Int Rev Sociol Sport, 23(4), pp287–303
United Nation's Declaration on the Right of Development (1986); https://www.un.org/en/events/righttodevelopment/declaration.shtml
Van Eekeren F (2006) Sport and development: How to succeed at difficult times. Int Counc Sport Sci Phys Educ Bull 43(4):19–21
Wang, Jian (2006) Managing national reputation and international relations in the global era: Public diplomacy revisited. Public RelatS Rev, 32(2), pp 91–96

Books

Bourdieu P (1986) Distinction: Asocialcritique of the judgement of taste. London: Routledge
Coakley J (2001) Sportin society: issues & controversies. NewYork: McGraw-Hill
Edwards Harry, Homewood (1973) Illinios Sociology of Sport, Oxford Academic-Social Forces, p 378
Jarvie G (2006) Sport, culture and society: an introduction. London: Routledge
Stones Rob (2005) Structuration Theory. Red Globe Press, p 240, Edition 1, ISSN 2947–4299
Coakley J (2009) Sports in society: Issues and controversies (10th ed). McGraw-Hill
De France M (1995) Sport and society in France. Routledge
Edwards H (1973) Sociology of sport. Dorsey Press

Giddens A (1984) The constitution of society: Outline of the theory of structuration. University of California Press
Houlihan B (2008) Sport and society: A student introduction (2nd ed). Sage Publications
Jarvie G, McGuire B (1994) Sport and leisure in social thought. Routledge
Stones R (2005b) Structuration theory. Palgrave Macmillan
Light R (2001) Bourdieu and the sociology of sport: Habitus, capital and field in sport and physical education. University of Melbourne

Web Pages

https://documents1.worldbank.org/curated/en/262201468285343550/pdf/485210v10SR0wh10Box338913B01PUBLIC1.pdf
https://archive.pib.gov.in/archive/releases98/lyr2001/rjun2001/20062001/r200620011.html
European Sport Management Quarterly. http://www.tandf.co.uk/journals/titles/16184742.asp
Leisure Studies. http://www.tandf.co.uk/journals/routledge/02614367.html, Sociology of Sport Journal, http://www.humankinetics.com/SSJ/journalAbout.cfmSport, Education and Society, http://www.tandf.co.uk/journals/carfax/13573322.html, Indian Sociological Society
http://www.insoso.org
International Sociological Association–Sociology of Sports. http://www.isa-sociology.org/rc27.htm
Ministry of Sports and Youth Affairs, Government of India http://www.yac.nic.in/index.html
Athletics Federation of India http://www.indianathletics.in/
Donnelly P, Darnell S, Coakley J (2007) The use of sport to foster child and youth development and education
Report prepared for the ontario ministry of health promotion
Ministry of Youth Affairs and Sports. (2008) Panchayat Yuva Krida Aur Khel Abhiyan Scheme Document. Government of India
Ministry of Youth Affairs and Sports. (2014). National Sports Policy. Government of India
United Nations (1959) Declaration of the Rights of the Child. United Nations General Assembly
United Nations (1986) Declaration on the right to development. United Nations General Assembly
United Nations. (2005). International Year of Sport and Physical Education. United Nations
United Nations (2006) Sport as a means to promote education, health, development and peace. United Nations General Assembly Resolution 60/9
United Nations (2015) Sport for development and peace: The UN system in action. United Nations Office on Sport for Development and Peace
United Nations (2020) World Youth Report 2020: Youth and the 2030 Agenda for Sustainable Development. United Nations
UNESCO (1978) International charter of physical education and sport. U N Educ, Sci Cult Organ

Chapter 23
Empowering Marginalized Minds: A Roadmap for Equitable Education Reform in India

Sudha Khokate

Abstract The issue of caste-based discrimination in education and the lack of representation of marginalized communities in the education sector in India has been a major concern for many decades. However, despite several efforts, the educational disparities faced by marginalized students in India remain a persistent challenge. This has resulted in an education gap between marginalized and non-marginalized communities. This paper aims to examine the significance of addressing caste-based discrimination in schools using a subaltern framework. Besides this, it argues that increasing the representation of marginalized communities in the education sector is crucial for ensuring that marginalized students have equal access to quality education and can realize their constitutional right to education. The paper concludes that community-based solutions, in addition to policy changes, are necessary for addressing the educational disparities faced by marginalized students in India.

Keywords Marginalized communities · Education policy changes · Community-based solutions · India

Introduction

In the labyrinthine narrative of India's sociological trajectory, the subaltern perspective emerges as a powerful prism refracting the nuanced struggles and triumphs within the realm of education. Within this framework, this chapter unfolds against the backdrop of the book "Hundred Years of Sociology in India: Evolving Issues and Emerging Trends." It endeavours to navigate the contours of educational reform through the lens of the subaltern perspective, shedding light on the intricate interplay between power dynamics, systemic injustices, and the quest for equitable education.

S. Khokate (✉)
Department of Sociology, Bangalore University, Bangalore, Karnataka, India
e-mail: drsudhakhokate@gmail.com

A. Chauhan et al. (eds.), *Hundred Years of Sociology in India: Evolving Issues, Emerging Trends*, https://doi.org/10.1007/978-981-96-1317-5_23

As we embark on this exploration, the subaltern perspective becomes our guiding compass, urging us to delve into the experiences and voices of those historically marginalized–the Dalits, Adivasis, and other disadvantaged groups. Rooted in the intellectual legacy of Antonio Gramsci, this perspective demands a departure from traditional narratives, imploring us to dismantle the structures that perpetuate inequality within the educational landscape. The subaltern, in this context, becomes the focal point, an agent of change, and a testament to resilience in the face of systemic challenges (Gramsci 1999).

Gramsci's ideas on education and culture are primarily found in his "Prison Notebooks," written while he was imprisoned by the fascist regime in Italy between 1929 and 1935. He introduced the concept of cultural hegemony to explain how dominant classes maintain power in society through the control of culture and ideas. He argued that ruling classes not only use political and economic force but also shape the cultural and intellectual life of a society to maintain their dominance. Gramsci saw education as a key battleground in the struggle for cultural and ideological dominance. He argued that schools and educational institutions played a crucial role in transmitting and reinforcing the values and beliefs of the ruling class. However, he also believed that these institutions could be sites of resistance and counter-hegemony (Gramsci 1999).

This research paper aims to examine the current state of education in marginalized sections of India through a socio-political approach. It begins with an overview of the Indian education system, including its history, structure, and challenges. The focus of the paper then shifts to the marginalized sections of society, including the Dalits (formerly known as "Untouchables"), Adivasis (indigenous communities), and other socially and economically disadvantaged groups. Despite constitutional guarantees of education for all, these marginalized sections continue to face systemic barriers that prevent them from accessing quality education. These barriers include a lack of government investment in education, the prevalence of "caste-based" discrimination in schools, and a lack of representation of marginalized communities in educational institutions and in the teaching workforce (Khera 2016a, b, c, d).

The paper also highlights the impact of these barriers on the educational outcomes of marginalized students. For example, data from the Annual Status of Education Report (ASER) shows that only a small fraction of Dalit and Adivasi children attend school, and even fewer complete their education (Pratham 2017). Additionally, marginalized students often face lower levels of academic achievement, higher rates of dropout, and limited opportunities for post-secondary education (National Commission for Scheduled Castes 2017). Given these challenges, the paper argues that addressing the educational disparities faced by marginalized communities in India requires a multi-faceted approach that incorporates both policy changes and community-based solutions. This includes increasing government investment in education, addressing discrimination in schools, and increasing the representation of marginalized communities in the educational sector. Additionally, the paper suggests that community-based organizations and civil society groups can play a critical role in advocating for the rights of marginalized students and providing alternative forms of education that are responsive to their needs.

An attempt is made in this paper to provide a socio-political analysis of the state of education in marginalized sections of India. Through an examination of the systemic barriers faced by these communities in accessing quality education, and the impact on their educational outcomes, the paper highlights the urgent need for action to address the disparities faced by the marginalized students and ensure their right to quality education. It, therefore, makes recommendations for addressing the educational disparities, marginalized students face in India. The paper also evaluates the role of community-based solutions and policy changes in addressing the educational disparities faced by marginalized students in India. It synthesizes and analyzes existing knowledge on the topic and identifies gaps in the literature that can be addressed through further research.

An attempt is made in this paper to provide a socio-political analysis of the state of education in marginalized sections of India. Through an examination of the systemic barriers faced by these communities in accessing quality education, and the impact on their educational outcomes, the paper highlights the urgent need for action to address the disparities faced by the marginalized students and ensure their right to quality education. It, therefore, makes recommendations for addressing the educational disparities, marginalized students face in India. The paper also evaluates the role of community-based solutions and policy changes in addressing the educational disparities faced by marginalized students in India. It synthesizes and analyzes existing knowledge on the topic and identifies gaps in the literature that can be addressed through further research.

The study is based on secondary sources and the inclusion criteria for the sources were limited to education among the marginalized communities. The literature reviewed was from sources such as peer-reviewed journals, books, and government reports on education and marginalized groups in India. The study has used a critical and interpretive approach to analyze the existing literature, drawing on relevant theories and frameworks to contextualize and understand the complexities of the issue. This methodology has allowed the study to provide a comprehensive overview of the Indian education system and the challenges marginalized communities face in accessing quality education.

Equity in Indian Education: Struggles of the Marginalized Communities

Education is often considered as a fundamental right and a powerful tool for social mobility. However, in India, the quest for educational equity remains elusive, particularly for marginalized communities facing systemic challenges. The review attempted here explores the nuanced issues surrounding equity in Indian education, drawing from a comprehensive review of studies that shed light on the struggles faced by marginalized groups. The analysis encompasses various dimensions, including caste-based discrimination, government policies, community-based solutions, and the imperative for a multi-faceted approach.

Khera (2016a, b, c, d) provides a comprehensive overview of the Indian education system and the challenges faced by marginalized communities in accessing quality education. This book argues that addressing the educational disparities faced by the marginalized students requires a multi-faceted approach that incorporates both policy changes and community-based solutions. One of the prominent themes explored in the literature is the pervasive issue of caste-based discrimination in Indian schools.

"Caste-based Discrimination in Schools: A Study of Dalit Children in Rural India" by Gautam and Srivastava (2013) provides a systematic analysis of the prevalence of caste-based discrimination in schools and its impact on the educational outcomes of Dalit children. The study concludes that addressing caste-based discrimination in schools is essential for ensuring that marginalized students have equal access to quality education. "The State of Education in Adivasi Areas in India" by Singh and Dey (2015) provides a comprehensive analysis of the state of education in Adivasi areas in India. The authors suggest that community-based solutions, in addition to policy changes, are necessary for addressing the disparities faced by Adivasi students.

"Education for the Marginalized: Experiences from Rural India" by Nair and Ramesh (2017) provides a qualitative study of the experiences of marginalized students in rural India. The authors are of the view that community-based organizations and civil society groups can play a critical role in addressing the disparities faced by marginalized students. "Access to Education for Marginalized Children in India: A Study of Government Schools" by Mukherjee (2018) provides a quantitative study of the access to education for marginalized children in government schools in India. The author suggests that increasing government investment in education and addressing discrimination in schools is necessary for ensuring that marginalized students have equal access to quality education.

"Caste and Education: A Study of Dalit Students in India" by Bhat (2019) gives a qualitative study of the experiences of Dalit students in India. The author suggests that addressing caste-based discrimination in schools and increasing the representation of Dalit communities in the educational sector is necessary for ensuring that Dalit students have equal access to quality education. "The Right to Education for Marginalized Children in India: An Analysis of Government Policies" by Raman (2020) provides a comprehensive analysis of government policies aimed at ensuring the right to education for marginalized children in India.

The literature review presents a comprehensive examination of the educational landscape in India with a focus on marginalized communities. "Education and Social Justice in India" (Khera 2016a, b, c, d) emphasizes the challenges faced by marginalized groups in accessing quality education, advocating for a multi-faceted approach that integrates policy changes and community-based solutions. "The Right to Education in India: Challenges and Progress" (Jain 2010) offers a detailed analysis of progress made in realizing education rights while identifying lingering challenges. Studies such as "Caste-based Discrimination in Schools" (Gautam and Srivastava 2013) and "The State of Education in Adivasi Areas in India" (Singh and Dey 2015) systematically address caste-based discrimination and disparities in Adivasi areas, advocating for a comprehensive strategy that includes both policy interventions and community engagement.

Qualitative studies like "Education for the Marginalized" (Nair and Ramesh 2017) delve into the experiences of marginalized students in rural India, highlighting the crucial role of community-based organizations. Quantitative research, such as "Access to Education for Marginalized Children" (Mukherjee 2018), stresses the importance of increased government investment and addressing discrimination in schools. Additionally, studies like "Caste and Education" (Bhat 2019) and "The Right to Education for Marginalized Children" (Raman 2020) underscore the necessity of tackling caste-based discrimination and enhancing representation in the educational sector for equitable access to quality education. Collectively, these studies form a compelling narrative advocating for a comprehensive, multi-dimensional approach to addressing educational disparities for marginalized communities in India.

In the realm of tribal education, numerous critical issues and challenges hinder the effective provision of learning opportunities for tribal children. One of the primary constraints is the medium of language, which poses a significant barrier, preventing tribal children from accessing education. The diversity of languages within tribal communities creates a challenge in delivering education that aligns with their linguistic backgrounds. The location of tribal villages presents another obstacle. Physical barriers often hinder children from attending schools in neighbouring villages, limiting their access to educational facilities. This geographic challenge compounds the difficulty of ensuring widespread and equitable educational opportunities for tribal children. Economic conditions further exacerbate the situation. The impoverished state of tribal communities results in a reluctance to spare children for formal education, as families may depend on their labour power to contribute to the household income. The immediate economic returns of education are not always apparent, leading parents to prioritize remunerative employment for their children over formal schooling (Sedwal & Sangeeta 2008).

The attitude of tribal parents towards education is shaped by these economic considerations. In remote tribal areas, the preference for engaging children in income-generating activities, rather than investing in education, becomes a prevailing mindset. This attitude contributes to a cycle of limited educational attainment within tribal communities. Teacher-related problems compound these challenges. Teacher absenteeism is a recurrent issue in remote tribal areas, significantly impacting the quality of education provided. The lack of consistent presence and engagement from teachers hampers the learning experience for tribal students (Sujatha 2002).

Furthermore, the lack of proper monitoring and coordination between the Tribal Welfare Department and the School Education Department exacerbates the situation. Poor coordination undermines effective oversight, making it difficult to implement targeted interventions and address the specific needs of tribal students. To address these multifaceted challenges, a comprehensive approach is necessary, encompassing linguistic considerations, geographical accessibility, economic empowerment, and improved coordination between relevant departments to ensure the holistic development of tribal education (Singh & Dey 2015).

Challenges of Marginalized Communities in the Indian Education System

In the analysis that ensues, the subaltern perspective acts as a critical apparatus, dissecting the systemic barriers that impede the educational journey of marginalized communities in India. It prompts us to scrutinize not only the overt manifestations of discrimination but also the subtle mechanisms that perpetuate educational disparities. Through this lens, we unveil the historical injustices, the intricate dance of caste-based discrimination, and the stark absence of representation within educational institutions and the teaching fraternity.

The Indian education system has faced several challenges in ensuring that marginalized communities have equal access to quality education. Despite constitutional guarantees of education for all, systemic barriers, including caste-based discrimination, inadequate infrastructure and resources, and poverty, prevent marginalized students from accessing quality education. This has resulted in significant disparities in educational outcomes between marginalized and non-marginalized students in India. The study aims to address the educational disparities faced by marginalized students in India and requires a multi-faceted approach that incorporates both policy changes and community-based solutions.

Caste-based Discrimination

The hypothesis that addressing caste-based discrimination in schools and increasing the representation of marginalized communities in the education sector is necessary for ensuring that marginalized students have equal access to quality education is supported by several studies in the field of education and social justice in India. For example, Gautam and Srivastava (2013) found in their study, "Caste-based Discrimination in Schools: A Study of Dalit Children in Rural India," that caste-based discrimination was a prevalent issue in Indian schools and had a significant impact on the educational outcomes of Dalit children. The study concluded that addressing caste-based discrimination in schools was essential for ensuring that marginalized students had equal access to quality education.

Similarly, Bhat (2019) in his qualitative study, "Caste and Education: A Study of Dalit Students in India," found that Dalit students continued to face systemic barriers, including caste-based discrimination, that prevented them from accessing quality education. The author suggested that addressing caste-based discrimination in schools and increasing the representation of Dalit communities in the education sector was necessary for ensuring that Dalit students had equal access to quality education. Furthermore, Nair and Ramesh (2017) in their qualitative study, "Education for the Marginalized: Experiences from Rural India," found that marginalized students continued to face systemic barriers, including poverty and inadequate infrastructure, that prevented them from accessing quality education. The authors suggested that community-based organizations and civil society groups could play a critical role in addressing the disparities faced by marginalized students.

These studies provide evidence to support the hypothesis that addressing caste-based discrimination in schools and increasing the representation of marginalized communities in the education sector is necessary for ensuring that marginalized students have equal access to quality education. Policy changes, as well as community-based solutions, need to be incorporated to address the systemic barriers faced by marginalized students and improve their educational outcomes.

Case Laws Related to Caste-based Discrimination in Education

There have been several important cases in India that have dealt with the issue of caste-based discrimination in education and the right to education for marginalized communities. One such case is the landmark judgment in the Unnikrishnan case (1993), which ruled that the right to education is a fundamental right guaranteed by the Constitution of India. The case recognized the importance of education in realizing the constitutional goal of equality and held that the state has a constitutional obligation to provide free and compulsory education to all children.

Another significant case is the Inamdar v. State of Maharashtra (2005) case, which dealt with the issue of reservation of seats for socially and economically marginalized communities in private unaided educational institutions. The case held that private unaided educational institutions must reserve a certain percentage of seats for socially and economically marginalized communities to ensure that these communities have access to quality education.

The T.M.A. Pai Foundation v. State of Karnataka (2002) case dealt with the issue of the admission of students from socially and economically marginalized communities in private unaided educational institutions. The case held that the state has the power to regulate the admission of students in private unaided educational institutions to ensure that socially and economically marginalized communities have access to quality education.

These cases demonstrate the importance of addressing caste-based discrimination in education and ensuring that marginalized communities have equal access to quality education. As stated by Khera (2016a, b, c, d), "addressing the educational disparities faced by marginalized students requires a multi-faceted approach that incorporates both policy changes and community-based solutions." Addressing caste-based discrimination in schools and increasing the representation of marginalized communities in the education sector is crucial for ensuring that marginalized students have equal access to quality education and can realize their constitutional right to education.

Community-based Solutions

The educational disparities faced by marginalized students in India cannot be addressed by policy changes alone. A multi-faceted approach that incorporates both policy changes and community-based solutions is necessary to effectively address these disparities (Khera 2016a, b, c, d). This idea is supported by research that has shown that community-based solutions can play a critical role in improving educational outcomes for marginalized students (Muralidharan & Sundararaman 2011). For example, community-based programs that involve parents and other members of the local community in the education process are effective in increasing enrollment and improving educational outcomes for marginalized students (Chudgar & Lavy 2010). These programs can help to create a supportive learning environment for marginalized students and address some of the cultural and social barriers that may prevent them from accessing education (Chudgar and Lavy 2010).

Similarly, community-based organizations and NGOs can play an essential role in advocating for the rights of marginalized students and working to address the systemic barriers that prevent them from accessing quality education. These organizations can work with the government and other stakeholders to develop and implement policies and programs that are tailored to the specific needs of marginalized communities (Muralidharan and Sundararaman 2011).

Addressing the root causes of these disparities, such as caste-based discrimination and systemic barriers, community-based solutions in addition to policy changes are necessary for addressing the educational disparities faced by marginalized students in India.

Suggestions and Recommendations

Below are some suggestions and recommendations for addressing the educational disparities faced by marginalized students in India:

The government can make policy changes to address the educational disparities, marginalized students face in India. For example, the government can make changes to the Right to Education Act, of 2009 to ensure that it is effectively implemented and monitored. The government can also provide financial assistance to the marginalized students to help them access quality education.

Community-based solutions can play a crucial role in addressing the educational disparities faced by marginalized students in India. For example, community-based organizations can work with local schools to provide support to marginalized students, such as after-school programs, tutoring, and mentorship programs. These organizations can also work with the government to provide financial assistance to marginalized students.

Parental involvement can also play a significant role in addressing the educational disparities faced by marginalized students in India. For example, parents can be encouraged to participate in school activities and advocate for their children's education. They can also be provided with information and resources to help them support their children's education.

Teacher training programs can also be implemented to address the educational disparities faced by the marginalized students in India. For example, teachers can be trained on how to identify and support marginalized students, as well as how to create a supportive and inclusive classroom environment.

Data collection and analysis can also play a crucial role in addressing the educational disparities faced by the marginalized students in India. For example, the government can collect data on the educational outcomes of marginalized students and analyze this data to identify disparities and implement targeted interventions.

Addressing the educational disparities faced by the marginalized students in India requires a multi-faceted approach that incorporates policy changes, community-based solutions, parental involvement, teacher training, and data collection and analysis. It is important to take a comprehensive and coordinated approach to ensure that marginalized students have equal access to quality education and can realize their constitutional right to education.

Conclusion

The subaltern perspective continues to resonate, guiding us towards a resounding call for transformative action. The roadmap unveiled for equitable education reform is informed by the principles of justice, inclusivity, and a commitment to dismantling oppressive structures. The subaltern, once relegated to the periphery, emerges as the protagonist in this narrative, charting a course towards a more equitable future.

As we reflect on "Empowering Marginalized Minds: A Roadmap for Equitable Education Reform in India," the subaltern perspective stands as a testament to the enduring spirit of those who have long been silenced. It beckons us to continue this journey beyond the confines of this chapter, urging sociologists, policymakers, and advocates to join hands in shaping a future where education is truly a liberating force for all, transcending the shackles of inequality. In the annals of sociology in India, the subaltern perspective beckons us to be not just observers but active agents of change, forging a path towards a more inclusive and equitable educational landscape.

In conclusion, the paper highlights the importance of addressing caste-based discrimination in education and ensuring that marginalized communities in India have equal access to quality education. The right to education is a fundamental right guaranteed by the Constitution of India and the state has a constitutional obligation to provide free and compulsory education to all children. The judicial pronouncements in the Unnikrishnan case (1993), Inamdar v. State of Maharashtra (2005), and T.M.A. Pai Foundation v. State of Karnataka (2002) demonstrate the significance of addressing caste-based discrimination in education and the need for reservation of seats for socially and economically marginalized communities in both public and private educational institutions.

Additionally, the research underscores the importance of community-based solutions, complementing policy changes, to address the educational disparities faced by the marginalized students, including tribals. Implementing measures such as teacher training programs and community outreach initiatives is deemed essential to ensure that marginalized students, particularly those from tribal backgrounds, have equal access to quality education and can realize their constitutional right to education.

In light of the above discussions, it is recommended that the government should take the necessary steps to address, both caste and tribal-based discrimination in education and ensure that marginalized communities have equal access to quality education, fostering an inclusive and empowering educational environment. This can be achieved through policy changes, such as the reservation of seats in both public and private educational institutions, and by implementing community-based solutions. The government should also take steps to ensure that educational institutions are made aware of the importance of addressing caste-based discrimination and the need for inclusive education.

References

Bhat M (2019) Caste and education: a study of dalit students in India. J Soc Justice Educ 8(2):127–139

Bhup SG, Mangal S, Tran V-P, Keerthiraj (2023) Law and legal methods. Evincepub Publishing

Chudgar A, Lavy V (2010) Community involvement in education: What does it mean for educational outcomes? J Dev Econ 92(2):330–344

Devaiah NG, Keerthiraj (2021) E-Governance in India: Challenges and Strategies. Orange Books Publ

Gautam M, Srivastava N (2013) Caste-based discrimination in schools: a study of dalit children in rural India. J Educ Pract 4(17):56–62

Gramsci, Antonio, 1891–1937 (1999) Selections from the prison notebooks of Antonio Gramsci. New York: International Publishers

Inamdar PA v. State of Maharashtra (2005) Supreme Court of India, 2(2), 1–15

Indian Council of Social Science Research (2015) Marginalized communities in india: a study of access to education. New Delhi, India: Indian Counc Soc Sci Res

Jain S (2010) The right to education in india: challenges and progress

Keerthiraj (2019) Isms in politics: political ideologies ruling the world. Evincepub Publishing

Khera R (2016a) Addressing disparities in education faced by marginalized students. Econ Pol Wkly 51(34):46–52

Khera R (2016b) Addressing educational disparities faced by marginalized students in india: a multi-faceted approach. J Educ Pract 7(5):1–10

Khera R (2016c) Addressing educational disparities in India: A multi-faceted approach. Econ Pol Wkly 51(8):43–51

Khera R (2016d) Education and social justice in India. Oxford University Press, New Delhi

Ministry of Human Resource Development. (2016) Right to Education Act, 2009. New Delhi, India: Government of India

Mukherjee P (2018) Access to education for marginalized children in India: A Study of Government Schools

Muralidharan K, Sundararaman V (2011) Community-based monitoring of schools: Evidence from a field experiment in India. J Public Econ 95(1–2):16–30

Nair R, Ramesh S (2017) Education for the marginalized: experiences from rural India. J Educ Dev 5(4):340–350

National Commission for Protection of Child Rights (2017) Caste-Based discrimination in education in India: a study. New Delhi, India: Government of India

Pratham (2017) Annual status of education report (Rural). Mumbai: Pratham Education Foundation

Raman K (2020) The right to education for marginalized children in India: an analysis of government policies

Sedwal M, Sangeeta K (2008) Education and Social Equity with special focus on Scheduled Castes and Scheduled Tribes in Elementary Education, NUEPA, New Delhi

Sujatha K (2002) Education among Scheduled Tribes. In Govinda R (ed), India education report: a profile of basic education. New Delhi: Oxford University Press

Singh R, Dey N (2015) The state of education in adivasi areas in India

T.M.A.Pai Foundation & Ors vs State Of Karnataka & Ors on 31. (2002, 10 31) Retrieved from Indian Kanoon: https://indiankanoon.org/doc/512761/

UNESCO (2017) Education for All Global Monitoring Report. UNESCO, Paris, France

Unnikrishnan JP (1993) Right to education as a fundamental right. Supreme Court India 1(1):1–12

Chapter 24
Environment Management Through Youth Volunteerism: A Study on Green Army, Trivandrum

K. A. Anoop

Abstract The paper is a study on the Green Army of the Trivandrum Municipal Corporation in Kerala, a youth volunteer umbrella group consisting of students, youth, working professionals, retired personals, and activists which has received world attention with its structure and activities and use of its voluntary service for waste management and environmental protection. The paper aims to understand the mission and activities of the Green Army as an Environmental Youth Volunteer group, how it mobilizes the volunteers for environmental volunteerism, and in what way the Green Army model can be applied to a sustainable environment in other states of India to understand and solve various environmental issues and challenges. Open-ended interviews were conducted with six Green Army volunteers to know about the vision and mission of the Green Army from the beginning to the present stage of its growth. The respondents were the founding youth volunteers and the stakeholders of the organization. The study concludes that youth Volunteerism is the most effective and useful way of tackling and resolving environment-related problems, not only in India but across the world where young people offer their time and effort freely and voluntarily for genuine concern of the society. In this sense, it provides additional information and a new dimension to the sociology of environmental movements. It seems that young people will lead the environmental movements of this century and the case of the Green Army in Kerala, as shown in this paper, substantiates this argument.

Keywords Volunteerism · Environmental volunteerism · Green Army · Waste management

K. A. Anoop (✉)
Department of Sociology, University of Kerala, Thiruvananthapuram, Kerala, India
e-mail: anoopsalphd@gmail.com

A. Chauhan et al. (eds.), *Hundred Years of Sociology in India: Evolving Issues, Emerging Trends*, https://doi.org/10.1007/978-981-96-1317-5_24

Introduction

Environmental volunteerism is an established form of volunteerism that is happening worldwide when people volunteer themselves for the benefit of the natural environment. As the environment and its sustainability are continuously affected by climate changes, pollution, industrialization, and various other factors, different governments are taking up the huge and necessary task of preserving the environment for future generations. As the problems are increasing, the challenges for achieving sustainable goals are also growing. Citizens' active participation, volunteer availability, and initiatives with sustainable attitudes and efforts are the need of the time (Pillemer et al. 2017). The traditional and governmental bodies are not so equipped and sufficient to meet the environmental issues and provide effective remedial measures. Therefore, many nations have accepted the role of volunteer groups and their outstanding involvement in environmental issues. A lot of organizations and voluntary movements are coming up, supported by government funds and project undertakings for solving environmental problems. It shows that individuals are aware of the problems affecting their environment which can be solved at their source by the initiatives at the local level (Donald 1997).

According to Learner and Reid, the Volunteer Environmental Stewardship Group (VESG) consists of a few people gathered into a group who dedicate their time and efforts to the wellbeing of the natural environment and participate in the activities for the said purpose voluntarily (Learner and Reid 1993). These groups engage in activities to restore, maintain, and preserve the environment and to create awareness among the local public. (Fisher et al., 2007). Among them, the Urban Environmental Stewardship Group of Volunteers concentrates on the urban areas and takes care of the parks, waterbodies, trees in the streets, footpaths, systems waste management, recycling, and other eco-system services (Boyer & Polasky, 2004; Barthel et al., 2006). These groups join hands with urban environmental management and governing systems spreading their network of activities with other agencies, non-governmental groups, local groups, and stakeholders (Ernstson et al., 2010; Newmann and Dale, 2007).

A few groups of volunteers engage in observation which is one of the important ways to help the professionals to make the policies and measures for preservation of the environment. The observation of the streams, natural habitats, the effects and miseries of the natural calamities from the primary sources, and the real situations of pollution with the chemical characteristics of the water, air, and atmosphere is made to provide real and reliable data for the state and the authorities. The observation of birds, insects, plants, fish birds, and other kinds of creatures in wildlife is precious and useful information that is impossible for the authorities to collect directly from the real sources for the departments to take further actions to protect them. These observations may help to better screen the real situations and understand the trends and tendencies to manage for better sustainable strategies for nature. The cleaning and collecting the plastic wastes from the water bodies, categorising the debris at the seashore and the forest peripheries, wildfire suppression, the immediate and effective help and evacuation at the time of floods and tycoons are not possible without the help of a good number of dedicated young environmental volunteers. The protection of water bodies, the campaigns against deforestation, nuclear wastes, and multinational companies that pervert nature, water, and air are only possible with a good number of environmental volunteers. The time and effort spent by a number of volunteers and non-profit organizations are behind the laws and regulations made by the state and other organizations for the protection and preservation of the environment.

Motivations for Environmental Volunteerism

Even though environmental volunteerism is an established social action worldwide, the motivations specifically for environmental volunteerism and the factors that are leading young ones to environmental volunteer activities are not separately studied. As the motivating factors of all the volunteer activities are almost well defined and are also applicable to environmental volunteers, the scholars always refer to the factors leading to all the volunteer activities to the environmental activities too.

However, the primary motivation of each and every volunteer who engages in free and unpaid activities for the environment is just to keep or preserve nature and the world for future generations (Erikson, 1994; Warburton and Gooch 2007). The survival instinct when the habitat and the surroundings are under threat always leads the human being to defend his own environment and nature. So, the most real and genuine motivation for young people to be involved in activities and volunteer behaviour to contribute their precious time and effort to the environment is the fear and concern for survival. It is a concern for the future not to leave the world worse than what we received from our ancestors (Moody 2008).

A kind of "sense of place" is working behind this motivation, which is explained as belongingness or a sense of attachment to the village, neighbourhood, communities, cities, and the world they live (Bushway et. al. 2011). This attachment makes the people promote themselves for the well-being of the places they live, by doing volunteer activities for the preservation of the resources, keeping the surroundings and the environment waste-free and pollution-free. Steadman et. al., (2004) and Kruger (2009) also posit that this sense of place and attachment to the world they live in always lead people to pro-environmental behaviours and activities. However, a few researchers are of the opinion that by continuous interaction with the environment and community, they live through volunteer activities belongingness formed in the mind of the young people so that they engage and sustain in volunteer activities. (McHugh & Mings 1996). A sense of belongingness or an attitude of steward or protector of the environment can be created in young minds.

However, the young people who are engaging in environmental volunteerism have a few more motivating factors as defined by the scholars who evaluated the motivations of volunteerism in general. These are found among the young people who are looking for a platform for their self-actualization for making their life useful and giving significant meaning to their life, who are looking for personal relationships and friendships, who have some monitory intentions, and who have just joined with the persuasion of a friend or an influential person or just for fun who engage themselves in environmental volunteerism (Kim et al, 2010, Shier 2020).

Modes of Environmental Volunteerism

Environmental volunteerism is a pro-social activity that is concerned with the protection of the environment, defending violations against the environment, and protecting wildlife. These modes are explained below.

Observation—Volunteers engage in observation of social and natural realities outside of their lives and bring the attention of the general public to these realities are one of the prominent groups of environmental volunteers. By visual and direct observations of the land, water, habitat, and living creatures like birds, animals, plants insects, etc. the youth volunteers provide first-hand information to make the remedies possible and effective. Collecting data and samples physically and directly is costly and difficult for professionals and scientists, so they rely on these environmental youth volunteers who observe the world around them and collect information spending their time and effort freely (Bushway et. al. 2011).

Activism—The mode of activism is more effective, and immediate and attracts more public participation. There are many people who are not even interested in other modes of environmental volunteerism, participate, and contribute themselves as partial or active activists for the protection of the environment. This mode is used as a political measure and turns easily to aggressive moods (Marris 2006).

Creating Awareness—Educating people and making them aware of how to protect nature and the surroundings is an important factor of activities for the well-being of the same. There are many volunteers who engage themselves actively in creating awareness in the rural and urban setting on how to protect nature, how to avoid the pollution of water, air, and atmosphere, how to manage and recycle waste, etc. There are many agencies and organizations that conduct events, conferences, street plays, and other art forms to educate people about the preservation of nature and best practices for sustainable development.

Environmental Assessment and Monitoring—The volunteers and the organizations constantly engage themselves in assessing and monitoring nature, natural resources, and living and non-living organisms in this mode. The organizations like Environmental Monitoring Group (EMG), Bombay Natural History Agency (BNHS), CONSERVE, Earthwatch, US Environmental Protection Agency, etc. are the best examples of this kind. The aim of these agencies is to continuously assess and monitor the environmental realities and challenges and provide support for the research; filling the gaps in the research on certain issues and helping to formulate Government policies to protect the environment.

Rebuilding the Environment—There are many volunteers and volunteer agencies working hard with great enthusiasm to restore nature and natural resources. The activities to restore the water bodies and waterways, the seashore and beaches, bushes, and forests, the rare species of animals and plants, the natural medicinal herbs, etc. are done by many volunteers to improve the environment again.

Barriers of Young People to Engage in Environmental Volunteerism

Youth volunteerism is a pro-social behaviour and like all prosocial behaviours the individual and groups who are engaged in it may have to face and overcome various barriers. These socio-economic and political barriers may continuously influence the initiation, progress, and sustenance of the volunteer attitude of young ones.

Money or financial constraints are a major barrier for the youth volunteers engaged in environmental volunteerism. Young people who are usually students, jobless, or job-seeking people are not able to spend much on volunteer activities. As the agencies cannot pay a nominal remuneration for their expenses, the young volunteers suffer the barrier of financial constraints to continue their career as volunteers.

Environmental volunteerism among young people is promoted only by adequate support given to them. Various agencies and governmental organizations support and provide funds and resources for these young volunteer contributions to the environment. Among them, there are organizations for the environment, various Non-Governmental organizations, entrepreneurs with their CSR funds, Governments with various grants and endowments, etc. There are numerous projects which are run purely by individual and independent funding. Sometimes these agencies and groups mobilize foreign funds from various foreign agencies. Fund raisings, personal money collection, people's funding or crowd fundings, etc. are also seen to be the financial backup of environmental volunteerism.

Green Army Trivandrum: The Beginning of a New Initiative

Green Army is an environmental Stewardship Group started in 2016 associated with the 'My City My Beautiful City Campaign' of the Trivandrum Municipal Council. The group began with a few young people with a volunteer spirit towards the preservation and sustainability of the environment and as an oriented group to solve a relevant problem faced by all the countries dealing with environmental issues- Waste and its management. At that time, the city was struggling a great deal to manage 80 tons of solid waste produced daily. So a few like-minded people gathered together to address this issue. The group was supported by V.K. Prasanth, the Mayor of the city, who himself was a young man with a lot of volunteer instinct to be an administrator of the city. The space was given by him to the group at the Municipal Corporation Office of Trivandrum City which became their meeting and planning room.

The environmental Stewardship group is the Green Army which began as a small group and later turned into an army of Students, Young people, Mentors, retired personnel, activists, and other NGOs working for environmental sustainability. It was a normal and spontaneous gathering that happened among a few like-minded young people who wished to do something about the environmental problems of the city and society. One of the respondents who was among the first ones and later became the active leader and coordinator of the Green Army and still keeps the spirit of the mission of the group, was from a family who were actively engaging in nativities of social reformation. Almost all of them, rather than creating an association or being official youth volunteers, gathered with a vision and desire to do something for society and the city. They were ready to spend the time they got from their busy schedule of study and career for solving a few radical problems affecting humanity.

Attukal Pongala (Festival of Women) and its Impact on the City Environment

The Attukal Bhagavathy Temple is considered to be a great pilgrim centre for women and so the Festival of the Temple which is celebrated in the Months of February and March is considered to be the biggest festival for women by a large number of women participants. They flock from all over the state and participate in it irrespective of religion, caste, and creed. The festival is celebrated for 10 days and the most important ritual is on the ninth day, on which women from all over the state gather in the city and prepare the oven with bricks (*pongalayaduppu*) to cook the "pongala" (the sacred food for the ritual to please the deity and to get the blessings). The this is called Attukal Pongala. This ritual is centred on the temple and women who gather in the city prepare the oven on the streets of the city centring the temple. The ritual happened in 1997 and made a Guinness World Record as 1.5 Million women participated in the festival and performed rituals. In 2009 a new record was made and it just continues as millions of women flow to the temple every year.

The impact of the festival on the city eco-system is huge and serious as the gathering of millions of women with their families dumb a huge amount of waste on the city. Cleaning and recycling this high amount of waste is a herculean task for the municipality. There are already tons of waste created daily by the city dwellers and the extra amount of waste from the visitors makes the burden unbearable for the authorities. The festival especially the ritual of cooking the festive food on the streets, the days after the festival are so burdensome for the municipal daily cleaning workers. This circumstance demanded a group of people who could voluntarily contribute their time and effort to work with the municipality to clean the city. According to one of the respondents, it was the first huge responsibility taken up by the Green Army volunteers.

The Small Group to an Army

The Group was not hierarchical not even structured into an organizational form. A few young people gather with the motivation of doing something for the well-being and wellness of the environment around them. At the beginning "everyone's voice was heard and taken up as important by all. There were no complexes or conflicts of interest. Each one had the same motto and motivation- to clean the city. And then was born the project—"My City, My Clean City" said one of the respondents. However, the number of volunteers was to be increased for better and more effective implementation of the programs and plans. Mayor V.K. Prasanth did not work as a leader but as a group member involved with the group and planned the programs. The decision to recruit volunteers from the Schools under the Trivandrum Municipality was revolutionary. The school environmental club named Green Army was formed in each school with a teacher member. The teacher member was directed by the Health Inspector and coordinated by the Green Army with the support of the municipality. A large group of individuals from different streams of life and various NGOs joined hands with this umbrella organization and worked hard for the environmental well-being of the city starting from campaigning, collecting, and managing the wastes created by Aattukal Pongala.

The Growth and Development of the Green Army

Every movement gets clicked and makes a significant impact on society at the first project on a relevant issue. The sustenance of that same impact on society can be achieved only by continuously being involved in various other pertinent issues happening in society. Green Army fortunately was so equipped after the first project with a number of volunteers and a strong Governing Body. The Trivandrum Municipality has given its immense support to the group and its honourable Mayor V. K. Prasanth was like a full-time mentor to the group. "He has given adequate letters and timely instructions when the organizations hunt the volunteers from Schools and other government Bodies, and moreover he was almost one among us", said a respondent.

Decentralization of Waste and My City, My Clean City

The Green Army was entrusted with the responsibility to make awareness among students and make them part of the army with the campaign for My City, My Clean City. The group has done it very successfully by adding thousands of students from various schools aware of the decentralised waste management which was the motto and vision of the campaign. Similarly, a small group at the beginning began to evolve as a great army with young people and students who were well aware of their responsibility to keep nature for the next generation waste-free and safe.

The Green Army mentor continuously visited schools to motivate and keep the students updated and aware of their duties and responsibilities with adequate training and classes on how to scientifically and responsibly handle waste. The vacation camps were equipped with classes and training on responsible waste management, other activities and competitions that promote the responsibility of the public to deal with their waste locally scientifically, the *Haritha ngarothsav*, where students were involved in gaming and other productive activities that spread the importance of decentralized waste management, etc. These were the major activities of the Green Army at the beginning stage. Green Army units were formed at various schools within the boundary of Trivandrum Municipal Corporation.

The Floods and the Covid 19

A volunteer organization cannot close its eyes and be indifferent when the world around us is struck by disasters and epidemics even though it is outside of its working area and focused themes. The Green Army started with the mission and vision to keep the Trivandrum city, clean and tidy by its timely involvement and centralized waste management campaigns with the help of the schools and various young volunteers, when the state of Kerala was struck by a sudden flood. On 16 August 2000, due to sudden rainfall, Kerala witnessed a heavy flood killing many people and destroying the lives of the people of almost all the districts of Kerala. The central Government has graded it as a 'Level 3 Calamity' or calamity of severe nature, and for the first time in history all the shutters of the Idukki Dam were opened, and also of various other dams. This caused unexpected but heavy water flow to the life and properties of people and lakhs of people were evacuated from their own homes and sent to the relief camps. Almost all of them lost their properties, household articles, and food storage. Trivandrum which is in the southern part was one of the less affected states, and the Green Army under the leadership of V. K. Prasanth and the District Collector, started a collection centre. The Green Army could distribute tons of materials and flood relief for the affected people with the help of the volunteers. Thousands of youth joined the Green Army and worked hand in hand with the volunteers. The packing center at Nisaghandi Auditorium, Trivandrum was full of dedicated volunteers, and the Green Army was growing bigger and bigger with their presence.

The Covid 19 was the next phase of the challenge when the Green Army showed its relevance and significance in the Kerala Society. By March 20th when the whole nation was locked down and was fighting for survival against the Noval coronavirus, the city of Trivandrum was also struck by a large number of deaths and disease. Green Army youth Volunteers were very active, participating in the campaign 'Break the Chain' and helping the community kitchen established by the Government of Kerala. The youth volunteers have been dedicatedly involved in all the COVID-19 rehabilitation processes and programs of the Government. The volunteers selflessly served in the rehabilitation and isolation centres even sacrificing their health and life.

The fame and spirit of the Green Army did not limit itself to the borders of the City. The District of Waynad later adopted the same model from the Green Army for their environmental issues. Internationally the concept was recognised as two schools in Indonesia and the Philippines adopted the model too. So Green Army has become a Young Induvial organization formed within the limit of a Municipality, but an International one, named Green Army International.

The Challenges Faced by the Green Army

From 2016 the volunteers are still there and the first volunteers are also active but the movement has gone through many changes as well as the nature of the volunteers and the motives. The projects and the leaders have changed a lot, according to one of the senior volunteers and mentors. The peer group which united all of them with the attitude of one and an atmosphere of everyone's voice was heard and taken as important. Some political involvements have overlapped. Even though the volunteer group was formulated without any political motto and influence in the Municipality, later the politicians and people with political agendas in the group began to create divisions and tried to dominate the groups for their political motives. These involvements have negatively affected the young volunteers with selfless aims and intentions. V.K. Prasanth, a leader and influencer of the Green Army Volunteers from the beginning phase was elected as the Member of Legislative Assembly, and so resigned from the office of the Mayor of the city. This impacted the upper hand of the Green Army in the Trivandrum Municipality Governance system and even resulted in losing their 'physical space' in the Municipality. Gradually the Municipality with its whole governance system showed its disinterest in pertaining and cultivating the relationship with the Green Army.

The so-called mafia, according to one of the founding mentors of the Green Army, who has their eye on the business with the accumulation of waste in the city began to work against the Green Army, which worked so effectively for the City Waste Management. The new volunteers who were recruited at the time of Flood Relief and Covid rehabilitation were ignorant about the original motto of Green Army, which is environmental well-being and sustainable development for the future. So, the group was disoriented to many secondary motives forgetting the original one which remained still firm in the first members. This disorientation also created division and deviations.

The young people who were involved wholeheartedly with the Green Army, over the course of time, became concerned about their studies and future. The new jobs, responsibilities, and higher studies made many volunteers with dedication, leave the Green Army as they were not able to contribute their time and effort fully to it as in the earlier days.

Conclusion

Youth volunteerism is the most effective and easy remedy for solving the radical and serious problems of society and the world around. Almost all countries use this free and energetic force to solve many of their issues and problems. The young people who are offering their time and effort freely and voluntarily for real and reasonable causes are really an asset to the Society.

As with all the concerns of society, environmental concerns also can be effectively addressed with the help of the Young Volunteers who have the attitude of preserving nature and conserving it for the better future. Many young people nurture a real and rich attitude towards the environment and are ready to dedicate their time and effort to the well-being of society. These young Environmental volunteers are involved in society through activities, observations, creating awareness, nature monitoring, and rebuilding the natural resources. Green Army was a typical Environmental Volunteer endower in which thousands of young people and students joined hands with the association of Trivandrum Municipality and a number of Government and Non-Governmental Organizations. As an environmental youth group, it has successfully educated the volunteers and the school children about decentralised waste management and zero scheme waste. Green Army Mentors comprised members of various NGOs, Government Professionals, and Youth volunteers. The focus on the children was because children are the future of every society and agents of future changes.

Through the vocation camps, awareness classes, competitions, discussions, and debates, the children and the society learned about how to preserve the environment from waste and pollution. The 80 tons of solid waste created by Trivandrum City in a day was considerably reduced by the involvement of the organization. Through workshops, activities, and discussions the Green Army formed Green Action Plans and Green Protocols. However, the political involvements, the division of power, and inordinate motivations over the original motivation of the well-being of nature and the future generation have destroyed the group dynamism, unity, and the genuine mentality of the organization. The irresponsibility of the mother authority and the supportive organizations has caused the withering away of the volunteers and hindered the volunteer's sustenance.

The young generation of today is more aware of the ecological issues and environmental concerns than in the older days, as the generation faces a lot of environmental challenges all over the world. As witnesses to all of these problems and challenges, they themselves are motivated to come forward as young volunteers to address and solve the issues. This genuine and original involvement on the part of the youth must be taken with much importance and must be encouraged with great care and reinforcement. By emphasizing on the role of the youth, voluntarism, and the motive of 'good for all', rather than only for a community or group, this paper brings a new form of social movement where issues concern all and are not limited by primordial ties or boundary limits. In the study of the sociology of movements, it shows the changing issues and perspectives in the discipline in the last few decades of its development.

In this century, as India is becoming a young country with its demographic dividend, having almost 79% of its population with young people, it is crucial to involve them in environmental issues and resolutions. The endeavours like Green Army, involving young leaders and mentors, including the young students and supervised by the government bodies like Trivandrum Municipality, is a novel concept and effective step. However, the continuity of the support and nurturing of the atmosphere for the growth and sustenance of the volunteers and volunteer initiatives is very important. According to McKey (2010), with exposure to environmental issues and disasters, the youth are convinced about what to do to solve them, and, young people will lead the environmental movements of this century. Green Army is the perfect example of this fact.

References

Barthel T, Dusuel S, Vidal J (2006) Entanglement entropy beyond the free case. Phys Rev Lett 97(22):220402

Boyer T, Polasky S (2004) Valuing urban wetlands: a review of non-market valuation studies. Wetlands 24(4):744–755

Bushway LJ, Dickinson JL, Stedman RC, Wagenet LP, Weinstein DA (2011) Benefits, motivations, and barriers related to environmental volunteerism for older adults: developing a research agenda. Int J Aging Hum Dev 72(3):189–206

Connolly, James J, Svendsen, Erika S, Fisher, Dana R, Campbell, Lindsay K (2013) Organizing urban ecosystem services through environmental stewardship governance in New York City, Landscape and Urban Planning, 109(1), 76–84

Donald BJ (1997) Fostering volunteerism in an environmental stewardship group: a report on the task force to bring back the don. Toronto, Canada 40(4):483–505. https://doi.org/10.1080/09640569712056

Erikson EH (1979) Dimensions of a new identity. WW Norton & Company

Erikson EH (1994) Identity and the life cycle. WW Norton & company

Ernstson H, Van Der Leeuw SE, Redman CL, Meffert DJ, Davis G, Alfsen C, Elmqvist T (2010) Urban transitions: on urban resilience and human-dominated ecosystems. Ambio 39:531–545

Fisher DR, Campbell LK, Svendsen ES (2007, June) Towards a framework for mapping urban environmental stewardship. In: International symposium on society and resource management, published abstract. http://www.docstoc.com/docs/50284639/List-of-Oral-Presentations-ISSRM-2007-(listed-inalphabetical) (accessed 01/28/2011)

Fisher DR, Campbell LK, Svendsen ES (2012) The organizational structure of urban environmental stewardship, environmental politics, 12(1), pp 26–48

Kim M, Zhang JJ, Connaughton DP (2010) Comparison of volunteer motivations in different youth sports organizations. Eur Sport Manag Q 10(3):343–365

Kruger J, Buchner DM, Prohaska TR (2009) The prescribed amount of physical activity in randomized clinical trials in older adults. Gerontologist 49(S1):S100–S107

Learner SC, Reid (1993) A Study of Ontario volunteer environmental stewardship groups, in S.C. Lerner (Ed) Environmental Stewardship: Studies in Active Earth keeping, Publication Series 39 (University of Waterloo, Department of Geography

Marris E (2006) Environmental activism: In the name of nature. Nature 443(7111):498–502

McHugh KE, Mings RC (1996) The circle of migration: Attachment to place in aging. Ann Assoc Am Geogr 86(3):530–550

McKay L (2010) Generation green. CRM Mag 14(4):12–13

Moody HR (2008) Environmentalism as an aging issue. Public Policy Aging Rep 18(2):1–7
Pillemer K, Wells NM, Meador RH, Schultz L, Henderson CR, Cope MT (2017) Engaging older adults in environmental volunteerism: the retirees in service to the environment program. Gerontologist 57(2):367–375
Shier ML, Larsen-Halikowski J, Gouthro S (2020) Characteristics of volunteer motivation to mentor youth. Child Youth Serv Rev 111:104885
Stedman RC (2002) Toward a social psychology of place: Predicting behavior from place-based cognitions, attitude, and identity. Environ Behav 34(5):561–581
Stedman RC (2003) Is it really just a social construction? The contribution of the physical environment to sense of place. Soc Nat Resour 16(8):671–685
Steadman EJ, Mitchell P, Highley DE, Harrison DJ, Linley KA, Macfarlane M, McEvoy F (2004) Strategic environmental assessment (sea) and future aggregate extraction: in the East Midlands region
Warburton J, Gooch M (2007) Stewardship volunteering by older Australians: The generative response. Local Environ 12(1):43–55

GPSR Compliance

The European Union's (EU) General Product Safety Regulation (GPSR) is a set of rules that requires consumer products to be safe and our obligations to ensure this.

If you have any concerns about our products, you can contact us on ProductSafety@springernature.com

In case Publisher is established outside the EU, the EU authorized representative is:

Springer Nature Customer Service Center GmbH
Europaplatz 3
69115 Heidelberg, Germany

Batch number: 08999295

Printed by Printforce, the Netherlands